# PEDDLERS ALL
## Stories of the First Ashkenazi Jewish Settlers in Barbados
## Revised Edition

### Simon Kreindler

Copyright © 2017 by Simon Kreindler
All rights reserved. No part of this book may be reproduced or transmitted in any form or by any means, electronic or mechanical, including photocopy, recording or information retrieval system, without prior written permission from the author except by a reviewer who may quote brief passages in a review.

Requests for permission to copy any part of this publication should be addressed to:
Simon Kreindler
240 Heath Street West, Unit #1003
Toronto, ON
Canada
M5P 3L5
iamsimonkreindler@gmail.com

Library and Archives Canada Cataloguing in Publication
Peddlers All – Stories of the First Ashkenazi Jewish Settlers in Barbados
978-0-9959294-0-1

Printed in the United States of America by
48Hour Books
2249 14th Street SW
Akron, Ohio 44314
www.48hrbooks.com

Cover Design by Nanjar Tri Mukti and 99Designs.com
Indexing by Clive Pyne, Book Indexing Services

# *DEDICATION*

To the 40 Founding Families of the Barbados Jewish Community[1] and the Barbados Government that welcomed them so hospitably

Henry and Hinda Altman and Family
Henry and Deborah Altman and Son
Simon and Rose Altman and Family
Jacob and Miriam Bernstein and Family
Leon and Kathlyn Bernstein
Shaul and Rivka Bernstein
Jozef Bomsztajn
Jacob and Miriam Brzozek and Family
Harry and Sonia Burak and Family
Ephraim Burak
Gustav Feldman
Joseph and Edith Friedman and Daughter
Loddi and Aranka Friedman and Son
Lazar and Bertha Gross
Aron and Marilyn Karp and Family
Bernard and Ethel Konigsberg and Family
Bunia and Sophie Korn
Joseph and Sara Kreindler and Family
Iancu and Toni Lazar and Daughter
Moses and Dyna Mass and Family
Paul and Vera Paster and Family
Oscar and Elka Pillersdorf and Family
Leib and Fanny Pillersdorf and Family
Naiman and Hannah Pulver and Family
Kiva and Esterea Pulver and Son
Martin and Anita Reingold and Family
Chaim and Mary Rosner and Family
Leo Rubin
Ernest and Jean Saunders and Family
Hersh and Hannah Silver and Family
Louis and Mary Speisman
Mr. and Mrs. Stamler and Family
Moses and Ellen Steinbok and Family
Lazar and Toni Spira and Son
Morris Taub
Abraham and Elfreida Templer and Daughter
Motel[2] and Evelyn Truss and Family
Abraham and Helen Wajchendler and Family
Jacob and Mina Zierler and Daughter
David Zlotowitz

---

[1] Identified as the "Founding Members of the Barbados Jewish Community 1931-1951" on a memorial plaque in the Shaare Tzedek Synagogue, Rockley, Christ Church, Barbados.
[2] That Motel Truss' name appears as a Founding Member of the Barbados Jewish Community 1931-1951, even though he arrived in 1953, probably reflects the high esteem in which he was held by the community.

## ACKNOWLEDGEMENTS

This book could not have been completed without the support and assistance of a wonderful group of contributors to each of whom I wish to express my deepest appreciation. The time and effort you expended in documenting your parents' and your stories will undoubtedly be valued by generations to come.

Assembling the book has also been personally enriching. The narratives drew me in and I developed a much deeper appreciation for the founding generation of the Barbados Ashkenazi Jewish community; the challenges they faced; and the creative ways in which they carved out new lives for themselves. I also learned a great deal about their children (many of whom are my contemporaries) and the successes they achieved from their parents' sacrifices.

My wife, Ruby, spent countless hours re-editing this revised edition, a truly formidable task given the many authors and their different literary styles. Any changes made were done for purposes of enhancing the manuscript and hopefully will not have unduly altered anyone's writing style. All footnotes in the book are mine.

I am particularly indebted to Jimmy Altman and Aaron Truss. Jimmy provided many helpful suggestions, photographs and documents from the early days of the Barbados Jewish community, as well as documents from his mother's personal papers. Aaron arranged contacts, shared correspondence, newspaper clippings and historic photos; facilitated the acquisition of Genevieve Adams' story in Chapter 7; and allowed me to draw on his extensive knowledge of the island's Jewish history.

Betty Konigsberg Feinberg, Marsha Altman Glassman, Leah Pillersdorf Gilbert, Clara Paster Halpern, Jack Mass, Ellen Konigsberg Schapiro, Paul Steinbok, Beverley Stock, Rachel Pillersdorf Weisman, Molly Rosner Mann, Paulette Tepper Beyer, Merlyn Mass, and Larry Rosenthal all helped with identifying photographs, documenting community events, and providing background information.

I have no doubt there were others who assisted me and who should be recognized for their contributions but whose names I have inadvertently overlooked. To each of you I offer heartfelt apologies. You deserve better!

Simon Kreindler
Toronto, October 2017

## TABLE OF CONTENTS

**CHAPTER 1**
*A Brief History of the Jews in Barbados*
Aaron Truss … 1

**CHAPTER 2**
*The Synagogue Block Restoration Project*
Joe Steinbok … 25

**CHAPTER 3**
*The First Ashkenazi Jews to arrive in Barbados*
Simon Kreindler … 27

**CHAPTER 4**
*Stories of the Early Ashkenazi Families* … 31

*The Altman Family*

| | | |
|---|---|---|
| Henry and Deborah Altman's Story | Sir Paul Altman | 32 |
| Mary and Louis Speisman's Story | Marsha Altman Glassman, Marlene Altman Sargeant and Betty Konigsberg Feinberg | 38 |
| Edna and Oscar Pillersdorf's Story | Leah Pillersdorf Gilbert | 42 |
| Rachel Pillersdorf Weisman's Story | Rachel Pillersdorf Weisman | 52 |
| Simon and Rose Altman's Story | Marsha Altman Glassman and Rose Diane Miller Altman, ז״ל | 59 |
| James Altman's Story | James Altman | 74 |
| Doris and Jack Kaplan's Story | Marsha Altman Glassman | 81 |

*The Bernstein Family*

| | | |
|---|---|---|
| Srul Jacob and Miriam Bernstein's Story | Paul Bernstein and Dan Raizman | 82 |
| Leon and Kathlyn Bernstein's Story | Paul Bernstein | 85 |
| Shaul/Szol Bernstein's Story | Paul Bernstein | 87 |
| Dan Raizman's Story | Dan Raizman | 88 |
| Jorge Raizman's Story | Jorge Raizman | 90 |

| | | |
|---|---|---|
| *Jakub Josef Bomsztajn's Story* | Aaron Truss, Leah Pillersdorf and James Altman | 92 |
| ***The Brzozek and Steinbok Families*** | | |
| Yehudah and Miriam Brzozek's Story | Beverley Stock, Ellen Steinbok and Clara Paster Halpern | 94 |
| Moses and Ellen Steinbok's Story | Ellen, Paul, Jerry, Eva and Martin Steinbok | 97 |
| ***The Burak Family*** | | |
| Harry and Sonia Burak's Story | Dorothy Rosenthal Burak and Louis Burak | 100 |
| Efraim Burak's Story | Dorothy Rosenthal Burak | 108 |
| ***The Feldman Family*** | | |
| Gustav and Kate Feldman's Story | Rolf Feldman | 109 |
| ***The Friedman Family*** | | |
| Joseph and Edith Friedman's Story | Clara Halpern and Hanna Templer Abramowitz | 112 |
| ***The Karp Family*** | | |
| Aron and Marilyn Karp's Story | Anne Karp Zeplowitz | 113 |
| Ron Karp's Story | Ron Karp | 125 |
| ***The Konigsberg Family*** | | |
| Bernard and Ethel Konigsberg's Story | Max Konigsberg | 127 |
| Max and Shirley Konigsberg's Story | Excerpted from "Max and Shirmax – More than a Love Affair" | 134 |
| Alex and Vivian Konigsberg's Story | Betty Konigsberg Feinberg and Vivian Tissenbaum Konigsberg | 143 |
| Betty and Jack Feinberg's Story | Betty Konigsberg Feinberg | 146 |
| Ellen and Peter Schapiro's Story | Ellen Konigsberg Schapiro | 151 |
| ***The Korn Family*** | | |
| Baruch/Bunia and Miriam Korn | | 157 |
| Chaim and Mary Korn Story | Molly Rosner Mann | 158 |
| ***The Kreindler Family*** | | |

| | | |
|---|---|---|
| Joe and Sara Kreindler's Story | Simon Kreindler | 167 |
| Peggy Kreindler Lancut's Story | Simon Kreindler | 176 |
| Simon and Ruby Kreindler's Story | Simon Kreindler | 180 |
| Maurice Kreindler's Story | Maurice Kreindler | 193 |
| Bertha and Luzer Gross' Story | Simon Kreindler | 199 |

*The Lazar Family*
Iancu and Tony Lazar — 201

*The Lebens Family*
Geoffrey and Edith Lebens' Story — Ann Lebens Abel — 202

*The Mass Family*
Dina and Moses Mass' Story — Merlyn Mass and Jack Mass — 205

*The Pasternak/Paster Family*
| | | |
|---|---|---|
| Paul and Wisia Pasternak's Story | Clara Paster Halpern | 214 |
| Jack and Ricky Pasternak's Story | Jack Pasternak | 218 |
| Clara and Norman Halpern's Story | Clara Paster Halpern | 225 |

*The Pillersdorf Family*
Leib and Fanny Pillersdorf's Stories — Sam, Florence, and Paulette Pillersdorf — 228

*The Pulver Family*
Naiman and Hana Pulver — 241

Kiva and Esterea Pulver — 242

*The Reingold Family*
Martin and Anita Reingold — Betty and Max Konigsberg and James Altman — 243

*The Rubin Family*
Leo and Catherine Rubin's Story — Simon Kreindler — 244

*The Saunders Family*
Ernest and Jean Saunders' Story — Harold Saunders — 245

Roberta (Robbie) Saunders' Story — Roberta Saunders — 248

*The Schor Family*

| | | |
|---|---|---|
| Salmon and Feiga Schor's Story | Simon Kreindler | 252 |

**The Silver Family**
| | | |
|---|---|---|
| Henry and Chana Silver's Story | Carole Joseph Silver | 255 |

**The Spira Family**
| | | |
|---|---|---|
| Lazar and Toni Spira's Story | Sidney Spira | 260 |

**The Stammler Family**
| | | |
|---|---|---|
| Hanna Templer Abramowitz,<br>Max Konigsberg, and Betty Konigsberg Feinberg | | 268 |

| | | |
|---|---|---|
| Morris Taub; Loddi Friedman | | 269 |

**The Templer Family**
| | | |
|---|---|---|
| Abraham and Elfreida Templer's Story<br>Hanna Templer Abramowitz | | 270 |

**The Truss Family**
| | | |
|---|---|---|
| Motel Truss' Story | Motel Truss | 276 |
| Misha (Moisey) and Musya Truss' Story | Misha Truss | 284 |
| I Remember When –<br>A Tribute to Evelyn Truss | Aaron Truss | 289 |
| Around My Mother's Table | Joe Truss | 295 |
| Leon Truss' Story | Leon Truss | 309 |

**The Wajchendler Family**
| | | |
|---|---|---|
| Abraham and Helen Wajchendler's<br>Story | Hannah Wajchendler Oliver,<br>Harry and Irving Wajchendler | 311 |

**The Zierler Family**
| | | |
|---|---|---|
| Rosie Zierler Weinberger's Story | Daniel and Joe Weinberger | 317 |

**The Zlotowitz Family**
| | | |
|---|---|---|
| David and Anne Zlotowitz's Story | Jack Pasternak and Clara Paster<br>Halpern | 324 |

## CHAPTER 5
*From Peddling to Retailing and Manufacturing*
Simon Kreindler 325

## CHAPTER 6
*Some Families who came to Barbados in the 1950s and later*     Simon Kreindler     333

| | | |
|---|---|---|
| Hy Bloom's Story | Hy Bloom | 334 |
| Hal and Michelle Blumenfeld's Story | Connecticut Jewish Ledger and Hal Blumenfeld | 336 |
| Eric and Penny Bowman's Story | Eric and Penny Bowman | 341 |
| Robert and Del Flam's Story | Karen Flam | 343 |
| Jacob Hassid's Story | Jacob Hassid | 345 |
| Stan and Joan Hoffman's Story | Leah Pillersdorf Gilbert | 348 |
| Paul and Priscilla Koves' Story | Leah Pillersdorf Gilbert | 349 |
| Jay and Leila Newman's Story | Leah and Benny Gilbert | 350 |
| Marshall and Anita Oran's Story | Gilda Oran | 351 |
| Growing up in our Bajan Shtetl | Gilda Oran | 354 |
| Kuk and Fela Pilarski's Story | Joseph Pilarski | 360 |
| Joseph Pilarski's Story | Joseph Pilarski | 362 |
| Sheldon and Laurel Salcman's Story | Sheldon Salcman | 367 |
| Goldie Spieler's Story | Simon Kreindler | 369 |
| Orial and Anthony Springer's Story | Orial Springer | 373 |

## CHAPTER 7
*Some Notable People and Interesting Events that impacted the Barbados Jewish Community*

| | |
|---|---|
| Errol Walton Barrow, Barbados' First Prime Minister and his possible Jewish roots | 375 |
| The Bendas of Islington, England: the Jewish ancestry of Genevieve Adams, wife of former Prime Minister, Tom Adams | 377 |
| Israel Brodie, UK Chief Rabbi (1948-1965) and Mrs. Brodie visit Barbados | 379 |

Memories of Hurricane Janet, September 22, 1965     381

The Rebbe and his Emissaries     390

## CHAPTER 8
### Where do We go from here? The Future of the Barbados Jewish Community
Simon Kreindler     394

## APPENDICES

### APPENDIX 1
### Leaders of the Barbados Jewish Community     397

### APPENDIX 2
### Group Photos of the Barbados Jewish Community from the 1940s to the 1960s     399

### APPENDIX 3
### Bar Mitzvah Photos 1930s -1960s     415

### APPENDIX 4
### Ashkenazi Burials in the Barbados Jewish Cemetery and Memorial Plaques for Former Members     423

Map of Barbados     424

*INDEX*     425

ABOUT THE AUTHOR     449

# PREFACE

In the summer of 2015, I learned that Rose Altman, the matriarch of the Barbados Jewish community, was seriously ill. I had known Rose since I was a child growing up on the island and what always stood out in my mind was her ability to relate to children as easily as she did to adults. When Rose asked you a question, she was always interested in hearing what you had to say. In 2015, she was one of two remaining members of the generation of Ashkenazi Jews who, like my parents, arrived in Barbados in the 1930s and 40s, and helped revive the island's connection to a Jewish past on the brink of extinction.[3]

A charming, effervescent lady blessed with an incredible memory, Rose's warmth and sincerity attracted others and they confided in her. She knew everything about the Barbados Jewish community and could recall details about people and events like no other. As I thought about her declining health, it occurred to me that no one had ever documented the stories of the founding Ashkenazi families in Barbados, brave souls who, like her, left their relatives and worldly possessions in pre-WWII Europe to seek a better future elsewhere for their children and themselves.

Undaunted by their inability to speak English, the Ashkenazi immigrant men initially worked as peddlers, lived frugally and sent for their wives and children as soon as they could. Most of them later went on to open retail businesses on Swan Street in Bridgetown. Some later got involved in manufacturing and a few invested in real estate and land development. Most of the women helped their husbands in business, and the men and women of the community did their best to preserve the Jewish traditions they brought from Europe.

Very early on, Rose's father-in-law, Moses Altman, created a place of worship in his home, "Macabee," on Harts Gap. The community gathered there for Friday evening and High Holiday services; later started a Sunday school for the children; and regularly raised money in support of the fledgling State of Israel. They were determined that Judaism would be perpetuated in whatever ways possible.

I felt it was important to document the stories of these brave, determined men and women as well as the stories of their children who had the good fortune to grow up in a free country. I believe these narratives represent an important chapter in Barbados' history and the history of the Jewish diaspora.

---

[3] A Sephardic community had flourished in Barbados in the late 17th and early 18th centuries but then began to decline. The last member of that community died in 1934.

I floated the idea for the book with several of my Bajan contemporaries. All offered encouragement and many offered to help. A few were skeptical and mentioned that what I was proposing had previously been attempted but had not succeeded. I chose to ignore this caution and set year-end 2016 as the deadline by which I would decide whether there was sufficient interest.

Within days Max Konigsberg had submitted his family's story, and shortly after, I received the Spira, Burak, and Truss families' stories. Meanwhile Aaron Truss and Jimmy Altman began sending me background information and helpful documents. Within three or four months it was clear there would be enough material for a book, although the undertaking turned out to be significantly more challenging than I had initially imagined.

Over the course of the next several months I made dozens of phone calls and had copious email correspondence with Bajans I had last seen when we were children growing up on the island. Ruby and I visited Barbados in May 2016 and were graciously hosted by Jimmy and Anita Altman. I interviewed Ellen Steinbok and about a dozen descendants of the founding families; talked with several newcomers to the island; and met with one black couple who had recently converted to Judaism and are active members of the Barbados Jewish community.

I had been very much looking forward to interviewing Rose, but unfortunately her health continued to decline and by the time we arrived on the island this was no longer possible. In fact, she died a week later, on May 9, 2016. Rose had been an icon of the Jewish community and it was difficult for those who knew her to imagine Jewish life in Barbados without her. Her funeral was a very sad event that left many of us with a profound sense of emptiness.

Simon Kreindler
Toronto, September 2017

# CHAPTER 1
## A Brief History of the Jews in Barbados
Aaron Truss

Aaron Truss, Barbados, 2016
(Simon Kreindler photo)

In 1627 the British colonized Barbados and in 1628 the first Jewish settlers arrived. The Jewish history of Barbados is an inseparable part of our heritage dating back 385 years. No attempt has been made to treat this subject in its entirety; this is merely a synopsis of the history of the Jews of the island.

**THE ARRIVAL**
Robert Schomburgh's *History of Barbados,* published in 1848, states, *"the settlement of Jews in Barbados dates from 1628."* This statement was based on a letter from London sent to James, Earl of Carlisle, Lord Proprietor of Barbados, stating, *"The island business has not yet yielded above 200 pounds, which* the *writer paid to Jas Maxwell."*[4] This letter, dated 22 September 1628, is signed by Abraham Jacob, a Jew, and is preserved among colonial state papers.

---

[4] Schaumburg had reason to believe that James Maxwell was Jewish.

Richard Ligon, an Englishman who lived in Barbados from 1647 to 1650 and who wrote *A True and Exact History of Barbados* published in London in 1657, refers to the failure of one of Barbados' inhabitants who was making bricks. *"There was an ingenious Jew upon the island whose name was Solomon, that undertook to teach the making of it, yet, for all that, when it came to the touch, his wisdom failed and we were deceived in our expectations."*

In 1654 the Brazilian seaport of Recife was retaken by the Portuguese. They supported the Spanish Inquisition and Jews were forced to leave Recife immediately. Fortunately, in that same year Oliver Cromwell opened all British domains to Jewish settlement and many of Recife's Jews came to Barbados. Evidence of their arrival was documented in the *Minutes of Council of Barbados* on November 8, 1654, when it was *"ordered that consideration of the Jews and foreigners brought from Brazil to the island be presented at the next sitting of the Governor and Assembly."* These minutes are preserved in the Government Registry.

In January 1655 the matter came up for consideration at a meeting of the Council and the following is taken from the Minutes – *"Upon the petition of several Jews and Hebrews, inhabiting in and about this island, it is ordered, that the petitioners having themselves civilly and conformably to the government of this island, and being nothing tending to the disturbance of peace and quiet thereof during their stay, shall enjoy, the privileges of laws and statutes of the Commonwealth of England and of this island, relating to foreigners and strangers."* These minutes are also preserved in the Government Registry.

As a result of a petition by the Jewish people in (what was to become) America to the Dutch West India Company, dated January 1655, to allow Jews to travel to British domains, Cromwell issued two passes in April 1655 to Dr. Abraham de Mercado, an elder of the Recife Jewish community and his son, David Raphael, to settle and practice medicine in Barbados.

## THE WORK OF EUSTACE M. SHILSTONE, A CRITICAL CONTRIBUTION TO OUR KNOWLEDGE BASE

In his foreword to E. M. Shilstone's 1956 book, *Jewish Monumental Inscriptions in Barbados*, Wilfred S. Samuel states *"public worship for the Jews of London came about in February or March 1657.... Shilstone shews grounds for selecting 1654 as the commencing year of the practice of Judaism on Barbados."* This is because the Jews of Barbados were allowed to publicly practice their religion three years before the Jews of London. Samuel also writes that Lewis Dias was the founder of the Bridgetown Synagogue sometime in August 1654 and based on *"Amsterdam synagogal archives ... two scrolls, a reading desk cover and curtains were handed over at Amsterdam in April 1657 to the agents for the Barbados Jews."*

Shilstone transcribed all the inscriptions on the old headstones in the Nidhe Israel Cemetery [5] and wrote, *"I cleaned and deciphered the inscriptions, English, Portuguese and Spanish.... I knew not a single Hebrew character and made no attempt to copy inscriptions in that language."* In 1938 Shilstone visited the U.S., met Edward D. Coleman, the Librarian of the American Jewish Historical Society and showed him the transcripts. Coleman visited Barbados on a cruise ship that stopped for a weekend later that same year and spent his time deciphering the inscriptions and checking Shilstone's copy. Coleman visited Barbados again in the spring of 1939 and spent a fortnight examining the transcripts, cross-referencing them with the inscriptions on the stones and adding all the Hebrew writing he could decipher.

Shilstone was a devout Anglican, an attorney, Deputy Clerk to the Legislative Assembly, and one of the founders of the Barbados Museum and Historical Society. All Barbadians are greatly indebted to him for helping to elucidate an important chapter of our country's history.

Shilstone's work revealed that the oldest tombstone in the Nidhe Israel Cemetery was the one that recorded the burial in 1660 of Aaron de Mercado. He writes that *"there is no exact record of the earliest existence of a synagogue in Barbados ... facts concerning the acquisition by the Jews of the site of the synagogue and the lands of the burial grounds are buried in obscurity. No such records exist."* However, in a Deed of Conveyance dated September 1, 1664, one of the boundaries mentioned is "the Jews' Synagogue." There also exists a plan, dated July 4, 1664, made by Andrew Norwood, Surveyor, with a sketch of the synagogue building shown as a boundary. This was published in the Journal of the Barbados Museum and Historical Society in February 1948.

---

[5] The Nidhe Israel cemetery will later be referred to as the Barbados Jewish cemetery when it pertains to burials of Ashkenazi Jews who began arriving on the island in the 1930s.

**Detail from a 17th century painting in the Barbados Museum showing a synagogue-like building with arched windows in Bridgetown**
(Jewish Museum, Barbados)

The Jewish congregation in Barbados was named "Kahal Kadosh Nidhe Israel," The Holy Scattered Congregation of Israel. This is because the Barbados congregation, although mainly Portuguese, came from all parts of the world, and by the end of the 17th century, numbered about 300 Jews and grew to over 800 by the mid-1700s. The Jewish community also built another synagogue in Speightstown, "Semach David,"[6] that was unfortunately destroyed by fire in 1738 after a non-Jew who crashed a Jewish wedding, was accused of theft by the host and a fight broke out.

## GROWTH AND DEVELOPMENT DESPITE HARDSHIP

In an article in the *Daily Nation* of March 1, 1989, entitled *History of the Bajan Jews*, Winston E. Layne[7] wrote *"the Jews were well entrenched, not only in the sugar business but also in trading and banking – with an outreach to much of the Caribbean – the Jews controlled nearly all of Barbados' commerce."*

Barbados produced more riches for Great Britain than any of its other colonies and it was dubbed 'Little England.' The island became rich because David de Mercado, a Dutch Jew living in Barbados, invented a new type of sugar mill to crush sugar cane. The juice that was extracted was then boiled to make molasses, then processed into sugar. The venture proved very profitable, and although the local authorities imposed a tax on all sugar manufactured by the Jews, they transformed the economy of Barbados. Even though the local Christian merchants complained and the House of Assembly enacted a law

---

[6] Offshoot of David
[7] Winston Layne was a Barbadian print journalist

restraining Jews from trading with the black population, they prospered and made Barbados 'The Gem of the Caribbean in the Crown of Great Britain.'

Layne also wrote the *"Jews were officially categorized as among the island's 'foreigners and strangers' and endured certain civil and economic constraints. They were taxed more heavily than others. They were denied full benefits of the island's judicial system because they were not allowed to testify against Christians since the Jews would not take the oath on the bible* (i.e., New Testament).*"* This was the plight of Jews worldwide from as far back as the Middle Ages when according to *Hallam's History of the Middle Ages*[8], *"The Jews paid exorbitant sums for every common right of mankind, for protection, for justice."* However, in the 19th century, Barbados was the first British colony to grant Jews full political rights and in 1976 (348 years after the first Jews arrived on the island), the first Barbadian Jew[9] walked up the steps of Parliament.

A Category 4 hurricane slammed into Barbados on August 10, 1831, destroying much of the island's economy, along with the synagogue. The synagogue was re-built and consecrated in March 1833. The editor of the *Barbados Globe* prophesied, *"It was a day that would ever stand eminently distinguished in the annals of the Hebrew community of the town."* The editor continued, *"There is indeed no portion of our civil, political or religious institutions which they (the Jews) have not contributed to improve, or benefit, and to them and their liberality, there is no charitable association of the island which is not deeply indebted."* Layne confirms this view and wrote, *"It is quite clear that the Jews of Barbados were well respected and involved themselves significantly in the island's activities."*

---

[8] Hallam, Henry. History of the Middle Ages, published by Colonial Press, 1899
[9] Aaron Truss

**Interior of the Nidhe Israel Synagogue after reconstruction in 1833**
(Reproduced from a photo in the Barbados Museum)

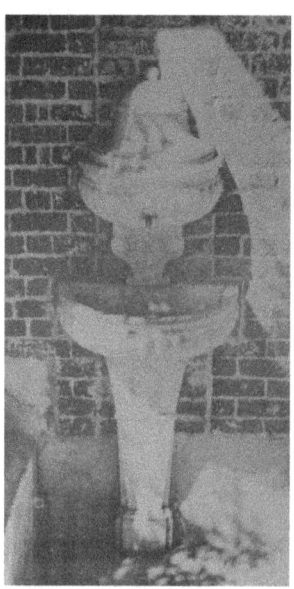

**Marble laver that once stood at the entrance to the
Nidhe Israel Cemetery in Bridgetown
and now in the Barbados Museum.
Jews traditionally wash their hands after visiting a cemetery.**
(Willie Alleyne photo)

It is also recorded in the *Journal of the Barbados and Historical Society* of 1942 that *"The Jews of those days long ago, in spite of the disabilities imposed on them showed the Christians of the land how to succeed in the face of distressing odds. More than that, at a time when there was a slackness in living and a weakness in morality, they (the Jews) by their compact and organized manner of life, set a bright example of piety, of religious enthusiasm and of the security and sanctity of family life."*

At the intersection of Coleridge and Pinfold Streets is the Montefiore Fountain[10] donated in 1864 by John Montefiore, a member of the prominent Sephardic family. At the corners of the fountain are four marble statues representing the qualities of Justice, Fortitude, Temperance and Prudence – each with the relevant inscription; "Do Wrong to None"; "Look to the End"; "Be Sober-minded"; "To Bear is to Conquer."

**Montefiore Fountain, Coleridge Street, with the Nidhe Israel Synagogue in background prior to restoration.**
(Willie Alleyne photo, 1986)

---

[10] The Montefiore Fountain was originally located in Beckwith Place, lower Broad Street, Bridgetown, but was subsequently moved to its present location at Coleridge Street in 1940 and no longer has running water. It was donated to the city by Jewish businessman, John Montefiore, whose father, John Castello Montefiore, was among the first Barbadians to die of cholera in 1854. John Castello Montefiore was a respected merchant described as being a free coloured. It is reported that for 40 years he had been one of the leading merchants in the city; had a wholesale and retail store in Swan Street; and was also the owner of Neils Plantation. The fountain is a fine example of neo-Gothic decorative art and is made from cast iron. It was opened to the public on November 2, 1865, and described as "a little gem of architectural beauty, there being nothing in Barbados to compare it with." (Adapted from the Barbados Pocket Guide)

In 1848 there were but 71 Jews on the island. Shilstone records that on May 6, 1869, a Deed of Settlement was made and executed by the then-members of the Jewish community by which document the synagogue and graveyard were conveyed upon trust for the use of the Hebrew community in Barbados until there should be no Jews residing on the island. By 1905 the trustees of the Deed had all died and the entire property was conveyed to Joshua and Edmund Baeza, two Jewish brothers who were prominent merchants in Bridgetown. When Joshua died, Edmund Baeza, the sole member of the Hebrew faith in Barbados decided to wind up the trust and dispose of the property.

**Nidhe Israel Synagogue, 1925**
(From a photo in the Nidhe Israel Museum)

## THE SALE OF THE SYNAGOGUE AND CEMETERY

According to Shilstone, the authorities of Bevis Marks Synagogue in London, England, approved Baeza's suggestion and he received a Power of Attorney from the wardens of Bevis Marks Synagogue to negotiate and sell the Jewish properties. "Delegatus est non potest delegare"[11] was the power granted to Baeza. This was most unusual in the case of trustees.

Henry Graham Yearwood, a Bridgetown solicitor, offered to purchase the synagogue for use as a legal library but wanted to level all of the headstones and remove those that were broken. This was reported in a letter from Mr. Baeza to Bevis Marks on July 28, 1927. The Bevis Marks authorities expressed their refusal to sell at any price because they would not be party on religious grounds to the destruction of existing memorials. It was then agreed that the graveyards be excluded from sale and remain in the possession of the Bevis Marks Congregation. Mr. Baeza was instructed by Bevis Marks in a letter dated September 16, 1927, to *"find means of disposing of the property, on conditions which do not affect the burial grounds in the manner suggested."* Thereafter, Mr. Baeza reported to Bevis Marks that agreement had been reached to sell the building but not the graveyard. He wrote, on January 12, 1928, *"The graveyards are excluded from the sale and remain in possession of the Bevis Marks Congregation."*

Shilstone had access to the correspondence between Bevis Marks and Baeza, and confirms that on April 27, 1928, Baeza sold the entire property, "including the graveyard" to Yearwood. "The purchaser covenanted for himself and successive owners to keep the walls around the burial grounds in repair and to keep in proper order and condition, the burial grounds and not to use or permit to be used for any purpose whatsoever."

However, in February 1929, the headstones had all been levelled to one height. It was clear in the purchaser's covenant that repairs to the enclosure walls and upkeep for the burial ground was the purchaser's responsibility. Mr. Yearwood, notwithstanding the covenant in the conveyance, had levelled the headstones, removed some of the broken stones and then made a sale of some of the contents of the synagogue. *"It is difficult to reconcile these circumstances with Bevis Marks' former views,"* writes Shilstone.

Suddenly in May 1934, Mr. Yearwood died and on June 4, Mr. Baeza also died. Shilstone notes that shortly afterwards the entire Jewish property changed hands again and was purchased by Mr. W. St. C. Hutchinson, another Barbados

---

[11] Latin for "a delegate may not delegate" and is the legal rule that an agent to whom an authority or decision-making power has been delegated by a principal or higher authority may not delegate it to a subagent unless the original delegator expressly authorizes it, or there is an implied authority to do so. www.businessdictionary.com

solicitor. He sold the remaining furniture, made some alterations and rented the synagogue as offices. "The old magnificent timber trees were felled and garages erected on the grounds." The walls of the synagogue were demolished and graves were desecrated to make a road to accommodate motor traffic. Shilstone warned Hutchinson "No good (will) come from (your) actions." Hutchinson replied, "What are you going to do, sue me?" It is clear that Hutchinson "repudiated the burden of the covenant to keep the burial ground and synagogue in proper order and repair." Suddenly Mr. Hutchinson died. It is rumoured to this day that Barbadians who knew the facts were convinced that Yearwood and Hutchinson were cursed because they abrogated the terms of the purchase covenant and desecrated the Jewish burial grounds. The same was said of Mr. Baeza for disobeying Bevis Marks' instructions not to sell the graveyard.

## THE ARRIVAL OF THE FIRST ASHKENAZI JEWS
According to Winston Layne, in January 1932 a new generation of Jews arrived in Barbados. *"Starting as peddlers, they plied their wares around the island. Soon they were successful enough to attract other family members, friends and friends of friends. Within two years, by 1934, there was once again a minyan."*[12] Layne writes, *"I believe it was Moses Altman, whom I recall as a youngster, living in Harts Gap, Hastings, who built a home there which also served as a synagogue."* After his death, his son, Simon Altman, lived in his father's home, 'Macabee,' in Harts Gap and continued to hold Friday night services and other services there. In the 1960s the Jewish community first rented and later purchased a house called 'True Blue' on Rockley New Road and converted it to a synagogue, 'Shaare Tzedec,' where services are still conducted to this day.

---

[12] A quorum of ten men (or in some synagogues, men and women) over the age of 13 required for traditional Jewish public worship (Google).

**Shaare Tzedec Synagogue, Rockley New Road, Barbados, 2016**
(Kreindler photo archive)

By the early 1950s a considerable community of Jews lived in Barbados and they sought burial in the graveyard. They were willing to assume legal control of the burial ground so that it might never again fall into secular use. After protracted negotiations over a period of years between Oscar Pillersdorf, the leader of the Jewish community; Eustace Shilstone, representing the Barbados Museum and Historical Society; other members of the Jewish community; and the owner of the ancient Jewish Burial Grounds[13], a petition was presented to His Excellency, Alfred William Lungley Savage, C.M.G., Governor and Commander-in-Chief of the Island of Barbados. It requested that the burial grounds be vested in the "Synagogue Burial Grounds Committee" with perpetual succession. The petition was signed by Oscar Pillersdorf, Lazar Spira, S. J. Bernstein, Paltyel Pasternak, H. Burak, J. H. Altman, and E. M. Shilstone. The Island's legislature subsequently passed a statute approving the request. These seven men deserve recognition for their role in facilitating the return of the cemetery to the Barbados Jewish community.

---

[13] The Hutchinson family

**Oscar Pillersdorf**     **Eustace M. Shilstone**

**Lazar Spira**     **Srul Jacob Bernstein**     **Paltyel Pasternak**

**J. Henry Altman**     **Harry Burak**

TO HIS EXCELLENCY ALFRED
WILLIAM LUNGLEY SAVAGE, C.M.G.,
Governor and Commander-in-
Chief of the Island of Barbados
&c.,      &c.,      &c.,

The humble petition of Oscar
Fillersdorf, Srul Jacob
Bernstein, Felyel Pasternak,
Harry Burak and Jacob Hersch
Altman, persons of the Jewish
Faith resident in this Island
and Eustace Maxwell Shilstone
representing for the purposes
of this petition The Barbados
Museum and Historical Society.

---

BARBADOS.                TO HIS EXCELLENCY ALFRED WILLIAM LUNGLEY
                         SAVAGE, C.M.G., Governor and Commander-in-
                         Chief of the Island of Barbados.
                         &c.,      &c.,      &c.,

The humble petition of Oscar Fillersdorf, Lazar
Spira, Srul Jacob Bernstein, Felyel Pasternak,
Harry Burak and Jacob Hersch Altman, persons of
the Jewish Faith resident in this Island and
Eustace Maxwell Shilstone representing for the
purposes of this petition The Barbados Museum
and Historical Society.

SHEWETH as follows:-

1. The present owner of the Ancient Jewish Burial Grounds situate in Synagogue Lane in the City of Bridgetown in this Island has at the request of your petitioners agreed to vest the said Burial Grounds in them to be used as burial grounds for persons of the Jewish Faith in this Island subject to the terms and conditions covenants reservations and stipulations to be contained and set out in the deed vesting the same in them.

2. Your petitioners deem it advisable in order to ensure the more convenient vesting of the said Burial Grounds and any other property real or personal that may hereafter be acquired by your petitioners for the benefit of persons of the Jewish Faith in this Island and also to ensure the effective administration of such property and the general conduct of their affairs that your petitioners should be incorporated under the name of "The

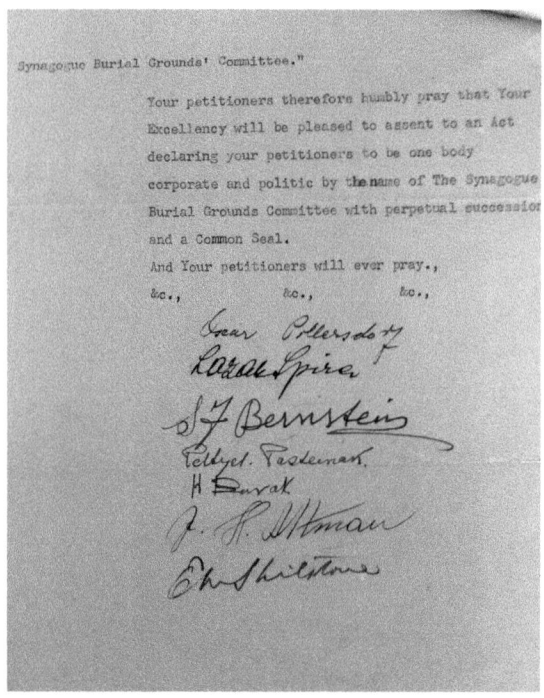

**Petition of the Barbados Jewish Community presented to Governor W. L. Savage**
(Photo courtesy of James Altman)

**THE PROPOSED CONSTRUCTION OF THE HALL OF JUSTICE**
In 1977 a decision was made by the Cabinet of Barbados to construct a much-needed "Hall of Justice" (Supreme Court). In March 1978, a plan of a parcel of land that included the synagogue and most of the Jewish cemetery was prepared by A. St.C. Hutchinson, Land Surveyor, on which is recorded, "Plan of a parcel of land, the estate of R. St.C. Hutchinson, which is to be acquired for the siting of a New Supreme Court and Registration Department. Surveyed by me with due authority in March 1978 at the instance of the Ministry of Housing and Lands." Signed A. St.C. Hutchinson, Land Surveyor. A copy of this plan is in the Government Lands and Survey Department. In 1979 the Cabinet formally agreed to build the Hall of Justice and in order to achieve this, the old office building that was once the Jewish synagogue; a large section of the cemetery; and properties on Coleridge Street, Magazine Lane and James Street were compulsorily acquired by government. It was also a requirement to widen Synagogue Lane by 10 feet since the entire area was required to build the Hall of Justice.

From the very beginning Prime Minister Adams was ambivalent because building the Hall of Justice at this location would destroy the ancient Jewish synagogue and its cemetery. Between 1979 and 1983 he had numerous meetings and discussions with Aaron Truss[14], a member of government and the Jewish community; spoke with the Leader of the Opposition, The Honourable Errol Barrow; sought advice and support from the Caribbean Conservation Association, The Barbados National Trust, and even Lord Bernstein from Granada TV, on using our Jewish heritage to promote Barbados.

Encouraged by this, the Barbados Jewish Community met and formally selected a committee to continue negotiations with the government. The committee members were Benny Gilbert, President of the BJC, Marshall Oran, Paul Altman, and Aaron Truss. Two meetings were held with government officials of the then-Ministry of Communications and Works and Housing and Lands during which the BJC committee strongly opposed the destruction of the synagogue and desecration of the cemetery. Meanwhile, the Prime Minister agonized over the decision and delayed the start of construction of the Hall of Justice. Finally on October 10, 1983, as Minister responsible for Town Planning, he listed the "Jewish Synagogue and Cemetery" as a "Building of Special Architectural or Historic Interest" and had a notice to this effect (Town and Country Planning Act, Cap. 240) delivered to Mr. James Altman, 8 Broad Street, Bridgetown, representing the Jewish community.

**Aaron Truss, James Altman, Tom and Genevieve Adams, 1977**
(James Altman photo)

---

[14] Aaron Truss was a member of the Barbados Senate 1976-1981; Member of Parliament from 1981-1986; Minister of State in the Prime Minister's Office from 1982-1984; and Minister of Tourism and the Environment from 1984-1986.

**1983 Notice to James Altman listing the Jewish cemetery as a "Building of Special Architectural or Historic Interest."**
(Document courtesy of James Altman)

## SAVING THE SYNAGOGUE AND CEMETERY

On March 13, 1984, Prime Minister Adams reported to Parliament that *"... Government had already paid $2 million for technical services for the building of the new Supreme Court ... to be built in a "Y" shape to accommodate the Jewish Synagogue which is to be restored as a tourist attraction."* He went on to say he *"was satisfied about a restored synagogue, maintained by a body interested in Judaism (The Barbados Jewish Community) and a museum of the history of the Jews of the Western Hemisphere, would be a new addition to the tourist facilities of Bridgetown"*.

The Leader of the Opposition, Mr. Errol Barrow, supported the project in Parliament and congratulated Mr. Adams on *"getting the Jewish community involved and interested in 'saving the synagogue.'"* Seldom do a Prime Minister and a Leader of the Opposition agree on the same thing, but in relation to this matter they did, as was reported in the *Barbados Advocate* and the *Nation Newspaper* on March 14, 1984.

**Benny Gilbert, President of the Barbados Jewish Community in 1984**
(Rachel Pillersdorf Weisman photo)

On March 28, 1984, Benny Gilbert, President of the Barbados Jewish Community, wrote to Prime Minister Adams commending him: "Your recent statement in the House of Assembly that the old Synagogue building will be saved and restored was received by the Jewish community with profound satisfaction and gratitude."

On January 15, 1985, Prime Minister Adams created the Ministry of Tourism and Environment and placed the "Restoration of the Jewish Synagogue" under it. It was the first time a project of this nature was given to a ministry other than the Ministry of Culture and was done because he believed that our Jewish historical heritage would play an important role in promoting tourism.

**WORLD JEWISH CONGRESS – JERUSALEM**
A booklet printed in January 1986 entitled *A Brief History of The Jewish Settlement in Barbados* was prepared for distribution at the 50th World Jewish Congress to be held in Jerusalem in February 1986. It was researched and written by Don Singh of the Public Relations and Marketing Department of the Barbados Board of Tourism to promote the Synagogue Restoration Project. The government of Barbados paid for Aaron and Jennifer Truss and Paul Altman to attend the Congress. Aaron addressed the 2000 delegates who attended and proposed the following resolution:

"Whereas Barbados was colonized in 1627 and it is recorded that the first Jewish settlers arrived in 1628, and whereas the first Jewish Synagogue, *Nidhe*

*Israel*, was built in 1654, be it resolved that at the 50th Meeting of the World Jewish Congress, the Commonwealth Jewish Council recognizes the importance of the restoration of the Jewish Synagogue in Barbados since it represents one of the two oldest synagogues in the Western Hemisphere. Be it further resolved that the Commonwealth Jewish Council undertakes to promote this most historic monument, thereby preserving our Jewish Heritage for future generations." The resolution was unanimously passed and officially launched the "Restoration of the Jewish Synagogue Project in Barbados."

The Jerusalem mission was intended "to make Jews aware of the synagogue" and "launch an appeal to Jews worldwide to contribute financially to the Synagogue Restoration Project in Barbados."[15] Over 10,000 copies of *A Brief History of the Jewish Settlement in Barbados* were distributed at the Congress and following the group's return to Barbados, an additional 20,000 copies were printed and distributed by the Barbados Board of Tourism in Germany, London, Paris, Canada, and the United States of America. This greatly assisted in galvanizing the support of the worldwide Jewish community and Jewish organizations which donated millions of dollars to assist in the restoration project.

**Israel's Minister of Tourism (left), Paul Altman,
Jennifer and Aaron Truss,
World Jewish Congress, Jerusalem, February 1986**
(Israel Ministry of Tourism photo, courtesy of Aaron Truss)

---

[15] A Brief History of the Jewish Settlement in Barbados, a booklet prepared by the Barbados Board of Tourism, 1986

**Restored Nidhe Israel Synagogue and Cemetery, 2016**
(Kreindler photo archive)

**Restored Interior of the Nidhe Israel Synagogue**
(Kreindler photo archive)

**Jewish Museum**
(Kreindler photo archive)

**Restored Mikvah, Nidhe Israel Synagogue**
(James Altman photo)

## AN INDEBTED COMMUNITY
The acquisition and subsequent restoration of the Nidhe Israel Synagogue and cemetery could not have been accomplished without the support and vision of His Excellency, The Right Honourable Errol Walton Barrow, Q.C., M.P., The Right Honourable J.M.G.M. "Tom" Adams, Q.C., M.P., and Sir Paul Altman.

**Above: Errol Walton Barrow (1920-1987)**
**Below: J. M. G. M. "Tom" Adams (1931-1985)**
(Google images)

**Sir Paul Altman, Barbados, 2016**
(Sir Paul Altman photo)

Sir Paul Altman[16] played a very important role in restoring one of the oldest synagogues in the Western Hemisphere. We are indebted to him and proud of the work he did raising the necessary finances while also supervising the renovation and refurbishment of this magnificent building. In addition, he was responsible for converting an old warehouse building into what is now the Jewish Museum. Thanks to his dedication, hard work and attention to detail, the synagogue and museum are now complete.

Archaeologists subsequently discovered under the site of the rabbi's house, a mikvah, the ritual bath used primarily by women before marriage, after childbirth, and after their monthly menses end. In Shilstone's book there is a plan of the entire area showing the synagogue, the site of the Rabbi's house, the graveyards, the original entrance on Synagogue Lane and the property previously owned by Mr. Kinch that is now the Jewish Museum.

In particular, the late Prime Minister, Tom Adams, deserves the highest praise for his vision and foresight in saving this historical monument for Barbadians and Jews alike. Although he was not Jewish, he had a 'Jewish heart.' He was an intelligent and well-read individual, versed in the history of ancient civilizations, including the valuable contribution Jewish people have made over the centuries.

---

[16] Paul Bernard Altman was awarded the Knight Bachelor in the Queen's 2016 New Year Honours List for service to the preservation of historic buildings and real estate development in Barbados.

His Excellency, The Right Honourable Errol Barrow ("Uncle Errol," as we lovingly called him in our household), a 'self-professed Jew,' also gave his full support to saving the synagogue. On many occasions he publicly stated that his name was originally 'Baruch,' later changed to Barrow. In 1972 when he visited Israel and was asked by Prime Minister Golda Meir about the rumour that he had Jewish ancestors, he informed her that his great-grandfather, Simon Barrow, was buried in the Barbados Jewish cemetery and confirmed that his great-great-grandfather's name was 'Baruch.' At the time he quipped, *"Where else did you think I got my brains from?"* There was great laughter and applause, and the story was reported in the newspapers of Jerusalem and Barbados.

The combined support of both Adams and Barrow was very significant in saving the synagogue and cemetery, as both men recognized the need to preserve our cultural heritage and simultaneously promote the island as a destination with historic attractions. As Professor Sir Henry Fraser[17] said, *"A city without a history is like a man without a memory."*

The Nidhe Israel Synagogue, the cemetery, the museum and the mikvah are now major tourist attractions. Their significance goes beyond Barbados to touch the lives of people everywhere who are interested in the preservation of their history. Today as Barbadians proudly celebrate the designation of Historic Bridgetown and its Garrison as a UNESCO World Heritage Site,[18] we need to continue our link with the past.

In conclusion, I would like to quote from Mark Twain, "If statistics are right, the Jews constitute but one percent of the human race. It suggests a nebulous dim puff of stardust lost in the blaze of the Milky Way. Properly, the Jew ought hardly to be heard of, but he is heard of, has always been heard of. He is as prominent on the planet as any other people, and his commercial importance is extravagantly out of proportion to the smallness of his bulk. His contributions to the world's list of great names in literature, science, art, music, finance, medicine and learning are also way out of proportion to the weakness of his numbers. He has made a marvellous fight in this world in all the ages; and had done it with his hands tied behind him. He could be vain of himself, and be excused for it.

The Egyptian, the Babylonian and the Persian rose, filled the planet with sound and splendour then faded the dream stuff and passed away; the Greek and the Roman followed; and made a vast noise, and they are gone; other people have

---

[17] Renowned Barbadian physician and expert in architectural history and heritage preservation
[18] http://whc.unesco.org/en/list/1376

sprung up and held their torch high for a time, but it burned out, and they sit in twilight now, or have vanished. The Jew saw them all, beat them all, and is now what he always was, exhibiting no decadence, no infirmities of age, no weakening of his parts, no slowing of his energies, no dulling of his alert and aggressive mind. All things are mortal but the Jew; all other forces pass, but he remains. What is the secret of his immortality?"

## ACKNOWLEDGEMENTS

Special thanks to Eustace M. Shilstone whose book, "Jewish Monumental Inscriptions in Barbados" provided a great deal of information from which I quoted extensively. My thanks to Edward Stoute, Winston E. Layne, Warren Alleyne, Robert Schomburg and Richard Ligon for the informative articles and books they wrote which greatly assisted me in my research.

Most of all, I must acknowledge the dedication and many hours of research that Don Singh of the Barbados Board of Tourism put into the booklet that the Ministry of Tourism produced in 1985. In addition to other research, much of what was written in "A Brief History of the Jewish Settlement in Barbados" was based on a speech I made in the Barbados Senate on Wednesday, June 18, 1980, which is documented in the Official Report of the Senate Debates.

In preparation for my visit to Israel in 1986, I formally presented a paper before the Cabinet of Barbados for approval and I am grateful to the Cabinet for supporting my Ministry in this endeavour.

Special thanks to Prime Minister Harold Bernard St. John for his support and encouragement in accomplishing Tom Adams' dream of a restored synagogue.

My deepest regards to Dr. Corin Bayley for his input and advice.

# CHAPTER 2
## The Synagogue Block Restoration Project
### Joe Steinbok

The Synagogue Redevelopment project is the final phase of the Synagogue Restoration project that commenced in mid-1985 under the direction of Sir Paul Altman. It included the restoration of the Nidhe Israel Synagogue, construction of the Jewish Museum and restoration of the mikvah.

In 2014 the Executive of the Barbados Jewish Community was facing a difficult problem. The Jewish cemetery had reached maximum capacity and additional burial space was needed. The two available options were either to seek approval from Government to acquire a portion of the car park adjoining the existing cemetery or to purchase additional burial plots at Coral Ridge Memorial Gardens in Christ Church.

Sir Paul was concerned that if Government was approached for only a small portion of the car park, they might subsequently be reluctant to contribute the additional property that would be needed to complete the larger Redevelopment Project. This concern led him to approach The Tabor Foundation (Barbados) that had previously been a major contributor to the Synagogue Restoration project as well as construction and outfitting of the museum.

The Tabor Foundation agreed to fund the entire project with the understanding that Joe Steinbok, with whom they had a longstanding professional relationship, would lead the project and that Steinbok Management Services Inc. would source and appoint the team of professionals who would do the work.

With this commitment in place, the final and largest phase of the Synagogue Restoration Project was implemented. It included restoration, adaptive reuse of buildings, and new construction. The work required Town and Country Planning approval and the services of a structural engineer, architect, quantity surveyor and a competent contractor.

The Synagogue Redevelopment project comprises:

1. Restoration of the artisans' workshop at the corner of Synagogue Lane and James Street.
2. Restoration of the old fire station at the corner of Coldridge and James Streets and its conversion into a museum; the addition of a new structure to house a café; and restoration of the courtyard.

3. Restoration of the Weights and Measures Building that will become an art gallery (with public restrooms).
4. Construction of a new social hall for the synagogue making it more attractive for hosting events such as weddings or Bar Mitzvahs that require catering service.
5. Extension of the cemetery.
6. The construction of a monument on the site of Codd's House. This was the site of one of the first Houses of Parliament from where the Emancipation Bill was proclaimed. Unfortunately, the building was destroyed to make way for the proposed Supreme Court.
7. The conversion of the existing car park into a new modern parking area with lots of trees and green space.
8. Elimination of vehicular access to the Synagogue and the restoration of the original pedestrian entry, including its gate and path.

On December 7th, 2015, the work on site commenced and was immediately met with challenges. Construction commenced with the Artisans' Workshop, and after removal of the rotted timber floor and excavating for new foundations, the contractor unearthed Jewish headstones. This meant that the building had to be redesigned so that the headstones were not covered again. This was done and a portion of the Artisans' Workshop building is now an enclosed cemetery for all to visit.

While excavating for the new Social Hall building, a Quaker headstone was found. Fortunately, it was just outside of the building's footprints. The headstone has been repaired and is prominently displayed.

The other areas of the project proceeded without any major surprises, and should be completed by the end of 2016.

Once completed, the entire property will be managed by a not-for-profit company that has representatives from all four parties involved. These include The Tabor Foundation (Barbados), The Barbados National Trust, The Barbados Jewish Community and the Synagogue Restoration Project.

The project is the first major development within Historic Bridgetown and its Garrison since receiving its UNESCO World Heritage status. The block will be one of the most historically significant places within Bridgetown and will be there for the enjoyment of all Barbadians and visitors alike.

# CHAPTER 3
## The first Ashkenazi Jews to arrive in Barbados
### Simon Kreindler

As readers of this book will discover, there are differing claims as to who was the first Ashkenazi Jew to arrive on Barbados and when he/she arrived. If ship manifests or lists of passenger arrivals in Barbados from the 1930s exist, they are probably buried somewhere in the island's archives and I had neither the time nor the resources to search them out. I was therefore forced to rely on secondary sources in trying to answer these two questions.

Over the years many articles have been published in newspapers and periodicals about the Barbados Ashkenazi community and many of them refer to Moses Altman as the first member of the community to have arrived on the island. However, available information suggests the answer is not quite so clearcut.

A memorial board that hangs in the Shaare Tzedek Synagogue in Rockley bears the inscription, "Founding Members of the Barbados Jewish Community 1931-1951." These dates imply that the first founding member(s) arrived in 1931.

Support for the 1931 date comes from two sources. One, an article published in the Canadian Jewish News in November 2006, entitled "Barbados, Home to a Fascinating Jewish History" in which Henry Altman is quoted as saying that his father, Moses, arrived in Barbados in 1931. The other is found in Henry and Deborah Altman's story[19] in which their son, Paul, indicates that his father arrived in Barbados in 1932, a year after his grandfather, Moses Altman.

Contradicting the 1931 date is a two-page handwritten document, entitled "Names of the New Settlers in Barbados" found by Jimmy Altman and his sister, Marsha Altman Glassman, among their mother's papers after her death in May 2016. Jimmy and Marsha believe the document was written either by their father, Simon Altman, or his sister, Mary Speisman. This document indicates that three people arrived together in March or April 1932 - Moses Altman, his niece, Dina Mass, and her husband, Moses Mass.

Support for this trio being the first to arrive can be found in the article "Sanctuaries in the Sand" published in "Caribbean Travel and Life" in September-October 1991. In it Henry Altman is quoted as saying that his father, Moses Altman, left Poland in 1932, together with his niece and her husband (Dina and Moses Mass) on a ship bound for Venezuela. "En route, the ship

---

[19] Chapter 4

stopped in Barbados. The three passengers got off, looked around, and thought it might be a good place for them...later that year Moses sent for his older son (Henry)."[20]

Additional support for the 1932 date can be found in Moses and Dina Mass' story[21] in which their son, Sam Mass, refers to his parents' arrival in Barbados from Poland in 1932. Given that Dina Mass was pregnant when she arrived, that her daughter, Doris Mass, was born in Barbados on October 6, 1932, and that the Masses and Moses Altman were travelling together, it seems reasonable to conclude that Dina and Moses Mass and Moses Altman were the first Ashkenazi Jews in Barbados and that they probably arrived about March or April 1932.

Contradicting this proposition is Paul Bernstein's firm assertion that his grandfather, Srul Jacob Bernstein, had always said that he and Moses Altman were the first Ashkenazi Jews to arrive on the island and that they had travelled from Poland to Barbados via British Guiana, arriving on the island in 1932.[22] Paul's assertion is contradicted by the New Settlers document that indicates "Jacob Birstain (sic) a friend of M. A. (presumably Moses Altman) and a landsman arrived on the 7th of November 1932...."

Although there is more support for 1932 as the arrival year of the first Ashkenazi Jews in Barbados, it is impossible to definitively resolve the issue. Hopefully, future archival research will uncover the answer.

I next turned my attention to creating a list of arrival dates for other members of the community. Rose Altman's list includes many names, some of which are followed by a year that I assume marks an arrival date. Unfortunately, some of the dates are clearly incorrect which makes it difficult to know just how accurate the others are. For instance, Rose's list indicates that the author's father, Joseph Kreindler, arrived in 1933 but in fact he arrived in 1934.

Similarly, Motel Truss' arrival date is given as 1954 but in his own story he indicates he arrived in 1953.[23] Ernest Saunders is listed as having arrived in 1950 but his son, Harold, says it was 1949; the author's aunt and uncle, Bertha and Lazar Gross, are listed as having arrived in 1968 but they actually arrived in 1947.

---

[20] Why Henry Altman would give his father's arrival date as 1931 in the 2006 article after having given the date as 1932 some 15 years earlier is unclear.
[21] See Moses and Dina Mass' story in Chapter 4.
[22] See Srul Jacob Bernstein's story in Chapter 4.
[23] See Motel Truss' story in Chapter 4.

The New Settlers document includes the following names and dates: Szymon Altman, Yehuda Brzozek, Harry Burak, Bernard Konigsberg, Buny Korn, Jacob Zierler, S--l Bernstein, Aron Karp (Dina Mass' brother), Joseph Friedman (1950), Herschel Silver, P. Paster, David Zlotowitz, Salomon Shor, Leib Speisman (1937), Motel Truss (1954), Oscar Pillersdorf, Moshe Steinbok (1946), --Abbadi, Jack Kaplan (1946), Lazar and Sydney Spira, Getzel Feldman, Ernest Saunders (1950),

Other names follow (in a different handwriting) and some are repetitions of names previously listed. They include: Harry Burak, --Greenbaum, Salamon Schor (1942), Joseph Friedman (1950), Burak (brother) –presumably Ephraim Burak, Abbedi (sic), Templar (sic), Stamler (sic), Gross, Lazar and Bertha (1968) (sic), Rubin, Spira.

Based on names and dates culled from various sources, including the New Settlers document, previously mentioned articles in which Henry Altman is quoted, and stories that make up the body of this book, I offer the following approximate sequence of arrival dates, countries of origin and/or ports of embarkation. The list is not comprehensive and I fully expect there are errors and/or omissions for which I apologize in advance.

About March/April 1932 - Moses and Dina Mass and Moses Altman from Poland via Holland
November 7, 1932 - Srul Jacob Bernstein from Poland
November 1932 - Henry Altman
1932 - Baruch/Bunia and Bertha Korn and daughter Myrla/Mary from Poland via Holland
1933 - Simon Altman from Poland
1933 – Miriam, Tola (12), Leon (8), Helen (3), and Samuel Bernstein from Poland
About 1933 – Solomon, Feiga and David Schor from Poland via Guatemala
1934 – Hinda, Mary, Edna, and Doris Altman from Poland
1934 - Yehudah Brzozek from Grajewo, Poland, via Guatemala and Honduras
May 1934 - Joseph Kreindler from Cernauti, Romania, via Curacao
1934 - Aaron Karp from Tarnow, Poland
January 1935 - Miriam, Ellen (9), Mary (7), Sara (5), and Sam Brzozek (3) from Poland
About 1935 - Szol/Shaul Bernstein from Poland
1936 - Bernard Konigsberg from Poland via Holland
1936 - Sara Gerstenhaber from Cernauti, Romania, via Guatemala
1937 - Ethel and Max Konigsberg (1½) from Holland
1937 - Jacob and Mina Zierler from Poland via Holland
1937 - Louis Speisman from Poland
1938 - Palteil, Vishka, Jack (4), and Clara Pasternak (3 mos.) from Poland

August/September 1938 - Harry and Sonia Burak from Poland
About 1938 - Hirsch and Chana Silver from Poland
1938/39 - David Zlotowitz from Poland
1939 - Joseph and Edith Friedman from Czechoslovakia
1939 - Leopoldo Tepper from Poland
Late 1930s - Jakub Josef Bomsztajn from Poland
April 1941- Lazar, Toni and Sidney Spira (13) from Germany via England and Trinidad
1941 - Gustav, Kate, Ruth (9) and Rolf Feldman (6) from Germany via England
1945 - Oscar Pillersdorf from Poland via Trinidad
About 1946 - Leib and Fanny Pillersdorf from Poland via Germany
About 1946 - Jack Kaplan from Chicago and the US army base in Barbados
Late 1946 - Moses Steinbok from Poland via Trinidad
About 1946 - Stammler family from Poland via Trinidad
1947 - Ephraim Burak from Poland via Detroit, USA
About 1947 - Luzer and Brancia Gross from Cernauti, Romania
About 1948 - Iancu and Tony Lazar and Felicia from Romania
1948 - Naiman, Hana/Anutsa, Molly and Vicky Pulver from Romania
1948 - Kiva and Esterea Pulver and Bernard (7) from Romania
1949 - Abraham, Helen and Hannah Wajchendler (2) from Poland via Germany, France, and Trinidad
1949 - Ernest, Jean, Harold (4) and Robbie Saunders (6 mos.) from Czechoslovakia via Jamaica and the US[24]
Feb 1950 - Abraham and Elfrieda Templer and Hanna (12) from Danzig via Trinidad
About 1951 - Paul and Priscilla Koves and Yvonne from Baltimore, Maryland
1953 - Motel Truss from Russia, via Romania, Poland, Germany, France, British Guiana, and Trinidad

---

[24] Ernest met and married Jean in the US after leaving Europe.

# CHAPTER 4
## *Stories of the Early Ashkenazi Families*
### Simon Kreindler

For the sake of simplicity, I have chosen to organize the stories that follow in alphabetical order by surname, grouping the stories of Founding Members, their children, and sometimes their grandchildren together. Because not all readers will be familiar with the many surnames, I have included maiden names of mothers and daughters in the hope that it will add clarity.

Stories of almost all the 40 Founding Members, written mostly by their children, are included here. Unfortunately, some families have no living descendants, or if they do, they could not be located or failed to respond to my efforts to reach out to them. A very few families chose not to contribute their stories and I have included only brief references to them to acknowledge that they were part of the community.

Many of the stories in this book are compelling. Some are sad and others light-hearted but almost all are inspiring. Most are coloured by the Holocaust and its impact on those who left family behind in Europe. Many of the fortunate ones who made it to Barbados had to grapple with survivor guilt. It is a testament to their resilience that they carried on and built new lives for their children and themselves. To the generation of my contemporaries who grew up on the island, I extend a hearty Yasher Koach.[25] Your stories are a tribute to your parents and grandparents and will undoubtedly be treasured by your children and grandchildren.

Anyone assembling a collection of stories such as this must be prepared for the inevitable criticism that there will be conflicting accounts of the same event, errors as to when the event took place, who was there, etc. I accept this criticism, knowing that human nature being what it is, different people may recall the same event differently and for different reasons. Hopefully, these occasional contradictions will not prove overly distracting for the reader.

---

[25] Literally the phrase means "May it be for strength ("koach" in Hebrew)," that is, may what you just did be a source of strength. www.jewish-language.org

# HENRY and DEBORAH ALTMAN'S STORY
### Sir Paul Altman

**Deborah and Henry Altman, Barbados, ca. 1940s**
(Sir Paul Altman photo)

Barbados was settled in 1627 by the British. It has been suggested that its Jewish heritage predates that year as the original name of our island, "Los Barbadoes," was a Portuguese name, and the only Portuguese settlers on record were the Maranos or "hidden" Jews, many of whose names are on the ancient tombstones in our graveyard next to Nidhe Israel Synagogue. Just over 300 years later, Moses Altman arrived here from Lublin, Poland, on his way to South America. Barbados, a British colony, offered an opportunity to become a citizen. A British passport would allow entry into Great Britain and the United States.

Moses had no reason to remain in Poland. Life was difficult and he was challenged in supporting five children – three daughters and two sons, the eldest of whom was my father, Henry (Judka Hertz) who arrived in 1932, one year after his father and became the second new arrival.[26] After Henry's brother, Simon, arrived, they and their father established Altman's Store. Moses Altman could easily be said to be a true Moses because as a result of his deciding to settle in Barbados, some 40 families followed just in time to avoid the Holocaust. This act could be interpreted as one that places him as "Hassid vanot haolam," "Righteous Among the Nations."[27]

---

[26] Discussion of who were the first Jews to arrive and the likely dates they did can be found in Chapter 3.
[27] Yad Vashem (www.yadvashem.org) describes Righteous Among the Nations as "an official title awarded on behalf of the State of Israel and the Jewish people to non-Jews who risked their lives to save Jews during the Holocaust."

The new Barbados Ashkenazi Jewish community was traditionally observant, and "Macabee," the home Moses built with Henry, became their centre for worship.

On a buying trip to London in 1947, Henry met Deborah Tintpulver through mutual friends, the Borensteins. There was a connection: The Borenstein family had been in the diamond business, which had taken them to Guyana and an extended visit to Barbados. Deborah who had been studying dentistry at London University, also knew the Borensteins. She came from a successful family in Warsaw where her elder sister had qualified as a lawyer and her identical twin sister had also completed university. As fate would have it, the War broke out and Deborah, stranded and alone in London, was the only survivor in her family. She was able to support herself by working at a chemical laboratory linked to a rubber factory producing materials for the war effort. She spoke of being on watches when the Germans were dropping 'doodlebugs' over London and having to take shelter in the London Underground.

Deborah and Henry married in London in May 1947, and as Deborah said, it did not matter where Barbados was. She was ready to start a new life anywhere! Deborah and Henry returned to Barbados determined to build a successful life. Paul, their only child, was born in March 1948. After a brief commercial venture with his brother and sister-in-law, Simon and Rose, Henry, together with Deborah, set out on their own to establish what would become a feature business on Broad Street, the Broadway Dress Shop. Its first location was at the top of Broad Street facing Nelson's Statue, possibly the most visible location for retail in Barbados. It occupied two floors with a dry goods retail business on the ground floor and a dress factory/sales showroom above. There was a third level that was occupied by the signature Bridgetown restaurant at that time, The Flying Fish Club. The dress factory was Deborah's way of expressing her creativity – and she brought elegance to her efforts – designing and using materials that became her signature style. It was a one-woman effort.

**Henry and Deborah Altman's "Broadway Dress Shop,"
Bridgetown, Barbados, ca. 1950s**
(photo courtesy of the Barbados National Trust, Fitzpatrick Collection)

It must be remembered that Barbados in the 1950s was not a tourist destination, but Deborah managed to attract almost every visitor who came to the island as well as the cream of Barbados' society with her unique style and her educated approach. Linen was the craze and also Sea Island cotton, African prints and embroidery. Venezuela was prospering and Deborah even had a sign in Spanish at the bottom of the stairway to her shop – "Vestidos para damas ariba." Whoever says that hard work does not reap rewards needs to think again. After work Deborah would play her piano accompanied by Henry on his violin. Paul was lulled to sleep with wonderful classical music.

The Broadway Dress Shop prospered and Henry's retail business grew. The need for more space encouraged the purchase of a large section of what is today Trident House. Again, Henry occupied the ground floor and Deborah had a new, magnificent shop and factory upstairs. There were 30 sewing machines and a well-organized production line. Henry's retail included shoes, shirts, hats (very popular at the time for ladies) and fabrics sold by the yard. This was the 1950s.

**Deborah, Paul and Henry, Barbados, ca. 1955**
(Sir Paul Altman photo)

By that time their new home, "Golf View," on Rockley New Road, was built and it still stands today overlooking the golf course. Golf became a focus for Paul who went on to play on the Barbados National Team and represented Barbados in The Caribbean Championship (Hoerman Cup) on several occasions. Paul also served as President of the Barbados Golf Association.

At that time Rockley New Road did not have government-supplied water so Henry dug a well and had a windmill installed. Water was pumped from 50' underground into holding tanks which supplied "Golf View" as well as several neighbours, including Henry's sister and brother-in-law, Edna and Oscar Pillersdorf, and their children, Leah and Rachel.

**"Golf View" with windmill in background, Rockley New Road, Christ Church, Barbados, ca. 1950s**
(Sir Paul Altman photo)

In 1956 Deborah encouraged Henry to purchase a beach property on the West Coast. It was unheard of at that time to live or own properties on the West Coast (in this case, Gibbs Beach). That decision was one of the most forward-thinking moves Henry made. It included a small house, originally called "In and Out," which sat on one of the most exciting locations with a stream (pond) in the garden. It was used as a weekend and school vacation place and became the family refuge – indeed the start of a new life. The West Coast was to become the Platinum Coast of Barbados. The friendships formed there with Barbadian and foreign families were to become meaningful and lifelong. There was a cross-section of religions, races, and professions. By 1996 Henry and Deborah had sold their Rockley home and the Broadway Dress Shop to a Barbadian entrepreneur, Sam Rollock. Rollock went on to combine several adjacent properties in Bridgetown and opened the 5-and-10 Discount Store with the first escalator on the island. Unfortunately, it did not succeed.

In 1965 real estate offered new opportunities. Paul had left Harrison College and was at the University of Miami. Henry and Deborah sold the old "Sea Isle" and built the new "Seashell" on land next door. They remained at "Seashell" until the late 1990s when Gibbs Beach had become a premium West Coast location. Henry had invested in other property and built Speedbird House in Bridgetown, named after its lead tenant, British Airways, that was flying the Concorde to Barbados. Other properties and land subdivisions continued to occupy him. Still, he did not allow them to interfere with his enjoyment of the "beach life" and winters in Miami where he and Deborah made new friends. There they also enjoyed their other passion, bridge, which they also played several times a week in Barbados with a wide circle of friends.

The synagogue was a centre of commitment for Henry and Deborah and they were always active members. Friday nights at "Seashell" were also special. This was carried forward from "Macabee," the house that Henry helped Moses build on Harts Gap and where Moses and Hinda lived until Moses died in 1949. "Macabee" subsequently became Simon's family's home. Paul celebrated his Bar Mitzvah there in 1961, and soon afterwards, the community acquired a house located halfway between "Macabee" and "Golf View" on Rockley New Road that became the synagogue (shul) that is still used today.

When Moses arrived in Barbados, he was made aware of the island's Jewish past. Several Barbadian people had quietly told him that they were descendants of the original Jewish settlers who had built a synagogue in Bridgetown. He was shown the cemetery and the synagogue that had been sold and converted into offices. They were owned by a lawyer, a Mr. Hutchinson, and his family. The cemetery had been maintained by another non-Jewish Barbadian lawyer, Eustace Shilstone. Shilstone turned over control of the cemetery to the new

Jewish community, and a committee that included Henry was formed to take over responsibility for it.

In the early 1980s the government acquired the synagogue building as a part of a larger compulsory land acquisition in the immediate area in order to build a new Supreme Court compound. No one knew the historic importance and past elegance of the Nidhe Israel Synagogue. It was slated for demolition and as well, the government indicated that they would need to relocate some of the graves because they needed more land. Henry Altman stood alone in his forceful stand and said, "Under no condition!" Paul, who had served as President of the Barbados National Trust, and his wife, Rachelle, knew that all of the late Mr. Shilstone's records were in the Shilstone Library housed in the Barbados Museum. After several days of research, they hit the jackpot – Shilstone photos and lots of other information, including some minute books, from the original 1654 Nidhe Israel Synagogue and community.

It proved to be a timely find because a truck, men, and equipment were on site ready to start the demolition. There was never a deliberate plan by Government to act against the Jewish community; they were simply building a new Supreme Court in a choice location. There was only one voice opposing, and no one, including Henry, knew anything of the real splendour and magnificence of the old synagogue, sold in 1925, six years before Moses arrived. What had upset Henry was the intention to move the graves. That had upset him so much that he said that the synagogue also should be saved. Paul was able to arrange a quick meeting with the then-Prime Minister Tom Adams, who quickly answered with the words, "If you can find the money, we will give the community the building and find another site for the Supreme Court." In the process, meetings were held with the Town Planning Department and letters were written to the press and the Minister for Planning. Once the significance of the synagogue was realized, there was a strengthening by Government to relocate the Supreme Court and support the restoration and beautification of the entire area.

The rest is history. The oldest synagogue in the Western Hemisphere was saved and restored, thanks to one man's determination. Henry continued to keep an office in Speedbird House until his 95$^{th}$ year. Deborah was the docent at the synagogue until her passing and was the first signature in the first visitors' book. They were most proud of their contributions. They moved to "Mallows" cottage in Sandy Lane where they spent their final days. Deborah passed in 1998 and Henry in 2008. Paul and Rachelle still live at "Mallows." Their daughters, Rina and Abby, live in New York and London, respectively.

## MARY and LOUIS SPEISMAN'S STORY
Marsha Altman Glassman, Marlene Altman Sarjeant,
and Betty Konigsberg Feinberg

**Mary and Louis Speisman, Barbados, ca. 1950s**

In 1934 Mary Altman arrived in Barbados from Poland with her mother, Hinda, and sisters, Edna and Doris, two years after her father, Moses, and brothers, Hersz/Henry and Simon. Louis Speisman came to Barbados from Poland in 1937. They were married in Barbados on February 25, 1939. She was 24 and he was 33 years old.

**Louis and Mary's wedding**

Mary and Louis never had children of their own but treated Rose and Simon Altman's children, Marlene, James, Marsha, and Steven, who lived next door as their own. In fact, Mary often told them they could come to her home and do whatever they wanted! Their other "children" were their dachshunds, Polly and Bobby, who also could do no wrong and who ruled the Speisman home. Mary's niece, Marlene Sarjeant, described her aunt as a devoted daughter to her parents, a caring sister to her siblings, and a non-judgmental lady who was always there with unconditional love for her siblings and her.

Louis was a Torah scholar and spent hours reading and studying in the back room of his home, surrounded by his beloved religious texts. Jewish observance was an important part of his and Mary's lives, and they celebrated Shabbat and all the holidays.

Louis probably started out in business with a small store in Swan Street although no one in his family remembers where exactly it was. Later he and Mary owned 23 Swan Street that they rented to Simon and Rose Altman, and 30 Swan Street, also rented to Simon and Rose, and later to Mr. Lazar.

Betty Feinberg whose father, Bernard Konigsberg, was a good friend of Louis recalled her father telling her how upset Louis had been when he learned that Arnold Toynbee, the famed British historian and specialist in international affairs, had labelled the Jewish people a "fossilized" civilization. Louis wrote to Toynbee to express his outrage. His unhappiness with the historian again surfaced in 1961 when Toynbee delivered a lecture at McGill University in which he questioned the right of the Jewish people to a state and asserted that the Zionist treatment of Palestinians was morally equivalent to the Nazi treatment of Jews. Toynbee was immediately challenged by Israel's ambassador to Canada, Yaacov Herzog, and the two of them subsequently engaged in a public debate. When it was over, the consensus was that Herzog had been the victor.[28]

Mary and Louis were ardent supporters of Israel and donated generously to many charities. On numerous occasions they hosted young Lubavitch rabbis who journeyed to the Caribbean and South America, promoting Judaism and raising funds to build yeshivas in the United States. In the 1950s Louis was instrumental in arranging for a Lubavitch mohel from Rabbi Schneerson's community in New York to come to Barbados to ensure that Jewish boys had a "kosher" bris and not just a circumcision by their family doctor.[29]

In the 1940s and 50s when the shul was still at "Macabee" and Yom Kippur services had concluded, it was a tradition that hot coffee was available in the Altman kitchen and the Speismans served challah with cream cheese or butter, ginger ale, soda water, Coke, etc., on their verandah at "Massiah."

---

[28] http://www.tabletmag.com/jewish-news-and-politics/161156/herzog-toynbee-1961
[29] See the story of the Rebbe and his emissaries in Chapter 7.

In the 1960s Louis was a leading supporter and financial backer of the community when it decided to purchase "True Blue," the house in Rockley that later became the Shaare Tzedek Synagogue.

**"Massiah," the Speismans' home in Harts Gap**
(Marsha Altman Glassman photo)

After Paul Paster left Barbados for Canada, Louis assumed responsibility for blowing the shofar on the High Holy Days, and his niece, Marsha, still remembers how he would get out of breath and very red in the face after doing so. She also recalled her uncle's warmth and kindness and the respect he was shown when he walked along Swan Street.

Louis enjoyed betting on the English horse races and it was a ritual for him to go to the betting shops every morning during the week to do so. He would often say, "This is how I make my daily bread" (and his winnings covered the costs of his cigarettes and coffee while he was in Bridgetown). On occasion, he would go to the Garrison Savannah to watch the horses and the people, all the while drinking coffee and smoking cigarettes.

Marsha recalled her uncle's ritual for making coffee that involved putting a teaspoon of coffee in a tall glass, placing the teaspoon in the glass then filling the glass with tap water. He would then give the contents a big stir. No hot water for him, just plain tap water! He also loved his scrambled eggs "runny," the runnier the better! When he wasn't studying or otherwise occupied, Louis could usually be found sitting in his rocking chair, chain smoking and listening to Rediffusion[30] or later, when TV came to Barbados, watching the screen for hours at a time. He particularly loved to listen to the singer, Roger Whittaker.

Mary loved animals, was involved with the SPCA, and was also president of the Barbados chapter of WIZO, the Women's International Zionist Organization, that helped raise funds for Israel and other causes. The women in the community gathered monthly in different members' homes to collect dues, raise money, and socialize. Canasta was their card game of choice while Poker and 66 kept their husbands busy.

Mary and Louis usually spent Sunday mornings at the Aquatic Club, Paradise Beach, or Sandy Lane where they mingled with the other Jewish families and friends and where Mary could often be seen taking a dip in the ocean with some of the other ladies.

Louis passed away on August 18, 1976, and Mary on May 5, 1985. Both are buried in the Jewish cemetery in Bridgetown.

---

[30] Wired radio broadcasting was first introduced to Barbados in 1934 and on the 24th October of that year a company called Radio Distribution (Barbados) Ltd. was formed. The first program schedule of Radio Distribution included delayed broadcasts from the BBC as well as wireless broadcasts from Canada and the United States. In 1951 Radio Distribution (Barbados) Ltd. was taken over by Rediffusion Services Ltd., a subsidiary of Rediffusion Ltd. London. Governments of Barbados realized the public good of mass communications and became one of Rediffusion's biggest clients, paying for some 53 loud speakers which broadcast Rediffussion in public places such as police stations, shops, schools, the General Hospital and several locations in Bridgetown. In 1999 Rediffusion ceased operations and was rebranded Starcom Inc. Though long gone as a media service many Barbadians have retained their (iconic) 'little brown box.' (Excerpted from the Barbados Museum and Historical Society's website)

# *EDNA AND OSCAR PILLERSDORF'S STORY*
## Leah Pillersdorf Gilbert

**Edna and Oscar Pillersdorf, Barbados, ca. 1953**
(Leah Pillersdorf Gilbert photo)

My mother, Edna, was born in Lublin, Poland, the third child of Moshe and Hinda Altman. She came to Barbados as a teenager in 1933, along with her mother and sisters. My grandfather had arrived a year earlier from Holland along with a few of his friends. They were on their way to South America. The ship stopped in Barbados to refuel and restock. The men liked what they saw and decided to stay. The family was comprised of three sisters, Mary, Edna/Elka (my mum), and Doris (Dyna), the youngest, and two brothers, Henry and Simon.

**The Altman family, Barbados, ca. 1934**
Back row: Hinda and Doris. Front row: Mary, Henry, Moses, Edna and Simon

My grandfather, Moses/Moshe, started off peddling for a living. Soon he rented a store on High Street called 'Royal Store" which my parents took over in due course. He was a carefree person who loved horses, dogs and fishing. My grandmother was a religious woman who hated Barbados, and the day after my grandfather died in 1948, she departed for Israel (then Palestine), leaving behind her children and me, Leah Rose, her only grandchild.

My father, Oscar (Schie Wolfe) Pillersdorf, was born in Rutki, Poland. He got his law degree in Poland but never practiced because a "numerous clausus" law that forbade Jews to be called to the Bar was passed shortly after his graduation.

In *Our Calypso Shtetl*[31], a book about the Trinidadian Jewish community, Oscar described his arrival in the Caribbean: *"I arrived in Trinidad in 1938 on my way to Venezuela. My relatives there, the Lustgartens, had visited my family in Lwow (Lvov/Lviv) shortly after the Polish government effectively barred young Jewish lawyers from opening offices or practicing their profession. In view of the bleak economic outlook and oppression in the country I agreed with the Lustgartens to go to Trinidad and wait there for them to arrange for me to join them in Venezuela.*

*After several fruitless attempts to get a visa and the outbreak of World War II, I was left stranded in Trinidad. At the time, (it) was a British colony with liberal immigration laws. New arrivals who deposited 60 British pounds with the harbour master could land and remain on the island. The deposits were later returned, but until they were, could be used to secure the purchase of goods from local merchants.*

*My first job was as a clerk in the store of J.T. Johnson on Fredrick Street in Port of Spain. Mr. Johnson put me in charge of a dry goods section where I organized the credit extended to the mostly-immigrant peddlers.*

*When WWII broke out and censorship was introduced, I worked as a censor for foreign languages at the Post Office. Later, with the influx of refugees from Austria, Germany, Holland and other countries, I assisted the Colonial Secretary in identifying bona fide Jewish refugees from possible planted German spies.*

*I also tried a variety of other occupations. I established an atelier producing miniature paintings of island scenes, shell necklaces, and other souvenirs which were purchased by the many sailors and soldiers passing through Trinidad. For a time I owned a very successful woodworking factory with Mr. Wolf and his*

---

[31] Oscar Pillersdorf's story in *Our Caypso Shtetl* (Immediate Impact Publishers, Toronto 1998) reprinted with the permission of Dr. Zeno Strassberg (who compiled the book).

son, Sami, an engineer, and later took over the management of "London Fashion" - a men's clothing factory established by Moses Chaim (Muniu) Gottfried of Aruba to create employment for his relatives, the Katz family, and his nephews, Shechter and Salo Gross."

Mrs. Chuma Averbuch, a member of the small Trinidadian Jewish community, wrote to the even smaller Barbados community to say there was an eligible bachelor there and to send the girls. My mother was the lucky one. Oscar and Edna met and married in Trinidad on July 28, 1943. When my mother became pregnant with me in 1945, they moved to Barbados to be near her family. I, Leah Rose, was born on February 4, 1946, and as the first Altman grandchild, was suitably spoiled.

We lived at "Macabee" on Harts Gap with the other members of the Altman family. Simon and Rose Altman had taken over the house from my grandparents and they had four children – Marlene, Jimmy, Marsha, and Steven. My Aunt Mary and Uncle Louis Speisman who had no children lived next door.

**Edna and Oscar's wedding, Trinidad, July 28, 1943**
(Leah Pillersdorf Gilbert photo)

After my sister, Rachel, was born on August 10, 1948, we moved to a house that my parents had built on Rockley New Road. Uncle Henry and Aunt Deborah lived next door with their son, Paul, who was close in age to Rachel. We were part of a close-knit Jewish community that in its heyday numbered over 40 families. Everyone was invited to all parties. The adults played cards in different homes at least once a week. We had a community centre on Country Road, Bridgetown, which was used as a venue for Sunday school for the kids and a rehearsal hall for the adults' Yiddish theatre group. Mr. Konigsberg taught the children until Geoff Lebens arrived on the island. Mr. Lebens, his wife, and two children, Anne and Ralph, came from England. He taught at Harrison College, the island's premier boys' school. By the 1950s we no longer had a community centre. Sunday School was held in a room at the back of "Macabee" that also had served as our shul from the inception of the Ashkenazic Jewish community. Services were held there every Friday evening/Erev Shabbos. Several of the men were sufficiently knowledgeable to serve as "Ba'al-Tiffilahs"[32], including Bernard Konigsberg, Aaron Karp, Louis Speisman, Simon Altman, and my father.

On the Yom Tovim[33] the living and dining rooms of "Macabee" were turned into a shul, with the men and women sitting separately. The children played outdoors in the Altmans' and Speismans' yards. We walked to shul from Rockley New Road and thought nothing of it.

In 1965 the community rented a house on Rockley New Road from Mr. Joe Carew and turned it into a shul. Previously, Peggy Kreindler and her husband, Sam Mass, had lived there with their two young sons. I would sometimes ride there to visit the boys when their mother was out playing cards. In 1969 the community bought the house and it is still used as a shul today.

My father and his brother, Uncle Leib, helped bring their younger brother, Kuk Pilarski, his wife, Aunt Fela, and their three sons, Richard, Joseph, and Alex to Barbados. My parents gave up the Royal Store on High Street to Uncle Kuk and his family, and I presume they took over the lease.

Daddy started the Reliance Shirt Factory on Palmetto Street, the first shirt factory on the island, and he also made uniforms for various government departments. He and my mother also opened the Colony Store on lower Broad Street that my mother managed. It was a small department store selling yard goods, hats, sewing accessories, tablecloths, etc., and it had a men's department. My parents worked hard five-and-a-half days a week and made a success of both businesses.

Sometimes on Saturdays and during school holidays, especially at Christmas time, Rachel and I would lend helping hands. There were very few ready-made dresses available so dressmakers abounded. I can fold a shirt professionally

---

[32] Those who lead and chant the Sabbath services.
[33] Jewish holidays

because of helping in the factory. The one thing I never did well was cut lengths of material because I cannot cut a straight line.

Behind our house was a hill that Rachel, Paul, and I climbed regularly. There were very few chattel[34] houses in our area and little else but sugar cane fields. We would walk to Club Morgan, a nightclub owned by Peter Morgan, where our parents would sometimes go dancing on Saturday nights. On New Year's Eve the Marine Hotel was the first choice to welcome in the New Year. As teenagers, we would ring in the New Year at the Crane Hotel and watch the sunrise from the hotel room our parents rented for the night.

On Saturday afternoons my mother would sometimes allow us to go to a film in Bridgetown at the now defunct Empire Theatre or the Plaza Cinema – long burnt down. Our father would have preferred us to spend the time studying Hebrew with him. In the early years of the Jewish community, many members met at the Aquatic Club for a swim and chat on Sundays. Water polo was played next to the Club's pier where the kids sat and watched. Dances were held and movies screened at the Aquatic Club. When the Club closed, down, we met at the Paradise Beach Club, and later at the Hilton Hotel where I spent many mornings when our sons were little. On Sunday afternoons many families in the community would drive to the Crane Hotel where the children would run around while the adults chatted and had tea. We also watched the horse races at the Garrison Savannah sitting on top of our car.

**Edna and Oscar with Leah and Rachel at the Aquatic Club, Barbados, ca. 1951**
(Leah Pillersdorf Gilbert photo)

During school vacations Rachel, Paul, and I rode our bikes everywhere, including to Accra Beach. We always had to let Mummy know where we were going and call her when we got home.

---

[34] Wooden houses that were occupied by plantation labourers and which were easily dismantled and moved from one location to another.

Rachel and I were given piano lessons by Gerald Hudson who also taught voice at Queen's College. We had ballet classes with Madam Ifill and later, Penny Ramsey, a Royal Academy teacher who came to the island from England. Our early dance classes were held upstairs at the Aquatic Club and later, at the hall of the Young Men's Progressive Club.

There were very few tennis courts for public use so Mum tried to become a member of the Royal Yacht Club (now just called the Yacht Club) so we could use their courts. However, she was told no Jews were allowed. This was in the 1950s. No blacks or dogs were allowed either! However, when U.S. marines visited the island and young women were needed to partner them at dances, they did not hesitate to call me! When Barbados became independent in 1966, the situation changed and we are now members of the Yacht Club. So are blacks, but not dogs!

My sister and I got our primary education at Mrs. Jones' School. To this day I still see her children. From there we went on to Queen's College, an all-girls school opposite Queen's Park. Academics were not my forte. Nevertheless, I was accepted at NYU in New York to study medicine. I declined, knowing I would never cope with all the bookwork. Instead, much to my parents' disappointment, I opted for The Hammond School of Dancing, a ballet school in Chester, England, where I spent two very happy, satisfying years. I did spend one term in Montreal at Outremont High School and stayed with former members of our Jewish community, Anutsa and Naiman Pulver and their daughters, Molly and Vicky. However, as soon as the cold weather arrived, I was very unhappy and returned home.

**Leah and Rachel, Barbados, 1955**
(Leah Pillersdorf Gilbert photo)

During part of my vacations in the UK, I spent time in London with David and Celia Bornstein, friends of my parents and who used to live in British Guiana, now Guyana. It was at the Bornsteins' that I met my husband, Benny Gilbert. I was only 17, but there was an immediate attraction. We had our official engagement party in Barbados with the entire community in attendance. In fact, when we arrived at the airport, half the community was waiting to see whom I had brought home. In those days there was an open area so people could see the passengers alighting from the plane. Everyone took an interest in the lives of the other members of the community and they approved of my choice. A year later in 1965 we married and lived for a year in Golders Green, London. We then moved to Toronto where my sister lived and my parents had an apartment. We stayed for two years and our oldest son, Ian, was born there in April 1968. I taught ballet, and Benny who had worked with diamonds in London started a diamond business. By December 1968 the winters drove us back to Barbados where our second son, Eli, was born in August 1972.

**Leah and Benny Gilbert's wedding, London, UK, September 1965**
(Leah Pillersdorf Gilbert photo)

The original community had dwindled. Many of my peers had left the island, mainly for Canada, and their parents had followed them. Still, there were enough people to immerse ourselves in the shul and social life. Within a few years of our return, however, the feel of the community changed. We were a Jewish community in name only, no longer a cohesive group.

From 1969-1985 I taught ballet and performed with the Barbados Dance Theatre Company. I toured with the company to Guyana for Carifesta (Caribbean Festival of the Arts) and to Albany, New York, where we performed at the Egg Performing Arts Center. I did voluntary teaching at the School for the Blind and Deaf for 17 years, and led them in performances at the Holetown

Festival and in an annual show that the disabled community put on. It was both a frustrating and rewarding task.

For five years I prepared young couples, along with the fathers, for the "Black and White Debutante Balls," held by the American Women's Club. The dress code was black tie and gowns. The affairs were beautiful, very successful, and enjoyable, and usually held at Sam Lord's Castle. For the last 35 years, I have held "Aquacise" classes for the over-40s – an easier form of exercise for those with aging joints. I think I was one of the first people in the world to initiate this type of exercise for people with orthopaedic problems and arthritis. I don't remember at what point I began volunteering for the Jewish community's Chevra Kadisha that helps prepare the dead[35] for burial, but am thankful the jobs are few and far between.

After my parents sold the store, the factory, and their home on Rockley New Road, they built a house on Rendezvous Ridge across the street from the Wajchendler family. Daddy couldn't just sit around. As much as he liked to read and learn, he had to keep his mind active and Benny joined him in a budding real estate company called Land Development and Building Ltd. that catered to the lower/middle classes. The two of them got on very well and the business flourished.

We lived in a rented house in Regency Park until we bought a lot in one of our developments in Atlantic Shores, Christ Church. We built a house there, moved in soon after Eli's birth, and still live there.

**Oscar Pillersdorf receiving the 1983 Silver Crown of Merit award from**

---

[35] The Chevra Kadish is a volunteer organization in which Jewish women prepare the bodies of women for burial, and Jewish men, the bodies of men.

**Sir Hugh Springer, Governor General of Barbados,
for building affordable housing for low-income Barbadians.**
Left to right, Oscar, Sir Hugh Springer, and Edna
(Rachel Pillersdorf Weisman photo)

After Moshe Altman passed away, Dad became the leader of the Jewish community. He was a true academic who spoke several languages, Polish, German, Yiddish, Latin and English. He taught himself Spanish and Hebrew and never hesitated to refer to a dictionary to find the most appropriate word whenever necessary. Visiting Israelis were amazed at his vocabulary and ability to speak Hebrew. Although he was known as an absent-minded professor and gave the impression he lived in a world of his own, he was very aware. He was an extremely successful businessman and a staunch supporter of Israel to which he and my mother travelled a few times in an era when it was not an easy journey.

Dad was the leader of the community until 1975 when Motel Truss succeeded him. After Motel, Benny became the President and in 1982 was also appointed the Consul for Israel. A few years later he was made Consul General for Israel in Barbados, a position he still holds today. Marshall Oran succeeded Benny as President of the Barbados Jewish Community, and after him Rochelle Altman and Joseph Steinbok served short terms. Jacob Hassid, who came to Barbados from Israel with his wife, Michal, to open Diamonds International, followed Joe Steinbok and is the current President.

My mother was a gregarious, hospitable, and capable woman. She constantly entertained both the local community and visitors. She was a wonderful baker and cook. We had guests at our table for every Yom Tov and most Shabbats, all this while she managed the Colony Store. Unfortunately, she suffered a severe stroke at age 64 and never recovered her speech. It was miserable for her and she passed away in 1990. At the time Ian was graduating from Emory University in Atlanta, Georgia. Dad moved between living with Rachel and Simon in Toronto and Benny and me in Barbados until he passed away in 1999. My parents were good, hardworking people and are terribly missed.

Ian now lives in Toronto with his partner, Tarra, and has his own business. Eli graduated from Queen's University, in Kingston, Ontario. He is married to Jodie and has two lovely children, Mya and Riley. They live in Oakville, Ontario, and plan to move to Kelowna, British Colombia.

Benny and I celebrated 50 years of marriage in September 2015 and still live in Atlantic Shores. However, we now travel during the summer and are in Barbados between October and June.

# RACHEL PILLERSDORF WEISMAN'S STORY
Rachel Pillersdorf Weisman

**Simon and Rachel Weisman, Toronto, 2013**
(Simon Kreindler photo)

My mother, Elka (Edna/Eda) Altman, the third of Hinda and Moses Altman's five children, arrived in Barbados from Lublin, Poland, at age 14. She spoke no English and was too old to attend high school so her father arranged for her to have a private tutor.

**Henry, Mary, Hinda, Doris, Edna, and Moses Altman,
Barbados, ca. 1940**
(Rachel Pillersdorf Weisman photo)

My grandfather, Moses, had a boat in which he used to go fishing and he also had horses. Mum used to tell us the story of how one of the horses once threw her while she was riding along Belleville Road and then raced back to the stable leaving her to limp home!

Bum (Abraham) Pillersdorf, who was killed in the Shoah, was my father's youngest brother. He used to call my dad, Shie Wolf, "Oscar" and the name stuck. Dad arrived in Trinidad on his way to Caracas, Venezuela, just as WWII broke out and met my uncle, Simon Altman, who was on a buying trip in Trinidad. There weren't many eligible bachelors in Barbados and Simon introduced him to my mother. After several visits and many letters between the two islands, they were married in Trinidad. Since it was during the war, only one person was permitted to travel with Mum for the wedding so her father, Moses Altman, accompanied her to Trinidad.

**Henry Altman, Oscar Pillersdorf and Simon Altman,
Barbados, 1940s**

**Hinda Altman, Oscar and Edna Pillersdorf, and Mary Altman, Barbados, 1940s**
(Rachel Pillersdorf Weisman photos)

After the war they moved to Barbados to be with Mum's family. Initially, they lived on Harts Gap with the rest of the family but later they built their own home on Rockley New Road, Christ Church, across from the only golf course on the island at the time.

Dad used to tell us a story of the time he had a pet rooster that would always greet him when he returned home. One day he didn't see the rooster. That night at dinner, he asked Mum what they were eating. It was the rooster. He did not eat!

I was born in the Barbados General Hospital on Bay Street, Bridgetown, on Tuesday, August 10, 1948, approximately six years after my parents were married. My sister, Leah Rose, is two-and-a-half years older than me. I understand she was very precocious. As a two-year-old watching a painter in the house, her oft-repeated famous words were, "Painter, painter, hold the brush, the ladder is falling."

When I was six months old, my grandfather, Moses, died of cancer after which my grandmother, Hinda, moved to Israel, leaving all her children and grandchildren in Barbados. For various personal reasons, she never liked being in Barbados, and although she died more than 10 years later, she only ever saw three of her children and two grandchildren who came there to visit her. I met my grandmother once when I was eight and accompanied Mum and her sister, Auntie Mary, to Israel.

My childhood was a very happy and, I believe, a lucky one. I had a devoted nanny, Margaret Alleyne, with whom I was very close and who took care of me until I started school at age five. She then left to work for my Auntie Fanny and Uncle Leib[36] who still had babies. Margaret's sister, Uraline Alleyne, then came to work for us, and although she was officially our cook and housekeeper, she also took care of me and I loved her. After I left home, she quit and eventually moved to New York where I visited her a few times and kept in touch until she passed away. We also had a washerwoman and a gardener, and from when I was nine or ten, a chauffeur who drove us to and from school and worked in the store the rest of the time.

**Leah, cousin Paul Altman, and Rachel, in school uniform, Barbados, 1957**
(Leah Pillersdorf Gilbert photo)

My cousin, Paul Altman, lived next door and we were very close friends. We also played with Jimmy, Jocelyn, Susan and Mark Paris who were black and lived across the street from Paul. We went to their birthday parties and they came to ours. Birthday parties were huge as can be seen from various photos. We had no choice in the matter, every Jewish child and their family was invited whether we wanted them or not. At Christmas, we joined the Paris family in exchanging gifts and drank sorrel[37] that Mrs. Paris made only at Christmas.

At Eastertime we had kite-flying competitions and in the summer we roamed the street and fields on foot and later on our bikes. We raced lizards that we

---

[36] My paternal uncle and his wife whom Dad had found in a DP camp after the war and brought to Barbados.
[37] A drink made from petals of the Roselle flower, a species of Hibiscus, native to West Africa.

collared with long grass, or picked dunks, ackees, gooseberries, tamarinds, cherries or golden apples, depending on what was in season. We'd fill paper bags with the fruit, return home to sit on our swing and eat and spit the seeds for the next hour or so. As we got older, we were permitted to ride where we liked, even to the beach as long as we were home in time for lunch. We didn't have watches and usually averaged the time by the position of the sun.

On Sunday mornings we met most of the Jewish community at what was then the Aquatic Club to swim and schmooze. Before going, however, we all attended Sunday school where we were taught basic Hebrew reading and heard stories about the Jewish holidays and heroes. After the beach, we returned home to a large lunch followed by a nap, except for those of us who preferred listening to records. In the late afternoon we would take a drive to the airport to watch planes land or to the Crane Hotel where we had tea and buttered toast fingers. Then we got to run around and play and watch the waves crash against the rocks. There were usually other Jewish families there doing the same thing, so we generally had other kids with whom to play.

At least twice a week the adults met in each other's homes for games of Canasta and Poker. I remember loving to stay up late to serve snacks and non-alcoholic drinks!

On Friday nights we all attended Shabbat Services at Simon and Rose Altman's home in Harts Gap. They later built on an addition in back of their home that was used specifically as a shul. After services Auntie Rose would play popular music from the U.S. and teach us all how to dance. I have a vague memory of being in a large yard during the High Holidays where services were being held. I remember Sonia Silver, Betty Konigsberg, and Rosie Zerlier, all at least 10 years older than me, and a man selling coconuts from a cart. I have since learned that when I was quite young, there used to be a Jewish community centre and maybe this was the place I remembered.

My parents had a dry goods store and a shirt factory. We wore uniforms to school but at home we usually hung out barefoot in shorts and tops. Each year before Rosh Hashanah, Leah and I got to choose from our parents' Colony Store two lengths of material we liked. Then off to our dressmaker, Esther, to choose the style of dresses we wanted from a large pattern book that was probably a few years old. Still, we were happy to have new dresses for Yontif[38] each year.

At age five I attended a private school run by Mrs. Jones in what must have been her garage plus another large room under the living quarters of her house. At recess we played in a field on a hill behind the house. We made cuts on some

---

[38] A Yiddish word meaning "holiday."

of the trees and collected the gum that oozed out by the next day. I don't know for what! Also at recess, the "sweet lady" came to the school and we usually had a few pennies our parents had given us to spend on sugar cakes and glacies - local homemade candy.

At age eight I took the entrance exam for Queen's College, and went to school there for seven years before leaving Barbados for Toronto, Canada.

When I was nine, Dad found his brother, Kuk, and family in Europe. Not long after, Kuk and his middle son, Joseph Pilarski, came to live with us. Very soon after there was a lot of Polish being spoken at home and I still remember at least 10 words! I think about a year later, Fela Pilarski and their other two sons, Richard and Alex, arrived on the S.S. Batory. We got to go on board to meet them and I remember having strawberries and smoked salmon. Later they moved into their own house.

When I was 13, Leah left for school in Montreal, although she was back by Christmas! At my request my parents started dropping me off at Accra Beach on Sundays where I met with friends, both Jewish and non-Jewish. I remember Aaron Truss playing guitar while we all sang and lay in the sun getting burnt. My parents would pick me up on their way home from whatever beach they were at. Often, we kids met again in the afternoon at the cinema to see a matinee or sometimes attended dances as a group, chauffeured by our parents. We listened to the Merry Men and the Young Ones (Joe Truss and a boyfriend of mine played in this group) among others and we danced! There were no liquor laws that I am aware of and we all drank rum and coke but no one got drunk - at least not at our table.

I attended ballet classes from age three, had lots of fun performing at various charity events, and continued with it after coming to Toronto until well into my 40s.

I did well in my O level exams at Queen's College and wanted to do A level science but Queen's College had no A level science program. I was accepted by Harrison College, a boys' school, but for a variety of reasons made a spur of the moment decision not to go there. Instead, I went to stay with my Aunt Fanny and Uncle Leib in Toronto and continued my education there. I completed grade 13 at Bathurst Heights Secondary School and then went on to the University of Toronto.

**Rachel and Simon Weisman, September 1972**
(Rachel Pillersdorf Weisman photo)

# *SIMON AND ROSE ALTMAN'S STORY*
Marsha Altman Glassman and Rose Diane Miller Altman, ז״ל

**Rose and Simon Altman, Barbados, 1967**
(Marsha Altman Glassman photo)

Some of us who lived in Barbados have beautiful memories of our island and warm, loving memories of the Jewish and non-Jewish communities that helped shape who we are today. Over the past 50-plus years, people have repeatedly asked me, "Being Jewish, how did your family end up in Barbados?" Here is our story.

My father's family originally came from Lublin, Poland. Our grandfather, Moshe Altman, after whom I am named, left Poland for Palestine in early 1930, but since it was under British rule, he was not granted permission to stay there. He returned to Poland and shortly thereafter, he and some of his Jewish friends/family, such as Yankel Bernstein, Dyna Mass and Moshe Mass (and others of whom we are not sure) left Poland on a freighter for South America.[39] On the way the freighter stopped in Barbados and Moshe Altman and his friends decided to remain there. They sent for their families in Poland a few years later and so began the revival of the Jewish community in Barbados.

Moshe Altman started out as a peddler as did most of the Jewish men who came to Barbados in the 1930s and 1940s. As soon as they had saved enough money,

---

[39] Available evidence suggests that Moses Altman arrived in Barbados in 1932 on the same ship as Moses and Dina/Dyna Mass. See Chapter 3.

they sent for their families in Europe. All of them were fleeing pogroms, persecution, and poverty in Europe.

Moshe met the Averboukhs when the freighter on which they were travelling stopped in Barbados on the way to South America. He knew Chuma Averboukh's father in Poland and Chuma spent two weeks with Moshe and Hinda in Barbados before joining her husband, Louver, in Trinidad.

Chuma Averboukh had a niece who in 1930 had come to New York from Wengrow, Poland, when she was seven. That niece was my mom, Rose Diane (Dyna Raizel) Miller, b. April 1, 1923. My mother's father, Simcha Bunem Monka, came to New York in 1923 and changed his last name from Monka to Miller (since Monka sounded like monkey). In 1930, he sent for his wife, Esther Malka Monka, b. March 10, 1898, in Wengrow, and my mother, Rose.

My mother and her parents lived with her maternal grandparents, Devorah and Jacob Rubin, in New York. My mother had two older sisters. The eldest, Pauline Monka, born in Warsaw, died of dysentery when she was an infant. Her other sister, Sara Lily, was not granted a visa to come to the United States of America because she had had tuberculosis as a child and was killed in Warsaw by Hitler.

After my mother's arrival in the United States, my grandparents had three more children, all born in New York. Harry on April 16, 1931; David, on February 12, 1933; and Anita on April 26, 1935.

On March 28, 1940, my grandmother, Esther Malka, died from leukemia, leaving her husband and four children. My mother, being the eldest, was responsible for her siblings as her father was not a responsible individual. After about three years of working and taking care of them, she placed them in Jewish foster homes but visited them faithfully each week.

**David, Anita, Rose, and Harry Miller, New York, ca. 1946**
(Marsha Altman Glassman photo)

In 1946 Chuma and Louver Averboukh invited my mother to come to Trinidad. Although my mother did not want to leave her siblings, she went anyway and subsequently flew with Chuma to Barbados where she met my father, Simon Altman. They married in Trinidad on October 26, 1946, returned to Barbados, and started their new life together there. As they say, the rest is history.

**Rose and Simon Altman's wedding, Trinidad, October 1946**
Back row: Moses Altman holding Leah Pillersdorf, Rose, Simon, Louis Speisman, Hinda Altman, Oscar Pillersdorf.
Front row: Edna Pillersdorf, Mary Speisman
(Marsha Altman Glassman photo)

In Barbados, Simon, Henry, Doris, and their mother, Hinda, worked at and had shares in the Broadway Dress Shop. Their father, Moshe Altman, and their sister, Edna (Elka), who had married Oscar Pillersdorf in Trinidad on July 28, 1943, worked at and had shares in the Royal Store. When Hinda moved to Palestine after Moshe's death, she was paid for her share, and when Doris married Jack Kaplan and moved to Florida, she was paid for her share.

Rose and Simon then rented the Bargain House, 30 Swan Street, from Louis Speisman who was married to Simon's sister, Mary Altman. When Louis Speisman built 23 Swan Street, Simon and Rose rented the building and called it Altman's. It had a dress shop upstairs and dry goods (materials) downstairs. In 1956 Rose bought the building at 8 Broad Street in Bridgetown, and Altman's Department Store was born. When Simon died on July 5, 1976, their eldest son, James, worked in the business with Mom until 1998 when it was dissolved and the building rented to Diamonds International.

When Mom and Dad were first married, they lived with Hinda and Moshe Altman at "Macabee," Harts Gap. After their eldest child, Marlene, was born, they lived in Elm House in Hastings. From there they moved to Lynnwood on Rockley New Road and then back to "Macabee." Later Rose built 24 Rendezvous Ridge in Christ Church and lived there for the rest of her life.

Our parents had four children. Marlene Estelle was born in Miami on September 9, 1947. The younger three children were all born in Barbados: James Chaim, b. September 20, 1948; Marsha, b. January 29, 1950; and Steven Lawrence, b. October 12, 1952. We were all raised at "Macabee," our paternal grandparents' home.

Several of the Jewish families in Barbados were related by blood. Henry Altman, Mary Altman Speisman, Edna (Eda) Altman Pillersdorf, Simon Altman, and Doris Altman Kaplan were all offspring of Moshe and Hinda Altman, and the Karp and Silver families were cousins. In 1963 Marshall and Anita Oran (Rose's sister) and family moved to Barbados.

The Jewish community consisted of about 25-30 families and was like one big family when I was growing up. For years "Macabee" was the meeting place for Friday night and High Holiday services, as well as other Jewish celebrations. Since there was no rabbi on the island, community members such as Bernard Konigsberg, Paltiel Paster, and Simon Altman conducted services. Sunday school was held in our home and taught by Mr. Geoff Lebens. Most of the

Jewish boys in the 1950s and 1960s prepared for their Bar Mitzvahs by learning their Haftorah[40] from a recorded tape.

In 1964 the Jewish community rented "True Blue," a house on Rockley New Road and converted it to the current synagogue, used from March through December for services and celebrations. In 1969 they purchased the property.

The downtown synagogue, Nidhe Israel, was constructed in 1654[41] and is the second oldest synagogue in the Western Hemisphere. It was restored to its original 19th-century splendour in the mid-1980s and is used during the tourist season from December through April. The Jewish cemetery on the grounds of Nidhe Israel has graves of Jews buried there from the 1660s.

Passover Seders and High Holiday meals at "Macabee" always required additional chairs and tables to accommodate our parents' many guests. No Jew was a stranger to our father, Simon. They were always invited and welcomed in our home whether it was for a Jewish holiday or a weeknight dinner. The United States servicemen who were stationed at the U.S. base often joined us for the Jewish holidays.

Our mother, Rose Diane, never disappointed anyone who sat down for a meal in our home. The delicious smells coming from the kitchen were a foreshadowing of what to expect and all of this was done with daily help, Griff-Griff, Braff-Braff, and Ki-Ki, throughout the years. Even though Mom worked side by side in the business with our Dad, she never failed to produce an outstanding meal for her family, friends, and guests. From her chopped liver and gefilte fish entrees to her strudel, honey cakes, cookies, and other delicious dishes, one could always expect to hear, "Second helpings, please!"

---

[40] A portion of the Book of Prophets chanted or read in the synagogue on the Sabbath and holy days. www.dictionary.com/browse/haftarah.
[41] Although 1654 is frequently used in referring to the completion of the Nidhe Isreal Synagogue, it is probably inaccurate as the arrival of significant numbers of Sephardi Jews from Brazil only started that year. See Chapter 1.

**KiKi, Rose's helper and later, Marsha Altman Glassman's helper**
(Rose Altman photo)

Mom was the treasurer of the local WIZO[42] chapter and the Jewish community for many years. She played canasta with the ladies on a weekly basis. For years Dad ordered the matzot[43] and kosher wine for Passover for the other Jewish families. Later on, Marshall Oran took over ordering the Pesach (Passover) products. Orders came to Altman's Department Store and were then distributed to each family.

Living next door to us in Harts Gap were our father's sister, Mary Altman Speisman, and her husband, Louis Speisman. Their home was called "Messiah." Aunty and Uncle never had children of their own and they treated us children, Marlene, Jimmy, Marsha and Steven, like their very own. Aunty was President of the WIZO chapter for many years and helped raise funds for Israel and other causes. She was also involved with the SPCA. Uncle was a wise and learned man who spent hours reading in his back room, surrounded by hundreds of books. He was very involved in the rituals of the Jewish community; enjoyed betting on the horses during race season; and was a heavy smoker who loved his scrambled eggs "runny" and his coffee in a big glass!

Our education began at Mrs. Hart's School where we were taught to read, write and do basic mathematics. From there my brothers progressed to Lodge School, and my sister and I to Codrington High School. Jewish students were a minority in both schools. The education was excellent but discipline was strict - writing lines or being given detentions for less serious offences or, as was the case at

---

[42] Women's International Zionist Organization
[43] A flat piece of unleavened bread resembling a large cracker eaten by Jews during Passover. According to the biblical account of Passover, G-d directed the ancestors of the Jews to eat unleavened bread rather than delay their departure from Egypt by waiting for bread to rise. Source: The American Heritage New Dictionary of Cultural Literacy, 3rd Edition. Houghton Mifflin Company, 2005.
http://www.dictionary.com/browse/matzot

Lodge School, being caned with a bamboo rod for more serious infractions. We did our best to be respectful of all, regardless of age, colour or creed; to be courteous and polite; and to study hard in order to avoid any and all discipline.

When we came home on weekends we spent time with our parents and socialized with other members of the Jewish community. On Friday nights Mom lit the Shabbat candles and said the blessings to welcome the Sabbath. Dad said the blessings before sitting down to eat Shabbat dinner, which consisted of chopped liver or gefilte fish, chicken soup with luckshon (noodles), boiled chicken, rice, peas, salad, and fruit compote or one of Mom's delicious baked products, such as strudel or cookies. Later we attended services and afterwards many of the teenagers would come to our home and Mom would teach us to dance. I especially remember her teaching us to square dance to music from the movie, Oklahoma, etc.

On Saturdays our parents worked in their business for half a day. Some Saturdays we were recruited to help with taking cash, selling merchandise, or wrapping packages. When we worked in the store we were taught that the customer weas always right. We were also taught to be polite and courteous, that it was a mitzvah to give tzdakah (charity) and to care about those less fortunate. These teachings were part of our lives growing up and are still with us today.

The upstairs of Altman's Department Store carried only women's wear such as bathing suits, dresses, skirts, and blouses, etc. Mom designed and cut women's formal and informal dresses and skirts. Her customers loved her taste and relied on her to select the most becoming outfits for whatever occasion they were going to be attending.

**Altman's Department Store, 8 Broad Street,
Bridgetown, Barbados**
(James Altman photo)

**Upstairs at Altman's Department Store**
(James Altman photo)

The downstairs of the store carried a variety of merchandise for local Barbadians and tourists, ranging from souvenirs to men's shirts, ladies' and men's hats, shoes, dry goods/materials, women's underwear, stockings, straw bags, and other merchandise.

After Saturday lunch, our big meal of the day, it was either off to the beach with friends (Accra or the Aquatic Club) or to the movies at the Plaza, Empire or Globe Theatres. On Saturday afternoons our Dad would usually rest while Mom continued doing things that only she could do after working in the store for half a day.

Sundays were family days. After breakfast we sometimes went to Paradise Beach Club or the Aquatic Club. We would swim, chat, play in the sand, and look for shells (especially popeyes). Our parents, except for Mom, would often take a dip in the ocean, then sit in the shade and catch up on the gossip. Paradise Beach had the best bar for Bentleys[44] served with extra cherries. In addition, their ice cream floats were out of this world.

When we were boarders at our respective schools, we came home on Friday afternoons and returned to school on Sunday afternoons. When we became day students, we were driven to school every morning and picked up every afternoon. The drive home was long and didn't leave much time for homework and all the other necessary chores before bedtime. Weekends were our only respite.

Gradually the Jewish community dwindled. Children were sent to Canada or the United States to further their education (there being no university in Barbados during the 1950s and early 1960s) and/or to meet prospective spouses. Eventually many of the parents followed.

Some of my memories of growing up in Barbados include visiting Humphrey's Bakery and inhaling the delicious aromas coming from their breads, jam puffs, rock cakes, penny loaves, and other delicacies. Sometimes we were allowed to go into the back of the bakery and walk around to see what was available and sample some of their products.

Other memories include climbing the ackee tree at "Macabee" and eating the ackees until they "tied up our mouths"; picking breadfruits that grew on the tree in the middle of our yard; picking avocados from the tree outside our kitchen window; and eating the acerola cherries that grew by the well in our backyard. Aunty Mary and Uncle Louis used to have pomegranates and tamarinds on their property that we also helped ourselves to whenever we wanted. Golden apples and dunks were often purchased from local vendors at the old bus terminal and tasted best when eaten in the ocean. Memories of eating local dishes such as cou-cou, salt fish, sea eggs and rice, flying fish, either steamed or fried, and

---

[44] A lemonade-like drink made with a shot of Angostura bitters and decorated with a maraschino cherry.

drinking Bajan tea with condensed milk and sugar still excite my palate to this day!

In 1963 our parents sent my elder sister, Marlene, to live with Mom's cousin in New York for the school year. Marlene didn't like the cold weather and went to Miami to continue her education. My brother, Jim, and I followed her there in 1964 for the last two years of high school and at one point all three of us were at the University of Miami.

In 1967 Marlene married Yerachmiel (Rachmi) Mutchnik. Their son, Mark Aron, was born on December 29, 1967. Marlene and Rachmi later divorced and she eventually returned to Barbados with Mark and lived with Mom and Dad. About 1979 she married Stan Langer in Toronto and their son, Simon Louis, was born on February 21, 1980. Marlene and Stan eventually also divorced, and about 2005 she reunited with Peter Sarjeant, her first boyfriend in Barbados. She and Peter married in Louisiana in 2006 and continue to live there. Marlene's elder son, Mark Aron, married Erica Kent (b. September 4, 1976) on December 1, 2008, and they live in Florida. Their son, Jackson Kent, was born September 27, 2010. Marlene's younger son, Simon Louis, married Ella Schondorf on May 13, 2007. They have a son, Liam Samuel, born on October 22, 2009, and they live in Toronto.

Jim, the second eldest child of Rose and Simon, attended yeshiva in Miami Beach from 1964-1965 and graduated from Coral Park Senior High School in 1966. While Jim was in his last year at the University of Miami in 1969, our Dad had a heart attack and Jim went back to Barbados to work in the business. The years passed. Jim married Mary Lea (Leah) from Montreal on March 18, 1989. They have two sons. Sean Noah, b. January 18, 1990, and Ryan Jacob, born June 2, 1991, both born in Montreal. After Jim and Mary Lea divorced, Jim married Anita Vatch (b. December 24, 1951) in Montreal on May 28, 2000. Jim and Anita split their time between Barbados and Montreal.

Sean Altman graduated from university with a Bachelor of Arts Degree, and Ryan, his brother, with a Bachelor's Degree in Business. Sean currently lives in Montreal with his girlfriend, Samara Wolofsky, b. November 13, 1987. Ryan is single and working in Los Angeles.

Anita was previously married and has two children: Adam Howard Silverman, b. December 12, 1977, and Lauren Shari Silverman, b. August 5, 1980. On June 22, 2003, Adam married Tali Chemtob, b. August 14, 1978. They have three sons, Gabriel, b. May 25, 2006; Joseph Dylan, b. September 4, 2008, and David James, b. June 15, 2013, all living in Montreal. On August 5, 2007, Lauren Shari married Noah Jason Pinsky, b. January 14, 1980. They have two children:

Drew, b. September 19, 2009, and Courtney Summer, b. July 29, 2011, all of them also living in Montreal.

I, Marsha, am the third of Simon and Rose's children. I met Daniel Glassman (b. January 8, 1946) an Israeli, at the University of Miami's Hillel House. We married in Barbados in a civil ceremony on August 14, 1969, and then in a Jewish ceremony on August 16, 1969, at the Hilton Hotel. Rabbi Alter Kriegel was brought in from New Jersey to officiate at our religious wedding. Rabbi Kriegel was related to very good friends of Mom and Dad's, Dr. and Mrs. Saul Shapiro.

**Daniel and Marsha Glassman, Barbados, August 16, 1969**
(Marsha Altman Glassman photo)

I graduated from the University of Miami in January 1970 and taught elementary school for four years. Daniel graduated from the University of Miami in 1973 and we moved to Minnesota in 1974 so that Dan could attend Northwestern College of Chiropractic. On December 9, 1975, our twins, Liat Dania and David Isaac, were born at Southdale Hospital in Edina, Minnesota.

Following Dan's graduation, we remained in Minnesota until 1981, then moved to Arizona and have lived there ever since. Dan established a chiropractic practice but is currently only working a couple of hours per week as he is on dialysis and waiting patiently for a kidney transplant.

In 1988 David celebrated his Bar Mitzvah at the Shaare Tzedek Synagogue in Barbados. Since the Jewish community was more traditionally Conservative with some Orthodox practices, Liat was not called to the Torah, and instead did a Havdalah service at her Granny Rose's home at 24 Rendezvous Ridge to celebrate her becoming a Bat Mitzvah. In honour of this momentous occasion, Granny Rose held a huge celebration for both Liat and David at the Hilton Hotel on December 24, 1988.

Liat and David graduated high school with honours in 1993 and from the University of Arizona in Tucson, AZ, also with honours, in 1996. Liat completed Master's degrees in Psychology and Education in Los Angeles and teaches elementary school in Culver City, CA. She married Dan Spitz on March 23, 2007, and they have two children: Kai Joseph (Hai Yosef), b. September 24, 2007, and Riley Alexis Lydia (Rachel Leah), b. January 13, 2011. Liat, Dan, and their children live in Venice, CA.

David attended Midwestern University, College of Osteopathic Medicine, in Glendale, AZ, and became a physician (obstetrician-gynecologist), specializing in gynecological surgery. He married Samara Lazarus on June 2, 2002, and they have two children, Eliana Nicole (Eliana Nurit), b. November 2, 2005, and Jesse Alexander (Yishai Alexander), b. May 20, 2009. Samara and David are now divorced, and he lives in Phoenix, AZ.

My younger brother, Steven, graduated from the Military Academy in Miami, Florida, and attended the University of Miami where he obtained his undergraduate and Master's degrees. He married Ellen Ganzman in Miami and they have a son, Adam Colin, b. November 9, 1974. Steven and Ellen divorced and he returned to Barbados. He married Donna Pooler and they have a daughter, Stacy, b. July 11, 1981. Stacy Altman married Danny Mansour on December 5, 2007. Steven and Donna were also divorced. He is single now and has established himself as a realtor in Barbados.

Over the years my family has returned to Barbados on many occasions. Liat and David were only seven months young when they made their first trip to Barbados. They have grown to love the island and met many of the Jewish families and their offspring. They are now taking their children (my grandchildren) to Barbados to absorb some of the culture and learn about their heritage. They are also meeting cousins and other Jewish and non-Jewish families whom we have known for many years. G-d willing, the cycle will continue.

Most of the information set forth here was given to me by my mother when her first great-granddaughter, Eliana Nicole Glassman was born. Since I had no documentation of our family history, I put together several questions and sent them to her. She answered for her side of the family and for Dad's side since there was no member of his family left to tell their story. I have additional documentation from Mom regarding names, etc., but it would take many more pages to tell it all.

Our mom, Rose Diane, was the eldest member of the Jewish community at the time of her death on May 9, 2016. She was an inspiration to us all and is greatly missed by her family and many close friends. Mom, thank you for sharing your memories, both the good and the not-so-good. You have certainly given our family a wealth of information that would otherwise have been lost.

They say you can never go back, but our memories are forever. We hope that our children, grandchildren, and great children, etc., will gain a little insight into their heritage and how we lived our lives in our beloved Barbados after reading the stories in this book.

Buried in the Jewish cemetery, Bridgetown, Barbados are the following family members of the Altman and Oran families:

**Moshe Altman** (Born 1888 and died 1949): Husband of Hinda Altman; father to Henry Altman, Mary Altman Speisman, Eda Altman Pillersdorf, Simon Altman, Doris Altman Kaplan; grandfather to Marlene Estelle Altman Mutchnik Langer Sarjeant, James Chaim Altman, Marsha Altman Glassman, Steven Lawrence Altman; great-grandfather to Mark Aron Mutchnik, Adam Colin Altman, Liat Dania Glassman, David Isaac Glassman, Simon Louis Langer, Stacy Altman Mansour, Sean Noah Altman, Ryan Jacob Altman; great-great-grandfather to Eliana Nicole Glassman, Kai Joseph Spitz, Jesse Alexander Glassman, Liam Samuel Langer, Jackson Kent Mutchnik and Riley Alexis Lydia Spitz.

**Hersh Silver** (b. Lublin, Poland, March 15, 1909; d. February 2, 1943): Husband of Chana Silver; nephew of Hinda Altman; father to Sonia and Leon Silver; grandfather to Sonia and Leon's offspring.

**Aron Louie Karp** (b. March 21, 1915; d. April 7, 1967): Husband of Marilyn Karp; nephew of Moshe Altman; cousin to Henry Altman, Mary Altman Speisman, Eda Altman Pillersdorf, Simon Altman, Doris Altman Kaplan; father to Rabbi Joel Karp, Stanley Karp, Ronald Karp, and Annie Karp Zeplowitz; grandfather to Joel, Ronald and Annie's children.

**Simon Altman** (b. May 19, 1920; d. July 5, 1976): Son of Moshe and Hinda Altman; brother to Henry Altman, Mary Altman Speisman, Eda Altman Pillersdaorf, and Doris Altman Kaplan; husband to Rose Diane Altman; father to Marlene Altman Mutchnik Langer Sarjeant, James Chaim Altman, Marsha

Altman Glassman, Steven Lawrence Altman; grandfather to Mark Aron Mutchnik, Adam Colin Altman, Liat Dania Glassman, David Isaac Glassman, Simon Louis Langer, Stacy Altman Mansour, Sean Noah Altman, Ryan Jacob Altman; great-grandfather to Eliana Nicole Glassman, Kai Joseph Spitz, Jesse Alexander Glassman, Liam Samuel Langer, Jackson Kent Mutchnik, and Riley Alexis Lydia Spitz.

**Louis Speisman** (b. November 25, 1906; d. August 18, 1976): Husband of Mary Altman Speisman; uncle to Marlene Estelle Altman Mutchnik Langer Sarjeant, James Chaim Altman, Marsha Altman Glassman, Steven Lawrence Altman; great-uncle to Mark Aron Mutchnik, Adam Colin Altman, Liat Dania Glassman, David Isaac Glassman, Simon Louis Langer, Stacy Altman Mansour, Sean Noah Altman, Ryan Jacob Altman; great-great-uncle to Eliana Nicole Glassman, Kai Joseph Spitz, Jesse Alexander Glassman, Liam Samuel Langer, Jackson Kent Mutchnik, and Riley Alexis Lydia Spitz.

**Mary Speisman** (b. April 5, 1915; d. May 5, 1985): Daughter of Moshe and Hinda Altman; sister to Henry Altman, Eda Altman Pillersdorf, Simon Altman, Doris Altman Kaplan; wife of Louis Speisman; aunt to Marlene Estelle Altman Mutchnik Langer Sarjeant, James Chaim Altman, Marsha Altman Glassman, Steven Lawrence Altman; great-aunt to Mark Aron Mutchnik, Adam Colin Altman, Liat Dania Glassman, David Isaac Glassman, Simon Louis Langer, Stacy Altman Mansour, Sean Noah Altman, Ryan Jacob Altman; great-great-aunt to Eliana Nicole Glassman, Kai Joseph Spitz, Jesse Alexander Glassman, Liam Samuel Langer, Jackson Kent Mutchnik, Riley Alexis Lydia Spitz.

**Anita Oran** (b. April 26, 1935; d. August 8, 1997): Daughter of Simcha Benum Miller and Esther Malka Rubin Miller; sister of Rose Diane Miller Altman, Harry Miller, Dr. David Miller; wife of Marshall Oran; mother to Gilda Maureen Oran and Scott Oran; grandmother of Daniel Oran, Justin Oran, Naomi Oran Puckett, Gabriel Oran, Max Oran, and Arel Oran; great-grandmother of Elijah Oran, Amelia Oran Puckett, Nora Rose Oran Puckett, Logan John Oran.

**Deborah Tint-Pulver Altman** (b. December 8, 1914; d. January 7, 1998): Wife of Henry Altman; mother of Paul Bernard Altman; grandmother of Abigail Altman and Rina Altman.

**Henry Judka Hersz Altman** (b. April 23, 1913; d. July 20, 2008): Son of Moshe and Hinda Altman; brother of Mary Altman Speisman, Eda Altman Pillersdorf, Simon Altman, Doris Altman Kaplan; father of Paul Bernard Altman; grandfather of Abigail Altman and Rina Altman.

**Marilyn Karp** (b. November 12, 1926; February 19, 2013): Wife of Aron Karp; mother of Joel Karp, Stanley Karp, Ronald Karp, and Annie Karp Zeplowitz; grandmother to Rabbi Joel, Ronald and Annie's offspring; great-grandmother to the grandchildren's offspring.

**Elka (Eda) Edna Altman Pillersdorf** (b. Lublin, Poland, July 30, 1917; d. May 15, 1990): Buried in Toronto, Canada. Daughter of Moshe and Hinda Altman; wife of Oscar Pillersdorf; mother of Leah Rose Pillersdorf Gilbert and Rachel Pillersdorf Weisman; grandmother of Ian Michael Gilbert, Eli Simon Gilbert, Jonathon Jacob Weisman, Sara Arielle Weisman Borer, and Gideon Solomon Weisman; great-grandmother of Mya Gilbert, Riley Eric Gilbert, Kalanit Yarden Borer, Nathan Joshua Borer, Rebecca Sophie Borer, and Eliana Aviva Borer.

**Oscar Schie Wolf Pillersdorf** (b. Rudki, Poland, November 8, 1908; September 4, 1999): Buried in Toronto, Canada. Husband of Edna Altman Pillersdorf; father of Leah Rose Pillersdorf Gilbert, Rachel Pillersdorf; grandfather of Ian Michael Gilbert, Eli Simon Gilbert, Jonathon Jacob Weisman, Sara Arielle Weisman Borer, and Gideon Solomon Weisman; great-grandfather of Mya Gilbert, Riley Eric Gilbert, Kalanit Yarden Borer, Nathan Joshua Borer, Rebecca Sophie Borer, and Eliana Aviva Borer.

**Rose Diane Miller Altman** (b. April 1, 1923; d. May 9, 2016): Daughter of Esther Malka Rubin Miller and Simcha Bunem Miller (Monka) / Sister to Harry Miller, David Miller and Anita Miller Oran / Wife to Simon Altman / Mother to Marlene Altman Mutchnik Langer Sarjeant, James Chaim Altman, Marsha Altman Glassman, Steven Lawrence Altman / Grandmother to Mark Aron Mutchnik, Adam Colin Altman, Liat Dania Glassman, David Isaac Glassman, Simon Louis Langer, Stacy Altman Mansour, Sean Noah Altman, Ryan Jacob Altman / Great Grandmother to Eliana Nicole Glassman, Kai joseph Spitz, Jesse Alexander Glassman, Liam Samuel Langer, Jackson Kent Mutchnik, and Riley Alexis Lydia Spitz.

**Marshall Channing Oran** (b. Jan 9, 1932; d. Feb 27, 2017). Son of Gilbert and Sarah Oran / Husband of Anita Oran followed by Yvonne Oran / Father to Gilda Maureen Oran and Bryan Scott Oran / Grandfather to Daniel Louis Oran, Naomi Rose Oran Puckett, Justin Emmanuel Oran, Max Jacob Oran, Gabriel Elan Oran and Arel Alfi Oran / Great Grandfather to Elijah Jonathon Oran, Amelia Mae Puckett, Nora Rose Puckett, and Logan John Oran.

# JAMES AND ANITA ALTMAN'S STORY
## James Altman

**Anita and Jimmy Altman, Barbados, ca. 2015**
(James Altman photo)

My story will begin as far back as my memory will recall. Had I known that one day I would be called upon to relate the story of the BJC, I would have taken notes from as early as I could write. In my day there were no hi-tech computers, etc., only paper and pencil.

I was born in 1948, the second of Rose and Simon Altman's four children. Our family lived in various homes but my earliest memories begin when we lived at "Macabee" on Harts Gap, Christ Church.

In 1955 Hurricane Janet passed over our island with much force and caused extensive damage throughout the island. The experience was one I have never forgotten. As a seven-year-old, I remember my parents physically carrying my siblings and me over to the Speismans' house next door. Aunty and Uncle's house was high off the ground and offered us dry accommodation in which to shelter. The Steinbok family was also there as their home was right on the beach and faced the full force of the hurricane. The street where we lived became a river and I remember neighbours rowing their small dingies up and down transporting people.

Our home was on two levels. Upstairs were four bedrooms, a bathroom, etc., and downstairs, the living room, dining room, an exterior patio the length of these two rooms, a full bathroom, kitchen, and a room attached to it that housed the shul of the Barbados Jewish community.

The shul was used every Friday night for Shabbat services and all the other Jewish holidays. The one exception was the High Holidays (the Jewish New Year and the Day of Atonement) when the community also took over our living and dining rooms. The ladies occupied the living room where they enjoyed low-volume conversations while the men conducted services in the dining room. Meanwhile the children played outdoors where there was lots of room to stretch their legs and fruit trees to climb.

High Holiday services, Jewish festivals, weddings or Bar Mitzvahs were led by learned members of the community who had come to Barbados from "the old country," most of them from Poland. The group included Bernard Konigsberg, Paul Paster, Yankel Bernstein, Louis Speisman, Lazar Spira, Simon Altman, Oscar Pillersdorf, and Motel Truss.

As the years passed, senior members of the community either relocated to North America or passed on to another world, and other Jewish families came to the island. Many of these men were also capable of conducting synagogue services. Even so, there came a time when the community had to seek out the services of individuals who could lead High Holiday services, and we brought in rabbis from as far away as South Africa, England, Toronto, New York, and Miami. Even though these appointments were a significant drain on the community's finances, they were most appreciated.

In the late 1950s Rabbi Schneerson, the leader of the Chabad Lubavitch movement in New York, sent young rabbis to the West Indies and South America to encourage Jews in these countries to study Torah and observe Jewish traditions. Part of their mission was also to raise funds to build yeshivas[45] in America. When Rabbi Schneerson learned that there were Jewish boys in Barbados who had been circumcised by non-Jewish doctors, he arranged for a mohel[46] to visit the island to "kosher" them! There were about 18 such boys who faced the scalpel. Ouch, bless my private part![47]

Schmuel Bogomilsky is probably the best remembered of these rabbis and he had a long association with the community. As a matter of interest, Rose and

---

[45] A Jewish institution that focuses on the study of traditional religious texts, primarily the Talmud and Torah (Wikipedia).
[46] A mohel is a Jewish man who performs the ritual of brit milah on a baby boy eight days after his birth. (www.judaism.about.com).
[47] For more on this, see "The Rebbe and his Emissaries," Chapter 7.

Simon Altman were guests at his wedding in New York and he later came to Barbados to officiate at my Bar Mitzvah in September 1961.

In the late 1950s the community ran a Sunday school that was led by Mr. Geoff Lebens, a teacher from England, who also prepared boys for their Bar Mitzvah. I was one of them.

If memory serves me correctly, when Jewish cruise ships such as the SS Shalom and SS Jerusalem visited the island, the entire Jewish community was invited aboard for dinner. Before the deep-water harbour was built, this was a major undertaking as guests had to be transported by lighter[48] to the ships anchored in Carlisle Bay.

In my teens I would cut the grass at the Jewish cemetery in Bridgetown. Back then the cemetery looked very different from what it looks like now. For one thing, most of the monuments from the years before the 1930s were not even visible and lay buried under many years of accumulated topsoil. Ironically, this made my job much easier. The buried monuments in the cemetery have since been excavated, cleaned and catalogued, thanks to the work of Evan Milner, a young Jewish man from England.

One Sunday after I had just finished cutting the grass and was closing the wrought iron gate, a taxi pulled up and a gentleman approached, asking if he could see the cemetery. I opened the gate and gave him a tour. It turned out he was Teddy Kollek, the then-Mayor of Jerusalem, Israel.

As my Dad added rooms to our home, the shul at Macabee was relocated to a larger facility on the property. Eventually, my dad informed the community that he was considering relocating to Israel and suggested that they find a new location. In the early 1960s the community found a small house, "True Blue," on Rockley New Road, Christ Church, owned by Mr. Hugh Carew. They arranged to rent it and use it as their shul.

After completing my academic studies in Miami and returning to the island in the late 1960s, I took it upon myself to prepare the Jewish boys in the community for their Bar Mitzvahs. Because they did not know any Hebrew, I transliterated the blessings, Haftorah, etc., which they needed to repeat and this allowed them to conduct their part of the service.

In 1969 the community purchased "True Blue" from Mr. Carew and redesigned the interior to make it more of an island-style shul. Bar Mitzvah services,

---

[48] Large barges rowed by several men, and normally used for transporting goods to and from cargo ships anchored offshore.

formerly held at "Macabee," now took place at True Blue" at 6:30 AM on Saturday mornings, giving every business owner ample time to drive into Bridgetown and open his store by 8 AM. During the 1970s Stan and Joan Hoffman lived on the island and worked for a manufacturing concern called Barbados Children's Wear. They also ran a Sunday school for the community's youth and Stan led services on Friday nights.

Some years ago the Barbados Board of Tourism started the "Holetown Festival," which was held in February on the grounds of Sunset Crest in St. James. The Jewish community participated in this fund-raising activity by preparing and selling homemade Jewish-style foods such as gefilte fish[49], strudel, stuffed cabbage rolls, and many other delights.

Most Barbadians knew my family was Jewish and they would always direct Jewish tourists to our store, "Altman's," at No. 8 Broad Street, in Bridgetown. In fact, when cruise ships arrived, one could always count on there being a minyan[50] at Altman's!

During the years I was in business in Bridgetown, a number of colourful individuals brightened our days. "Easy Boy" was one. He always had a newspaper tucked under his arm as he slowly strolled the streets, never saying a word to anyone. The mystery man, "Gearbox," was another, as was "King Dyal" who wore colourful suits while riding his bicycle through town. Dyal was a serious cricket fan and travelled the world while following the West Indies cricket team on their international tours. Finally, there was the enterprising gentleman with a peg leg who drove a donkey cart and enhanced his financial standing by welcoming visitors to have their photos taken with him.

---

[49] An Ashkenazi Jewish dish made from a poached mixture of ground, deboned fish, such as carp, whitefish or pike, eggs, and seasonings which is typically eaten as an appetizer (Wikipedia).
[50] The 10 adult Jewish males required to hold a Jewish prayer-service

**Gentleman with peg leg and his donkey cart
in front of Altman's Dept. Store, Bridgetown, 1960s**
(James Altman photo)

In the 1950s the community used to gather on Sunday mornings at the Aquatic Club for a swim. The adults socialized and the children enjoyed being treated either to a Bentley or a soft ice cream cone. After many years at the Aquatic Club, the community relocated to the Paradise Beach Club, and in 1966 to the beach at the new Hilton Hotel.

During the time that the US Government maintained a naval station on the island, we were pleased to entertain many young Jewish servicemen who were stationed there.

In the early 1980s the Barbados Labour Party under the leadership of Tom Adams saved the old synagogue building on Synagogue Lane in Bridgetown from being demolished. On Friday, December 18th, 1987, the restored Nidhe Israel Synagogue was rededicated with members of the World Jewish Congress in attendance. Since then the synagogue is used for Friday night services from late December through the early part of March. During the rest of the year, Friday night and High Holiday services are celebrated at Shaare Tzedek Synagogue (True Blue) on Rockley New Road, Christ Church.

With the loss of its original leaders, the community had to seek outsiders to lead prayer services and officiate at life-cycle events. One of the first Jewish weddings to take place in the restored Nidhe Israel Synagogue occurred on December 25th, 1994, between film producer, Jeffrey Chernov, and Jacqueline Sirignand, a student from New York. Rabbi David H. Lincoln officiated.

In 1997 Leah Gilbert, concerned about the plight of children affected by the Chernobyl nuclear disaster, encouraged the community to collect funds to help them. The response was sufficiently positive that it led to an invitation to attend an historic event at the United Nations where I, as the BJC's treasurer, represented the community and where I had the pleasure of meeting Rabbi Yossie Raichik and his wife, the founders of the program.

Also in 1997, after years of bringing rabbis from various countries to the island to lead High Holiday services, I contacted Rabbi David Blumenfeld of the United Conservative Movement of America to try and establish a more permanent relationship. When he heard the name, Barbados, he mentioned that his daughter-in-law had come to the island as a child together with her family. He offered to ask his son, Hal, if he was interested in the job. Needless to say, Hal Blumenfeld and his wife, Michelle, were happy to accept our invitation. They and their three children have been travelling to our shores for the past 20 years, and he officiates at Shaare Tzedek Synagogue for Rosh Hashanah and Yom Kippur services. The Blumenfelds have now made Barbados their holiday home.

About 2000 an organization known as the Women's Multi-National Group started a fund-raising program to help subsidize the many poorly-financed children's homes on the island. The one-day event was held on the grounds of the Governor General's home and thousand of visitors and locals attended. The Barbados Jewish community participated by selling imported Israeli food products and jewelry, as well as barbecued kosher hotdogs brought in from Miami. Our efforts were a tremendous financial success and all for a good cause.

The Barbados Jewish Community celebrated the 350th anniversary of a Jewish presence on the island in December 2004 with a week of planned activities and Hal Blumenfeld conducted the Friday evening service at Nidhe Israel Synagogue.

The BJC is regularly updated about the situation in Israel through that country's various ambassadors who have visited the island. In the 1980s the State of Israel appointed our own Bernard Gilbert as their Honorary Consul in Barbados. Over the years we have had numerous visits from Jewish people stationed here while working for various offshore companies as well as others who started their own businesses. Membership in the Jewish community varies from year to year due to the constant movement of expats and others who have only short-term employment contracts.

As the senior members of our community pass on, it appears the Yiddishkeit our parents and grandparents brought with them from Europe in the 1930s will soon be lost. Many in the younger generation have intermarried, and there has been a decline in their practice of Jewish traditions and dedication to the synagogue. Unfortunately, I do not foresee the continuation of a meaningful Jewish community in the future.

## DORIS AND JACK KAPLAN'S STORY
Marsha Altman Glassman

**Jack Kaplan** (from an old group photo) **and
Doris Altman Kaplan, Barbados, 1952**
(Dina Truss photo)

Doris (Dyna Ita) Altman was the youngest of Moses and Hinda Altman's children. She was born in Poland on April 24, 1924, and came to Barbados with her mother and siblings in 1933. Doris met Jack Kaplan who was a sergeant in the U.S. Air Force weather service stationed in Barbados during WWII. Jack was born in Chicago on August 2, 1921. Doris and Jack were married in Barbados on May 4, 1946, and subsequently moved to Florida. They had two sons, Martin and Michael.

Martin Spencer Kaplan was born on July 24, 1947, and was last known to reside in Jerusalem, Israel. Michael Slater Kaplan was born on January 3, 1952, and on April 6, 1975, married Marjorie Ann Slater, b. March 8, 1952. Michael and Marjorie have two children, Leah Rebecca Kaplan and Matthew Ari Kaplan. Leah's DOB is February 17, 1980, and Matthew's DOB is February 15, 1983.

Jack Kaplan died on May 26, 1993, and Doris, on August 4, 2000, both in Miami, Florida.

# *SRUL JACOB AND MIRIAM BERNSTEIN'S STORY*
Paul Bernstein and Dan Raizman
(Interviewed by Simon Kreindler in Barbados, May 2016)

**Srul Jacob and Miriam Bernstein, Barbados, ca. 1960**

According to Paul Bernstein, his grandfather, Srul Jacob Bernstein, told him that he came to Barbados from Poland on the same ship with Moses Altman in 1932. When they boarded ship, the two men only knew it was going to "America" and when it docked in British Guiana[51] (now Guyana), they got off. One of the first things they saw was a reservoir where the local people were getting their drinking water. When frogs jumped into the water and started swimming, the two friends looked at each other and agreed that British Guiana was not for them. They returned to the ship and got off at the next port that turned out to be Barbados. As Paul likes to say, his grandfather's decision to come to Barbados was determined by frogs!

Both Paul Bernstein and Dan Raizman say their grandfather told them that he and Moses Altman were not the first Ashkenazi Jews to arrive on the island but that it was Moses Mass who arrived first in 1930 or 1931.[52]

According to the "New Settlers in Barbados" list, Srul Jacob arrived in Barbados on November 7, 1932, several months after his friends and landsman[53], Moses Altman and Moses and Dina Mass. Srul Jacob's wife, Miriam, and their children, Tola, Leon, Helen, and Sam arrived in 1933.

---

[51] None of the Altman family stories make reference to Moses Altman travelling to Barbados via British Guiana.
[52] The best evidence we have suggests that Dina and Moses Mass and Moses Altman arrived in March or April 1932. See Chapter 3.
[53] A Yiddish word for someone who came from the same town or village in Europe.

Srul Jacob did not speak any English when he arrived, but a very nice Bajan whom he had met, a Mr. Emtage, was very helpful and showed him around. When he learned some English, he began peddling and eventually opened a store on Swan Street called "The Shopping Centre" near where the Barbados Hardware store is currently located.

Srul Jacob was one of the Founding Members of Barbados Jewish community and played an active role in it for the rest of his life.

Miriam Bernstein died in Barbados in 1967 and Srul Jacob, in 1974. Both are buried in the Jewish cemetery in Bridgetown

**The Bernstein and Tepper families at Issy Tepper's 1961 Bar Mitzvah**
Back row, L to R: Helen Bernstein Raizman, Leopold Tepper, Rochelle Tepper, Tola Bernstein Tepper,
Miriam Bernstein, Kitty, Dina, and Leon Bernstein.
Front row: Srul Jacob Bernstein, Paulette Tepper, Issy Tepper (in dark suit).
Sitting: Paul and Anne Bernstein
(Paulette Tepper Beyer photo)

**Dina, Joan, Miriam, and Kathlyn (Ginger) Bernstein,
Tola Bernstein Tepper, and Srul Jacob Bernstein, ca. 1960s**
(Paulette Tepper Beyer photo)

# LEON AND KATHLYN BERNSTEIN'S STORY
**Paul Bernstein**
(Interviewed by Simon Kreindler in Barbados, May 2016)

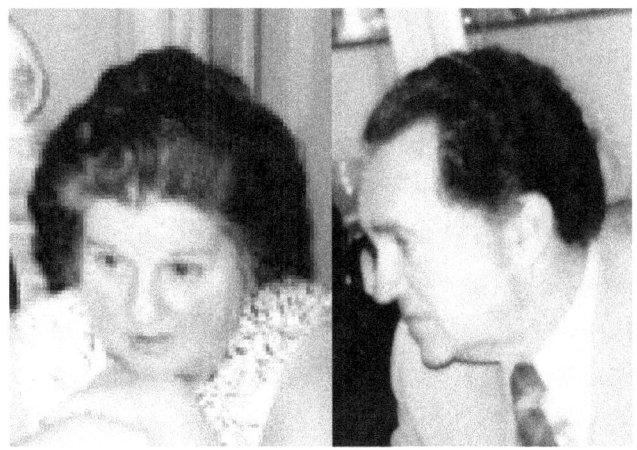

**Kathlyn and Leon Bernstein, Toronto, 1981**
(Simon Kreindler photos)

Leon Bernstein was born in Poland in March 1924 and was eight years old when he arrived in Barbados in 1933 together with his mother, Miriam, and siblings Tola, Helen, and Samuel. In 1937 Miriam returned to Poland because she needed to have a kidney removed. Leon accompanied her and celebrated his Bar Mitzvah there.

Back in Barbados, Leon followed in his father's footsteps and opened a store on Swan Street near Roebuck Street. He met and married Kathlyn/Kitty Gonsalves about 1941. She was born in British Guiana but had grown up in Barbados along with her nine siblings.

In addition to his retail business, Leon sold life insurance on the side and used to joke that unlike his store, the insurance business didn't require his having to worry about carrying stock. As the insurance business grew, Leon concentrated on it and left Kitty in charge of the store.

Leon and Kitty had five children, twin daughters, Kathlyn and Joan, followed by Dina and Paul, all born in Barbados. In 1953, Leon moved his family to Trinidad where their youngest daughter, Ann, was born in 1956.

Leon was so successful selling life insurance that he was eventually made manager of Crown Life Insurance Company's operations in Trinidad and the

Leeward and Windward Islands.[54] Although his insurance business was very lucrative, he didn't like all the travelling it entailed and decided to focus his energies on Trinidad and Barbados. After his mother died in 1967, he gave up the insurance business, and in 1969 returned to Barbados where he built some apartments and invited his father to move in with him. Leon's sister, Helen Raizman, and her children all lived on the same street and the cousins developed close relationships.

When the Barbados Development Bank was founded in 1969, Leon, a close friend of the then-Prime Minister, Errol Barrow, was asked to become its first Chairman. He was the first Barbadian Jew to be appointed to such an important government position, one he held until 1976.

Leon died in Toronto in 2000, and Kitty, in Barbados in 2012.

---

[54] The islands of the West Indies can be divided into the Greater and Lesser Antilles. The Greater Antilles include the four largest islands - Cuba, Hispaniola (Haiti and the Dominican Republic), Jamaica, and Puerto Rico. The smaller islands of the Lesser Antilles are divided into the Windward and Leeward Islands. The Leeward islands (those away from the wind) include the US and British Virgin Islands, Anguilla, St. Martin, Saba, St. Eustatius, St. Barts, Antigua, Barbuda, St. Kitts, Nevis, Montserrat, Guadeloupe, Dominica. The Windward islands (those exposed to the northeast trade winds) include Martinique, Saint Lucia, Barbados, St. Vincent and the Grenadines, Grenada, Trinidad and Tobago, Aruba, Curacao, and Bonaire. www.rumshopryan.com

## SHAUL/SZOL AND RIVKA BERNSTEIN'S STORY
### Paul Bernstein
### (Interviewed by Simon Kreindler in Barbados, May 2016)

Shaul Bernstein was born in Poland on May 7, 1907, and brought to Barbados by his older brother, Srul Jacob. Shaul was probably in his late 20s when he arrived. He married a Trinidadian woman, Rivka Medveier[55], but the marriage didn't last. He later married a Barbadian "woman of colour" whose surname was Heinam. They had three children, Louis, David, and Sonia, all of them still living in Barbados and all married to black partners.

For many years Louis worked for Barbados Hardware and later for Carter and Company, another hardware business. Louis has two sons and two daughters. One son graduated from Harrison College and immigrated to the U.S. The other, Matthew, is a nurse at the Barbados Psychiatric Hospital in Black Rock, St. Michael. One of his daughters works at Carter and Company and what the other is doing is unknown.

David worked with Paul Bernstein at the Barbados Knitting and Spinning Mills when Ernest Saunders first started the business. Later he worked for Purity Bakeries driving one of their vans and selling bread. David has two sons, one of whom works for a car rental company and the other sells bread.

Shaul's daughter, Sonia, has a daughter, Shanika Blackman, who is married to a Mr. Cumberbatch in Barbados.

Shaul and Rivka are listed among the Founding Members of the Barbados Jewish Community (1941-51). Shaul died in Barbados on September 6, 1974, and is buried in the Jewish cemetery.

---

[55] The spelling of Rivka's surname is uncertain.

# DAN RAIZMAN'S STORY
### Interviewed by Simon Kreindler, Barbados, May 2016

**Dan Raizman, Barbados 2016**
(Simon Kreindler photo)

Dan is the middle of three sons of Helen Bernstein and Mauricio Raizman. Mauricio was born in Argentina, but Dan believes Mauricio's parents were from Lublin, Poland.

Mauricio came to Venezuela about 1950 when he was in his early twenties. A wealthy Jewish family there took him under their wing and he prospered in business. Dan did not know how his parents met, but they married in Barbados and returned to live in Venezuela where Dan and his brothers, Jorge and Martin, were born. The family enjoyed a comfortable life and Dan recalled that he and his brothers each had their own nanny when they were growing up.

Early on, Mauricio had a few stores but when business deteriorated, the family moved to Barbados in 1965. Dan was eight years old and his parents enrolled Jorge and him in Mapps College in St. John.

Initially, the family lived near Accra Beach and because Dan and Jorge loved to surf, they "lived in the sea." School couldn't compete with surfing, playing music with various bands, and chasing girls. Dan described Jorge and himself as "wild kids." Their younger brother, Martin, attended Lodge School and would tag along with them, but he was six years younger, much more studious, and ultimately went on to become an engineer.

When their parents returned to live in Venezuela, the three brothers remained in Barbados and lived with their grandparents, Srul Jacob and Miriam Bernstein. They saw their mother, Helen, only periodically when she visited from Venezuela. Helen eventually left Mauricio and came to live in Barbados but he followed her and they reconciled for about six or eight years.

Helen and Mauricio ran the Coronation Store at 15 Swan Street that had earlier belonged to Bernard Konigsberg and later, Abraham Wajchendler. Ironically, Dan now owns the property. After Helen and Mauricio divorced, she got involved in a drapery and furniture business with a partner. With help from her brother, Leon, and Leon's son, Paul, Helen bought out her partner and gradually expanded Drapery Specialists.

After graduating from high school, Dan and Jorge completed grade 13 at St. Michael's College School in Toronto and could have continued to university but neither was interested. Dan returned to Barbados and started working with his mother while Jorge moved to Venezuela, married, and worked there for a few years. Martin completed an engineering degree in Florida, returned to Barbados, married, and took an engineering job with "Bizzy" Williams.[56]

Eventually, Helen and Dan invited Jorge and Martin to join them at Drapery Specialists and together they expanded the business even more. After about 20 years, Jorge left the company and went into business with the Amway Corporation. Dan and Martin continue their partnership at Drapery Specialists.

Helen Bernstein Raizman died in Barbados in 2011. Mauricio Raizman is still living in Venezuela.

---

[56] Ralph "Bizzy" Williams is the Founder and Chairman of Williams Industries Incorporated and is the holder of an Electrical Engineering degree from the University of the West Indies. A visionary and calculated risk-taker, he has had an uncanny ability to spot business opportunities in the bleakest of circumstances. Over the last 40+ years, his knack for selecting skilled leaders and dedicated staff has helped him build one of the Caribbean's leading conglomerates on a foundation of integrity, honesty, and determination. www.williamsind.com

# JORGE RAIZMAN'S STORY
## Interviewed by Simon Kreindler, Barbados, May 2016

**Jorge Raizman, Barbados, May 2016**
(Simon Kreindler photo)

Jorge is the eldest son of Helen Bernstein and Mauricio Raizman. Born in Venezuela in 1955, he came to Barbados in 1965 and attended Mapps College in St. John, initially as a boarder and later as a dayboy.

Jorge has fond memories of regularly attending Friday night and High Holiday services at "Macabee" in the company of his Bernstein grandparents when he was younger. He also remembers the delicious gefilte fish his grandmother, Miriam, prepared.

After graduating from Mapps College in 1971, he completed grade 13 in Montreal, then spent a year studying music at Duquesne University in Pittsburgh. He wasn't interested in academics, however, and returned to Barbados. For a time, he played lead guitar and back-up vocals in several bands including High Times, Super Slave and Frequency. He eventually gave up music and went to work with the Jolly Roger Organization in Bridgetown, making souvenir key rings for tourists taking cruises on the company's ship.

After marrying his Venezuelan-born wife, Calena, and working there for a few years, Jorge returned to Barbados in 1985 and joined his mother and brother, Dan, in their business, Drapery Specialists. Although the business prospered, Jorge left in 1995 to go into network marketing with Amway Corporation. He now does business throughout the Caribbean and parts of the United States.

Sadly, Calena died in September 2016 but their children, David and Raquel, continue to work with him in the business. Although they were always more aligned with their mother's Catholic beliefs they are not churchgoers. Jorge feels the Jewish community in Barbados has lost some of its earlier cohesiveness and regrets that he and his family have lost some of their previous Jewish connectedness.

# JAKUB JOSEF BOMSZTAJN'S STORY
Aaron Truss, Leah Pillersdorf Gilbert, and Jimmy Altman

**Jakub Josef Bomsztajn, Barbados, ca. 1954**

According to his grave marker in the Jewish cemetery in Bridgetown, Jakub Josef Bomsztajn was born in Ostrowiec-Kielecki, Poland, on January 22, 1899. He probably came to Barbados in the 1930s (although no one in the current community knows exactly when) and his name is included in the list of Founding Members of the Barbados Jewish community.

Some of the authors have childhood memories of Jakub trying to scare them during High Holiday services at "Macabee" by making strange noises or pretending he was going to lurch at them. Aaron Truss described him as "cruel" and recalled how he would pinch him and his brother, Joe. Jimmy Altman also recalled Jakub pinching his ears.

Leah Pillersdorf Gilbert's parents, Edna and Oscar, regularly invited Jakub to their home for Friday night dinner but stopped doing so after he was diagnosed with leprosy. In fact, Edna got rid of the chair Jakub used to sit on after she became aware of his illness.

After Jakub was diagnosed he was interned at the leper colony in Black Rock, St. Michael. Aaron Truss recalled accompanying his mother, Evelyn, on her regular Saturday trips to visit him there. Jakub lived at the leper colony and received treatment there until his death in 1968.

**Jakub Josef Bomsztajn's headstone, Jewish cemetery, Bridgetown**
(James Altman photo)

## JUDKO/YEHUDAH AND MIRIAM BRZOZEK'S STORY
Ellen Brzozek Steinbok, Paul, Jerry, Eva, and Martin Steinbok, Beverley Stock[57], and Clara Paster Halpern

**Miriam and Judko Brzozek, Poland, ca. 1925**
(Clara Paster Halpern photo)

Judko Brzozek was born in 1898 in Grajewo[58], Poland. He married Miriam Gittel Winogora, born July 1899, in Nuir, Poland. They had four children, Ellen, Mary, Sarah, and Sam.

Shortly after Ellen's birth in 1926, Judko immigrated to Guatemala where a friend was living. He worked and periodically returned to Poland for vacations. After their daughter, Mary, was born ca. 1928, Miriam took Ellen and her to live in Guatemala. They stayed a couple of years and Sarah was born there in 1930. When Miriam became pregnant with Sam, she and the three girls returned to Grawejo where Sam was born in January 1932.

In the early 1930s Judko left Guatemala. He tried living in Honduras but did not like it and moved to Barbados, where the friend[59] who had earlier

encouraged him to move to Guatemala was then living. In 1935 Miriam and the four children travelled from Grawejo to Barbados via Holland to join Judko.

---

[57] Beverley Stock is the daughter of Mary Brzozek and granddaughter of Judko and Miriam Brzozek
[58] Judko/Judah Bzozeck's mother and Clara Paster Halpern's paternal grandmother were cousins. Both were from Grajewo and Clara believes it was because the Brzozeks were living in Barbados that her family immigrated there in 1938.
[59] The author believes Judko's friend was probably Shlomo/Salomon Schor, who was also from Grajewo.

The family lived in Rockley and Ellen attended Mrs. Kinch's Private School. Mary and Sarah went to Queen's College and Sam later went to Harrison College.

Judko had probably learned the leather business in Grajewo, and together with Miriam had a small leather store on Palmetto Street[60] in Bridgetown. He imported leather from Guatemala and sold it to local shoemakers for making alphagattas, leather-soled sandals with woven cord uppers that many local people wore. He also supplied leather to local shoemakers.

Because he was unable to get his driver's license, Judko got around on a bicycle. Apparently, he had difficulty reversing a car and used to say, "Driving is for going forward. Why do I need to know how to reverse?"

Judko was a learned Jew and officiated at the wedding of Joseph Kreindler and Sara Gerstenhaber in Barbados on September 15, 1936.[61]

**The Brzozeks in Barbados, ca. 1946**
Standing: Sam, Ellen, Mary and Sarah. Seated: Miriam and Judko
(Paul Steinbok photo)

In 1948, a year after Ellen married Moses Steinbok, Judko sold his leather store to Mr. Paster and the family immigrated to Australia. Yehudah, "went into business there selling things connected to the rag trade - accessories and so forth. At first the family lived in North Fitzroy, part of the Jewish ghetto of the 1950s, but later moved to Malvern where they had a draper's shop in their

---

[60] Information from Clara Paster Halpern whose father bought the store from the Brzozeks when they left Barbados.
[61] See Joseph and Sara Kreindler's story.

home. Most of their business, however, was carried out at the Victoria Market where they had a stall in what was then known as K shed. I remember my father helping them take the materials to the market as (Yehudah) never had a car." [62]

At age 72, Yehudah had a heart attack. He died peacefully at home on June 13, 1970, after asking Miriam for a cup of tea. Miriam died on November 17, 1988, at age 89. Both are buried in Melbourne.

According to Paul Steinbok, his grandparents had hoped the move from Barbados to Australia would give their children better opportunities for finding Jewish spouses and they were right. Mary married Jack Stock on June 12, 1951. Sara married Leon Aarons in the 1950s but subsequently divorced him in the 1960s, and never remarried. Sam married Anna Rubenstein in 1957. All three lived out their lives in Melbourne. Sam died in 2009, Mary in 2014, and Sara in 2015. All are buried in Melbourne.

**Yehudah and Miriam Brzozek's graves, Melbourne, Australia**
(Beverley Stock photo)

---

[62] Beverley Stock, Yehudah Brzozek's granddaughter

# MOSES AND ELLEN STEINBOK'S STORY
Ellen Brzozek Steinbok, Paul, Jerry, Eva, and Martin Steinbok

**Moses and Ellen Steinbok, Barbados, 1960**
(Dina Truss photo)

Moishe/Moses Steinbok, was born in Ostroviecz, Poland, one of four children. His father, Pinchas, was in the leather business and died of a brain hemorrhage. His mother, Chava Bauer, was originally from Warsaw. Moses' brother, Jacob/Yankel, married Toby in Poland, and with the help of her family in Trinidad was able to emigrate there. When he had saved enough money, he brought Toby and later Moses there in 1935. Unfortunately, Chava Steinbok and her two daughters died in Majdanek concentration camp during WWII.

According to Ellen Steinbok, her husband, Moses, used to race pigeons in Grajewo and was very successful at it. His arch competitor was the local chief of police whose birds he always defeated. When Moses decided to leave Poland, he obtained exit papers by bribing the chief with his prized pigeons. He arrived in Trinidad in 1935 and lived with his brother, Jacob, his sister-in-law, Toba, and their two daughters, Cecelia and Sonia.

In 1946 Ellen Brzozek met Moses Steinbok when the entire Brzozek family travelled to Trinidad for the wedding of the daughter of a friend Judko had known in Guatemala. The Brzozeks never said anything to Moses about Ellen being deaf when they met him, but according to Paul Steinbok, "offered him the world to marry her." In those days, a deaf child was regarded as retarded, and had Ellen's deafness been known, it would have seriously limited her marriage prospects. Ellen and Moses were married in Barbados on January 7, 1947, spent their honeymoon at the Crane Hotel, then returned to Trinidad where Moses worked at London Fashions, a business owned by a Mr. Katz and a partner.

Ellen came back to Barbados to give birth to their first child, Paul, born October 6, 1947. According to Paul, his father only realized his mother was deaf after he was born and when it became clear she could not hear him crying! Ellen returned to Trinidad briefly with the baby, but after Jerry's birth in Barbados in October 1948, she and Moses made the island their home. In addition to Paul and Jerry, Ellen and Moses had five other children - Eva, Abraham, Joe, Martin and Esther.

After Ellen's family left Barbados for Australia in July 1949, Moses and Ellen rented a house on Palm Beach Gap near the ocean. Although they did not own the house, Moses was happy living by the beach and enjoyed sitting out in the evening, watching the sunset and telling stories. Although he had opportunities to buy a home, he would not purchase a property away from the water.

Moses initially made a living peddling. On paydays, he would drive to the various sugar plantations to sell clothing on credit to the workers. The amount owing to him was noted on cards and workers would pay 25 cents or more each time he visited until their debt was repaid.

Paul remembers accompanying his father on some of these trips. He also recalls the time his father bought him a size 2 shirt, took it apart and made a pattern from the various parts on pieces of soft white cardboard. For the size 4 shirt he added an inch to each piece and for the size 6, another inch, etc. Moses used the garage next door to their house on Palm Beach to spread out layers of cloth, placed the patterns on top, then cut out the pieces with a large scissors. The cut pieces were then sent to various people who would sew them into garments. Jerry often delivered the pieces of cloth on his bike, sometimes to homes on Culloden Road, two miles away. Moses then collected the finished garments and sold them.

Moses' factory, the Eileen Shirt Factory[63], initially occupied the house next door to the family home on Palm Beach. It was later moved to the second floor of a building on Roebuck Street (behind Harrison College) where Moses maintained a small retail outlet on the ground level. Paul remembers when the factory was still at Palm Beach, his father made some clothes for the Australian cricket team that was visiting Barbados for a series with the West Indies in 1955. The team later paid the Steinboks a visit at home.

---

[63] Named after Moses' wife Ellen.

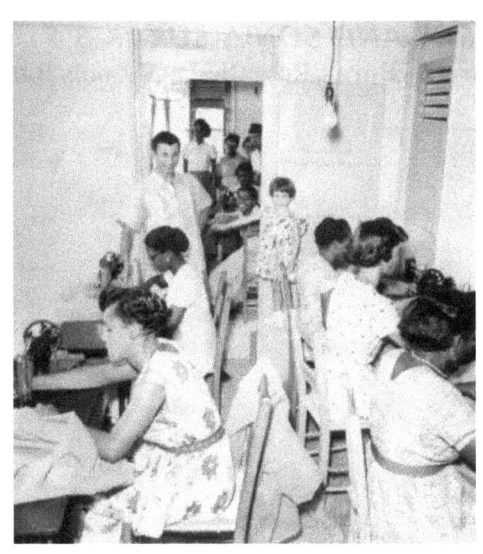

**Moses Steinbok with daughter, Eva, and workers
at the Eileen Shirt Factory,
Palm Beach, Barbados, ca. 1954**
(Paul Steinbok photo)

**The Steinbok family, Barbados, ca. 1960s
Back L to R: Jerry, Eva, and Paul
Front: Ellen holding Esther, Martin, Abraham, Joseph, and Moses**
(Paul Steinbok photo)

## *HARRY AND SONIA BURAK'S STORY*
**Dorothy Burak Rosenthal and Louis Burak**

**Harry and Sonia Burak, ca. 1937**
(Dorothy Burak Rosenthal photos)

Our paternal grandparents, Avraham Yitzhak and Dora Burak, lived in Dabrowa, Suchowolska, Poland. They had a flour mill, were prosperous, and lived comfortably. They had 11 children including Nissel, Helen, Ephraim, and our father, Zvi ben Avraham Yitzhak, also known as Harry, who was born November 5, 1905.

When Harry was a youngster, his father travelled for business and ended up dying in another town. The story came back to the family that he took ill and no doctor was available, but in those days, it was very dangerous to be Jewish and the family believed he likely was robbed and killed.

Harry was raised in a large family with many cousins. The family took vacations together, a rarity for people of that era, and Dorothy even remembers seeing a picture of her father at a resort hotel in Europe. He was among the fortunate to leave Poland before the War, as were Ephraim and Helen who made it to Detroit, and Nissel who went to Buenos Aires, Argentina. The rest of Harry's family perished in WWII.

Our maternal grandparents, Leib Frydman and Faige Malke Lachover, lived in Grajevo, Poland. Our mother, Sonia, was born there on December 25, 1912. Her siblings were Solomon, Morris, Chaim, and Mina. Our grandfather, Leib, used to travel with a horse and buggy to earn a living, and one day when Sonia was about three years old, the horse and buggy returned to the shtetl without him. The family believed he was murdered.

Our Uncle Morris was about 12 years old at the time, and because Jewish children were being forced into the Polish army, he and his friends decided to leave for to Palestine, a journey they made on foot and that took them about two years. After living there for a while Morris made his way to New York, married, and later moved to Pamplico, South Carolina.

Our Uncle Solomon was also able to escape Europe and was able to make it to Buenos Aires, Argentina. His brother, Chaim, fought with the partisans and died during the Warsaw Ghetto uprising. Our grandmother, Faige Malke, and our aunt, Mina, probably perished in the Majdanek concentration camp.

Dorothy remembers her father telling her that he had spent two years in Paris when he was a young man and had also visited Guatemala and Barbados where two or three other Jews were living at the time. He told them he was returning to Poland to find a wife and get married, and promised he would bring them a Torah on his next trip. Harry was introduced to Sonia in Poland and they were married there on August 8, 1938. After honeymooning in London, England, they purchased tickets to go by ship to Barbados, and planned to bring the rest of Sonia's family there after they got settled.

Sonia and Harry arrived in Barbados in 1938. As promised, Harry brought the Torah with him. They tried to rent a room on Roebuck Street near downtown Bridgetown. They did not have any money but Harry had gold nuggets and asked the homeowner if he would keep a piece of gold until he could acquire some money to pay the rent. The owner agreed and they moved into the room with their possessions, including Harry's leather briefcase that Louis has to this day.

Our father knew that he had to find a way to make money. He obtained several lengths of clothing fabric on credit from local merchants and walked around for hours until he sold all that he had. The next day he went back to the merchants, paid for what he had taken the day before and was able to get more material. After a few weeks, he had enough money to pay the rent and take back the gold. Time passed and he could buy a bicycle that enabled him to ride around the island selling his wares.

**Torah that Harry Burak brought to Barbados from Poland in 1938, now in the Nidhe Israel Museum, Bridgetown, Barbados**
(Kreindler photo archive)

Louis was born on May 12, 1939, and around the same time Harry and Sonia moved into their first home on 7th Avenue, Belleville, in the Parish of St. Michael. Business was going well and Harry opened The Lucky Store on Swan Street where many of the Jews who had arrived from Eastern Europe had established businesses. According to Louis, he subsequently opened two other stores on the same street.

Louis remembers his early life in Barbados as a very happy time. On Sundays his parents would ride their bicycles to the Aquatic Club, with him sitting on the handlebar. He would swim, although his father never went in the water due to his asthma.

After Dorothy was born on October 30, 1941, the family moved to 9th Avenue, Belleville, across the street from Saint Cyprian's Church. Next door to the church stood the original St. Winifred's School where Dorothy later attended elementary and high school. Louis recalled how as young children they played outdoors and knew only one season, summer.

**Louis Burak and Betty Konigsberg
with Jack and Clara Paster in back of them, Barbados, 1942**
(Dorothy Burak Rosenthal photo)

When Louis was eight and Dorothy six, the family moved to a beautiful new home in Navy Gardens, the construction of which their father had personally overseen. Shortly after, their uncle, Ephraim Burak, a widower in poor health, came from Detroit to live with them. In early February 1951 Ephraim had a heart attack and died. A week later on February 27, 1951, Sonia gave birth to Fred who was named after Ephraim.

**Louis Burak, Bar Mitzvah portrait, Barbados, 1952**
(Dorothy Burak Rosenthal photo)

According to Louis, "When life goes smoothly, we sometimes take it for granted." At age eight, he developed severe abdominal pain. Several doctors examined him but could not find a cause. "One morning at 6 AM, we went to see Dr. Skeete whose office was next to his large two-story house on Upper Beckles Road. "He examined me in his clinic and diagnosed acute appendicitis. He told my parents I required emergency surgery and they should take me to the hospital immediately. He would follow. Before the surgery could begin, my appendix ruptured, I became septic, and my condition became critical. My recovery was a very long one since antibiotics were not readily available on the island. I do not remember this as I was in a coma and there was fear I would not survive. All the men of the community came together to pray for me. They even changed my Hebrew name so that the 'evil eye' would not find me. Eventually I got stronger and could go home. I recuperated slowly. I was weak and had lost a lot of weight. My sister and friends were afraid to look at me because I looked so different."

A year after Louis' surgery, Harry developed ulcers and travelled to the Mayo Clinic in Rochester, Minnesota, for treatment. Sonia looked after the children and the two stores.

Louis described his parents as a team. They worked long hours in the stores Mondays to Fridays from 8 AM to 5 PM and on Saturdays from 8 AM to 1 PM, but when they came home it was family time. Dorothy described her mother as a beautiful, elegant lady who enoyed singing. An avid reader, she joined the Barbados Public Library soon after she arrived on the island. She was very good with a needle and made beautiful petit points. She embroidered and crocheted, and before Fred was born, made him a beautiful layette.

Louis remembered his mother loved music and song and was part of the theatre group that performed for the community. He remembered Purim plays and her performances in Shalom Aleichem plays. The Empire Theatre in Bridgetown was the venue where she participated in a WIZO fundraiser for Israel.

Ephraim Burak was the first relative Dorothy had ever met from either side of her family but not long after he died, our uncle, Solomon Frydman, came to visit from Argentina. Our mother was happy because she hadn't seen anyone from her family since leaving Poland. It was a wonderful visit and an amazing experience to meet another uncle. He brought beautiful presents for us, including a gold watch I treasure to this day. Solomon was very artistic and every night the community would gather at our house to listen to him sing and recite poems. He would speak to me in Spanish and I would answer in English. We may not have understood each other but we had a strong connection.

Another time Uncle Morris (Frydman) came to visit. He was an intellectual and would discuss books and events. He always took great interest in what each of us was involved in and what we were learning. It was wonderful spending time with him and when he returned to South Carolina, we received a huge box of toys and games that he had sent from his store. Fred got a toy train and I got a beautiful doll that I named Princess Margaret in anticipation of the Princess' visit to Barbados.

Harry Burak was a very learned man and a member of the Religious Committee of the Barbados Jewish community. This Committee took care of funerals and the cemetery. He could read the Torah and lead High Holiday services. Louis recalled his father travelled abroad to purchase goods for the stores, buying textiles from Montreal companies such as Bruck Mills, Associated Textiles, Dominion Textiles, and visiting other textile companies in New York. To further increase sales, he had men's shirts cut and manufactured in Moishe Steinbok's factory in Barbados which proved profitable for both.

Louis attended Harrison College in Barbados. He earned swimming and life-saving badges in Sea Scouts and became captain of the school's water polo team. In 1956 the team won the championship and he still has the replica silver championship cup the team was awarded.

**Fred Burak and his nanny, Barbados, ca. 1954**
(Dorothy Burak Rosenthal photo)

Dorothy attended St. Winifred's, an all-girls private school. She participated in after-school tennis, played netball, was a Brownie and later, a Girl Guide. The highlight of her school year was the Guides' summer camping trip during which they would pitch tents and live on the school property for a week. St. Winifred's also held an annual school fair with a merry-go-round and other rides. Parents sold homemade cakes and students would sell their fancy needlework. Sonia was always asked to make her specialty pie with lattice topping.

**Betty Konigsberg, Dorothy Burak, and Rosie Zierler, Barbados, ca. 1954**
(Dorothy Burak Rosenthal photo)

**Paul and Vera Paster, Sonia Burak, Solomon Frydman, Harry Burak, Toni Spira, Dorothy Burak and Lazar Spira, Barbados, ca. 1957**
(Dorothy Burak Rosenthal photo)

Betty Konigsberg and Rose Zierler were Dorothy's best friends and every Saturday morning the three of them took ballet lessons at the Aquatic Club. In the afternoon they would dress up and go to a movie matinee. Dorothy recalled that even as youngsters it wasn't unusual for them to travel around town alone.

On Sunday mornings most of the Jewish children attended Hebrew School classes at the Altman home in Harts Gap. The teacher was Geoff Lebens, an Englishman who also taught at Harrison College. In the afternoon they either went swimming at the Aquatic Club or drove to the Crane Hotel, Silver Sands Beach, Oistins, or Sam Lord's Castle. Sometimes they would stop along the way for a drink or tea before returning home for supper and bed. This was how the Jewish community lived...we made plans, participated in activities together and had a wonderful childhood.

In the fall of 1956 Louis left Barbados to attend university in Montreal and Dorothy followed in 1958. Louis recalled that when children began leaving to study/work overseas, it put a strain on some families. Painful memories of leaving Europe and becoming separated from their own families prompted many to follow their children to keep their family together. This was also the case for the Buraks. As Louis recalled, his brother, Fred, remembered the loneliness of being without his siblings all too well. In early 1961 Harry, Sonia, and Fred moved to Montreal. It was a big change from the idyllic life the family had enjoyed on their "Island in the Sun" but at least we were a family again. I'm sure our parents missed what they left behind, but several members of the Barbadian Jewish community were then also living in Montreal, including our old neighbours, the Konigsbergs, and that helped. Still, life was not what it had been in Barbados.

Louis married Barbara Rosmarin in 1964 and they had three children, Brian, Michelle, and Elana. Barbara died in 1997, and Louis married Belle Clarke ca. 1998. Belle has three sons from her first marriage, Jeremy, Lewis and Howard.

In 1961 Dorothy married Larry Rosenthal. They have three children, Florence, Martin, and Shawn. Florence and her husband, Howard Dubarsky, have two daughters, Haley and Miranda; Martin and his wife, Tina Apfeld, have four children, Samantha, Catherine, Arieh, and Amanda; and Shawn and his wife, Annat Jivotovsky, have a son, Liam. Dorothy and Larry now have seven precious grandchildren, three wonderful children and two special daughters-in-law. "Everything in life is good and I am blessed."

Fred and Charlene Turner were married in 1980 and are the parents of Joshua and Adam.

Harry Burak passed away in Montreal on May 5, 1987, and Sonia Burak on January 1, 1995. Both are buried in Montreal.

# EFRAIM BURAK's STORY
### Dorothy Burak Rosenthal

Ephraim was one of Harry Burak's younger brothers. He was born in Dabrowa, Suchowolska, Poland in 1906. After losing his family in the Holocaust he went to Detroit and lived there with his sister, Hellen Burak Stein. When he became ill, he came to Barbados, hoping the fine climate would be beneficial to his health.

Ephraim was a quiet man not unlike his brother, Harry. I remember him living in our home and going to work with my late father. He wanted to settle in Barbados and (with my father's help) get established in a business. Unfortunately, that was not to be, as he suffered a heart attack and died in February 1951 at age 45 just months after his arrival.

For a brief spell my father was reunited with his brother, and Louis and I had the pleasure of meeting our uncle. He is buried in the Jewish cemetery in Barbados.... May his Soul rest in peace.

**Ephraim Burak's gravestone, Barbados Jewish cemetery**
(Dorothy Burak Rosenthal photo)

# GUSTAV AND KATE FELDMAN'S STORY
Rolf Feldman

**Gustav and Kate Feldman, Barbados, ca. 1957**
(Rolf Feldman photo)

Prior to WWII my parents, Gustav and Kate Feldman, were in the fur business in Germany and did quite well. By 1936 they recognized the political situation in Germany was deteriorating, so they took my sister, Ruth (then four years old), and me (then one year old), and travelled to Paris and later London. In November 1941 in the middle of the Blitz we departed Liverpool as part of a convoy hoping to avoid the German submarines that were prowling the North Atlantic. Our ship eventually docked in Bermuda on December 6, 1941 (the day before the Japanese attacked Pearl Harbour), then continued on to British Guiana, and finally brought us to Barbados. After all these years, I still find it hard to believe that our parents had the courage to travel to such an alien culture where they did not speak the language and had only limited finances.

We lived on Garden Gap across the street from the Pasternaks. Our father tried various businesses, including making macaroni and starting a tannery, but both failed and he ended up in a retail business at 50 Swan Street. Our mother bred, groomed, boarded and trained thoroughbred dogs, and her work gained her an international reputation. At one time she was even President of the RSPCA.

I attended Harrison College, completed ten GCE[64] ordinary-level subjects, then studied advanced-level science. I received two distinctions and came third in

---

[64] General Certificate of Education

the island, narrowly missing out on a Barbados scholarship.

I was an avid sportsman and a member of the senior A water polo championship team. I would have been on the National Team had I not left the Island to attend the University of the West Indies in Jamaica whose water polo team I captained. I was also a member of a Barbados gym run by my "guru," Delbert Bannister, a fine man who discouraged me from ever starting to smoke even though I was only 13 years old at the time.

**Rolf Feldman seated between an unidentified young woman and Rose and Simon Altman at Louis Burak's Bar Mitzvah celebration, Barbados, 1952**
(Dorothy Burak Rosenthal photo)

My sister, Ruth, left Barbados in 1951 to study radiography in England. She subsequently returned and worked at the Barbados General Hospital where she was widely respected for her work. She now lives in Vancouver.

I went on to complete a Master's degree in science and engineering at the University of Toronto and was later granted a D.Sc. from the University of London. Before retiring, I was a Senior Research Scientist at the National Research Council in Ottawa.

Our mother died in 1965 and our father in 1978. Both are buried in Barbados.

I have two daughters, Kirsten and Nichola and a son, Julien, from my first marriage and two stepdaughters, Leslie and Carolyn, the children of my second wife, Verna Schwartz, a former Montrealer.

**Rolf and Verna Feldman**
(Rolf Feldman photo)

# JOSEPH AND EDITH FRIEDMAN'S STORY
## Clara Paster Halpern and Hanna Templer Abramowitz

The Friedman family, Barbados, ca. 1945
Back row: Joseph and Edith Friedman and Sara Kreindler
Front: Ingrid Friedman, Simon and Peggy Kreindler
(Kreindler photo archive)

Joseph Friedman was born in Mali Paludzka, Czechoslovakia, on October 20, 1903. He and his wife, Edith, and their daughter, Ingrid, probably came to Barbados in the late 1930s. They lived in Navy Gardens and Joseph managed the Bata shoe store on Broad Street.

Hanna Templer Abramowitz recalled meeting Ingrid soon after she arrived and together they took the bus to St. Winifred's School each morning.

Joseph died on January 5, 1950, and is buried in the Barbados Jewish cemetery. Hanna believes Edith subsequently sold their home and emigrated to Israel with Ingrid.

# ARON AND MARILYN KARP'S STORY
## Anne Karp Zeplowitz

**Aron and Marilyn Karp, Barbados, ca. 1950s**
(Anne Karp Zeplowitz photo)

Over the course of my adult years, many an eyebrow has been raised when I mention that I was born and raised as a Jew in Barbados. Whenever this comes up, a barrage of questions ensues and I try my best to recall the details of my parents' arrival on our beautiful little island in the sun.

My father emigrated from Poland and was one of the first Jews to arrive on the island. Unfortunately, my parents' generation never spoke of the Holocaust and even my mother knew very few details of our father's family in Europe. I now understand that those memories must have been too painful for my father to recount and that he wanted to protect us from the horror of the atrocities inflicted upon the Jewish community in those years. However, I am deeply saddened that not only did our grandparents and so many aunts, uncles, and cousins perish in the Holocaust, but our father never shared any memories with us that could be passed on to future generations.

I am the youngest of four children born to Aron and Marilyn Karp (nee Berman). My father arrived in Barbados in 1934 with his uncle, Moshe Altman (his mother Raizel's brother)[65]. He was from Tarnow, Poland, and like so many other Jews left Europe, seeking a better life. Although several of his passports indicated than his birthdate was December 26, 1913, he always celebrated his birthday on March 21, and said he was born in 1915. We believe he changed his date of birth so that he would be old enough to obtain

---

65 Moshe/Moses Altman probably arrived in Barbados in March or April 1932. See Chapter 3.

any necessary travel documents. My siblings and I were never told the exact details of his journey, but I believe that my father, along with his uncle and cousins, were on their way to South America when their ship made a stop in Barbados. Barbados was British and offered a safe haven to those fleeing persecution and so they stayed.

My father was about 18-20 years old when he arrived. Although he never spoke of his family in Europe, I believe he had about 6 or 7 siblings, many of whom were married and had children. Family responsibilities made it even more difficult for them to leave Europe when Hitler came to power and conquered Poland. One of Aron's sisters, Dina, did escape the Holocaust, married Moshe Mass, and had five children: Doris, Helen, Sam, Jack, and Joseph. They eventually settled in the United States. Unfortunately, my father's parents, Joseph and Raizel Karp (nee Altman) and the rest of their children and grandchildren perished during the Holocaust. My three brothers and I are named for my father's murdered parents and siblings. My Hebrew name is Hannah, after my father's youngest sister, who was said to be very beautiful. My oldest brother, Joel (*Yosef* in Hebrew) was born on September 9, 1950, and named for our father's father, Joseph. Stanley, born on March 31, 1952, and Ronald, born on October 19, 1953, were named for two of our father's brothers.

When Aron decided that he was ready to marry, he travelled to New York to find a "nice Jewish girl." He felt it was up to him to marry someone Jewish and to have Jewish children who would carry on the family name. A cousin in New York introduced him to Marilyn Berman, an attractive young woman who was born in the Bronx on November 12, 1926. She was almost 12 years younger than Aron, worked as a secretary, and lived in Brooklyn with her parents, Morris and Gussie Berman (nee Rosenkavich), and younger brother, Jack.

Aron and Marilyn married on April 17, 1948, in New York and travelled back to Barbados by ship. Their cousin, Rose Altman, loved to tell the story of how Aron fell asleep in their cabin filled with their wedding gifts. Marilyn wanted to explore above deck but did not want to leave their gifts in an unlocked room. Not wanting to wake Aron, she locked him in the room along with the gifts. Aron woke up, trapped in the cabin and was none too pleased!

**Marilyn and Aron Karp's wedding,
New York, April 17, 1948**
(Anne Karp Zeplowitz photo)

Shortly after their arrival in Barbados, my parents left for British Guiana where my father worked in a lumber company for about three years. He was a wonderful story-teller, and when we were young children would entertain his friends and us with stories of snakes and sharp-toothed piranhas that they encountered while living in "the bush." During their time in Guiana, they met Motel and Evelyn Truss who would eventually also settle in Barbados and become their life-long friends.

**Marilyn and Aron Karp at the Courentyn Timber Co.,
British Guiana, ca. 1948**
(Anne Karp Zeplowitz photo)

**Marilyn and Aron Karp, Evelyn Truss and Aron's nieces,
Doris and Helen Mass,
Kissing Bridge, British Guiana, ca. 1948**
(Anne Karp Zeplowitz photo)

In his early years in Barbados, Aron made a living as a peddler with a pushcart. He was an enterprising young man and eventually bought a car. When he returned to Barbados from Guiana, he opened his own store, The London Shop[66], on Broad Street in Bridgetown. Early on, the store specialized in men's clothing. Aron imported fine materials and accessories, including underwear, swimsuits, shoes, socks, shirts, and ties from England and later from North America. He also hired tailors to make men's suits and uniforms to order. The store hours were generally 8am-4pm, Monday through Friday and 8am-1pm on Saturdays. However, whenever tourist ships were in port, he extended the store's hours to maximize sales.

---

[66] The initial location of the London Shop is uncertain. The second was at 29 Broad Street and its final location was on lower Broad Street.

**The London Shop, 29 Broad Street, Bridgetown**
(Anne Karp Zeplowitz photo)

**The London Shop, lower Broad Street, Bridgetown**
(Anne Karp Zeplowitz photo)

My mother always worked alongside my father in The London Shop. Over the years she introduced an interesting variety of clothing items, including Guyabera (Cubavera) shirts or "shirt-jacs" and dresses with African prints. A skilled secretary, she was responsible for the correspondence with agents and vendors at home and abroad. I clearly remember her typing at her desk in the store. Not only did she share in the responsibilities of the business, but every week she would type a long, newsy letter to her parents back in New York, describing the details of our lives in Barbados.

Aron and Marilyn initially lived in Belville and then Rockley before buying a lovely home in Marine Gardens called "Las Palmas" shortly before I was born in 1957. They hired a nanny, Ruby Kellman, to help care for the children: four of us were a handful! Ruby was beloved and feared by all. Besides keeping the boys and me in line, she and Prescod – who was hired to do the washing and ironing – kept a spotless home for our family. Ruby was like a second mother to me in those formative years. When I was 13 years old, she left our family to marry and live in New York where she worked as a nurse's aide in a home for the aged until she retired.

As skilled as our mother was in business, her talents did not extend to the kitchen. Ruby would prepare Bajan dishes including fried flying fish, red snapper and dolphin (mahi-mahi), rice and peas, deliciously seasoned curries, and spicy pepper-pot, a local delicacy. Breadfruit – cut into chips and fried or cooked and mashed into a cou-cou – was one of our favourite dishes. Our father, who would cook breakfast on weekends, passed on Ashkenazi recipes such as chicken soup and *knaidlach* (*matza* balls), roast chicken stuffed with a delicious mixture of soaked Sodabix crackers, onions, celery, and herbs, and potato *kugel*. Ruby became an expert at preparing many Jewish dishes and we almost always had chicken soup with *knaidlach*, followed by roast chicken on Friday evening before leaving for *shul*. To this day, it is a favourite meal of our families. Our mother always lit candles before Shabbat while we stood quietly watching, dressed in our finest clothes. Then our father would make *Kiddush* over the wine before we sat down to enjoy our dinner.

Our parents loved to entertain, both for the Jewish holidays and for Sunday lunch, which was typically a big meal enjoyed after a morning at the beach. There were few restaurants in those days and so families often gathered at each other's homes to eat and enjoy each other's company. We regularly invited friends from the local and the Jewish communities to join us. I clearly remember our parents' hospitality. If they happened to notice a customer in their store or even someone on the beach wearing a *Magen David* or a *Chai*[67], they would immediately strike up a conversation and invite them for Friday night dinner or to join us for Shabbat services at "True Blue," the synagogue in Rockley.

Shabbat services were generally led by Simon Altman, Louis Speisman, or in earlier years, by my father. Although there were no assigned seats and no *mahitzah* (separation between men and women worshipers), regular attendees tended to sit in the same spot from week to week. During Yom Kippur there were always smelling salts and Alcoldo Glacial – an invigorating menthol

---

[67] The word, "chai" is Hebrew for "life."

splash lotion – to revive those who felt faint from fasting. Just thinking about that smell makes me feel both nostalgic and queasy all at once. Women would stand in the kitchen, preparing food for the break fast, but as quickly as we buttered the bread, those who could not make it until the end of the fast would sneak away a slice.

On occasion my parents hosted emissaries from the Lubavitch community. Once we were entertaining a couple of young men who noticed that we had a chicken coop in our backyard. Ruby, Prescott, and I stood by laughing as they chased a chicken, hoping to catch and butcher it - their only hope for kosher meat on the island. They feasted that evening.

Though we had a strong connection to the Jewish community, my brothers and I were fully integrated into Barbados life. When I was a youngster, I attended Mrs. Smith's Primary School on Rockley New Road and later, Queen's College, which was at the time situated in Bridgetown. Joel and Stanley attended Foundation School on Church Hill and Ronald attended Harrison College in Bridgetown.

**The Karp family, Barbados, 1960**
**L to R: Joel, Marilyn, Aron, Anne, Ronald, and Stanley**
(Anne Karp Zeplowitz photo)

When I was about five or six years old, my parents built a house at the bottom of the hill leading down to the Paradise Beach Club in Black Rock. We split our time between the new house and Las Palmas. We would live in Black Rock for months at a time and it was there that we celebrated my brother Stanley's Bar Mitzvah. At the time my parents were very friendly with the Prime Minister, Errol Barrow, and his wife, Carolyn, a talented artist who painted a portrait of me as a child. They were so close, in fact, that the Barrows built a replica of our Paradise Beach home just next door for themselves! The friendship was representative of the close connections formed between the Jewish and Barbadian communities. In fact, while I was searching through one of my parents' old albums, I found pictures of Errol and Carolyn Barrow during their visit to Israel. The photographs capture Errol meeting with Israeli dignitaries and laying a wreath at Herzl's grave.

**Errol Barrow laying a wreath at Herzl's grave, Israel 1972**
(Anne Karp Zeplowitz photo)

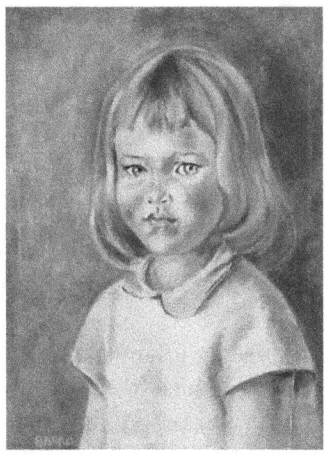

**Carolyn Barrow's portrait of Anne Karp**
(Anne Karp Zeplowitz photo)

In the same way that Bajans developed relationships with members of the Jewish community, so did the Jewish community try to do the same with them.

My father was deeply connected to his fellow islanders and was a member of the Free Masons in Barbados. Although we would beg him to tell us what the Masons did at their meetings, he remained loyal to his brothers and never revealed their secrets.

**Stanley Karp's Bar Mitzvah, Barbados, 1965.
L to R: Joel, Sheryl Kassner, Aron, Ronald, Doris Kassner,
Anne, Marilyn, and Stanley**
(Anne Karp Zeplowitz photo)

My father had a larger-than-life personality. He was well-loved by his family, the Jewish community, and his many Barbadian friends. Yet tragically he was taken from us far too soon. On April 7, 1967, at the age of 52 he suffered a heart attack and died in his sleep. My family was devastated. I have clear memories of the night he died. At 2 o'clock in the morning, his cardiologist and close friend, Dr. Graham, drove to our house, hoping to save our father. Unfortunately, he arrived too late and my father died shortly after. The entire Jewish community came to our house to be with our mother. Everyone was in shock and cried inconsolably. Whether related by blood or by love, there was a feeling that we were all one family.

As devastated as my brothers and I were to lose our father at such tender ages, it was especially hard on our mother. Aron's friends were also saddened by his loss and many years after he died, both Motel Truss and Abraham Wajchendler asked my mother for permission to be buried next to him. My mother agreed and I can imagine them continuing to play Poker together just as they did in life.

Despite losing her husband, my mother continued to run The London Shop for many years until her retirement. For business and pleasure Marilyn loved to shop, not only for herself and her family but also for others. Ever the bargain-shopper, she came to know all the sales people in Bridgetown who would give her insider information about upcoming sales. It was well-known that if anyone needed a gift or a prize, they could come to our home to choose from pieces that my mother bought on sale and then resold at a small profit.

Marilyn was a kind woman with a generous heart. A couple of years before she passed away, she introduced me to an elderly gentleman walking with a cane while she was shopping in a local grocery store. He was one of her former customers. Although she was in her 80s by then and retired for many years, she told me that she still went into Bridgetown to purchase clothes for him as he had trouble getting around. She did this for others as well. When I asked her why, she said she was happy to go into Bridgetown rather than be shut in at home. She continued to go into Bridgetown until her death on February 17, 2013.

After completing my "O" Level exams in Barbados, I convinced my mother to allow me to go to school in Canada. I lived with Fela and Kuk Pilarski for a year while attending Grade 13 at William Lyon McKenzie High School in Toronto. Kuk was Oscar Pillersdorf's brother, and Oscar's wife, Edna, was Aron's first cousin. The following year I was accepted by the University of Toronto where I earned a Bachelor's degree in Liberal Arts and met Irwin Zeplowitz, the man I married on August 5, 1979.

Irwin grew up on Grand Island, New York, between Buffalo and Niagara Falls. Following his life-long passion, he was ordained as a Rabbi in 1984 by the Reform Movement, Hebrew Union College-Jewish Institute of Religion. Irwin and I have lived in many places where he served as spiritual leader and rabbi, including Chicago, Illinois, from 1984-1989, Hamilton, Ontario, from 1989-2003, and our current home in Port Washington, New York. When we settled in New York, I attended Hofstra University where I received my Master's Degree in Speech and Language Pathology in 2008. I currently work as a speech therapist for preschoolers with special needs.

Irwin and I are blessed with three beautiful children - Abigail, or Abbie, born on February 14, 1986; Deena Leora on December 21, 1987; and Nathan Avi on June 13, 1990. Our children have visited Barbados many times and feel a close connection with our family that still lives there. In fact, when Abbie married Danny Moore on December 30, 2014, we all travelled to Barbados for the wedding. Although Danny never had the opportunity to meet my mother in person, they "met" on Skype and he learned that he had grown up only a couple of blocks away from where Marilyn lived in Brooklyn. It felt *beshert*[68] that Abbie and Danny had found one another.

My brother, Joel, left Barbados when he was about 18 years old and became a Ba'al Teshuvah[69] in the Lubavitch[70] community in Crown Heights, New York. He married Basya Lesser on August 17, 1980, and they are the parents of five children: Aaron (Ari), born May 29, 1981; Chaya Raizel, born June 6, 1982; twins Moshe and Sarah born, May 24, 1983; and Shmuel, born Oct 7, 1984.

My brother, Stanley, had many gifts as a young man. He was a talented artist and painted beautiful pictures of hibiscus and other flora. He was also a bee-charmer and kept a beehive, supplying our family with delicious honeycomb. Perhaps most notably, he was a champion swimmer for Barbados. The entire family would drive out to the Olympic pool at North Point to cheer him on at swim-meets much to his chagrin (as he was a modest boy). Our parents were extremely proud of his achievements and the top of the piano in our living room was covered with his trophies. Unfortunately, in his teenage years, Stanley was diagnosed with schizophrenia. While he continues to swim for pleasure, he never married and currently lives in a long-term care facility in New Jersey.

As a teenager, my brother, Ronald, studied at a yeshiva in Miami for about six months and finished high school at Miami Military Academy before returning to settle in Barbados where he is now the owner of Ron Karp Realty Ltd. He was previously married to an English woman, Caroline, and they had five children: Alexander Louie Karp, born July 14, 1986; Matthew Jason Karp, born February 27, 1988; Jessica Michelle Karp, born May 19, 1989; Jonathan David Karp, born February 23, 1991; and Samuel James Karp, born July 22, 1993. After Ron and Caroline divorced, he married Theresa (Terry) in 2010. She is originally from Illinois but fell in love with Barbados, its warm climate, and of course, with Ron.

---

[68] A Yiddish word most often used to mean a soulmate – the one person whom an individual is divinely destined to marry. www.momentmag.com
[69] The Baal Teshuva movement is a description of the return of secular Jews to religious Judaism.
[70] A movement embracing old-world Orthodox Judaism that was relatively small and little known when Rebbe Menachem Mendel Schneerson became its leader in 1951. During his 43-year tenure, Schneerson pioneered a system of *shluchim,* or emissaries, charged with going out into the world to open Chabad centers and spread knowledge of the Torah and Judaism. Some feared the movement would dwindle after his death in 1994 but today Chabad-Lubavitch, headquartered in Crown Heights, Brooklyn, has more than 3,000 centers in 70 countries—nearly half of them founded after the rebbe's death. http://ngm.nationalgeographic.com/ngm/0602/feature4/

**Yusel (Joel), Stanley, Anne and Ronald Karp, New York, 2010**
(Anne Karp Zeplowitz photo)

# RONALD KARP'S STORY
## Interviewed by Simon Kreindler, Barbados, May 2016

**Ron & Terry Karp**
(Ron Karp photo)

Ron was born in Barbados on October 19, 1953, the third of his parents' four children. His family was living on Rockley New Road at the time but later rented a house across the street from the Accra Hotel, and, in the mid-1950s purchased a home in Marine Gardens.

Ron attended Miss Smith's School in Rockley; Dorothy Smale's Primary School near the Garrison Savannah; and then spent a couple of years at Harrison College. He celebrated his Bar Mitzvah in 1966 and following the death of his father in 1967, attended the Miami Military Academy and Hebrew School on Miami Beach.

After graduating, he returned to Barbados and worked briefly for his mother and his cousin, Jimmy Altman. With financial help from his uncle, Simon Altman, he joined his cousins, Marlene, Marsha and Steven Altman at the University of Miami and after four-and-a-half years there returned to Barbados in 1980. He worked for a real estate company on the west coast until 1985, then started his own business, Ron Karp Realty.

Ron married his first wife in 1986 and they had five children - four sons and a daughter. They divorced in 1999, and about 2006 he met his present wife, Terry, an American with two adult children from a previous marriage. They married in 2011.

Ron's eldest son, Alexander, is a mature student in economics and finance at the University of the West Indies and periodically helps him with various projects at the office; Matthew, 28, is the bar manager at Limegrove[71]; Jessica, 26, is a real estate agent who works out of Ron's office; Jonathan, 25, is currently helping his mother (Ron's ex-wife) at the Coffee Barbados Café, adjoining the George Washington House at the Garrison Savannah; and Samuel/Sam, 23, is studying computer science at the UWI.

---

[71] A high-end shopping mall on the island's west coast

# BERNARD AND ETHEL KONIGSBERG'S STORY
## Max Konigsberg

**Bernard and Ethel Konigsberg, Barbados, 1940**
(Max Konigsberg photo)

Ethel and Bernard Konigsberg both came from poor Polish families that had been subjected to racial persecution and pogroms after World War I. My mother's name was Ethel Schiffman. She left Poland with her cousin, Mina Adler, and went to Holland when she was 19. The two of them chose Holland because it was more tolerant of Jews and they thought there would be more opportunity to make a living there than in Poland. They ended up in the city of Leiden where they survived by working in a factory as sewing-machine operators. Both met their husbands-to-be in Leiden.

My father's family name was Spergel. However, when he applied for a passport to leave Poland, the regime in power at the time questioned the legality of his parents' marriage. Tracing his origins back to a great-grandmother whose name was Konigsberg, he changed his name from Spergel to Konigsberg. When he was 14, Bernard left home and moved to another village where he got a job in a shoe store. Like my mother, he was 19 when he set out for Holland.

My parents met at a Jewish social club in Leiden where Jewish newcomers would get together. When they married in 1934, my father was 23 and my mother 26. They lived in a small room with little more than the bare necessities. Their bed was a pile of straw on the floor and they eked out an existence as peddlers until I was born on July 6th, 1935. My mother bought a sewing machine soon after I was born. She did home sewing in their room for a manufacturer and stayed home with me while my father continued to peddle. That was our life in Holland — barely getting by.

In the late '20s Hitler began making a lot of worrying noises and by the early 1930s his threats were becoming ominous. My father and some of his friends were convinced that Hitler was dangerous and conceived a plan to leave Europe. It wasn't easy for a Jew to leave Europe in those days because there were few countries willing to accept them and those that did, such as countries in South America, were half a world away. By 1935 both Canada and the United States were already closed to Jews. Leaving Europe meant leaving family and friends behind with the real prospect of never seeing them again, not an easy thing to do!

None of my father's friends had much money, but one of them, Moishe Altman, decided to be a pioneer. In 1931, he and his eldest son, Hershel, left their family, boarded a ship and set out for South America.[72] The ship made a stop in Barbados by which time they had had enough of sea travel. They got off the ship and didn't get back on. Mr. Altman decided to make Barbados home and started peddling. In a short time, he saw the prospect for making a living and eventually was able to send for the rest of his family.

As the pioneer, Mr. Altman had agreed to keep in touch with the other members of the group and to let them know whether they should follow him or not. So as soon as he was settled, he wrote to his friend, Yankel Bernstein, my father's best friend, and told him it was all right for him to come and Mr. Bernstein followed Mr. Altman to Barbados. After Mr. Bernstein was settled, he wrote letters to three people in Europe, one of whom was my father, and said: "I am peddling here and it's OK for you to come, so make your arrangements and come." And he did just that.

I was one year old in 1936 when my father left my mother and me in Holland and set out for Barbados. When it was time for him to board the ship, he was a young man of 25 with only a few pennies to his name. He was a smoker and he was hoping to use what little money he had to buy a few cigarettes on the voyage. But as he was going up the gangplank, he looked back at my mother on the dock with me in her arms and he took out his small packet of coins — literally all the money he had in the world — and threw it to her. I can only guess that he was overcome by the grim realization that he might never see us again as he set out alone and penniless for Barbados.

In 1936 Barbados was not the place it is today. The island was relatively primitive and undeveloped. Ninety-three per cent of the population was black and although the basic language was English, Bajans had their own dialect that

---

[72] Moishe/Moses Altman probably arrived in Barbados in March or April 1932 and his son, Hershel/Henry in November of that year. See Chapter 3.

was difficult even for an English-speaking person to understand. My father didn't speak English, let alone understand the Bajan dialect. He had no money when arrived in Bridgetown and I doubt that he had ever seen a black person before. Moreover, he had to make a living; in fact, he had to make an entirely new life for himself.

Like those who came before him, my father became a peddler. He was desperate to get my mother and me out of Holland as soon as possible, booking passage for us before I was two years old so that he would not have to pay a full fare for me. Fortunately for us, the few Jewish men in Barbados at the time pooled their resources and helped him finance our passage.

My mother and I arrived in Bridgetown, Barbados, in the spring of 1937, just before my second birthday. Shortly after, my Aunt Mina and her husband, Jacob Zierler, followed us to Barbados where they also made their home and where their daughter, Rose, was born.

My father initially earned a living as a peddler. He had a big bike that he rode all over the island. It had a heavy metal carrier attached to it in which he carried a suitcase filled with assorted items for sale. It was a very hard way to make a living. After a few years, he opened a small dry-goods store, the Coronation Store, on Swan Street in Bridgetown and for the rest of the time he lived on the island, made a modest living from that store. My mother also worked in the family business and, in fact, my father relied heavily on her. He was the brains behind the business and she managed the store.

About a year after my mother and I arrived in Bridgetown, my brother, Alex, three years my junior, was born. My sister, Betty, was born the following year and my younger sister, Ellen, was born eight years later.

**Ethel Konigsberg standing behind Max, Alex and Betty Konigsberg with Rosie and Mina Zierler, 9th Avenue, Belleville, Barbados 1942**
(Betty Konigsberg Feinberg photo)

We had a very rich Jewish life in Barbados. Our parents spoke Yiddish at home and so we all grew up understanding the language. We had Shabbat dinner every Friday night with our mother's homemade challah, raisin wine, and egg noodles. My mother taught our housekeeper, Mahon, to cook gefilte fish for those dinners. It was the one night we all had to be well washed and wear our best clothes - dresses for the girls and clean shirts for the boys. We have fond memories of being around the table together as a family, the Shabbat candles burning, singing the bruchas (blessings).

After Shabbat dinner our family joined the rest of the Jewish community at Simon and Rose Altman's house in Harts Gap for Friday night services. At the time, there was no synagogue but a room attached to the Altmans' house that was used for Friday night services and all the Jewish holidays.

Our father had received a very sound Jewish and Hebrew education as a young boy. He loved Judaic studies, was very serious about them, and was very learned in Jewish history and the Torah. Also, he had a beautiful singing voice and was a khazan[73], officiating at religious services all his life. He prepared my brother, Alex, and me for our Bar Mitzvahs. He was one of the leaders of our Jewish community in Barbados and very highly respected by his peers.

---

[73] The Jewish religious official who leads the musical part of the service.

**Rosh Hashannah services at "Macabee" 1945
L to R: Moses Altman, Ephraim Burak, Yehudah Brzozek,
U.S. army serviceman, Bernard Konigsberg and Srul Jacob Bernstein**
(Betty Konigsberg Feinberg photo)

Our Tanta (aunt) Mina Zierler taught all the Jewish children at Hebrew Sunday School. For two hours every Sunday morning before heading to the beach, we learned Hebrew, learned to dance the hora and learned many Hebrew and Yiddish songs. Like all the other Jewish events, Hebrew School was held at the Altmans' house.

There were 25 Jewish families in our community and we all lived in the same neighbourhood close to each other. Most of the seniors had come from Europe and had similar traditional Jewish backgrounds, so everyone, young and old, kept the traditions, celebrated and enjoyed all the Jewish holidays and festivals. My sister, Betty, has fond memories of dressing up for Purim along with the other children.

Socially, the seniors kept to themselves. There was no assimilation with the non-Jewish community. Moreover, they were very protective of us young people. By that I mean there was no social intermingling of Jewish children with non-Jews – especially those of the opposite sex.

Most of the community elders had lived in Europe before the War and had experienced extreme anti-Semitism. They had lived with both the experiences and the effects of pogroms as well as the reality of the Holocaust during World War II and were therefore wary of all non-Jews. For them, the thought of intermarriage between Jews and non-Jews was not merely intolerable, it was heresy! Obviously, we Jewish youngsters associated with non-Jews in school and in sports, but that was as far as it was allowed to go. A Jewish boy or girl having a non-Jewish girlfriend or boyfriend was absolutely forbidden.

We were certainly not well off financially so we didn't have many luxuries or extras but we never wanted for our basic needs. Most of our food was grown on the island and it was not expensive. We did not need heating and needed very little clothing.

We lived in a small house on Dayrells Road in Christ Church. I shared a room with my brother, and my sisters shared a room as well. Although it was small, our home was always very clean, tidy, and well ordered. Mahon was our housekeeper and nanny. Our parents worked very long hours at the store, so it was really Mahon who ran the household and she ran a very tight ship. We also had another lady named Beryl who came and helped with the cleaning and laundry, as there were no washing machines and all washing was done by hand.

We had excellent schools as Barbados was part of the British education system. My brother and I attended Harrison College, an all-boys school. My sisters attended St. Winifred's, an all-girls school. Both schools were very strict. We had uniforms and proper conduct was highly valued and enforced. At the time Barbados was very insulated from the outside world. There were no televisions or magazines and what we learned about the outside world we were taught at school.

In 1945 after the War in Europe ended, our father made a special effort to track down one of his relatives, an uncle, who he believed was living somewhere in the United States or Canada. It took our dad several years to locate him, but he eventually found him living in Montreal under the name of John Spergel. In 1951 he invited him to visit us in Barbados. I was 16 years old when our great-uncle John came to visit.

One evening my uncle asked our dad what his plans were for me when I finished high school. He suggested that my dad consider sending me to McGill University in Montreal to study accountancy. While our parents and the other Jewish immigrants had managed to create lives for themselves on the island, opportunities for us children were limited. Sending us off the island after high school was a way to counter this as and give us a better chance of meeting and marrying other Jews.

So in 1953 at age 17, after finishing my schooling at Harrison College, I was the first of my siblings to leave our home in Barbados. I moved to Montreal to study accounting at McGill. Two years later in 1955, my brother, Alex, followed and enrolled at McGill to study law. My sister, Betty, arrived a year after that in 1956. After we moved away, our parents felt they could not live without their children. In 1959 our father liquidated all his assets in Barbados and with our mother, and my youngest sister, Ellen, followed us to Montreal.

We all still have a great attachment to Barbados. We are so very grateful to have grown up on the island. We continue to visit every year sharing our roots with our children and grandchildren.

# MAX AND SHIRLEY KONIGSBERG'S STORY
Excerpted from "Max and Shirmax - More than a Love Affair" [74]

**Max and Shirley Konigsberg, Barbados, May 2016**
(Kreindler photo archive)

Max was born in Holland in 1935, and the following year his father left his mother and him there and travelled to Barbados. At that time, the island was undeveloped and insulated from the outside world. Most of the population was black and although the official language was English, they used a dialect that was difficult to understand, even for an English-speaking person. Max's father didn't speak English, let alone understand the dialect. He had no money and had to find a way to make a living.

Like the other Jews who had arrived there from Europe in the few years preceding him, Max's father became a peddler. He was desperate to get his wife and Max out of Holland as soon as possible, and it was very important to book passage for the two of them before Max turned two years old to avoid having to pay a second fare. They arrived in Barbados in the spring of 1937 just before his second birthday.

As Max told the story, "I still find it difficult to reconcile what my father had to do as a peddler with the man I knew. He was not particularly strong and had always had two left hands. He was not mechanically inclined and as best I remember couldn't easily balance himself on a bicycle. Yet he somehow managed a heavy bicycle with a heavy metal carrier attached to it in which he carried a suitcase filled with the assorted items that he sold. After a few years, he was able to open a small dry goods store on Swan Street in Bridgetown and for the remainder of the time he spent on the island was able to make a modest

---

[74] Max Konigsberg's book.

living.

About a year after my mother and I arrived, my brother, Alex, was born. My sister, Betty, arrive the following year and my sister, Ellen, eight years later.

My mother's influence on our lives was almost inconsequential. I think the fact that her mother had died when she was very young and that she had been sent away from home at an early age had a profound effect on her. She had never experienced parental love, was never nurtured or given an education. She had no role models, and so never had the opportunity to develop the feelings and skills needed to become a nurturing and supportive mother. We receive most of our nurturing and support from our father. Where our mother was most comfortable and effective was in the business and my father relied heavily on her. He was the brains behind the business but my mother managed the store.

Like my mother, my father was not very demonstrative. Neither was able to show sympathy nor were they receptive to our complaints that we were tired or didn't feel well. They didn't permit themselves to express those feelings and didn't allow us to either. They considered showing affection or being tired or unwell to be signs of weakness. I'm not suggesting that we thought they didn't love us. We knew they did and that they would take care of us, but we were expected to be strong, not to complain, or to feel sorry for ourselves.

We had a wonderful life in Barbados. Because I had nothing to compare it to, I probably did not appreciate it enough. Other than when I was in school, I lived as a barefoot beach boy wearing only bathing suits or shorts and enjoying the wonderful climate and the sea.

We were part of a small, tight, caring Jewish community and I had a solid Jewish upbringing. I had good friends, both Jewish and non-Jewish, and my life mostly revolved around sports - cricket, soccer, and water polo as well as sea scouts - and was a true Bajan boy.

**Max's 1948 Bar Mitzvah portrait and in cadet corps uniform ca. 1952**
(Max Konigsberg photos)

Some segregation between blacks and whites was a fact of life at the time. Although I had both black and white friends, I do not remember ever experiencing any anti-Semitism. In retrospect, I feel privileged to have grown up in Barbados, an experience most young people today can only dream about.

Culturally, we had a very rich Jewish life even though we were not very religious and did not keep kosher. It was impossible to keep kosher because kosher foods were not available in Barbados. However, we were very traditional. There were 25 Jewish families in our community and we all lived in the same neighbourhood. Most of the parents had come from Europe, had similar traditional Jewish backgrounds, and they all kept the traditions and celebrated the Jewish holidays. Socially, they kept to themselves and did not mix with the non-Jewish community. However, the children all had non-Jewish friends at school.

As a youngster, I suffered from a serious lack of self-esteem. There were two main reasons for this. I was not a good student and always sensed there was something wrong, but didn't know what. I concluded I was just not very smart. Years later I discovered I had a learning disability that caused my difficulty with reading. In those days, however, people didn't know about learning disabilities and no one suspected I had a problem. A youngster with this type of difficulty just got passed over and that was what happened to me. Most of my teachers paid me no attention and just wrote me off. I think they decided I just wasn't very bright and I became known as a "dunce."

The other reason for my low self-esteem was my relationship with my father. In many respects, he was a very gifted man. He had a photographic memory and an amazing mind. He was mostly self-taught but he was a scholar nonetheless. He was very learned in Jewish history and the Torah, and had a beautiful singing voice. He was a chazzan, was highly respected by his peers, and was one of the leaders of the Jewish community. However, he had his shortcomings and unfortunately never looked for ways to make his children feel proud of themselves. It is interesting that he often talked about how he never got a word of approval from his father and yet he always found reasons to put us down, especially me, his firstborn.

He was inept as a mentor and a teacher. When time came for me to prepare for my Bar Mitzvah, he was my teacher. His method consisted of coming to the table with a strap and every time I made a mistake, I got a whack! Unfortunately, my fluency in Hebrew was no greater than it was in English so instruction was one whack after another. Somehow, I managed to muddle through what I had to do and say for the ceremony and got it over with.

For a European Jewish father, a good education was paramount. Given my lack of scholastic ability, it was clear that I was a disappointment to him. He believed I would never amount to anything and he would often look at me, shake his head and ask in Yiddish, "Whatever is going to become of you?" Unfortunately, I could not shine in those areas that were closest to his heart and felt I had no way to prove myself.

There was, however, another side to my father. He could be very sensitive and kind. When I failed the same grade for a second time and had to bring home my report, I didn't know how I would face him. I was scared out of my mind. Then he showed his other side. Many of my friends had bicycles and I wanted one also. I had been asking my dad for months but he kept telling me he didn't have the money. When I came home and showed him my report card, he looked at it but said nothing. I knew he was very upset. That night before I went to sleep, he came to me and said, "I want you to come downtown with me tomorrow morning." I went to sleep thinking he had decided to take me out of school and was taking me to look for a job. I was petrified and it took me a long time to fall asleep. Next morning, he took me to a bicycle shop! Not once did he say anything about my failure. He knew I was hurting enough.

Although my father rarely displayed affection, he had his ways of letting me know he loved me. I loved him with all my being, and there was nothing I wanted more than to please him and make him proud of me. I credit him and his unorthodox ways for all I have accomplished, for giving me my "drivenness," and for inspiring me to excel.

When I was 15, I had a lucky break. I was attending Harrison College, an all-boys school, when the school decided to put together a water polo team to compete in the Barbados Water Polo League. I had played some water polo when I was with the Sea Scouts, but I was not big or physically strong, and I was only a mediocre player. I was afraid of getting hurt but because I had played before, they selected me for the team.

Two years before I finished school and left Barbados, the Barbados Water Police put together a team and joined the island's water polo league. One of their players was Lorenzo Best, a powerful black man, about six feet six inches tall with a great body and broad shoulders. He was a strong swimmer and from the day he joined the league, water polo in Barbados changed. Although he didn't have much finesse, he was so strong and so fast he could bulldoze his way past anyone. If he got his hands on the ball, the goalkeeper had little chance of stopping it. From his very first game, he consistently scored lots of goals and seemed unstoppable.

Eventually, our team came up against his. Everyone on our team was around 16 years old and we were all lightweights. Best played forward and so did I. Within no time he had scored four goals. It was humiliating and my teammate who was defending against him said, "I don't want anything more to do with him." So we decided to take turns playing defence and every time Best scored a goal, we'd change places. He soon scored four more goals and it was my turn to mark him. He was playing forward and I was now on defence. Best terrified me. Although I was marking him, I stayed as far away from him as possible, not wanting to get hurt. No one in the league other than Best could hold the ball in one hand - no one had big enough hands. Best could pick up the ball like it was a baseball. He would grab it, wind up, and fire it at the net. Suddenly while I was thinking I was far enough away from him to be out of his way, he brought his arm all the way back, and his hand and the ball were in my face! So I just tapped the ball out of his hand. This happened once.....twice....three times! What can I say? Best scored eight goals in the first half but none in the second half when I was defending against him. It was the first time anyone has ever held him scoreless.

Next day the headlines on the sports page of the local newspaper read, "Konigsberg holds Best scoreless!" As the season progressed, Best continued to score lots of goals in every game he played except when he played against Harrison College. For whatever reason, I psyched him out and for the next two years he never scored against me.

My water polo career ended during my last month in Barbados. As it happened, Harrison College and the Water Police were the finalists that year and we played for the championship cup. The Aquatic Club was packed with people who had come to watch the game and my father happened to be sitting next to the referee. Shortly before the game, Best came along yelling, "Where's Mr. Konigsberg?" The crowd made way for him and when he was face-to-face with my father, he said, "If you let your son into the water today, I'm going to kill him!" Best was not a hurtful or malicious person so I am sure he said this just for effect, but the referee witnessed it all.

When the whistle blew, the teams swam towards the centre. Best always swam with his head down and his arms churning like a mix-master. I was swimming towards him from the opposite end but I got too close and his hand came down and caught me in the eye. I put on a terrific show. I sank to the bottom came up, then went down again! The referee ordered Best out of the game. We went on to win the game and the cup. That was my last game for Harrison College but not my last encounter with Lorenzo Best.

In my last year at Harrison College I had another important learning experience. Sports Day was the highlight of the school year. Many of the students from other schools on the island came to watch. My father was there and so was my girlfriend. Since it was my final year I wanted to do something special. I wanted to leave some kind of mark that I had been there. Since I wasn't going to leave my mark scholastically, I decided to try to qualify for the 400-metre race. I bought a pair of running shoes and started running. I would get up in the morning and run and run and run. I won my qualifying heat and when Sports Day came, there was a lot of excitement and anticipation in the air.

I mentioned earlier that I had been afraid of Best because he was big, but neglected to say I was also intimidated because he was black. The truth is I was intimidated because I knew, as did most of us white guys, that black guys were much stronger and faster than white guys! I knew that as if it were really so. At the gun I got off to a good start. After 200 metres I was in third place and with 100 meters to go, I was in second place. The runner in front of me was black and without any thought, I just cruised in behind him and finished in second place. My teacher ran up to me when the race was over. I will never forget the expression on his face as he shouted at me, "Konigsberg, what did you do? You didn't even try!" I was absolutely stunned by what he said. I realized that because the guy in front of me was black and because I believed that black guys were stronger and faster, I had let him win and hadn't even tried. That experience always haunted me and made me promise myself that in future I would always do my best! That commitment became one of my prime motivators.

Near the end of high school, I became aware that my father was thinking of sending me to Israel after I graduated. He apparently believed that the only thing I was capable of was driving a truck. Being a truck driver in North America would make me a third-class citizen, but in Israel where everyone was considered equal, I could drive a truck and still be a first-class citizen. My uncle who was visiting from Montreal suggested that my father consider sending me to Montreal instead, and told him he had recently attended a graduation ceremony at McGill University where one of the deans had made a speech in which he mentioned the shortage of accountants in Canada. My father told him I was not a student and I could never be an accountant. Next morning I learned he had reconsidered his decision and was going to send me to Montreal to study accounting.

Recognizing that I would need help if I were to pass my final exams and get accepted at McGill, my father hired a tutor. He was an amazing man who worked with me on all my subjects and always found a way to explain things that I had never before been able to understand. His patience, encouragement, and skill were crucial to my eventual success on the exams and my getting accepted by McGill.

Another aspect of growing up in Barbados warrants telling. Socially, the entire Jewish community was very protective of its young people. There was no social intermingling of Jewish children with non-Jews, especially those of the opposite sex. Most of the community's elders had lived in Europe before the War and had experienced extreme anti-Semitism. They had lived with pogroms and the reality of the Holocaust, and were wary of non-Jews. The thought of intermarriage was intolerable. Although we Jewish youngsters associated with non-Jews in school and in sports, that was as far as it was allowed to go. It was absolutely forbidden that a Jewish boy or girl to have a non-Jewish girlfriend or boyfriend. A couple of years before I left the island, this consorting with non-Jews got me into big, big trouble.

My father knew that I socialized with girls and although it concerned him from time to time, he generally turned a blind eye. However, when I was 16, I became involved with a Christian girl whose name was Fleur. She became my girlfriend and our relationship continued for the last two years I was in Barbados. With the connivance and support of my brother, Alex, and my sister, Betty, I managed to keep my relationship with Fleur secret. However, when my father finally found out, all hell broke loose! I promised him I would stop seeing her. Things calmed down for a while but I couldn't break off the relationship. A few months before I was scheduled to leave the island, my father found out I was still seeing her. He refused to talk to me and the atmosphere at home became very strained.

The day I was to leave Barbados I got up early and went to say goodbye to Fleur. When my father awoke and discovered I was not in the house he went berserk. When I came home he started to rant and rave and accused me of being his "final destruction." All my family came to the airport to see me off and Fleur was there too. Someone noticed her and said, "Look who's here." My father looked over, saw her and promptly passed out in the middle of the terminal building. Everyone looked at me as if I had shot him. My brother was speechless and my sisters were hysterical. Suddenly the boarding announcement blared out on the PA system followed by a silence in the middle of which my mother looked straight at me and said in a voice that everyone could hear, "You will not be happy until you kill him." I turned, walked to the plane, and never looked back.

One of the first things I did when I got to Montreal was to sit down and write my parents a letter. I apologized for the scene at the airport and for the havoc I had caused those last two years. I got a nice letter back from my father thanking me and saying he was glad to hear it was over. I also wrote to Fleur to say goodbye and to apologize for all the hurt I had caused her. Fleur attended the same school as my sisters. Ellen was six years old at the time and was pretty much an appendage of Betty's. Soon after I sent the letter to Fleur, she met Betty at school and told her she had received a letter from me. Ellen overheard the conversation and that evening asked my parents "Did you get a letter from Maxie?" When they said they had not, she told them Fleur had received one. My father was devastated. He wrote to me immediately, telling me I had always been untrustworthy and that my word meant nothing. He never wanted to see or hear from me again. He told me I shouldn't try to contact anyone in the family and that I should change my name so I wouldn't disgrace them any longer. He stopped eating, lost weight, wouldn't shave and wouldn't even go to the store. Weeks went by. I kept writing but he wouldn't open my letters.

After about three months one of his friends, Joe Kreindler, visited Montreal and came to see me. He was very polite but very firm. "Max," he asked, "What are you doing? You're destroying your family and at this rate your father is going to die." I told him my story. I told him I had done the proper thing and that I had to write the goodbye letter to Fleur. I also told him I had had no contact with her ever since and the relationship was over. Mr. Kreindler went back to Barbados and somehow managed to get my father's ear. A short while later, my father came to Montreal to see me and patch things up. It was a very special visit. We were both hurting and needed to put the entire episode behind us. His visit was especially memorable because it was a clear acknowledgement for me that I was important to him and I saw it as a sign of his affection and love. I certainly needed some of both at the time.

**Max and Bernard, Montreal, 1955**
(Max Konigsberg photo)

## *Addendum From the jacket cover of "Max and Shirmax-More Than a Love Affair"*

In 1953 Max left Barbados for Montreal and married Shirley Mauer in 1956. He and Shirley opened their first store in 1957 and built that business into the Shirmax fashion organization, a national chain of more than 250 stores. Shirmax was best known for its maternity divisions – Shirley K and Thyme Maternity – and its Plus-size division – Addition-Elle.

Max's 45-year career in the Canadian fashion industry included spectacular highs and heart-stopping lows. Through it all he claimed to have been guided by a guardian angel and considering his remarkable career, even the most skeptical are often inclined to agree with him.

In 2002 Max sold Shirmax to the Reitmans Corporation.

# ALEX AND VIVIAN KONIGSBERG'S STORY
Betty Konigsberg Feinberg and Vivian Tissenbaum Konigsberg

**Alex and Vivian Konigsberg**
(Google images)

Alex Konigsberg was born in Barbados on June 2, 1938, the second of his parents' four children. He and his siblings were a close-knit group, spending a lot of their spare time together, sharing everything, participating in their childhood mischief, and always protecting each other.

Alex, like all Barbadians, was a typical island boy. His first love was cricket. The family has vivid memories of him carrying around a cricket bat and playing with his friends after school, on weekends, and on holidays. He spent all his spare time at the ocean with friends and family and also enjoyed being a Boy Scout and member of the school cadet corps at Harrison College. When he was older he played water polo, another favourite pastime, for his school team.

Alex was introduced to historical novels by his father and developed a love and appreciation for reading that he enjoyed all his life. He never went on vacation without a small bag packed with novels.

Alex left Barbados for Canada in 1955 and attended McGill University where he received his Bachelor of Commerce and Law degrees, as well as a BA degree from Concordia University. These afforded him the opportunity to distinguish himself in his career and in his private life. Alex had a fairly serious nature until later in his life. He had an analytical mind and was always conscious of doing the right thing. His principles were never compromised.

**Alex and Jumble in the Konigsbergs' backyard, Barbados, 1951**
(Betty Konigsberg Feinberg photo)

Alex met Vivian Tissenbaum, at Camp B'nai Brith of Ottawa, where he was first a tripping counsellor and later became the Camp Director. He and Vivian married in 1965 and had two children, Lori and Jonathan, who later gave them five grandchildren. Lori and Howard Manis have three daughters, Jordyn, Sydney, and Lindsay. Jon and Natalie Konigsberg's children are Hannah and Charlie. Alex's children and grandchildren lit up his life and in his later years he left each grandchild a book offering advice on how to live a moral and happy life. He was determined that they each learn how important it was to do the right thing in every situation.

Alex and four associates of diverse languages and cultures opened the first law firm of its kind in Montreal – Lapointe, Rosenstein, White, Le-Maitre Auger and Konigsberg. During his lifetime, the firm expanded and became known internationally. Alex practiced corporate law with a specialty in franchising, particularly on the international level. He made many friends and contacts worldwide and was consulted by governments and colleagues alike. His reputation was impeccable and his ethics beyond reproach. He was admired and respected for his morals and exacting standards.

For some years he lectured in corporate law at McGill University where he was Managing Editor of the Law Journal and served as President of the Faculty of Law. He also taught in the Master's program in the Faculty of Law, Université du Montréal, and at the McGovern School of Law, Austria.

Alex was an advisor to several governments and international institutions and made scholarly presentations in over 40 countries. He also advised such agencies as the OECD (Organization for Economic Cooperation and Development) and UNIDROIT (Institut International pour l'Unification du Droit Privé --International Institute for the Unification of Private Law).

The author of over 70 legal articles and a classic text, "International Franchising," Alex negotiated international commercial agreements in over 70 countries and in 1990 was the only non-American to appear as an expert witness on franchise legislation before the US House of Representatives' Committee on Small Business.

In 1990 Alex was honoured as the "Franchising Personality of the Year" by the Quebec Franchise Association. In 1993 he was a recipient of a Merit Award from the Canadian Franchise Association. He was also listed in "Best Lawyers in Canada" and in the "International Who's Who of Franchising Lawyers."

Alex was appointed a Queen's Counsel in 1987; sat on the Board of Directors of several Canadian and foreign companies; and served as Chairman of the Board of Immunotec Inc., a Canadian public corporation, from 2007 until his death in Montreal on August 9, 2010, at age 72.

After Alex retired, he continued to maintain an office at La Pointe Rosenstein and started his own consulting business that he named Royalmount, a linguistic similarity to the name "Konigsberg." With less responsibility and greater satisfaction with this type of work, he was more relaxed and surprised his family with his wonderful sense of humour that remained with him for the rest of his life.

After so much world travel Alex and Vivian were happy to rekindle their relationship with Barbados and spent many wonderful vacations there, both alone and with their family, particularly at The Crane.

Alex's life came to an end in August 2010 after a diagnosis of melanoma. Until his last days he claimed he had climbed all his mountains and achieved every success in his field. He was so grateful for his extraordinary life with his wife and children. His footstone reads: "A man whose life can be measured by the depth of his soul."

# BETTY KONIGSBERG FEINBERG'S STORY
Betty Konigsberg Feinberg

**Betty Konigsberg and Jack Feinberg, 1959**
(Betty Konigsberg Feinberg photo)

I was born in Bridgetown, Barbados, on August 6, 1939, the third of my parents' four children. Max was born July 6, 1935, in Holland; Alex, on June 2, 1938, in Barbados; and Ellen on August 25, 1947.

**Betty Konigsberg and Rose Zierler, Barbados, 1941**
(Betty Konigsberg Feinberg photo)

Some of my earliest recollections go back to Ninth Avenue in Belleville where we lived. When I was six years old we moved to a small home named "Overdeen" on Dayrells Rd., Christ Church. My two brothers shared a room and I shared the other with my Mom and Dad. In 1947 my Dad built a house, also on Dayrells Road, just across from "Overdeen" and Ellen was born there shortly after we moved in. Her arrival took me completely by surprise as I did not even know Mom was pregnant. Still, I was fascinated and excited with the new baby. I spent a lot of time with her when I was not in school, took her with me wherever I went and only left her at home when I had to.

Our home was very Jewish. We celebrated Shabbat every Friday night with my Mom's homemade chicken soup, gefilte fish, wine, and candles. My aunt and uncle, Mina and Jacob Zierler, and my cousin, Rose, were with us on Shabbat and all the Jewish holidays. My dad davened[75] beautifully and after supper we sang Hebrew and Yiddish songs.

Rosh Hashanah, Yom Kippur, Chanukah and Purim were all celebrated at the home of Moses Altman in Harts Gap. After his passing, his son, Simon, and Simon's wife, Rose, took up residence there and a room was added to the back of the house that served as our shul[76]. Every Sunday we had two hours of Hebrew school. Our teacher was my aunt, Mina Zierler, and she put a lot of effort into teaching us to read Hebrew, sing Hebrew and Yiddish songs, dance the Hora and learn to sing Hatikvah[77]. I have wonderful memories of these times, especially Rosh Hashanah when we would all get dressed up in our finery. On Yom Kippur, we broke the fast at the Altman home with hot coffee and buttered challah[78], homemade by Channa Silver[79], a special treat!

I started school when I was five years old. I attended St. Winifred's, a small private, all-girls school very close to our home in Belleville and next door to the old but beautiful Saint Cyprian's Anglican Church. Most of my teachers came from England and I remember them being very kind to me. A few years later our school moved to a larger facility on Pine Hill, a lovely old home that had been renovated to accommodate the growing enrolment.

---

[75] Prayed
[76] Yiddish word for synagogue.
[77] "The Hope," the Israeli National Anthem
[78] The traditional egg bread served on the Jewish Sabbath.
[79] Another member of the Jewish community.

**Betty in St. Winifred's School uniform, Barbados, 1947**
(Betty Konigsberg Feinberg photo)

I remember my experiences in school as very positive. When I was eight years old I joined a Brownie pack and went on to Girl Guides when I was 11 as part of an after-school program. When I was 15, I became a leader in the "Forget Me Not" Girl Guide patrol. It was a great experience and I learned many things that moulded me in very positive ways. While I was in Girl Guides I had the privilege of marching in a parade at the Garrison Savannah when Princess Margaret made an official visit to Barbados. My brother, Max, marched with the Barbados Cadets, and Alex with the Boy Scouts that same day. It was very exciting.

St. Winifred's was very rule-oriented and the environment quite strict. Manners, politeness, pride in our uniform, deportment, and shouldering responsibility were very much part of the school's culture. I became a prefect in the fourth form and truly learned what responsibility was all about. My experience at the school was very positive and I was proud to have been a student there until I left Barbados for Canada in 1956.

I had a great childhood growing up in Barbados. We were not exposed to life other than what we saw around us. We did not have toys and made our own games. My brothers made kites, played water polo and cricket, and they rode bikes. My aunt made me a rag doll. During school holidays we had fun at the beach.

In May 1948 when I was nine years old, I remember my father waking me up and hurriedly taking me, still in my pajamas, to a rum shop that had a radio on

Bay Street. Some of the other men in the community, including Mr. Brzozek, Mr. Paster and Mr. Burak were also there, waiting to hear the outcome of the vote at the UN regarding the creation of the State of Israel. When they heard the final vote, they all began laughing, crying, hugging, and dancing. I was too young to understand the enormity of the news but the memory has always stayed with me. I am also reminded of how close our community was and what a positive thing it was for us growing up. We did not socialize very much outside the community although I still have many friends who are former school mates and try to keep in touch with some of them when I vacation in Barbados.

**Sonia Silver, Betty Konigsberg, Dorothy Burak, and Rose Zierler, Barbados 1955**
(Betty Konigsberg Feinberg photo)

My brother, Max, moved to Canada in 1953, Alex in 1955, and I in August 1956. My parents and Ellen moved in 1959. It was not an easy move for any of us, but with time we adjusted and Montreal became our new home.

When I arrived in Montreal I lived with my sister-in-law's parents, Lucy and Harry Mauer, and their son, Michael. They were the most wonderful, kind and caring people. Michael was 15 years old and we were like brother and sister. I lived with them for three years until my parents and Ellen arrived from Barbados.

During those three years I worked in an office in the garment industry, learned bookkeeping and became the assistant office manager. It was a Jewish firm and I was treated very kindly, although with my accent, no one believed I was Jewish.

Two years after I moved to Montreal, I met Jack Feinberg who was from Brooklyn. We were married in August 1959 and moved to Brooklyn for a year before returning to Montreal. Jack then went into business with my dad and my brother, Max. Our first son, Howard, was born on April 18, 1962, and our second, Ronald, on July 7, 1965. I became a stay-at-home mom and enjoyed making a home and bringing up my two wonderful boys.

Our families remained very close. My brothers, Max and Alex, my sister, Ellen, and our respective children spent lots of time together. We vacationed together and spent all the Jewish holidays together. We also returned to Barbados with our children whenever possible, mostly during their Christmas holidays. We felt it was important to show them where we grew up, the history of their grandparents' lives in Barbados, and the amazing Jewish community that continues to be very active.

Montreal has been our home for a long time. Our families have grown and we are part of a very tight Jewish community here. Our son, Howard, met and married Diidi (Dyan) Ellen in November 1989 and they have two wonderful boys, Shayne, born June 5, 1991, and Nolan, born March 22, 1994. Shane is a graduate of the Molson School of Business and Nolan is following in his brother's footsteps in the same program at the same college. Our two sons, Howard and Ron, are in the menswear fashion business together and Ron also has his own computer business. We are very happy for all the good things in our lives and feel truly blessed.

# *ELLEN KONIGSBERG SCHAPIRO'S STORY*
## Ellen Konigsberg Schapiro

**Ellen and Peter Schapiro**
(Simon Kreindler photo)

I was born in Barbados on August 25, 1947. My parents, Ethel and Bernard Konigsberg, were born in Poland, moved to Holland, and immigrated to Barbados in the 1930s. In Barbados my father and mother worked in their store and my father was also the chazan [80] of the Jewish community.

My three older siblings, Max, Alex, and Betty, were very close in age and I was born many years after them. My father built the house in which I was born and where we lived until our move to Canada. It was located on Dayrells Road in Navy Gardens, Christ Church. The house and its gardens were a source of great pride for my father, and I remember him taking great care tending the roses, orchids, bougainvillea, and crotons.

---

[80] A cantor in a synagogue (The Free Dictionary)

**The Konigsberg family on the occasion of Alex's Bar Mitzvah, Crane Hotel, Barbados, 1951**
(Ellen Konigsberg Schapiro photo)

**Ellen, Betty, and their parents, Dayrrels Road, Barbados, ca. 1954**
(Ellen Konigsberg Schapiro photo)

Behind the house we grew bananas, mangos, tomatoes, and spinach, and my mother had a patch of dill for her pickles. At the side of the house we had a great big gooseberry tree and we made delicious stewed gooseberries with its fruit. We also had chickens and ducks. Everything we ate was grown fresh and there was no such thing as canned food or bottled drinks. My mouth still waters at the memory of tasting fresh fruit picked from the trees in our backyard.

I look back at my happy childhood and consider myself privileged to have grown up on such a beautiful island surrounded by blue sea, white sandy beaches, and the sound of the palm trees rustling in the wind. The familiar sounds of crickets and whistling frogs lulled me to sleep at night. Living in Barbados, we developed a love and respect for the land, nature, and the environment. We learned about different flowers, under which conditions they would grow best, about weather systems, and the wonders and perils of the ocean.

I took ballet, piano lessons, played a lot of sports in school, and had very close friends, both Jewish and non-Jewish. Above all, my favourite activity was going to the beach and swimming with my friends. Although I did not grow up with material excess, I was taught about the importance of family life, to be a good human being and to have respect for all people, no matter their colour, race or social status. In Barbados people never passed each other on the street without greeting each other, good morning…good afternoon…good day, etc. These values were embedded in our education and upbringing.

My parents worked very long hours in their business, The Coronation Store, 15 Swan Street, in Bridgetown, and were often not home. However, I had the good fortune to be brought up by my nanny, Mahon, a wonderful, warm and loving human being. She taught me proper etiquette, personal hygiene, how to conduct myself in public, and how to be a lady. Simply put, she taught me "how to be" and she was my go-to person.

**Ellen and her parents, Barbados, 1957**
(Ellen Konigsberg Schapiro photo)

**Ellen flanked by Mahon on right and her daughter, Angela, on left.
Ellen is holding Angela's daughter. Barbados, 1966**
(Ellen Konigsberg Schapiro photo)

After my brothers and sister left the island, it was lonely. When my parents went out in the evening to play cards with their friends, it was comforting staying with Mahon. She taught me how to sew, read to me from her bible, and often slept in my room. I look back at those times with feelings of warmth and fondness.

I attended St. Winifred's School with my sister and received a very strict British education. In addition to the English, Math and Science curriculum, the school emphasized the importance of kindness, respect, and pride in oneself. We were expected to uphold these ideals and any transgressions were taken very seriously. I have only the highest regard for the education I received in Barbados.

**Ellen Konigsberg and Dorothy Burak in St. Winifred's School uniform at the Konigsbergs' "Coronation Store," Swan Street, Bridgetown, ca. 1956**
(Ellen Konigsberg Schapiro photo)

Although our Jewish community was very small, my Jewish upbringing had a powerful impact on me. Although I did not consider my family religious, we were traditional and my parents instilled in us a very strong Jewish identity. We celebrated all the holidays, and Friday night dinners were particularly memorable. I remember sitting in our dining room, dressed in Shabbat attire, and often we had guests. The table was set beautifully with a white damask tablecloth and on it were flowers, challah, wine, and Shabbat candles. Brachas[81] were said and Shabbat songs sung. My mother was an excellent cook and she prepared many traditional Jewish-Polish dishes.

After dinner, the Jewish community attended services at the little synagogue in back of the Altmans' house in Harts Gap. Afterwards, the children would gather in the Altmans' living room where Mrs. Altman would play records and I would dance with my good friends, Leah and Rachel Pillersdorf. I specifically remember dancing the polka.

---

[81] Blessings

On Sundays I attended the Hebrew school taught by Mr. Lebens. After Sunday school the Jewish community gathered at the Aquatic Club and in later years at Paradise Beach. The children were all close friends and developed strong bonds with each other. Today we consider each other family. Although I left Barbados for Montreal when I was quite young, I have always felt I had one foot on the island, and Barbados is still very much a part of me.

My husband, Peter (Pedro) Schapiro, was born in Chile. We met in Montreal and were married there on September 1, 1969. My daughter, Michelle, was born on November 19, 1972; my second child, Robert, July 27, 1975; and my youngest, Bram, November 18, 1979. Michelle married David Burak on September 7, 1997, and they live in Montreal with their two children, Erin, 13-½ years old, and Emma, 10. Robert married Caroline Beaudoin on August 25, 2006. They have two sons, Mathieu, seven, and Alex, four-and-a-half. Robert currently lives in Longmeadow, Massachusetts, with his two sons. Bram married Saren Weinstein on May 31, 2009, and they live in Atlanta, Georgia, with their two daughters, Livia, four-and-a-half, and Hallie, three.

**Bram, Ellen, Peter, Michelle and Robert Schapiro,
Accra Beach, Barbados**
(Ellen Konigsberg Schapiro photo)

Since they were babies, our children have spent winter vacations with us in Barbados. They continue to do so now with their own children and regard Barbados as their second home. My Jewish identity reflects the Jewish upbringing I was privileged to have in Barbados and I am proud to be a part of the Jewish history of the island.

# BARUCH / BUNIA AND BERTHA KORN

**Baruch and Bertha Korn, Barbados, 1946**
(Molly Rosner Mann photo)

Baruch and Bertha Korn were among the Founding Members of the Barbados Jewish Community. See Myrla/Mary Korn Rosner's Story (below).

# CHAIM AND MYRLA ROSNER'S STORY
Molly Rosner Mann

**Chaim, Myrla, Linda, and Molly Rosner, Barbados, ca. 1954**
(Frank Watkins photo)

Barbados...beautiful Barbados...in my heart, still my home. After so many years living away from Barbados it is hard to understand why Barbados is still so central to my life and still evokes such warm feelings for me.

My mother, Myrla/Mary Korn, an only child, was born in Przemysl, Poland, and lived there with her parents, Baruch and Bertha Korn, until she was seven years old. They moved to Holland in 1930 to escape the hardships and anti-Semitism growing in Poland. Around the same time, a group of my grandparents' friends left Poland; some immigrated to Barbados and some to Trinidad.

Things continued to worsen in Europe so my grandfather sent a letter to his friend, Srul Jacob Bernstein in Barbados to ask whether he should pack up his family and come there. During this time, several other friends and family members of the original group that had immigrated to Barbados were asking the same question. Mr. Bernstein worried that if too many of them came to Barbados there would not be enough work for everyone so he wrote to my grandfather saying that things were not great in Barbados and that he should wait and not come. At the same time, he wrote a letter to his brother to say that Barbados was a paradise and that he should pack his family and come immediately! Mr. Bernstein mailed both letters but accidentally put the wrong letter in the wrong envelope. My grandfather received the letter that was intended for Mr. Bernstein's brother, and having no reason to believe his friend would tell him something different than he would tell his own brother, packed up the family and immigrated to Barbados in 1932. Only when my grandfather arrived did Mr. Bernstein realize his error. Unfortunately, it was too late to let his brother know, and he and his family perished.

In Barbados my grandfather made a living peddling and subsequently opened a general store on Swan Street in Bridgetown. So many Jews opened similar stores on the street it became known as Jew Street.[82]

**Myrla Korn (second row, third from left) and classmates, Przemysl, Poland ca. 1930**
(Molly Rosner Mann photo)

My father, Chaim Rosner, was born in Orzechowce, Poland, in 1912 and lived there with his parents, Linda and Jacob, and his six siblings. He was the youngest child and Herman, the eldest. His family was quite religious, and as a boy Chaim studied to be a cantor.

My father was conscripted into the Polish army in his early 20s. Because his family understood the dangers of being a Jew in the Polish army, when he came home on leave in 1938 they arranged for him to go and visit his brother, Herman, in Trinidad. Herman had immigrated to Trinidad with his family around 1930 when the first group of families left Poland for the West Indies and was married to my mother's paternal aunt, Gertie Korn. Once my father got to Trinidad, Herman would not allow him to return to Poland as the situation for Jews was becoming increasingly precarious. In fact, in so doing, Herman saved my father's life, as the rest of the family was lost in the Holocaust. This was very painful for him and he carried the guilt for the rest of his life.

---

[82]Swan Street was actually known as Jews' Street in the 17th Century when many of the Sephardic Jews who had come to Barbados from Brazil had established businesses there.

My parents met when my mother came to Trinidad to visit her aunt, and my father was staying with his brother there. They fell in love and were married in Barbados on November 10, 1946.

**Myrla and Chaim Rosner's wedding, Barbados, November 1946
L to R: Bertha Korn, Chaim and Myrla Rosner and Bunia Korn**
(Molly Rosner Mann photo)

## Myrla/Mary Korn and Chaim Rosner's 1946 Barbados marriage certificate

My father worked as a peddler in Barbados and helped my grandfather in his store. My mother was at home, as was common during that time. In 1949 my sister, Linda, was born and then I, Molly, in 1950. We continued to live in Garden Gap, Christ Church, Barbados, until 1959. My memories of growing up in Barbados are so positive. The Jewish families formed a close community. Our parents' friends were always called "Aunty" and "Uncle," and they were our extended family.

**Linda, Molly, and their nanny in Barbados, ca. 1953**
(Molly Rosner Mann photo)

Education was very important to our family and to all of the Jewish families. We attended private British schools. Most of the Jewish girls went to the same school, St. Winifred's. In fact, the educational level of the general population in Barbados is the highest in the world. I remember that during my first geography class, the teacher told us to take the sharpest pencil we had and to make the tiniest dot on a piece of paper. That, she said, was the size of Barbados in relation to the rest of the world. We never felt that smallness. Our world was filled with love and community, and we were happy.

**Molly receiving award at St. Winifred's School, Barbados, ca. 1957**
(Molly Rosner Mann photo)

We were not rich but we did not know that. Appreciating what we had and living frugally was our way of life. We learned old-fashioned values that shaped who we are today - kindness and respect for everyone, an openness and acceptance of the differences in people, love of community and how to live enriched lives without being 'rich'. Because so much was imported to the island, everything was very expensive and so we used local produce, raised chickens and pigeons in our yard, made cheese from milk, etc. We were careful not to be wasteful and we were grateful for what we had in our lives.

In fact, I think that this attitude is what makes all of the Bajan people so special. They are not bitter or angry but kind-hearted, honest and hardworking. They value education and work hard to be able to support their families. They are gentle and believe in God and fate.

All the families who immigrated to Barbados during this period shared the desire and commitment to maintaining their Jewishness and passing it on to their children. At first the synagogue was in the Altman home but subsequently the Jewish community bought a private home and converted it to a synagogue. The children would play in the courtyard as the fathers and grandfathers prayed inside. At important moments in the service, someone would come out to call us to come in to hear the shofar or listen to a special song or prayer. Services were held every Friday night because most of the community members had retail stores and they worked on Saturday. Everyone came to Friday night services and during holidays everyone made something for the kiddush following services.

Every Sunday the stores were closed. All the families in the community gathered at the Aquatic Club to swim, talk, play, and be together. My grandfather would bring mangoes to the beach and take us into the ocean to eat them. This was because mangoes stained our clothes and the ocean was the only place our mother allowed us to eat them. We left the beach around lunchtime and returned home to eat and rest. In the late afternoon, many of the families drove to The Crane Hotel where the parents talked and played cards while the children played outside. There was only one swing in Barbados that I remember - and it was at The Crane. We all took turns on the swing. Sundays were the best!

My memories of life in Barbados are mostly anecdotal - going to Bathsheba and seeing the only mountains in Barbados; my grandfather putting freshly laid pigeon eggs on our eyes to protect them when we got the whooping cough; taking the bus to the Purity Bakery to buy freshly baked goodies; going to the cricket games at the Savannah; my father waking up early every morning to go to the goat farm to get my sister milk, as goat milk was the only milk her stomach tolerated; my father drawing the outline of our feet on paper so he could buy us the right size shoes; stopping at the coconut stand along the street to drink fresh coconut water out of the coconut shell with a straw, etc.

Being Jewish was a pivotal part of our lives. My mother lit candles on Shabbat. We celebrated all the holidays together and learned Yiddish just from listening to our parents talk amongst themselves. The Jewish community was our extended family. It was important to all the families that we know our heritage and embrace our Jewish identity. They also wanted us to have a good education and to have opportunities they didn't. This fear and desire drove many families to leave Barbados in the late 50s. Many went to Montreal or Toronto, as it was easier to get into Canada than the United States if you did not have relatives to sponsor you. My father left for Montreal in 1958 to get a job and my mother, sister, and I followed him in May 1959. My mother went to work for the first time in her life at Canada Steamship Lines. We lived in an apartment and bought our very first black-and-white TV. In large part, our close community life was broken.

For a few years the families who came to Montreal from Barbados rented a room near the Van Horne Shopping Centre and held services there that were led by Mr. Konigsberg. This only lasted a few years as some families had other relatives in Montreal, their children were older and got married, or they had other commitments. Life took us in different directions, and being together the way we were used to was no longer possible.

We had very few relatives who survived the war. My father's brother moved with his family to New York and we had a cousin who lived in Israel. We made new friends and developed new relationships but we were always a bit sad at holiday time; we were together but we were alone. My father never forgot his family who perished in the War. Every spring when the new telephone directory was delivered, my father would open it up to R and would sit at the telephone and call every Rosner in the book, hoping and praying that one of them might be a member of his family. He never found one.

We missed Barbados but were only able to go back a few times after immigrating to Canada. My grandfather would sometimes bring my mother and us to Barbados for a few weeks in the summer. My grandmother passed away in 1952 when I was just a baby and my grandfather remarried soon after. This was very difficult for my mother so we did not see them often. My grandfather died after suffering a stroke while visiting NY in 1966.

Linda and I had never seen snow before we moved to Montreal. We did not know what it meant to be cold. We learned to ice skate, make snowmen and to adapt to our new home. We went to school, made friends and grew up. Often our new friends did not know Barbados even existed and had no idea where it was. I remember a few weeks after we arrived in Montreal, walking home for lunch with Linda. Some of the kids from our school had grouped together along the way and were waiting for us. When we got close, they formed a circle around us and started to do a war dance, clapping their hands to their mouths and making chanting sounds. We were scared and did not understand what they were doing. Because we came from the West Indies, they thought we were native Indians!

Being Bajan and especially being a Jew from Barbados was often a source of notoriety. In my early 20s I travelled to Europe and Israel. When I arrived in Greece, they looked at my Barbados passport and brought out a globe to ask me to show them where Barbados was located. They would not believe that Barbados was a part of the British Commonwealth and kept us at Customs for quite some time until they could confirm it. Later in Israel, whenever I had to show my passport to identify myself, there was always a buzz about the Jewish girl from Barbados who could speak Yiddish.

Linda lived in Montreal until 1980, then moved to Atlanta, Georgia, with her husband, Steve, and her son, Corey. Corey married Kellie and following the 9-11 terrorist attacks, Corey enlisted in the U.S. army, motivated by a duty to protect and serve his country. He has done several tours in both Iraq and Afghanistan. He and Kellie have a seven-year-old son, Patrick.

I stayed in Montreal and married Harry. We worked and raised our two sons, David and Jonah here. My parents lived in Montreal until their deaths - my father, Chaim, died in 1985 at the age of 73 and my mother, Myrla, in November 2011 at age 88.

Unfortunately, we were only able to visit Barbados twice while our sons were young but in 2011 Harry and I planned a Barbados vacation with their wives, Melissa and Laura, and them. We toured the island, went to our old house in Garden Gap, talked with the Bajans, visited the old synagogue for a community Chanukah party, visited the restored synagogue for Friday night services and fell in love with Barbados. Some other members of the expat Bajan Jewish community were also vacationing with their families at the same time. Betty Feinberg (née Konigsberg), recounted many stories about life in Barbados to my children and told them about their great-grandparents who helped establish the Jewish community there. They were very touched by the stories, with the result that Barbados has now become a special place for yet another generation.

Two years later we returned with our children and our new granddaughter, Lyla. She was only 16 months old at the time, but for months after would ask to me to sing the song "Beautiful Barbados" and always inquired when we were going to take the plane to "Bar-dy-ba-dos."

Sadly, I do not get to see the other members of the Jewish Bajan community often, even those who live in Montreal. However, every time we do, there is a special feeling, a bond that is always present. They will always be my extended family and an important part of my community. Barbados has a special place in my heart and will in some ways always be home for me.

# *JOSEPH AND SARA KREINDLER'S STORY*
## Simon Kreindler

**Sara and Joe Kreindler, Barbados ca. 1950s**
(Kreindler photo archive)

My father, Joseph Chaim Kreindler, was born in 1910 in Okna, a shtetl in the southeast corner of the Austro-Hungarian Empire. He was the youngest of his parents' eight children. When WWI broke out in 1914, his father was drafted into the Austrian army and because Okna was on the front line of the warring Russian and Austrian armies, his mother took his siblings and him to safety in Vienna. They remained there until the War ended in 1918, then settled in Cernauti[83], Romania (which before the War had been Czernowitz, the capital city of the Austrian Province, Bukovina).

Joe left Cernauti in 1930, intending to join his two older brothers in New York, but when he got to the port in Hamburg, Germany, he discovered that the Johnson-Reed Immigration Act, enacted by the US Congress in 1924, precluded immigrating there. Determined to escape the anti-Semitism and restrictive measures facing Jews in Romania, he boarded a ship bound for Curaçao in the Dutch West Indies. He spent a year there peddling until his brothers could get him a visitor's visa to join them in New York.

In 1933 after the last of his visa extensions expired, Joe had to leave the U.S. He returned to Curaçao but couldn't find work there. He heard there were opportunities on the neighbouring island of Aruba and eventually secured a job there in the commissary of the Lago Oil refinery.

---

[83] At the end of WWI, Romania annexed northern Bukovina including its capital, Czernowitz. The city's name was changed to Cernauti. Today it is part of Ukraine and known as Chernivtsi.

In Aruba Joe met a Bajan by the name of Wilkie who told him about Barbados and what a wonderful place it was. He quit his job, returned to Curaçao, and four days later booked passage for Barbados. On board the ship he realized he had not thought to ask Wilkie why he was in Aruba if life in Barbados was so good! What if Wilkie had sold him a bill of goods? What if all his talk about the island's beautiful beaches, attractive women, and good-natured people was just talk?

On arrival in Bridgetown, Joe inquired about inexpensive accommodation, took a bus to the Ocean View Hotel in Hastings[84], and purchased room and board for a week for $4. His eagerness to see the island was tempered by the knowledge that he had very little money and had to make some soon. He was very familiar with peddling from his time in Curaçao and knew he could do it again if he could find appropriate merchandise. He took the bus back to Bridgetown and bought some straight pins, sewing needles, spools of thread and combs in one establishment, and ribbon, lace, and dish towels in another. He packed everything into the battered brown suitcase that had accompanied him from Europe and started walking in the direction of Fontabelle[85], knocking on doors along the way.

Homeowners were surprised to see him at their door. Most had never encountered a peddler and Joe's highly-accented English made him something of an oddity. Still, most people greeted him cordially and were interested in seeing what he was selling. Before long he made his first sale and breathed a sigh of relief! Within months he had saved enough to buy a second-hand bicycle with a carrier rack that allowed him to extend his range to Black Rock[86] and beyond.

Joe first encountered the Ward family while peddling near Paradise Beach.[87] "Brother" Ward was a fundamentalist Christian who knew about Jews from the Bible but had never actually met one until encountering Joe. He was curious about where Joe was from and what had brought him to Barbados. He invited Joe in and they talked. The following week they talked some more. Over time a friendship developed and the Ward family ultimately invited Joe to stay with them.

Gradually Joe got to know some of the store owners in Bridgetown and met Moses Altman, Srul Jacob Bernstein, Shlomo Schor, Yehudah Brzozek, Bunia Korn, and Aron Karp, all of whom had arrived in the preceding two years and most of whom were also peddling. Although all were Ashkenazi Jews, the other

---

[84] A distance of about 2.5 miles, southeast of Bridgetown
[85] A residential neighbourhood about half a mile northwest of Bridgetown
[86] Another residential neighbourhood about 3 miles northwest.
[87] An enclave of homes and rental cottages on a beautiful beach about 3.5 miles northwest of Bridgetown.

men shared a Polish background that was different from Joe's Austrian heritage.

By 1936 Joe's English had improved and he was making a living peddling. His customers generally treated him with respect and seldom defaulted on their obligations to pay for goods purchased.

Meanwhile 2,000 miles away in Guatemala, Central America, Joseph Gerstenhaber and his wife, Bertha, recent immigrants from Cernauti, Romania, were also struggling to get established. After failing at several business ventures, Joseph was running out of options when a friend suggested he open a bakery and offered to introduce him to a baker who was willing to teach him the business. Lacking a viable alternative, Joseph decided to give it a try. Baking turned out to be very hard work and the hours were brutal, but the couple had three children to support and no one to turn to for help.

In 1935 fortune smiled on them. Joseph won $2,000 in a lottery, and he and Bertha breathed a sigh of relief. However, the following year they were dismayed to discover that the son of the country's Minister of War was showing an interest in their 15-year-old daughter, Sara. While they would never entertain the idea of her marrying a non-Jew, they realized the only way not to offend the young man and his family was to leave Guatemala. Sara was saddened by her parents' decision. She didn't want to leave her many girlfriends and although she hardly knew the young man, she found his attention exciting and enjoyed receiving the messages he was sending her. At the same time, Sara could not argue with her parents' conviction that the gifts the boy's mother had started sending her would probably soon lead to a marriage proposal.

Bertha and Joseph had known Shlomo Schor and Yehudah Brzozek before they left Guatemala for Barbados in 1933/34. With Joseph's lottery winnings, they purchased tickets on the next ship headed there and arrived in Bridgetown in May 1936. Within days Shlomo Schor had introduced Sara to Joe Kreindler and they were soon seeing each other regularly.

**Joseph Gerstenhaber, Joe Kreindler, Edy Gerstenhaber,
and Shlomo Schor
at Paradise Beach, Barbados, 1934**
(Kreindler photo archive)

At 26, Joe was undoubtedly anxious to find a wife and start a family. On the other hand, marriage was probably the last thing 15-year-old Sara anticipated when she arrived on the island. Her parents had not come there expecting to marry her off but at the same time they were realists and did not discourage it, especially given the alternative in Guatemala.

Because Sara's first language was Spanish and Joe was still perfecting his English, they communicated mostly in Yiddish, their one common language. Sara's parents were concerned about the 11-year age difference but had only heard positive things about Joe and his family from when they had previously all lived in Cernauti. This helped set their minds at ease.

Four months after they met, Joe proposed, and in September 1936 he and Sara were married. Yehudah Brzozek, then the most-learned Jew in the community, conducted the service. Not long after the wedding, Joseph and Bertha returned to Guatemala with their two younger children, Edy and Dina, and resumed running their bakery.

**Sara and Joe, Barbados, 1936   Wedding photo, September 15, 1936**
(Kreindler photo archive)

Joe initially rented a house on River Road in Bridgetown and hired a tutor to teach Sara English. Although he continued peddling, he was anxious to open his own store, but needed capital and did not qualify for a conventional bank loan. He approached Harcourt Carter, a Bajan whom I believe he had met while peddling and who had built a successful optical business in Bridgetown. After hearing Joe's dilemma, Carter pointed to the safe in the corner of his office and told him, "Joe, take as much money as you need!" With Carter's support, Joe opened the Jubilee Store on High Street about 1935, very close to Carter's optical business.

The 1929 stock market crash in the U.S. and the subsequent Great Depression reverberated around the world and people everywhere felt its impact. In Barbados it led to unemployment, strikes, and a drastic fall in the standard of living. People didn't have money to buy goods and retailers struggled to stay afloat. Somehow Joe managed to keep the Jubilee Store going and by the time Peggy was born in 1937, he and Sara were living in a rented apartment in Pavilion Court, Hastings. A couple of years later they moved to a nicer place in Aquatic Gardens, adjacent to the Aquatic Club.

When WWII started in 1939, German submarines prowled the Atlantic looking for ships to torpedo and making it almost impossible to get merchandise from England and North America. Retailers suffered as did their customers, even those who had money.

**Joe Kreindler at the Jubilee Store, High Street, Barbados, ca. 1936**
(Kreindler photo archive)

As Europe was engulfed by the Holocaust many of my parents' relatives in Czernowitz disappeared, never to be heard from again. Some who were considered members of the bourgeois because they owned property were deported to Siberia when Russia captured the city in 1940. Others were interned in the ghetto when the Romanians retook the city in 1941 and were later deported to Transnistria[88]. In October 1941, my father's sister, Brancia, and her husband, Luzer Gross, were deported to Moghilev in Transnistria but somehow managed to survive. When the War ended, Joe and his brothers located them in a Displaced Persons' camp in Italy and brought them to Barbados about 1947.

When I was born in 1940, my parents were renting in St. Lawrence Gap. In 1942, they purchased "Breezely," a spacious one-and-a-half storey house close to the beach on Maxwell's Coast[89], Christ Church.

---

[88] Transnistria, an artificial geographic entity created in WWII, was a part of Ukraine that was conquered by German and Romanian troops in the summer of 1941. It was used as a concentration point for the Jews of Bessarabia, Bukovina, and northern Moldavia who had been expelled by the Romanian dictator, Ion Antonescu. Deportation of Jews to Transnistria began in September 1941 and continued until the fall of 1942. Between 150,000 and 185,000 Jews were murdered or starved to death in the area's camps and ghettos. Transnistria ceased to exist after the Soviet army reconquered southern Ukraine in 1944.
[89] A residential neighbourhood about five miles southeast of Bridgetown

**Joe and Sara, Simon, and Peggy at "Breezely," ca. 1943/44**
(Kreindler photo archive)

When WWII ended, business improved and Joe opened a larger store, the Modern Dress Shoppe on Broad Street in Bridgetown. He imported and sold a variety of ladies' and children's clothing as well as hats and handbags. After my brother, Maurice, was born in 1947, Sara joined him in the business.

**Modern Dress Shoppe, Broad Street, Bridgetown, ca. 1950s**
(Kreindler photo archive)

The prosperity that followed the War resulted in a steady increase in tourism and Barbados became a preferred destination for airlines and cruise ships. Although Sara and Joe were quick to exploit this new market, they never abandoned their loyal Bajan customers who continued shopping at the "The Modern" for the latest styles from Montreal and New York.

About 1949 Joe purchased G.W. Hutchinson Ltd., a hardware business at 29 Broad Street, directly across the street from the Modern Dress Shoppe. He gradually sold off its hardware inventory, modernized the space, and when the CIBC purchased the Modern Dress Shoppe's property to build a new head office, he moved the business across the street and Hutchinson's became the "new" Modern Dress Shoppe.[90]

**The "new" Modern Dress Shoppe, 29 Broad Street, Bridgetown**
(Kreindler photo archive)

By the time my youngest brother Jerry was born in 1954, Joe was having more and more difficulty with what he thought was hay fever, but which later turned out to be asthma. Believing that flower pollen was the cause, he and Sara tried renting houses in various locations before deciding that the wind-swept Atlantic (East) coast would be the best place to live. In 1958, they purchased "Gibraltar," a much smaller bungalow in Cattlewash[91].

My sister, Peggy, left Barbados in 1955 to attended McGill University in Montreal. I followed her in 1957 as did my brothers, Maurice in 1964 and Jerry in 1971.

Eventually, Joe and Sara began to think about joining us in Canada but first needed to dismantle the business. The 1969 fire that ravaged Fogarty's Department Store on Broad Street and subsequently spread to several other

---

[90] Initially, one-half of the building was rented to Aron Karp and was the location of The London Shop.
[91] A sparsely-populated community of mostly vacation homes in St. Joseph Parish on the Atlantic side of the island.

businesses in Bridgetown, including the Modern Dress Shoppe, clinched the decision. By the early 1970s, downsizing the business had been accomplished. Sara was living in Montreal much of the time and Joe was commuting back and forth to Barbados. Because business had been his life for such a long time, Joe felt at loose ends and was delighted when Plantations Ltd., one of the island's larger businesses, invited him to become one of their buyers. Later, C.F. Harrison and Co. Ltd., another of Bridgetown's major players, made him a similar offer.

In 1976 Sara was diagnosed with breast cancer. In the early 1980s, after living 10 years in Montreal, she and Joe moved to Toronto and purchased a condo on Torresdale Avenue. Sara died in 1994 after an almost-18-year battle with cancer. Joe had meanwhile developed Alzheimer's disease and spent the last four years of his life in a nursing home. He died in 1996. The two of them are buried side by side in Mt. Sinai Cemetery, Toronto.

Sara and Joe were blessed with a warm and loving relationship that lasted 58 years. In all the time I was growing up in Barbados and subsequently as an adult, I never once heard either express an angry word to the other. They were affectionate with each other and with us children and their teamwork in business was exemplary. We were truly blessed to have had them as parents.

## *PEGGY KREINDLER LANCUT'S STORY*
### Simon Kreindler

**Peggy Kreindler Lancut, Israel, 2015**
(Kreindler photo archive)

Peggy was born at Pavillion Court, Hastings, Christ Church, on October 29th, 1937, the eldest of our parents' four children and their only daughter. She and I grew up together at "Breezely" on Maxwell's Coast Road and I am writing her story for her as she can no longer to do it herself.

Peggy attended St. Winifred's School from kindergarten through third form, then went on to Codrington High School as a weekly boarder. After she graduated in 1955, she spent two years at McGill University in Montreal but was very unhappy, dropped out, and returned home.

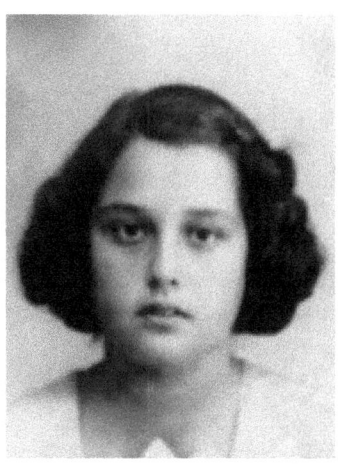

**Peggy Kreindler, Barbados, 1954**
(Kreindler photo archive)

Peggy struggled with obesity from her teens and would periodically diet, but her sweet tooth always overcame her good intentions. At McGill she seldom dated and felt very lonely. Both played important parts in her decision to quit university. Her unhappiness continued in Barbados and she was the source of a great deal of stress for our parents.

**Young adults of the Bajan Jewish community at Crane Beach, ca. 1954
Standing: Sonia Silver, Clara Paster, Alex Konigsberg,
Peggy Kreindler, and Dorothy Burak.
Sitting: Sidney Spira, Rosie Zierler, Louis Burak, and Betty Konigsberg**
(Rosie Zierler Weinberger photo)

In 1957 Peggy met Sam Mass. He had been born in Barbados, grown up in British Guiana and later, New York, and had come to the island to visit his aunt and uncle, Marilyn and Aaron Karp. Very soon after they met, Peggy and Sam got engaged and were married in September 1957. After their wedding, they moved to Miami where Sam worked for his brother-in-law, Richie Kassner, at his gas station. Peggy and Sam's elder son, David, was born in Miami on April 17, 1959. By 1960 they were having serious marital problems and moved back to Barbados. Alan was born in Barbados on April 8, 1961, and not long after his arrival, Peggy and Sam separated and later divorced.

In 1963 Peggy left the boys with Sam who was then living in California and emigrated to Israel. Sam was briefly married to Rochelle Tepper[92] and lived with her in California but the marriage didn't last. He subsequently married Merlyn Foss, and with her help, raised David and Alan.

---

[92] Rochelle Tepper was the eldest of three children of Tola Bernstein and Lejzor Tepper and a granddaughter of Srul Jacob and Miriam Bernstein.

Peggy met Shalom/Shlomi Lancut in Israel and they married in January 1968. Their daughters, Shelley and Sharon, were born in 1968 and 1972. Shlomi died suddenly in July 1997 and Peggy never remarried. Shelley and Sharon were dedicated daughters and were always very attentive to their mother. In early 2016 they helped her move into an assisted care residence in Gedera where she died in late December 2016.

David Mass was a bright child but I suspect he had unrecognized learning difficulties and struggled in school. After serving in and being discharged from the U.S. army, he moved to Florida, and contact with his family became sporadic. Alan, on the other hand, did well academically and built a successful career in the hotel industry. He was twice married and divorced, has two children with whom he has a close relationship, and is a general manager with Hyatt Hotels in San Francisco.

Sam Mass died in California in 2010 at age 74. His wife, Merlyn, still lives there, has since remarried and keeps busy with a variety of interests including stamp collecting, researching her family history, scrapbooking, and feeding a small flock of hummingbirds that have befriended her.

## SIMON AND RUBY KREINDLER'S STORY

**Ruby and Simon Kreindler, Barbados, 2016**
(Kreindler photo archive)

When I was born in 1940, my parents, Sara and Joe Kreindler, were renting a house on St. Lawrence Gap on the south coast of the island. In 1942 they purchased "Breezely," a spacious one-and-a-half story home close to the beach on Maxwell's Coast[93] in Christ Church. It was the first home they had owned and after living in many rented houses, they must have been happy to finally have a place of their own.

My father worked long hours at his store in Bridgetown and our mother stayed home with Peggy and me. Growing up, I spent my time playing in the back yard and sometimes "helped" my mother with her gardening. At other times Peggy and I went to the beach with our nanny. As far as I knew, life was about as good as it could possibly be.

---

[93] A residential neighbourhood about five miles southeast of Bridgetown

**Joe, Simon, and Peggy, 1941, Sara and Simon, 1944,
Peggy and Simon, 1944**

Sundays the store was closed and our father often took us swimming. Because Sara was self-conscious about her varicose veins and did not like being seen in a bathing suit, she seldom went. Sometimes Joe took us to the beach near Breezely, sometimes to the Aquatic Club, but most often we went to Paradise Beach where his very old friends, the Ward family, lived. Peggy and I liked the ice-cold springs at Paradise Beach that bubbled up through the sand under our feet and we also enjoyed being treated to "Bentleys" which our father would have the bartender, Manning, make for us. It felt very grown up having a drink that resembled ones the adults drank, and the fact that it was decorated with a maraschino cherry made it even more so.

Picnics were outings Sara enjoyed more. Sometimes we went to Farley Hill, a plantation in St. Peter overlooking the island's rugged East Coast. More often we went to Southpoint Lighthouse because it was much closer to home. The lighthouse sat on a rugged spit of land where the Atlantic Ocean and the Caribbean Sea merged. It was painted in alternating bands of red and white, and there was a row of stubby Casuarina trees on either side of the long driveway leading to it from the main road. As soon as Peggy and I had eaten our sandwiches and finished our lemonade, we would go off to play. One of the things we most enjoyed was lying on our backs at the base of the lighthouse and looking up at the sky to experience the illusion of the building falling on us.

On rare occasions Sara and Joe took us for a weekend to Powell Spring Hotel on the East Coast. It might seem odd that living in an "island paradise" we still took vacations, but Joe worked very hard and sometimes needed a break. Powell Spring filled the bill. It was off the beaten track and the rugged scenery surrounding it was a feast for the eyes. As a child, I loved breakfast at Powell

Spring, served on tables covered with starched white tablecloths and gleaming silverware. Fresh orange juice arrived in tiny tulip-shaped glasses, followed by eggs, hot buttered toast, and marmalade. Ever since then, orange marmalade and toast have been breakfast favourites of mine.

The movies were Sara's passion, and she and Joe regularly took us with them on Saturday nights to the Empire Cinema or the Plaza in Bridgetown. Back then people dressed up to go to the movies - men in suits and ties, and ladies in fancy dresses. White people generally sat upstairs in the balcony and black people downstairs. The most expensive seats in the house were the "boxes" at the front of the balcony and the cheapest were in the "pit" closest to the screen. On the way in, Joe would often buy us treats from one of the vendors in the foyer, usually a small bag of unshelled peanuts, guava cheese[94] wrapped in wax paper, or a Cadbury chocolate bar with nuts and raisins. Movies always began with everyone standing and singing "God save the King" (George VI). Then came the Movitone News (a brief synopsis of world events), a cartoon, trailers for coming shows, and finally, the main feature. People seated in the balcony usually conducted themselves with decorum but those downstairs were quite uninhibited and whenever there was a scene that was even slightly steamy, the pit would erupt with catcalls and whistles.

Sara's love of the cinema stood in sharp contrast to Joe's indifference but he knew how much she looked forward to going and always accommodated her. Typically, he fell asleep as soon as the theatre went dark and when he started to snore, she would gently prod him to wake up. In retrospect, I suspect he probably suffered from sleep apnea although the condition was unknown at the time.

Arriving home late after one such movie outing, I recall Sara asking if I felt like having some fried onion rings. I did not know what they were, but they sounded good so I said yes. I watched as she cut and separated the onion rings, dredged them in beaten egg and flour, then deep-fried them to a crispy-brown. It was the first and only time I ever remember her making them but they were delicious. I suspect she felt a yen for them and offered to make them for me to have an excuse to indulge.

When I was about six and Peggy about eight, Joe offered to get us a horse. It was soon after the War ended and bicycles were still not available. Peggy and I liked the idea and for a while we had a brown Shetland pony named "Nellie." Joe probably rented her from Mr. Pilgrim, a black gentleman who lived in a

---

[94] A jelly-like candy made from guava fruit.

chattel house[95] not far from Breezely and who owned several other animals. Every so often Mr. Pilgrim would bring Nellie over and would walk next to us as we took turns riding her. When the novelty wore off and bikes again became available, Joe got bicycles for each of us.

**Simon riding Nellie with Mr. Pilgrim at Breezely, 1946**
(Kreindler photo archive)

One day our cook invited Peggy and me to go with her to say goodbye to a friend who lived in one of the chattel houses near Breezely. We walked to the house, but when we arrived, no one answered our knock. Cook turned the doorknob, walked in, and we followed. I had never been in a chattel house before and was intrigued to see how the owner had made such a warm, cozy home in so small a space. The parlour into which we stepped was sparsely furnished with a table and some chairs, and white lace curtains covering the windows fluttered in the breeze. Cook's friend, a substantial woman, was lying on the sofa, beautifully dressed in her Sunday best and very dead! This was the first time I had seen a corpse but it seemed quite natural. Although children today seldom have this experience, in years gone by death was not something mysterious that happened in hospital, but a normal part of the life cycle, an event that children learned about and understood from when they were quite young.

When I had no one with whom to play at Breezely, I would amuse myself in

---

[95] A small wooden house that working-class Barbadian families occupied. The term goes back to plantation days when the labourers who worked the sugar can fields had to have houses that could be easily disassembled and moved from one plantation to another.

the backyard. Sara kept chickens there in a wire-enclosed hen house. I once bought a hen from her and struck a deal to sell her all the eggs it produced. Each time the bird got on its nest, I rushed upstairs to watch with my binoculars. The moment it laid an egg, I ran down to retrieve it and claim payment.

Sometimes I played with my toy boats in the gutter that ran around the back of the house. I would block the far end near the septic well[96], turn on the water until the gutter was filled, put the boats in and then unblock the far end. As the water rushed out, I would race after the boats as they headed towards septic doom, grabbing them just before they disappeared into the well.

We had a variety of fruit trees in our backyard including mango, golden apple, pawpaw (papaya), sugar apple, banana, and avocado. All of them regularly produced fruit except for the avocado tree. Sara had been given any number of recommendations to make it produce fruit, including driving an iron stake into its trunk, but none worked. Then one year blossoms appeared and the tree was covered with fruit. Some could be reached from the garage roof, but most were too high and had to be cut down by the yard-boy using a knife tied to a cobweb broom. Sara and the cook stood below and caught them in a sheet as they fell. That year we had so many avocados we didn't know what to do with them.

I began my education in 1946 at Miss Hart's Primary School in Worthing[97]. I joined about 30 other students who were divided by age into three classes. In addition to "Tootie" Hart, a wiry, austere-looking, 50-year-old spinster, there were two other teachers, Mrs. Gonzalves and Mrs. O'Neale, both gentle, caring ladies.

---

[96] Prior to 1982, when a government-operated solid waste system came to Barbados, homeowners relied on deep pits (or wells) in their backyards to handle sewage.
[97] A neighbourhood on the south coast of the island about halfway between Maxwell's Coast and Bridgetown.

**Miss Hart's School, Worthing, Christ Church, Barbados, 1946. Simon crouching in front row, extreme left** (Kreindler photo archive)

At Miss Hart's we learned reading, writing, and basic arithmetic. We wrote with slate pencils on slate boards and erased our mistakes with a finger dampened with saliva! Regular lead pencils were available but they were more expensive so we didn't use them. At lunch break we played outdoors in front of the school. Sometimes we played marbles or "catch" or just climbed the huge sea grape tree next to the driveway.

It was at Miss Hart's that I first met Doug MacKenzie. He was a year older than me but also lived on Maxwell's Coast Road. After our mothers began carpooling, we became friends and on weekends I would walk up the street to his home to play. The MacKenzies lived at "Dalney," a rambling, five-bedroom bungalow on a couple of acres with several hundred feet of beachfront.

Doug's father, whom everyone called "Mr. Mac," ran the Ford Motor agency in Bridgetown. A tall, imposing man with a deep, booming voice, he was quite deaf and communicating with him was a challenge. He smoked a pipe and kept a double-barrel 12-gauge shotgun in the corner of his bedroom. Even as kids we understood it was meant to warn the help that burglary would have serious repercussions. In contrast to Mr. Mac with whom we children had little interaction, Mrs. Mac was a warm, sweet lady with a great sense of humour who always treated me like one of her own.

Although I never thought about it back then, I practically lived at Dalney growing up and the fact that Doug's mother was so welcoming made it seem very natural. Years later my father revealed that he had first met Mrs. McKenzie when he was peddling and whenever he stopped at Dalney, she would offer him a cold drink. Because cold drinks were not readily available back then, he never forgot her kindness. Later, whenever she shopped at the Modern Dress Shoppe, he always made sure she received special attention.

When Doug and I were not in school, the two of us would spend our time swimming, hiking up and down the beach, or "hunting" in Dover Woods near Breezely. If I had a cold and my mother wouldn't let me swim, Doug would "accidentally" push me in the water and we would carry on as before. As we got older, we made "gutterperches" (slingshots) with which we planned to repel predators that for some reason never materialized; built sailboats with lead-weighted keels that we raced in the ocean; and made kites made from strips of cedar shingles and coloured tissue paper. We collected sea eggs[98] on the reef near Dalney; caught fish and roasted them in pits on the beach; and pilfered guavas and ackees from Mr. Eckstein's house across the road from Dalney. It was truly an idyllic time.

My brother, Maurice, was born in 1947 and by the time he was a toddler, I was away at Lodge School much of the time. This, in addition to the seven-year age difference between us, meant we never really got to know each other until much later. In 1954 my youngest brother, Jerry, was born. If the seven-year age difference between Maurice and me was an obstacle, the 14-year difference with Jerry presented an even greater challenge.

In 1949 I entered Lodge School as a boarder. Although there were other good schools closer to home, such as Harrison College in Bridgetown which most of the other Jewish boys attended, I wanted to be in the same school as Doug. About 350 boys attended the school, the majority of them black. Three-quarters of them were "day boys" who walked or took the bus to school each day. The rest were boarders, almost all white, who lived at the school during the week and went home on weekends. A handful of boys came from other islands and returned home for Christmas and summer vacation.

I was the only Jew in the school and while I never encountered any overt anti-Semitism, I recall feeling uncomfortable when I first became aware that many Christians held Jews responsible for Jesus' crucifixion, something that was occasionally referenced (although I do not remember by whom).

When I entered the school, I was a skinny, self-conscious nine-year-old. I did not know any of my classmates or any of the boarders except Doug. I followed the rules and studied diligently for tests and exams - a genuine "browner," although the term had not yet been coined. Classes included English, history,

---

[98] White sea urchins whose roe was a delicacy that was usually prepared by frying it with onion and serving it with rice.

geography, arithmetic, Latin, and New Testament scripture. I could have been exempted from Scripture but did not want to draw attention to myself and so chose not to. Ironically, I found the subject quite interesting and at year's end got top marks, mostly because of a drawing I did depicting Jesus raising Lazarus from the dead!

I am not sure which was more problematic, the scratchy slate pencils we had used at Miss Hart's or the "dip" pens[99] Lodge expected us to use. In contrast to the refillable cartridge or ballpoint pens that succeeded them, dip pens were cumbersome, but the school had used them forever and was in no hurry to change. Because I was a "lefty" and wrote "upside down," the ball of my hand would smudge everything I wrote unless I kept a piece of blotting paper between it and the paper on which I was writing. In the mid-1950s the school finally gave in and permitted us to use ballpoint pens or "dry writers," as Bajans called them. I breathed a huge sigh of relief and got rid of my stash of blotting paper.

Punishment at Lodge came either as lines, detentions, or canings. Being assigned 100 or 200 lines was not an uncommon consequence for being late for an activity or for not handing in work. Detentions were reserved for more serious infractions and canings for the worst of all. They were administered either by the headmaster for school-related matters or the housemaster for infractions in the boarding establishment. Although some boys might have pretended to the contrary, caning was a punishment feared by all. Today it would undoubtedly be regarded as child abuse, but back then it was an extremely effective deterrent to any adolescent ready to challenge the rules.

The boarding establishment operated on a rigid routine from the morning wakeup bell until lights out at night. There were set times for getting up, showering, dressing, eating, studying, sports, homework, and bed. Privileges came with age, junior boys having the fewest, and prefects the most. The bell woke us at 6:30 AM. We washed, brushed our teeth, dressed and went down to the dining room for cocoa or tea and biscuits (soda crackers), followed by an hour of "prep" (homework). When the bell signalled the start of the school day we assembled in the quadrangle. After the headmaster recited the Lord's Prayer and made any necessary announcements, we went to our respective classrooms.

Boarders returned to the dining room for lunch – meat drowned in thick gravy; rice or rice and peas; white or sweet potato and a vegetable, most often green beans or okra. If you didn't like what was served, there was always the tuck shop where you could purchase hot dogs or "fish cutters" (fried salt-fish patties

---

[99] A tapered cylinder of wood fitted with a metal nib that one dipped into a bottle or "pot" of liquid ink. You wrote five or six words then needed to "dip" again.

slathered with hot sauce and served on a "penny loaf"), and a cold drink. While boarders were eating indoors, day boys ate their lunch outdoors in the shade. When classes ended, boarders were again served cocoa, tea, and biscuits. Then it was back to the dormitory to change into whites and running shoes or cleats for the compulsory afternoon sports program. Depending on the season, we played either cricket or football (soccer). Dinner was essentially a repetition of lunch.

On days when rain precluded cricket or soccer, we would go on a cross-country run led by a prefect. These runs were lots of fun because high jinks along the way were inevitable. On one such run, Freddie Bethel stopped at a shop, had a drink of rum, and when he got back to school was totally drunk. We tried shaking him and walking him around the dorm but it did not help. The deadline for dinner was approaching and we had to be dressed and in the dining room when the bell rang or we would all be in serious trouble. Starting to feel increasingly anxious, we sat him in the shower and let the water run but even this didn't help. Then someone remembered hearing that squeezing lemon juice into the ears of a drunk could make them sober. In no time at all, one of the boys climbed the fence and retrieved a lemon from the orchard behind the dorm. We squeezed the juice into Freddie's ears but he just lay there like a beached whale. In desperation, we dragged him out of the shower, dressed him, walked him to the dining room and propped him up during the meal, all the while praying that the master in charge would not notice. Somehow we got away with it and after dinner we walked him back to the dorm and rolled him into bed.

**Simon in Lodge School dress uniform, Barbados, 1949**
(Kreindler photo archive)

When games ended, we showered and changed into our evening uniform, long-sleeved white shirts, grey flannel wool pants (shorts for the younger boys and slacks for the older ones), silver and blue school tie, and navy-blue wool blazer with the school crest.

Sunday was the one evening with a different routine. Because the weekly boarders returned in the afternoon and there was no evening prep, we were usually treated to a movie outdoors under the stars.

The end of the school year always culminated with the "Funeral," a ritual that was approved by the administration and which probably had more to do with symbolically burying the school year than anything else. As the time for it drew closer, hushed references only served to heighten the apprehension and foreboding among the youngest boys who had no idea what was involved and undoubtedly feared the worst. On the designated day, one of them was snatched and put in the "coffin," a large wooden box normally used to store rifles for the cadet corps. At that point, I suspect the unlucky nine-year-old probably expected he was going to be sacrificed in some strange ritual or buried alive in one of the sugar cane fields that circled the school. When all the boys had assembled in the quadrangle, the coffin and its human cargo was hoisted aloft onto the shoulders of four senior boys who led a noisy procession that wended its way to the main road about half a mile away. There it was lowered to the ground and a classic scholar was called on to conduct the "service." He climbed onto the coffin and in his best possible Latin proceeded to read passages from Virgil's Aeneid, pausing after each phrase to allow the assembled gathering to respond - which they did with loud yells and cheers. The service concluded about half an hour later at which point the coffin was again hoisted aloft, marched back to the school and the poor devil inside released.

I spent the year 1952/53 in Miami preparing for my Bar Mitzvah that was celebrated in Guatemala so that my mother's parents could share in the simcha. Although the year in Miami was an exciting and eye-opening experience, learning Hebrew in congregational school was anything but. I worked hard at acquiring proficiency in chanting my Haftorah[100] but something was missing. Reflecting on it more than 60 years later, I realize it was the absence of Yiddishkeit[101] at home when I was growing up. We had a mezuzah on our front door, attended High Holiday services at the Altman home in Hart's Gap, and Joe always lit yahrzeit candles on the anniversaries of his parents' deaths. We fasted on Yom Kippur and I knew that doing work that day was forbidden. However, we did not observe Shabbat, and although I sat with my father during High Holiday services, the experience was pretty meaningless as he never explained much about the ritual or prayers and I understood next to nothing. During Passover we ate matza, imported from the U.S. for the entire

---

[100] The Haftarah reading follows the Torah reading on each Sabbath and on Jewish festivals and fast days. Typically, it is thematically linked to the Torah portion that precedes it.
[101] Refers to the quality of being Jewish, the Jewish way of life or its customs and practices. In a more general sense, it has come to mean the "Jewishness" or "Jewish essence" of Ashkenazi Jews and the traditional Yiddish-speaking Jews of Eastern and Central Europe.

community, and I was aware that bread was prohibited, but we never had a traditional Seder.

In spite of the above, I was aware that Jewish continuity was very important to Sara and Joe. The problem was there was a gap between what they espoused and what they practiced, something I have struggled to make sense of. I am sure neither felt confident about instructing us but why not let others do so? There were, after all, knowledgeable Jews in the community and for several years there was even a Sunday School. Part of the problem was my father's disengagement from the Jewish community. While Sara enjoyed socializing with the women, Joe was not close with any of them apart from his business dealings with the men. I suspect he may have felt their shared Polish background left him out in the cold. There may also have been other reasons but whatever they were, the fact that we lived on Maxwell's Coast and that all four of us attended boarding school undoubtedly contributed to the community's perception that "we" were not part of "them." Consequently, Peggy and I had limited contact with the other Jewish kids, although I have fond memories of picnics at Crane Beach when we were teens and of the dance classes organized by Clara Paster, Betty Konigsberg, and Rosie Zierler at the Konigsbergs' home on Dayrell's Road.

From when I was quite young, I regularly helped my parents in the store on Saturdays. Initially, I would bring payments from customers to the cashier and later I sold merchandise or accompanied the porters to various stockrooms around town to recover goods that needed to be replenished. In my teens, I told my parents I hoped to eventually join them in the business but my father quickly put the idea to rest. He wanted all of us to continue our education in Canada, hopefully become professionals, and marry Jewish partners.

Peggy went off to McGill University in Montreal in 1955 but dropped out in 1957 and married Sam Mass in Barbados. They subsequently settled in Miami. I left for McGill in 1957, Maurice followed me in 1964, and Jerry followed him seven years later. As we children gradually left the nest, Joe and Sara began to think more seriously about immigrating to Canada. After dismantling the business in the 1970s, they gradually transitioned to living in Montreal.

I met my wife, Ruby, shortly after arriving in Montreal in 1957. She came from an observant Jewish family and I credit her parents and her with teaching me much of what I know today about being a Jew. After completing my undergraduate studies, I entered medical school at McGill and we got married in 1962 after my first year.

**Ruby and Simon, Montreal, 1958**
(Kreindler photo archive)

After graduating medical school in 1965, I interned at the Jewish General Hospital in Montreal and our son, David Michael, was born in Montreal in 1966. I spent the next five years doing a residency in adult psychiatry and a fellowship in child psychiatry at the Menninger School of Psychiatry in Topeka, Kansas, and our daughter, Lisa Sharon, was born there in 1969.

Ruby and I had planned to return to Montreal in 1971 but the antics of the separatist FLQ party[102], combined with the Quebec government's introduction of a health insurance plan the Province's physicians found totally unacceptable, made us change our minds. Instead, we moved to Toronto where our younger son, Jonathan Andrew, was born in 1973.

We have lived in Toronto for the past 45 years during which time our three children have married wonderful partners and given us eight beautiful grandchildren. They all live in Toronto and we regularly spend time together. Who could ask for more?

---

[102] Front du Liberation du Quebec

**The Kreindler family, Lake of Bays, Ontario, Summer 2016**
Back row: Kevin Green, Jonathan Kreindler, Simon,
David Kreindler, and Jacob Fenichel Kreindler
Middle row: Adam Green, Lisa Kreindler (Green), Matthew Green, Noah
Kreindler, Ruby, Debbie Fenichel, and Eliana Fenichel Kreindler
Front row: Samara Green, Corry Kreindler,
Kayla Kreindler, and Aden Kreindler
(Kreindler photo archive)

## *MAURICE KREINDLER'S STORY*

**Maurice Kreindler**

Born in Barbados in 1947, I was Joe and Sara Kreindler's contribution to the post-war Baby Boom. Except for nine months when I lived in Miami Beach to attend Hebrew School and have my teeth straightened, I spent my formative years in Barbados. At 17, I left the island to attend McGill University in Montreal, so my recollections are those of a child and adolescent growing up in an idyllic setting.

My earliest memories are of days filled with vistas of white sandy beaches and the sparkling blue waters of the Caribbean Sea. I remember spending time at the beach on Maxwell Coast Road, where my parents lived in a beautiful house named "Breezely". I have fond memories of picking golden apples ("Spondias Dulcis" or Jew Plum) from a huge tree in our yard and eating them in the salty water on the south coast.

**Maurice Kreindler, Barbados, 1950/51**
(Kreindler photo archive)

As I grew older, I attended Sunday school every week at the home of Rose and Simon Altman. Our teacher was Geoff Lebens, a handsome and soft-spoken British expatriate who in lay life managed a department store on Broad Street. When classes were over, all the Jewish families took their children to the Aquatic Club to swim and run wild over the elevated ballroom and jetty, and where I fished and watched cruise liners and freighters make their way to the port of Bridgetown. I have vivid memories of passing the walled property of the Barbados Yacht Club on the way to the Aquatic Club, wondering what went on inside and not understanding that it did not exist for Jews because we were not welcome. Then for some reason unknown to me, we stopped spending Sundays at the Aquatic Club and relocated to the gorgeous Paradise Beach Club. It was memorable because the warm and salty seawater was punctuated by cool springs of fresh water bubbling up from the sandy sea floor.

My first experience with Bajan rum occurred at the Crane Hotel when I was only 10 years old. The special occasion was the wedding of my sister, Peggy, to Sam Mass, an American ex-GI who swept her off her feet. While everyone was busy dancing, I convinced the hotel bartender to slip me a rum and coke because I told him that my father was paying for the wedding. Later that evening I woke up in the back seat of my father's Plymouth with no recollection of how I got there. At the Paradise Beach Club three years later, I engaged in protracted and ultimately unsuccessful negotiations with the hotel barman to add rum to my fruit punch so I could drink the same rum punch as the adults. Even though I bragged about my prior drinking experience, the barman held his ground. As an older teenager, I remember spending Sunday with my parents on the pristine white beach of the renowned Sandy Lane Hotel. There after hours in the beautiful blue water, we enjoyed an elaborate brunch buffet, featuring endless quantities of foods and desserts that would be daunting to most, but not to this teenage boy!

Most of the Jewish families in Barbados sent their sons to school at Harrison College in Bridgetown. My parents, however, chose to send Simon as a "boarder" to Lodge School in remote St John's parish. Boarders lived at the school from Sunday afternoon until Friday afternoon, coming home only on weekends. They made this decision because Simon had close friends somewhat older than him who were already enrolled at Lodge. Unfortunately for me, Simon's positive experience at the school encouraged my parents to send me, and then my younger brother, Jerry, there as well. I started classes at Lodge at the tender age of eight where I received a world-class education that I still appreciate, but my extracurricular life there was miserable. I was a pudgy child and from the age of six, needed very thick glasses to correct my severe astigmatism so I was constantly picked on and bullied. At Lodge I also had my first experience with anti-Semitism when I was accused of being a "Christ-killer" even though I was a pacifist and had never even met Christ! For this reason, I decided to study Scripture at Lodge even though the kindly priest who taught the class offered me an exemption because of my Jewish faith. Scripture became one of my favourite subjects in school and even today, my Jewish and Gentile friends are surprised at my familiarity with the New Testament. For me, being a boarder at Lodge five days out of seven was a very isolating experience. I looked forward to Fridays and was sad on Sunday afternoons when I had to go back to school. For decades after I left Lodge, I felt wistful and sad on Sunday afternoons.

**Maurice Kreindler's 1960 Bar Mitzvah,
Ocean View Hotel, Rockley, Christ Church**
L to R: Marlene Altman, Maurice Kreindler, Ann Lebens,
Florence Pillersdorf, Paul Altman, Richard Pilarski, Issy Tepper,
Aaron Truss, and Jerry Steinbok
(Kreindler photo archive)

My father suffered from asthma most of his life, and close to the time I was sent to Lodge, he moved the family to Bathsheba, a remote, windswept and picturesque part of the island, which was 30 minutes from Bridgetown by car. We moved there when I was 10, one of only two families who lived in Bathsheba year-round. The other 30 houses were rented out occasionally as "beach houses" or vacation homes. Lacking playmates, I became a voracious reader and loyal patron of the Barbados Public Library. By 13, I had read everything in the children's section. At the librarian's suggestion, my mother signed a permission slip enabling me to borrow books from the adult library. There I was thrilled to discover a great new world of literature. My parents were concerned that I spent too much time reading, and decided that I also needed more physical activity. I tried horseback riding but gave it up after I was either thrown from or fell off the horse. After my brief equestrian career, they suggested I take up golf. Despite many lessons and playing multiple rounds with Paul Altman on the Rockley Golf Club course, I realized I wasn't a "natural" and gave it up.

Starting at 13, whenever I came home from Lodge for the weekend, I volunteered to go to my dad's store, the Modern Dress Shoppe, on Broad Street. Initially, it was an attractive alternative to doing nothing in Bathsheba, but I soon found that I really enjoyed the responsibility of being the store cashier and honed my math skills on the job! I developed a genuine affection for the staff, and they for me, and soon I was working not just on weekends, but whenever I had vacation time. By the time I was 15, my parents had so much confidence in my "managerial abilities" that they took a three-week trip to Europe and left me in charge of the business! It was a somewhat ludicrous situation, being chauffeured daily to the store and back home because I was too young to have a driver's license. Also, because of my youth, my dad's bank would not let me sign cheques, so I had to pay the employees in cash which I found very stressful. One of the highlights of working there was celebrity sightings even though I was not always aware of their fame. I remember meeting Claudette Colbert and pretty Charmian Carr (Leisl from The Sound of Music) and most precious of all, I got the autograph of Tarzan (a.k.a. Johnny Weissmuller).

I remember fondly our most eccentric customer, an expatriate, aristocratic English lady named Mrs. Drummond. My mother supervised the production of ready-made clothing in our store, but the customers who had idiosyncratic requirements wanted custom-made dresses. Mrs. Drummond would come into the store twice a year and order six expensive silk dresses at a time, insisting that the fabric be reversed so the silky side would be against her body. For me, that was proof of my dad's aphorism that "the customer was always right" and "there's a customer for everything!"

In 1961 with the opening of the Barbados Deep Water Harbour, the tourist business surged and boatloads of American tourists, many of them Jewish, came to visit the island. My father quickly realized that there was money to be made in catering to these tourists, and the Modern was busy selling embroidered dresses and shirts in colourful tropical prints. My parents often conversed in Yiddish when they didn't want their kids to eavesdrop, so over the years I learned to understand most of what they were saying. I remember American tourist customers being surprised when they were conversing amongst themselves in Yiddish and then realizing that I understood them. They were also stunned to hear that I'd had a Bar Mitzvah in Barbados and that my older brother was attending McGill medical school.

At 17 I finished my education at Lodge and was accepted to McGill University. When friends asked why I went to McGill, I jokingly replied that all Kreindler kids went there because our parents did not know of any other universities. McGill was such a freewheeling environment (after so much structure at Lodge) that my freshman year was nothing short of wonderful. I spent much of my class time socializing, going to the movies or playing hearts, bridge and pool. Unfortunately, I also managed to fail my first year, even though when I deigned to attend classes, I found the subject matter easy after my British boarding school education. My parents were unexpectedly accepting of my failure, but McGill was not! The dean of students suggested that I take a year off in the hope that I would mature. My parents allowed me to spend that year in Montreal on the condition that I would be self-supporting. I landed a job with the Royal Bank, went to school at night, and had another socially-rewarding and maturing year in Montreal.

Every summer I loved going back to Barbados to help my parents in the store. Even though I missed my friends in Montreal, I remember telling my dad when I got my BA that I wanted to come back home and work in the business. He replied that I needed to get a profession because "no one" could not take it away from me. I have never figured out who "no one" was. Years later when I graduated from Law School and passed the Bar exam, I told my dad that I still wanted to work in the store and would be happy living in Barbados. He looked at me, smiling and said, "You're a professional now, you can't work in a store!" In retrospect, he was right. I have always loved the famous lyric in the song, "Beautiful Boy," written by John Lennon for his son, Sean, that goes "life is what happens to you when you're busy making other plans."

After 20 years practicing law and not feeling fulfilled, I made a career switch and became a real estate developer. I specialized in developing urban retail properties and over the years have had the good fortune to meet and befriend many small business owners who remind me of my parents and my roots.

# *BRANCIA AND LUZER GROSS' STORY*
Simon Kreindler

**Brancia and Luzer Gross, Cernauti, Romania, 1938**
(Kreindler photo archive)

Joseph Kreindler's sister, Brancia/Bertha, was born in Okna, Bukovina, in 1906, the sixth of her parents' eight children. When WWI broke out in 1914 and her father was drafted into the Austrian army, her mother took all the children with her to live in Vienna. When the war ended in 1918, they settled in Cernauti, Romania (formerly Czernowitz, Austro-Hungary).

In 1922 Brancia married Luzer Gross in Cernauti. When WWII broke out in 1939, Romania allied itself with Germany. In 1941 most of Cernauti's Jews were rounded up and forced into a ghetto. The Romanians subsequently deported 30,000 of them to Transnistria,[103] including Brancia and Luzer who were sent to the Moghilev camp. Many of the deportees died of exposure, starvation or disease or were murdered by Romanian or German units. Somehow Brancia and Luzer survived. When the War ended, my father and his two older brothers in New York located them in a Displaced Persons' Camp in Europe, and in 1947 they came to live with us in Barbados.

After Luzer learned to speak some English, my father wanted him to start

---

[103] Following the German invasion of the Soviet Union, Romania re-annexed Bessarabia and northern Bukovina, which had been seized by the Soviets a year earlier. After the conquest of the Ukraine by German and Romanian troops in July and August 1941, Romania was given the territory between the Dniester and Bug Rivers. Romanian authorities established a military administration there and dubbed the region Transnistria.

working as a peddler but he regarded this as beneath him and would have no part of it. After he and Brancia moved to their own apartment near the Garrison Savannah, my father set Luzer up in a small store at 7 Swan Street in Bridgetown and gave him merchandise to sell. However, nothing was good enough for Luzer and it soon became evident he had no interest in improving his lot in life. He complained about everything but was unwilling to do anything to make things better.

When I was growing up, our parents would take my siblings and me to visit them on Sunday afternoons. Branch and Luzer had no children and our visits were the highlight of Brancia's week. Luzer was totally disinterested in us and would usually just sit in his rocking chair and say nothing other than to answer the occasional question about his blood sugar! The moment we arrived, Brancia would greet us with a barrage of wet kisses that my siblings and I hated. Not long after, she would serve the varenikas[104] she always made and frequently, also a layered torte she had baked. No matter how much we ate, it was never enough and it was almost impossibl to escape her entreaties to eat more.

In 1954 my father's older brother, Willie, who lived in New York, offered to help Luzer get established in Montreal where he was then doing business. Luzer and Brancia went to Montreal to hear what he had to say, but Willie had much the same experience as had my father. He felt Luzer expected to be handed everything on a silver platter but wasn't prepared to extend himself in any way. In December 1954 Brancia and Luzer returned to Barbados via Venezuela where they visited Luzer's brother.

Luzer died in Barbados in 1968 and is buried in the Jewish cemetery. After his death, Brancia emigrated to Montreal where she lived in a seniors' building in Cote St. Luc and supported herself on reparations from the German government. She died in 1982 and is buried in the Chevra Kadisha section of the Back River Cemetery of Montreal.

---

[104] Stuffed dumplings known as kreplach in Yiddish, varenikes in Ukranian and pierogi in Polish. While there are many variations, the basic ingredients are the same in all three cultures and they are usually filled with meat, cheese or potato.

## IANCU AND TONY LAZAR

**Iancu and Tony Lazar, Barbados, ca. 1950s**
(Rachel Pillersdorf Weisman photo)

Iancu and Tony Lazar are listed among the Founding Members of the Barbados Jewish Community and came to the island from Romania ca. 1948.

Iancu died in Barbados in 1992 and Tony in 1997. Both are buried in the Jewish cemetery in Bridgetown.

# GEOFF AND EDITH LEBENS' STORY
Ann Lebens Abel

**Edith and Geoffrey Lebens, Barbados 1954**
(Dina Truss photo)

Geoff Lebens was born and grew up near Manchester, England. His family, Orthodox Jews, had come to the UK from Russia. Edith was born in Vienna and grew up in Zagreb, Croatia. Her parents were interned during WWII and she, her brother, and sister were brought to England on the Kindertransport.[105]

Geoff and Edith met at a Jewish youth club in Leicester, England. She was quite young but they kept in touch even after he went off to study at Oxford and got married right after he graduated. However, Geoff suffered with asthma and it led to him taking a teaching job in Jamaica at Monroe College in the Blue Mountains. He and Edith travelled there about 1945/46 and all three children were born there: Ann in 1947, Ralph in 1952, and Stephen in 1953.

In 1953 Ann was six and needed to start school so the family relocated to Barbados. Ralph took a teaching contract at Harrison College and Ann enrolled at Queen's College. Very soon after the family arrived on the island, Geoff got involved with the Jewish community and started a Sunday School.

---

[105] Kindertransport (Children's Transport) was the informal name of a series of rescue efforts that brought thousands of refugee Jewish children to Great Britain from Nazi Germany between 1938 and 1940.

**Geoff Lebens and children of the Barbados Jewish community, ca.1954**
Back row: Louis Burak, Simon Kreindler, Abraham Truss. 2nd row: unknown girl holding Steven Altman, Betty Konigsberg, Geoff Lebens, Dorothy Burak, Rosie Zierler. 3rd row: Mary Speisman and Leah Pillersdorf. 4th row: Paul Altman, Harold Saunders, Jimmy Altman, Maurice Kreindler, Ann Lebens, Paul and Jerry Steinbok. Front row: Marsha Altman, Robbie Saunders, Rachel Pillersdorf, Marlene Altman, Ralph Lebens

Geoff taught at Harrison College for about 10 years. Prior to Ralph and Stephen's Bar Mitzvahs, he sent them off to England to board and study at Carmel College[106] but by 1964, his concern with the cost of their education led him to quit Harrison College and take the position as manager at Fogarty's Department store on Broad Street. The boys returned to Barbados for their summer vacation, and Ralph and Edith would periodically see them in England when they went there on buying trips for Fogarty's.

---

[106] Carmel College was a predominantly Jewish co-educational boarding school in England, that operated between 1948 and 1997. It was Europe's only Jewish boarding school and had a very small number of day pupils who were not of Jewish descent. The school practised mainstream Orthodox Judaism; had a substantial number of students from Europe and the Americas; and had an ethos of respect, diligence and social responsibility. Its aim was to turn out international students who were both secular and had an appreciation of religion. It closed in July 1997 because of declining enrollment and severe financial difficulty broght on by the Labour government's termination of government-assisted places. (Wikipedia)

Ann graduated from Queen's College in 1966, won a Barbados scholarship, and studied Latin and French at Oxford. After graduating and getting her teaching qualifications, she got married and went to live in Nigeria where she taught French for four years. While there, she and her husband separated, and he was subsequently killed in a car accident. Ann returned to England about 1970, and Geoff and Edith returned from Barbados about 1971/72. Geoff got a job as a housemaster at Carmel College and he and Edith lived there until Geoff retired.

Ann taught French in England and France, and met her second husband, Malcolm, on a skiing vacation in Switzerland. They were married in 1979. Their daughter was born in 1981, their son in 1983, and they now have two grandchildren. Ann is now a magistrate[107], does some volunteer work, helps with her grandchildren and goes to the gym when she has time. She and Malcolm live in Manchester.

Ann's brother, Ralph, was an architect who specialized in passive solar energy, wrote a book on the subject, and for a time was at MIT in Boston. According to Ann, he "had two sons with whom we sadly have lost touch. He went off the rails after getting divorced and became a Rastafarian." He died in 1994 when the camper/trailer in which he was touring the U.S. caught on fire.

Stephen trained as a quantity surveyor, later became ill with schizophrenia, and lived near his mother in Reading. In 2007 he developed oesophageal cancer. Ann retired from teaching so she could take her mother to visit him prior to his death later that year.

Geoff whom Ann described as a "fabulous father and a good man who never said an unkind word about anyone" died in 2001 at age 80. Edith is now 92, and while she still has all her faculties, is quite frail. She recently moved into a seniors' facility near Carmel College near where she and Geoff lived after they returned from Barbados.

---

[107] Magistrates do not have legal training but act on panels as lower-court judges. Ann deals primarily with minor crimes, e.g., assault, traffic, and burglary, as well as family matters such as removing children from unsuitable homes and putting them up for adoption.

## DINA AND MOSES MASS' STORY
Merlyn Mass and Jack Mass

 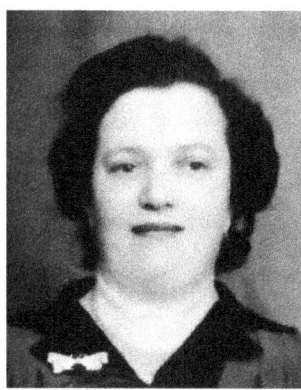

**Moses and Dina Mass, Georgetown, British Guiana, 1946**
(Jack Mass photos)

Moses Mass' parents, Samuel Mass (1879-?) and Dora Padriski (1887-?) married in Odessa, Russia, in 1900, and then moved to Bialystok where Moses and Hyman were born on May 10, 1903, and ca. 1904, respectively.

**Dora and Samuel Mass with sons, Hyman and Moses
Bialystok, Russia, ca. 1910**
(photo courtesy of Merlyn Mass)

When Moses was about 14, his parents were anxious to get him out of the way of the Russian Revolution and put him on a ship. He apparently spent the next nine to ten years at sea and only took up residence in Holland about 1926/27.

Dina Mass' parents, Joseph Karp and Rose Altman, were from Lublin, Poland. Joseph was born there in 1884 and Rose in 1885. Lublin was a small town with narrow streets and houses with thatched roofs. Schooling was mostly done at home although the rabbi did hold some classes for the children. Joseph and Rose married in 1903 and Dina was born on May 15, 1906.

In 1927 Joseph and Rose were feeling increasingly uneasy about the political climate in Poland and decided to send their children, Aaron and Dina, to live with friends in Holland. Aaron went first in 1927 and Dina followed in 1929. Before they could send any others or get out themselves, Germany invaded Poland and the remaining family perished in the Holocaust.

Dina Karp and Moses Mass met in Holland and married in 1930. As war clouds gathered, they secured visas to go to Barbados and travelled there in 1932. According to Doris Mass Kassner, her mother was pregnant with her when they arrived, and she was born in Barbados six months later on October 6, 1932.[108]

Unlike most of the other Jewish men who came to Barbados from Europe, Moses Mass did not start out as a peddler but opened the Russian Store at 9 Swan Street in Bridgetown that had crossed British and Russian flags over the door. Dry goods filled the front of the store and in back was a bar with a few tables and chairs where ginger beer, rum, and grog were sold. Moses worked in the store and sometimes also Dina.

Jack Mass recalled that when he visited Barbados in 1960, he searched for his father's store. At the time, it was owned by Mr. Spira who offered him a job. Jack found a hand-painted sign in the back of the store decorated with crossed flags and an inscription that read "Moses Mass, Proprietor." In retrospect, he regretted not having asked Mr. Spira if he could keep it but at the time didn't think to do so.

The older four Mass children were all born in Barbados - Doris in 1932, Helen in 1934, Sam in 1936, and Jack in 1939. At various times, the family lived on River Road, Swan Street, Roebuck Street and the Esplanade. The children attended Miss Kinch's School (run by two spinster sisters) which had beautiful gardens and ponds, as well as fruit trees the children would raid.

---

[108] This suggests that Moses and Dina probably arrived in Barbados in March/April 1932 and gives Doris Mass the distinction of being the first Barbados-born Ashkenazi Jew.

Sam remembered catching cockroaches, tying a string around them, tying the string to a matchbox and trying to race them. When the roaches wouldn't move, the kids would try to encourage them by lighting a match and holding it near them! Other times they raced wooden sewing spools that were notched with a stick in the middle, wound tight with a rubber band.

Sam also recalled that people got around on buses, bicycles, and donkey carts although the latter was usually used for hauling goods. The buses were small, had wooden benches and no windows. When it rained, the conductor rolled down a tarp that was stored on the roof and which would cover the sides. However, the tarp blocked out all light except for what came in at the front. Inside it was so hot that it felt like a spa. When it rained on the island, everything came to a halt, although the rain usually only lasted a few minutes.

Sam's best friends, Bert and Richard Evelyn, lived behind them and he remembered well the time Richard accidentally hit him on the head with a hoe, leaving an indentation he carried for the rest of his life.

Jack Mass noted that his mother returned to Poland with Doris, Helen, and Sam about 1936/37, but he did not know why. At some point a relative there sensed that something bad was going to happen and convinced her to return to Barbados. She did and in 1939 the Nazis invaded Poland.

**Helen, Dina, Sam, and Doris Mass in Poland, ca. 1936/37**
(Jack Mass photo)

In 1941 Dina became ill, required surgery, and had to travel to Trinidad. While recuperating she stayed with her relatives, Mr. and Mrs. Averboukh. According to Sam Mass, the pictures below were taken aboard ship when his parents and Moses Altman were returning to Barbados from Trinidad.

**Above: Moses and Dina Mass**
**Below: Moses Altman with Dina and Moses Mass**
**returning to Barbados from Trinidad by ship ca. 1941**
(Jack and Sam Mass photos)

In 1943 the Mass family left Barbados for Georgetown, British Guiana. Jack, five years old at the time, remembers getting seasick on the schooner, and worrying it might capsize. The trip took three days and Sam recalled there was water in the living quarters most of the time. Dina had to keep a tight rein on the children and keep them out of the way of the other passengers.

**The Mass family home, 179 Waterloo St., Georgetown, British Guiana**
(Photo courtesy of Merlyn Mass)

The family lived at 179 Waterloo Street in Georgetown opposite the Parade Ground and not far from the Botanical Gardens. It was a large house with nine bedrooms. Dina, Moses, and the children occupied the four downstairs bedrooms and the five upstairs bedrooms were rented out.

Moses went to work for his brother-in-law, Aron Karp, at his "lumber grant" in the interior where trees were harvested and cut into timber at his sawmill.[109] Dina and the children sometimes visited Moses there and other times Sam and Jack would go together for an overnight.

In Sam's 2010 obituary[110] his family recalled how "throughout his life he would share vivid memories of summers in the jungle working in the family's lumber company." The following is excerpted from Sam's recollections:

"Everything needed for the two-month (summer) stay would be packed except food. We didn't have a car or truck so we took a cab or bus to the paddleboat dock that was about three miles from home. It took most of a day to travel the 70 miles upriver to the lumber camp at Ampa Bay.

---

[109] Guyana, formerly British Guiana, is one of the most forested countries of the tropics. Over three-quarters of the national territory of 21.5 million hectares is covered in some kind of forest of which some 14 million hectares are considered to be loggable...Until the second half of the 19th century there was little exploitation of Guyana's forests due to the limitations of labour, transport, infrastructure and overseas markets. As markets developed and technologies improved, logging of coastal forests and those along the banks of the lower rivers commenced, but even until the 1960s, extraction from interior forests was limited by the absence of roads or other means of getting timber downriver past the major falls.
http://wrm.org.uy/oldsite/deforestation/LAmerica/Guyana.html
[110] San Mateo Times, June 16, 2010.

The paddleboat never stopped on the way to Bartica, the last stop before it turned around and returned to Georgetown. The river was not deep enough for it to dock at Ampa Bay, and if it didn't follow the channels, it would become grounded on sandbars.

Canoes came out from settlements along the river to meet the paddleboat and when they were close enough, the canoes would be lashed to it with ropes to transfer passengers and provisions. After the transfer was completed, the canoe was set free and returned to its pier at the lumber camp. The camp's office, storeroom, and living quarters were a few hundred yards away in a large wooden building that stood on concrete pillars to prevent wild animals such as tigers, iguanas and boa constrictors from getting in. When workers needed provisions from the storeroom, they either paid cash or their purchases were recorded and the amounts deducted from their pay at the end of the month.

**Transporting people and provisions to the lumber camp**
(Photo courtesy of Merlyn Mass)

Living conditions were primitive. Candles or kerosene lamps provided light for the living quarters and water from the river was boiled for drinking. There was an outhouse but no toilet paper – only newspaper or pages from a catalogue. One could bathe in the river but only at low tide because to do otherwise was to run the risk of encountering piranhas – the river's garbage disposal system. Cooking was done on wood-burning stoves with fuel that came either from the sawmill or was gathered in the forest. The camp was not a place for women although some aboriginal women did work there. They lived with their husbands in thatched roofed houses, cooked outdoors on stone stoves, and caught fish to supplement the provisions they could buy at the office. They cleaned the living quarters and collected wood for cooking.

**Aboriginal workers at the lumber camp, British Guiana**
(Photo courtesy of Merlyn Mass)

The lumber company covered hundreds of acres. Aborigines (called Bucks) cut down the trees with axes and handsaws. The fallen trees were trimmed, then brought by truck to the sawmill near the water's edge. Flat-bottom schooners would then ease their way to the beach, load the cut timber and take it to Georgetown."

Jack described his father as a tough, authoritarian man with whom it was not easy to get along. His mother, on the other hand, was a warm, giving, nurturing lady who made friends with everyone and was also a great cook. When the family later moved to New York, visiting friends and relatives always wanted to stay with Dina, even those who could afford the finest hotel.

Moses Mass had a Torah at home that was stored in a mahogany cabinet and used during High Holiday services. Jack didn't know where it came from or what became of it subsequently, but recalled that when the chaplain at the US Air Force base at Atkinson Field[111] heard that his family was Jewish, he contacted them to arrange for the Jewish service men and women stationed there to attend High Holiday services. These men and women would bring the

---

[111] After the commencement of World War II, the English Parliament agreed to allow the US to establish bases on some Caribbean Islands and in British Guiana for the protection of the hemisphere. Hyde Park was the site chosen for the Air Force Base, named Atkinson Field, 25 miles from the capital, Georgetown. Source: "Atkinson Field and WWII a memoir 1943-46" by Ivan O. Carew, Guyana Review, July 2011.

family gifts from the base commissary and Jack remembers them bringing him his first Hershey chocolate bar!

**Jack, Sam, Moses, Dina, Doris, and Helen Mass,
Georgetown, British Guiana, ca. 1945**
(Jack Mass photo)

In 1947[112] Aron Karp sold his lumber business. Needing alternate employment, Moses went to nearby Venezuela and worked as a salesman. Jack remembers how quiet the house was when his father wasn't there!

Moses and Dina had always wanted to immigrate to the US, and in 1948 the family applied for US visas at the consulate in Georgetown. Ironically, when their number finally came up, Dina was pregnant with Joe and could not travel. At that time Moses' brother, Hyman, and his wife, Esther, had a tailoring and drycleaning business in Jersey City, New Jersey, and they sponsored Doris to come and live with them. This allowed the rest of the family to maintain their position in the immigration queue, and they arrived in New York on June 22, 1949.

Doris graduated high school around the same time and moved to live with the family in Brooklyn. Shortly after, she met Richie Kassner who lived on the same block. Moses went to work as a tailor, a trade he had practiced in Europe, and Dina stayed home with the younger children. Sam, 13, was enrolled in public school but Moses enrolled 10-year-old Jack in a yeshiva, Toras Emes. Jack hated yeshiva life and particularly resented having to give up Saturday afternoon movies that were his greatest pleasure. He still remembers being

---

[112] This date is totally at odds with what Aron Karp's daughter, Anne Karp Zeplowitz, recounts about her parentts' stay in British Guiana. In her account, Aaron sold his lumber business about 1951/52, shortly before he and Marilyn returned to Barbados to start their family.

slapped across the face by the yeshiva's principal after a classmate told him he had seen Jack going into the cinema one Saturday afternoon.

After Doris and Helen completed high school, they worked for Grayson-Robinson, a clothing manufacturer in New York where they ticketed garments and did other clerical work. Doris married Richie Kassner in June 1951 and Helen married Alan Steinberg (later Sands). Both couples later moved to Miami, and in 1959 so did Moses and Dina. Moses Mass died in Miami in 1967 and Dina in 1970.

After graduating high school, Sam briefly worked for Grayson Robinson then also moved to Miami. For a while he and Helen's husband, Al, were partners in a service station, and later when he bought out Al's share, he and Doris' husband, Richie Kassner, became partners.

Sam met Peggy Kreindler in Barbados while visiting his uncle and aunt, Aaron and Marilyn Karp, and they married in Barbados in 1957. They lived in Miami and their son, David, was born there in 1959. Their second son, Alan, was born in Barbados in 1961. Sam and Peggy's marriage didn't last. Sam was very distressed and decided to move to San Francisco where he had been offered a job with relatives. He left the children with Peggy and moved there in 1962. The following year Peggy brought the children to San Francisco, left them with him and emigrated to Israel.

About 1964 Sam married Rochelle Tepper, but that marriage also failed and they were divorced in 1969. The following year he met Merlyn Foss who was managing the apartment building where he and the children were living. They married on June 1, 1972, and this time Sam got it right – the marriage lasted 38 years until his death in 2010.

Jack Mass went to work for Paramount Pictures straight out of high school and after completing a liberal arts degree at the University of Miami in 1965, he returned to New York and worked in the advertising business until his retirement in 2000. He now lives in Florida.

Joe Mass developed juvenile diabetes and it plagued him all his life. After graduating high school in Miami, he worked at his uncle's gas station and in 1968 took over ownership of it. He was a collector of stamps, coins and currency, and loved food and gambling. Eventually, his diabetes got the better of him. His marriage failed, he had to go on dialysis and required an amputation of one leg. He died on May 20, 1996.

# PALTYEL AND WISIA PASTERNAK'S STORY
### Clara Paster Halpern

**Paul and Wisia Pasternak, ca. 1930s**
(Clara Paster Halpern photos)

Paltyel (Paul) Pasternak was born in 1904, the youngest son of Chaim and Esther Pasternak. He married Wisia (Vera) Ribakovsky, born in 1906, the youngest daughter in her family. Both came from well-to-do families in Grajewo, Poland.

Paul's parents left Poland for New York in 1932 with two of their children, Jimmy and Fanny. The Ribakovsky family stayed in Grajewo, except for one son who left for Palestine and two others who went to Mexico.

Paltyel could see that things were deteriorating for the Jews in Poland and he also wanted to leave, but Wisia did not want to go since her parents refused to do so. Paltyel and Wisia got married in 1934 and left Grajewo in 1937 with their two children, Jack (two-and-a-half years old) and Clara (three months). They wanted to immigrate to New York to join their family there but quotas for Jews were already filled and their application was rejected.

Instead, with encouragement from their Brzozek cousin in Barbados, they made their way there with the children. They had no money and only a *shofar* which had belonged to Paltyel's father. They were in complete shock when they arrived. They had not imagined Barbados would be such a small place, they spoke no English, and had never before seen a black person. Because Bajans had difficulty pronouncing "Pasternak," they came to be known as the Pasters.

**Pasternak passport photos from 1937**
(Clara Paster Halpern photo)

**Wisia, Paltyel, Clara and Jack Pasternak, Barbados, 1938**
(Clara Paster Halpern photo)

Paltyel started out peddling *shmates* (dry goods) door-to-door on a bicycle and eventually saved sufficient funds to purchase a leather goods store on Palmetto St. from his cousin, Yehudah Brzozek, who was about to leave for Melbourne, Australia, in search of a better Jewish life for his family.

Wisia was an avid reader and was blessed with a marvellous singing voice. In her spare time, she could often be found reading with a dictionary at her side, wanting to improve her English vocabulary. When Paltyel purchased the leather store on Palmetto Street, she managed it and he then opened a dry goods store at 42 Swan St. that also proved successful.

The Jewish community was very close-knit. While most members were business competitors during the week, on Sundays they would usually gather at the Aquatic Club to swim and gossip, then drive to The Crane Hotel for afternoon tea. They would then meet in the evening to play Canasta and 66.

In 1942 Wisia's parents were rounded up with the rest of the Jews in Grajewo and transported to Treblinka for extermination.

**Ryan Peters lighting a candle for his Ribakovsky great-grandparents' family at the memorial for the Jews of Grajewo, Treblinka, Poland, July 2016**
(Clara Paster Halpern photo)

In Barbados Paltyel always blew the *shofar* that he brought from Grajewo on High Holiday celebrations. After he left for Canada, the community continued using it until 1996 when it was returned to Clara. She gave it to her granddaughter, Noa Teal, named after her great-grandfather, Paltyel, on the occasion of her baby naming.

**The shofar Paltyel Pasternak brought to Barbados from Poland in 1937**
(Clara Paster Halpern photo)

Wisia developed breast cancer in Barbados and went to Montreal for treatment in 1958. Paltyel returned to Barbados, sold their home and businesses, and returned to Montreal in 1959 to be with her. Sadly, Wisia passed away in October 1959 at the young age of 49. In 1960 Paltyel married a lovely lady, Roza/Zozo Hirsch, who had emigrated to Montreal from Romania via Israel. Their marriage lasted until 1992 when Paltyel died at age 87. Zozo died four years later in 1996.

# *JACK AND RICKY PASTERNAK'S STORY*
## Jack Pasternak

**Ricky and Jack Pasternak, Toronto, 2013**
(Kreindler photo archive)

As an adult now living in London, Ontario, I continue to be amazed when I think of the bravery, courage and foresight my parents showed when they left their home in Grajewo, Poland and boarded a ship with no knowledge of their destination, leaving family, home and possessions behind. It was around November 1937 and to them, the future of Poland was dark.

The Pasternak family, Paltyel (Paul), his wife Visha (Vera), and their children, Jack, age three, and Clara, age 1, arrived in Barbados and joined other Jewish families fleeing from various European countries when it became clear that war was on the horizon and anti-Semitism was becoming more intense. The Pasternak name was shortened to Paster on arrival in Barbados.

The Jewish families in Barbados before World War II (from memory) were the Spiras, Konigsbergs, Buraks, Altmans, Brzozeks, Kreindlers, Bernsteins, Speizmans, Pillersdorfs, Zierlers, and the Pasters. Other Jewish people who arrived during the war or just after included David Zlatow who lived with us for a few years, the Feldmans, and the Saunders.

I think of my parents, speaking only Yiddish and Polish, finding their family and themselves on a most unusual, colourful island. The people on this island were typically kind to newcomers. My father was given a bicycle and merchandise to peddle and after a while opened his own business.

Most of the Jewish families established businesses on and around Swan Street and Broad Street. The Paster store was at 42 Swan Street and like most Jewish couples, my parents worked in the store together. I remember my father as a man of high energy and a keen business interest. In addition to his dry goods store, he invested in other ventures and purchased a leather store from the Brzozeks, importing leather from other countries that would be made into shoes by the native population. It was my mother who managed this store.

My father was a successful businessman, although not all his undertakings went well. He had an idea that the local flying fish, a "Bajun" delicacy, could be canned for export and set up a pilot plant in our garage, complete with machinery and printed labels. It turned out to be an impossible task because of the texture of the fish and it was a big disappointment for my Dad.

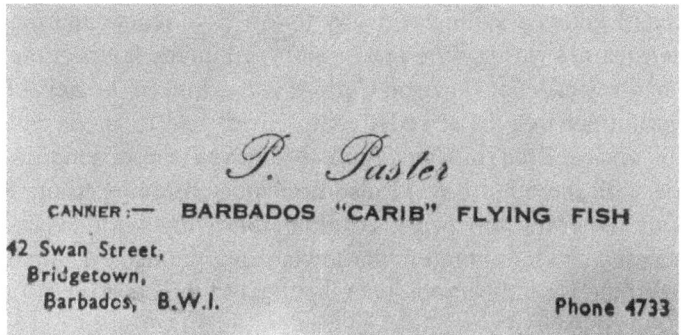

**Paltyel Paster's Carib Flying Fish business card**
(courtesy of Clara Paster Halpern)

He also invested with other Jewish members of the community in a small manufacturing business to produce "Sea Island Cotton" shirts that was more successful.

My mother was of a quieter nature. She liked to read and easily learned English, while my father had a harder time grasping it. My mother wrote poems celebrating special family occasions. The Sabbath was observed in our home and my mother taught the household help, Erla, a woman who was with us for many years, to cook Jewish dishes. I sometimes saw my mother crying and I did not know why. As someone who had escaped the Holocaust, she never spoke of the loss of her parents, family members, and friends whom she left behind in Europe.

The Barbados Jewish community was a close knit one, with regular religious services on Friday nights (after store closing hours), initially at the Altman home. My father blew the shofar on High Holidays and I remember him practicing those very familiar sounds. There was an active social life with various card games in the evenings. The Aquatic Club was a popular meeting place for a swim and "shmooze" on Sundays. Over the years many events were held to raise monies for Israel after the United Nations voted it into existence.

Life in Barbados for Jewish children was idyllic, with friends in the community and plenty of sunshine and beach time. Education was always important. Girls and boys were separated in school and uniforms were mandatory. I started kindergarten at age three in Mrs. Webster's one-room school on 8th Avenue in Belleville near our home. Later I attended Harrison College in Bridgetown. By then my parents had moved to Worthing, Christ Church, and I bicycled to school every day. After school, I played cricket on the beach with friends, then and now a very popular activity in Barbados.

On weekends I enjoyed sailing with my fellow Sea Scouts and played water polo for their team. I was an avid reader and spent many hours at the library. I trained as an army cadet at Harrison College and achieved the rank of corporal. During the summer months at cadet camps, I learned to shoot with an army "303" rifle and a Bren machine gun. I enjoyed these activities and the camaraderie with the other boys. I also remember listening to our shortwave radio with my father for long periods of time, following world events that were widely discussed and monitored in the Jewish community. I remember both of us listening to the United Nations vote that lead to the creation of the State of Israel.

Education in Barbados was on the English school system and highly regarded. I graduated from Harrison College with an Oxford and Cambridge Higher Certificate at the age of 16 and my application to McGill University was readily accepted.

My Bar Mitzvah was celebrated at the Ocean View Hotel in Christ Church, Barbados. It was customary to invite the entire Jewish community to such celebrations as well as any tourists who happened to be on the island. Special guests at my Bar Mitzvah were Mr. A. J. Alexandor and his wife. He was a prominent furrier in Montreal and had a significant influence in my life. His mother-in-law, Mrs. McCormack, had a boarding home in Montreal, with rooms for three students. Mr. Alexandor encouraged my father to contact him should I attend McGill University in the future and he would arrange housing for me. This plan came to fruition when I later moved to Montreal in 1950. I lived with Mrs. McCormack in the Town of Mount Royal for five years. I returned to Barbados every summer to be with my parents and one of those summers worked in a sugar refinery.

I graduated from McGill with a Bachelor of Chemical Engineering Degree in 1955 and was immediately accepted into the McGill postgraduate faculty, earning a Ph.D. degree in Chemical Engineering in 1959. My thesis research led to the publication of three papers that were well accepted by the scientific community. While in my postgraduate program, I shared an apartment for a time with my sister, Clara, who had come to Montreal from Barbados. Clara married my good friend, Norman Halpern, in 1957.

During my years at McGill, I joined a Jewish fraternity and ate my meals at Hillel House during Passover. It was there that I met Rowena (Ricky) Wiseman who had graduated with a Bachelor of Arts degree and was working on a Master's Degree in Psychology. We began dating and I visited her home in North Bay on several occasions, spending time with her family there. Her parents had a cottage on Lake Nipissing that I thoroughly enjoyed, but the North Bay winters were even colder than Montreal weather - a totally new experience for me.

Ricky and I were married in 1958 at the Chevrah Kadisha Synagogue in Montreal and we rented an apartment near the university. We received our graduate degrees together in 1959, with both sets of parents, along with an uncle from Israel, attending the graduation ceremony.

Sadly, my mother was already very ill with breast cancer at the time of my graduation. She and my father moved to Montreal where she received treatment at the Jewish General Hospital but she died in 1960. They had been married for 26 years. After her death, my father remained in Montreal, busied himself with a new career in the construction business and joined a synagogue and other Jewish organizations. He met and married his second wife, Zozo, a Holocaust survivor from Romania, and they remained together until her death 31 years later. My father died in Montreal at the age of 87 but had the pleasure of meeting his first great-grandchild, Ryan, Clara's grandson.

After my graduation in 1959, I accepted a position in the Research Department of Imperial Oil Limited in Sarnia, Ontario. After a wonderful month travelling through Europe, Ricky and I moved to Sarnia. I spent 32 years with Imperial Oil. By 1973 I had achieved the highest technical rank of Research Advisor and then became the Polyvinyl Chloride Plastics Technology Manager for Esso/Exxon worldwide, which involved extensive travel to the United States, Greece, Belgium and Japan.

Ricky initially worked for The Children's Aid Society and was then hired by the Ontario Government to establish, along with a psychiatrist, the first Mental Health Clinic in Lambton County. It was an experience she enjoyed. This clinic later became the outpatient service of the new Psychiatric Department of the Sarnia General Hospital where she worked until our move to New Jersey. Sarnia had an active Jewish community and I became President of Ahavas Isaac

Synagogue, a position I held for 30 years. Our two sons were born in Sarnia, Stephen in 1965 and Andrew in 1968. Both boys attended Hebrew classes after their regular days at school.

In 1976 I accepted a position, on loan from Imperial Oil, as Laboratory Director and Division Manager in Exxon's Corporate Research Facility in New Jersey. We spent eight years living in Short Hills, New Jersey. I was involved with directing scientists defining new science and technologies that could be commercialized by Exxon. It was an exciting time in our lives, especially living so close to New York City. Both boys celebrated their Bar Mitzvahs at Temple Beth Shalom in New Jersey, and many friends from Sarnia, along with family members, including my father, joined us. Ricky attended Seton Hall University and achieved a Master's Degree in Education specializing in Learning Disabilities as well as a Ph.D. in Clinical Psychology. Stephen graduated from high school and was accepted at Massachusetts Institute of Technology (M.I.T.) in Boston.

In 1984 we returned to Sarnia where I became Manager of Imperial Oil Lubes and Specialty Products Technology, Canada-wide. In total, I had a very rewarding career while with the Esso/Exxon organization. I was able to author or co-author 22 patents and publish 10 scientific papers. I was elected a Fellow of the Chemical Institute of Canada and received the U.S. Inventors' Hall of Fame Medallion as one of Exxon's scientists with the most patents. I was also awarded the Queen's Jubilee Medal marking the 25th anniversary of Queen Elizabeth on the throne. In addition, I was presented with a Medal and a Citation for an Outstanding Contribution to Chemical Engineering in Canada. On behalf of the Canadian Department of External Affairs, I had a wonderful two-week experience touring Japan, fact-finding on Advanced Ceramics. Because of my active involvement, I was elected Vice President of the National Executive of the Canadian Society for Chemical Engineering, but resigned before leaving Canada for New Jersey.

After retiring in 1991, a colleague and I were appointed as Co-Executive Directors of a Research Institute, Environmental Science and Technology Alliance Canada (ESTAC) that operated out of Sarnia. We created a consortium of 26 industrial companies that funded specific research of direct interest to the companies at universities across Canada. In 10 years, we awarded grants totalling $27 million, monies from the companies, matched by Federal and Provincial grants. At the same time, I became active in several organizations in Sarnia. I served on the Board of the Victorian Order of Nurses and the Board of the Family Counselling Centre. I was the Board President of the Sarnia YMCA and President of the 90-member Rotary Club of Sarnia. In my involvement with the latter, I was presented with a plaque naming me a Rotarian of the Year. I chaired the Bluewater Health Foundation Board that helped raise funds to build a new $400 million hospital in Sarnia. In addition, I was appointed as Chair of the Board of BioIndustrial Innovation Canada (BIC), an organization created in Sarnia-Lambton, funded by a $15 million federal grant to define and create green (plant-based) technologies that could be commercialized for the increased prosperity of Sarnia and Canada. I was appointed to the Mayor's Honour List for "outstanding service to the people and city of Sarnia." All these activities occurred while I was President of our Sarnia synagogue that had incorporated the Port Huron synagogue (across the border in Michigan) which could no longer exist independently.

On our return to Sarnia from New Jersey, Andrew completed two years of high school and attended the University of Michigan at Ann Arbor in the Chemical Engineering Department. At the same time, Ricky opened a private practice in clinical psychology. It became a very busy, full-time practice that she maintained for 30 years until we moved to London, Ontario. During our years in Sarnia we were able to enjoy world travel, often with the good friends we made in New Jersey. We are still travelling with them. In 2013, we moved to London, Ontario, where we could be closer to our sons and their families, to participate in the many activities of Or Shalom Synagogue and to avail ourselves of the cultural life of a larger community, including Western University (University of Western Ontario). Ricky and I have been able to see our sons achieve their own successes and they are our legacy.

Our son, Stephen, who now lives in London, Ontario, graduated from M.I.T. with degrees in both Chemical Engineering and the Health Sciences. He returned to Canada to attend McGill University where he received his M.D. and Ph.D. degrees. His specialty is neurology with expertise in Alzheimer's disease. He carries out research at the Robarts Research Institute, an arm of Western University, and has a clinic for patients suffering from Alzheimer's disease at Parkwood Hospital, London, where he also runs clinical trials related to Parkinson's disease. He is a tenured professor at Western University. He and his wife, Andrea Hirscheimer, a family physician, have three daughters, Emily, Melissa, and Alana, born two years apart. Emily, age 19, completed her first year at the University of Toronto in 2016.

Our son, Andrew, lives in Toronto and graduated from University of Michigan, Ann Arbor, with a degree in Chemical Engineering, followed by a Ph.D. degree in Biochemical Engineering from Northwestern University, Chicago. He returned to Canada and completed an M.B.A degree at University of Toronto. He now holds the position of Director of Commercialization and Business Development for Green Centre Canada,

bringing together universities and industries across Canada and USA. His career allows him to use his skills in both science and business management.

He and his wife, Maxine Katz, who has a postgraduate degree in Speech Pathology, have a son, David, who is an energetic five-year-old.

Ricky and I feel fortunate to have had the wonderful life experiences we have enjoyed. We are mindful of the support and encouragement received in Barbados so many years ago and under circumstances which could have been very difficult, but instead provided joy, a positive outlook, and high standards, which we believe shaped our destinies. We are very grateful.

# CLARA AND NORMAN HALPERN'S STORY
## Clara Paster Halpern

**Clara and Norman Halpern, Toronto, 2013**
(Kreindler photo archive)

Clara lived most of her early life at "Bognor" in Garden Gap, Christ Church. She had a very caring nanny, Erla, who looked after her while her parents worked very long days in their stores, and she often spent time with Erla and her family at their home. Her love of flowers and gardening developed from watching the family's gardener, George, and Clara still enjoys spending time in her own exquisite Toronto garden.

Clara loved her time growing up in Barbados, and as she says: "I would do it all over again if I had the opportunity." Although her family was not especially religious, they maintained Jewish traditions, and her parents closed the stores and observed all the Jewish holidays. Clara particularly looked forward to Rosh Hashannah and Yom Kippur, celebrated at the synagogue at the Altman home, and enjoyed preparing the coffee and buttered challah that was served to break the fast.

Growing up, Clara was a Brownie and later, a Girl Guide – even having had the pleasure of being introduced to Princess Margaret during one of her visits to Barbados. She took piano and dance lessons, swam, played netball, tennis, water polo, and generally led a very active life. She even learned to play cards with her mother's friends — age not being a barrier!

At age 10, she entered Queen's College where she received a wonderful English education. Her parents had insisted she attend a mixed-race school rather than an all-white one like most of her peers, but did not permit her to socialize with her non-Jewish friends after school for fear of intermarriage.

**The Paster family, Barbados, 1947**
(Clara Paster Halpern photo)

**"Bognor," the Paster family's home on Garden Gap, Rockley,**
(Photo of a painting by Lisa Litowitz)

**Clara's Toronto pride and joy**
(Clara Halpern photo)

After graduating from Queen's College, Clara was sent to stay with her ultra-Orthodox grandparents in Brooklyn, New York. It was culture shock, but she managed to survive a few weeks before being rescued by her Aunt Edda and Uncle Jimmy who invited her to stay with them in Albany, New York.

She returned to Barbados after four months, took several secretarial courses and was very involved in managing her parents' Swan Street store. In 1955 she left Barbados to live in Montreal with her brother, Jack, who had been there for the previous five years studying chemical engineering at McGill. In Montreal, she attended Sir George William College briefly before going on to work at several wonderful jobs.

Clara's brother, Jack, introduced her to Norman Halpern, one of his chemical engineering classmates and they were married in 1957. They have two daughters, Wendy (b. 1964) and Karen (b. 1966), along with four magnificent grandchildren – Ryan, Danielle, Talia and Noa.

As a result of Norman's occupation as a management consultant, they moved homes several times after leaving Montreal – to Toronto, Sarnia, Winnipeg, and finally back to Toronto. In the process, they had the opportunity to travel all over North America, Europe, Australia, Singapore, and China.

At the time of this writing (July 2016), Clara and Norman have been married for 59 years and have visited Barbados for 56 of those years - sometimes twice per year, often with their daughters, their spouses, and their four grandchildren. To quote Clara, "I still consider Barbados my home away from home!"

# LEIB AND FANNY PILLERSDORF'S STORIES
## Sam, Florence, and Paulette Pillersdorf

**Fanny and Leib Pillersdorf, Barbados, ca. 1950s**

## *Leib Pillersdorf*

Leib was born in Rudki, Poland, in 1919, the youngest son of Shlomo Korman and Rachel Pillersdorf. His parents, like many Jews in rural Eastern Poland, were married religiously, but not civilly, hence the adoption of his mother's last name as our family name. Daddy's eldest sibling was Faigy, followed by Oscar, Avraham ("Buom"), and Naftalie ("Kuk").

As a student, Leib was quite a troublemaker. Once when his teacher fell asleep in class, he took a clove of garlic and ground his teacher's beard into the desk with this all-natural glue. When the teacher woke up and could not extricate his beard from the desk, the first name he called out was Leibel Pillersdorf. Then there was one Pesach Seder night when Daddy and his friends waited outside a neighbour's house with a goat. Upon seeing the door open to allow Elijah the Prophet in, they squeezed the poor goat's testicles,

only to have the goat dart inside the house and wreak havoc on the Passover table!

A pivotal episode in my father's life occurred on the soccer field when he was a youth. It was raining and the upper part of his shoe separated from the sole. It was the only pair of shoes he had and he knew he would be in serious trouble the next day when he had to go to school. When he got home, he went straight to bed without any dinner. His parents realized something was up and after searching the house, discovered the shoe. This was a catastrophe for a family who was barely able to eke out a living. Leib received a beating, and then and there vowed never to let a lack of money adversely affect his life.

At age 10, he turned to commerce with determination. He wanted to help at a stall in the market place but no one would have him. He offered to work for the day and if he were useful, the stall owner could pay him whatever he felt like. At the end of the day he got paid and the stall keeper asked him to return the next day. After a short time, he realized that he could sell his own goods and travelled to a wholesaler in L'vov who carried second-hand scarves. He must have managed to impress the store owner who said, "My child, how can I give you credit? Do you have an adult to sign for you?" He ran to get his older brother, Oscar, who was about 20 at the time and studying in L'vov to sign for him. Eventually Leib became quite successful and his father joined him in the business. Little did he know that being a merchant who needed to become proficient in Russian, Ukranian, and Polish would supply him with the tools to survive WWII.

At the start of WWII, the Germans conquered Poland. The eastern part of Poland was handed over to the Russians as payment for not getting involved in Poland's defense. On Yom Kippur night in September 1940, Daddy was inducted into the Russian army. He said goodbye to his parents, not realizing it would be the last time he would see them. They, along with Faigy and her daughter, as well as Buom, were killed in the Belgitz concentration camp. I used to look forward to Yom Kippur night because Daddy would always tell parts of his life story in synagogue after Kol Nidre, first to me (Sam), and later to his grandchildren (my sisters missed out because there was separate seating for women). That same night in Sept. 1940, he had a chance meeting at the train station with his brother, Kuk, who was in the Russian Army as a military policeman.

Daddy went through training as an artillery solider. Translation: he looked after the horse pulling the mobile artillery gun. After basic training, he was shipped by train to White Russia in the eastern part of Belarus. He and the Russian soldiers found themselves leaderless in German-occupied territory. He wandered in the woods, burying his identification papers and having nothing to eat for days. When he was captured by the Germans, he assumed the identity of a Ukranian soldier, Stephan Billie, who had been sent home for bed-wetting.

By then he was fluent in Ukranian. The captured soldiers were marched back to Germany and Daddy used the time to listen and learn German. He knew that if he spoke a word of Yiddish, he would be killed. He had to endure many marches throughout his years in captivity. Many of his fellow prisoners died from cholera, a disease characterized by uncontrollable diarrhea. Daddy always said he was 'fortunate' enough to have been constipated all his life, and this was the reason he did not die then.

When he reached Germany, all the surviving prisoners were lined up to determine if they were circumcised. If you were, you were obviously Jewish and killed on the spot. After each person was inspected, they were allowed to go to sleep. When the inspection started, my father turned to his comrades and said, "We know there are no Jews among us. When someone goes to his bed from the far end of the line, one of us should also go. If we wait for them to check us, it will be hours before we get to bed". Unbelievably, his comrades listened to him and he avoided the inspection.

Conditions were terrible for the prisoners. There was not enough food and many died of malnutrition and infection. Daddy became so ill he was placed on the pile of dead bodies. Luckily, someone saw him move and managed to get him some extra food for a few weeks.

He was chosen to work on a farm outside Frankfurt am Main and because he understood German, acted as translator for the POWs and the farming community. This was the first time he had volunteered that he understood German, and it created suspicion. Why didn't he admit to knowing German before? Was he Jewish? He managed to convince those in charge that prisoners of war don't volunteer information.

One Saturday he felt unwell and couldn't work. He was told, "Stephan, relax. Don't work. It's your Sabbath - you Polish Jew." Daddy said, "Look, the Jews are circumcised." He pulled down his pants and said, "Look, I am not Jewish" and temporarily bluffed his way out of trouble. Unfortunately, later that week all the prisoners were rounded up and an SS officer asked, "Where is Stephan, der Polish Jude?" My father told us he saw the angel of death in front of him. He was beaten senseless, maintaining he was Stephan Billie from the Ukraine. As he was attacked, the SS officer drank more and more. At one point the officer asked for a towel to wipe his hands clean from the dirty Jew. Daddy didn't know what happened, but he awoke the next day. People referred to him as "der Polishe Jude", and he lived in terror for the next week. Days later the SS officer returned and lined everyone up asking for 'der Stephan.' Daddy approached the officer with great trepidation. The officer put his arm around Daddy's shoulder and asked "Vie geits, Stephan?" (How is it going?) Then he asked about the food. He told my father to do good work and then sent him back to the lineup. Everyone saw the interaction and asked Daddy what they had talked about. Daddy said he had received regards from his parents and siblings in the Ukraine but never understood why the SS officer hadn't killed him.

Daddy survived the war by his quick wits, his luck, and by the kindness of certain people. Near the end of the war, he was placed in a unit that broke down factories in captured territories and shipped them back to Germany. He was the translator and the head prisoner. He had a tattoo of an eagle placed on his forearm because all the other prisoners were doing it and he couldn't afford to be different. He was eventually liberated by the Americans and the area was passed over to the Russians. He found himself in Berlin where he met a Jewish girl named Fanny. Thinking she was the last Jewish girl alive, he proposed and they got married after their second date. The Russians wanted to make him part of the KGB but he and Fanny managed to escape to the Allied part of Berlin and ended up in a work camp in France. Daddy was able to make contact with his brother, Oscar, who had managed to leave Europe before the war. Daddy eventually joined him in Barbados. Many of our extended family came through Barbados at some point on their way to a new life.

With Fanny's help, Daddy thrived as a businessman. Florence, Paulette and Sammy were all born in Barbados. What a marvellous life it was compared to the horrors of Nazi Europe! Barbados had a small, tight-knit Jewish community where every Jewish adult was automatically your uncle or aunt. There was freedom to pursue all aspects of life and there was the beach. What more could you want? When Florence reached university-age, the family moved to Canada.

In Toronto, Daddy opened a textile store on Spadina Road that was later taken over by Uncle Jack (Auntie Yetty's husband) when Daddy became a real estate investor. I found myself attending Eitz Chayim School instead of going to the beach. My parents were not happy when they became aware that I was helping our neighbours decorate their Christmas tree.

So what kind of man was Leib Pillersdorf? Daddy was determined. When he made up his mind, he acted. If he thought it was right, he did it. He was quick-thinking, as evidenced by his survival as a prisoner of war. He was a shrewd businessman who recognized good assets when he came across them. He staunchly supported Israel, maintaining that if Israel had existed to defend us, there would not have been a Holocaust.

Our parents supported many charities and worked to improve the community. They were both avid supporters of Holocaust education. Daddy had an intense love for traditional Jewish customs. He was a man of his time and often commented on the changes he had seen in his lifetime. The village in which he grew up had one washroom that was used by everyone but he lived to see the technological marvels of today. What a spectrum!

Daddy was funny and liked to pull people's leg, even while he was sick. When my son, Daniel, came to see him at the hospital with his girlfriend, Jenna, Daddy held her hand, looked at Daniel and asked, "So, Daniel, are you jealous?" Later the same week Fanny came to visit him. As they held hands, one of the nurses asked her if she was his wife. Daddy looked at the nurse with a straight face and said, "No, this is just my girlfriend."

Daddy claimed to never have lost or misplaced an object in his 95 years. At one point, not long before he died, he became extremely worried that his address book and $1800 had indeed been misplaced. He obsessively asked us where the money had gone, who took it, and why we had been irresponsible and lost it. Later someone asked him how he was feeling. Instead of his usual, "A little bit much better," he responded, "You know, I feel like someone who just lost $1800." Even when he was deathly ill in hospital, his humour lurked just beneath the surface, waiting to declare itself.

Daddy loved spending time with his grandchildren, Daniel, Sarah, and Ben. Even at the age 88, he would sit with them and watch the afternoon trifecta of Judge Judy, Jerry Springer, and Maury because to him it was "fun."

Some of his grandchildren's fondest memories include Zeidy playing soccer in the hallways with Daniel; picking at the crispy parts of potato cholent with Sarah, or as he called it, the real McCoy; and eating Bubby's fresh homemade challah with Ben.

Our parents were married for approximately 70 years and even when they bickered or fought, they did it lovingly. Fanya, as he called her, was flamboyant, eccentric, and to put it lightly, strong-willed. Leib always acted as her buffer and she put up with his attempts to keep her in line. The two were a match made in heaven. As the grandchildren have pointed out, their connection was so deep that even without being told of Leib's passing, Fanny was admitted to hospital with heart problems less than an hour later. It was as if her heart had broken with sadness.

As you can see, Leib Pillersdorf was first and foremost a family man. He loved and supported Fanny with whom he built a life. He supported Florence, Paulette, and me in every endeavour we attempted and took great joy in his grandkids. He loved his brothers, sisters-in-law, nieces, and nephews. Simply put, he was a gentle man and a role model that we strive to emulate.

**Fanny Pillersdorf**

Fanny was born in Benjin, Poland, the eldest of three sisters of Shaindel and Yosef Friedman, a poor baker. Growing up, she would often look after her younger sisters, Tzeitel and Perel. When she was 11 years old, the family moved to Dombrova. It was before the War that Mommy purportedly would lead her same-aged Auntie Yetty and Uncle Sidney into all sorts of mischievous escapades. She was daring, ahead of her time, and would dye her hair blue as a teen.

Neither my sisters, Florence and Paulette, nor I know much of Mommy's history during the Holocaust. For most of our youth we understood that we could not ask questions about it because recounting her history would give Mommy nightmares and keep her up most of the night. Somewhere along the way she did a complete reversal and made a point of sharing her experiences with as many people as she could. She became active in Holocaust education and was a Madricha (leader) on many March of the Living trips, including a few with family members.

At the time of the Nazi occupation, Mommy was in her early teens. Her father signed her up to shovel snow for the city thinking it would be safer for her if she were doing something useful. Unfortunately, one day she and the other workers were rounded up by the Nazis and sent to the first of many labour camps. When the Nazis asked if there was anyone who had nursing experience, Mommy lied and said she was a nurse's aide. Her daring saved her. She maintained she survived the deadly typhus outbreaks in the camps by dipping her arms up to her elbows in lye even though it meant her arms were constantly red and irritated. At that time, she noted that the doctors were treated better than the other prisoners and survived when other Jews were killed. Is it any wonder why all three of her children ended up in the health care profession?

Mommy was moved around from work camp to work camp. At one, they were looking for people with experience in sewing garments. Translation in Mommy's mind - I can thread a needle; therefore, I have experience. She volunteered. The female German overseer didn't say a word about Mommy's inability to sew or that she was learning how to do so from the other ladies. This overseer would often leave her a piece of bread in the sewing machine drawer. One day a group of tall men entered her workplace, some dressed in uniforms, others in suits. It was the SS. Mommy was terrified even before she was made to undress. She was young and good-looking and was selected to go to the puffhouse, a place full of young women that the German soldiers could visit to have sex. This was a death sentence, as generally girls chosen to go to the puffhouse would soon become pregnant and then be murdered as a method of birth control. Her overseer started shouting that she had quotas to fill and if they took her workers away, she would not be able to do so. She made such a fuss that the men left everyone at their sewing machines. Mommy was grateful that this woman had once again saved her life.

Towards the end of the war Mommy was part of a death march. She survived and was eventually put on a train. At those times, train rides usually led to a death camp. Fortunately, the train had to stop along the way and Mommy and a few other girls managed to escape. They survived by hiding on a farm during the last few months of the War.

Mommy met our father, Leib, after the War and they decided to get married on their second date. They thought they were the only young Jews left in the world. While they were in Berlin in the American Zone, our father thought he was safe. He was out for a walk with his new bride when the Russian police carried out a sweep looking for defectors. He was blond, blue-eyed, was wearing a leather jacket with high boots - a typical Russian. Daddy was running away from the NKGB, the precursor to the KGB, that had unilaterally decided to enlist his services. The Russian police surrounded them and demanded to see their papers. Daddy saw his life flash before his eyes and uncharacteristically couldn't speak. Mommy started yelling in German at the top of her lungs, attracting a very large crowd. The Russians eventually had to leave them alone, saying, "Ah, fritz". Translation: Leave them alone. They are German, not Russian. They moved to a displaced persons' camp, then to a French work camp, and finally to Barbados where Leib was reunited with his brother, Oscar.

Growing up in Barbados, my sisters and I remember the numerous knocks on the kitchen door and the requests for food from strangers we did not know. They were always invited to sit at the table as Mommy served them a meal. Having survived the Holocaust and routinely being hungry, she was always concerned with people having enough to eat. This concern manifested itself in charitable deeds, but also in other less conventional ways. When she went on a car trip, she always took a healthy portion of food with her, whether it was a trip to Montreal or a trip to Yorkdale, a Toronto shopping centre.

Some people may think Mommy was far ahead of her time with respect to medical practices. After all, she survived the camps using basic principles of hygiene and believed in vitamins well before they became fashionable. She also had her own treatments that were somewhat unconventional. If Vicks Vapour Rub was good to rub on the chest, then it was doubly good to ingest, despite the bold "Do Not Ingest" warnings on the bottle. My sisters and I use to dread having a cold as we were forced to consume pieces of chocolate dipped in Vicks Vapour Rub!!!!

Mommy's approach to eye care was also unique. When we got an eyelash in our eye, she would hold our heads in her vice-like grip and suck on our eye. It was amazing how effective that was, as none of us subsequently ever admitted to ever having something in our eyes again!

Our favourite activity as children was going into our parents' bedroom and watching Mommy tickle Daddy. Every Sunday we would beg Daddy to raise his arm so that Mommy could tickle him. He always had a straight face and would never laugh, but Mommy would always be laughing uncontrollably and that in turn caused us to laugh hysterically. We loved it.

Determination is defined as a tendency to move in a fixed direction, or firmness of purpose. Stubbornness is defined as having or showing determination so as not to change one's attitude or position despite good arguments or reasons to do so.

I remember looking forward to going to a movie when I was very young. When we got there, the show was sold out much to everyone's disappointment. After Mommy had a chat with the manager, we were placed on the steps in the aisles of the cinema and watched from there. I have no recollection of the movie or whether we were uncomfortable sitting on those steps. What I do remember is Mommy's determination or stubbornness, forged by her formative Holocaust experiences. It has been a model to my sisters and me ever since. Maybe that is why we are still somewhat confused about the difference between determination and stubbornness.

On another occasion while on a trip to Barbados, we were about to visit the Governor General who had been our old family doctor. Right before we were to step into his office, Mommy with a look of horror on her face shouted, "Oy, Leibeshe, hob fergeson de versht!" (Translation: "Oh, Leib! I forgot the salami!") Imagine visiting the Governor General of Canada with all the pomp and circumstance and being concerned about not being able to offer him a salami!!!

Mommy was often larger than life, and there are too many Fanny stories to relate here. But some stories capture the vibrancy of life she possessed more accurately than anything else, so we will recount a few.

Mommy had a vain streak. She dyed her hair strange colours when she was young. She wore leopard skin patterned clothes, bird feathers and sequins. There are many pictures of Mommy with movie stars or with famous politicians. Polly (Paulette) likes to tell this story: One day she (Polly) was driving down Bathurst Street in the inside lane. Traffic was heavy and she wondered whether there was an accident in the other lane as cars were only moving about 5 km an hour. She eventually got to the car that was slowing things down which turned out to be Mommy's. She was having difficulty driving while simultaneously applying lipstick, putting on nail polish, and eating a tuna fish sandwich.

Mommy used to be invited to many charity lunches and teas. Florence says that at that point in her life she found them quite tedious. Mommy would want Florence to go with her, but Florence would always decline. Mommy would tell her that Paulette had already confirmed that she was coming, so in the end Florence would give in and agree to go. Yes, you know what is coming. Mommy would then call Polly to invite her to the tea because Florence was coming and how could she not come.

Mommy loved animals and used to spend many hours with her dog, Lockshen, on her lap while Farfel use to sit with Daddy. A little-known quality that Mommy possessed was her ability to foretell the future. After all, she named her parrot-loving child, Polly. Mommy's compassion towards animals manifested itself in quite a humorous story. On an outing to Monkey Jungle in Florida, Mommy was really enjoying feeding peanuts to some caged monkeys. When the bag of peanuts was depleted, one of the monkeys stole the spoon that she was using to eat her yoghurt. Mommy demanded her spoon back but the monkey had other plans. Mommy got so upset with the monkey that she cursed the monkey with great vehemence, "Behama bist tu!" ("You are a wild beast!") Sammy's wife, Rebecca, couldn't stop laughing. Insulting a monkey that in Mommy's mind was raised to near-human status and was being demoted again to the status of wild beast because it stole Mommy's spoon was so absurd that we all had to laugh.

Mommy was not afraid to promote her own or other people's issues. On one occasion, she ordered a car with special gold trim and put down a deposit. Unfortunately, the gold trim was discontinued and the dealership wanted to substitute another finish. Mommy wasn't getting what she wanted so she requested that her money be returned which the dealership refused. So what was she to do? Hire a lawyer? Get an ombudsman to get involved? Report this travesty to the press? Not Mommy! She stood outside of the dealership with a sign saying the dealership stole her money, and suggested as much to every car that drove in until the dealership gave back her deposit.

When Mommy was in her late 70s and 80s, she decided to take on another project. She had previously been a "shadchen" (marriage broker) and had several marriages to her credit. Now she decided to put her sewing skills to good use. She collected seconds from several clothing manufacturers, and as Auntie Yetty has recounted, worked tirelessly replacing missing or defective zippers, mending tears and repairing holes. She sold these garments out of her basement for about $7-$15 on average. After a few years she was able to donate a six-figure sum to Israel through Hadassah.

Mommy's grandchildren, Daniel, Sarah, and Benjamin, remember her fondly. They remember her insistence that the family be together for Friday night dinners. Ben and Daniel remember her raisin challahs, while Sarah enjoyed her potato cholent. Ben always recalls how much he would enjoy visiting his Bubby and Zeidy in Miami. Bubby developed Alzheimer's late in life. It was Jenna and Daniel who provided a focus that allowed Bubby to grill them on the status of their relationship. Sarah was the only one who could make Bubby smile the last few months of her life. It was Ben who would always go over to take care of Bubby and would text from Massachusetts wanting to know how Bubby was doing. All the grandchildren went out of their way to visit her in her latter months despite her inability to communicate.

You may already know that Mommy was found unconscious the day Daddy passed away. This was without having been told about his passing, but that sort of communication is possible after 70 years of marriage. She never quite recovered after that. When I think of Daddy, I think of humour, quick wit, support of Israel and responsibility. Although Mommy had her share of quick wit, to us she represented determination or stubbornness, courage to try things with little fear of failure, charity, nurturing of the mind in the form of education, nurturing of the body in the form of food, and support for Israel. Fine qualities for a Jewish mother and grandmother to leave as part of her legacy.

## *BARBADOS MEMORIES (next generation)*

My name is **Florence** and I am the eldest sibling. My parents lost their first child, Ruhel, as a result of a high fever and convulsions. They did not have the means to purchase the needed medication and consequently were overly vigilant, especially my mother, regarding our wellbeing.

My memories of life in Barbados are as follows:

- Initially we lived in the soldiers' barracks at the Garrison.

- On Sundays the whole community went to the Aquatic Club and later, Paradise Beach Club.

- One of my earliest memories: My sister, Paulette, and I looking up at our brother, Sammy, while my mother was holding him in her arms under the shower at the Aquatic Club. The water running between the wet, dark-brown floor boards to the sand below.

- Sunday AM before going to the beach – Closing all the windows and doors, my father spraying the entire house with a can of Flit so that when we returned all the cockroaches would be dead.

- Sunday afternoon naps and drives to the airport where we would share a ham sandwich and drink a 'Bentley.'

- Seeing the billboard for Macaw Rum on arriving and exiting the airport.

- Saying the names of the streets as we drove past them.

- Early education at Mrs. Jones' School.

- Being driven by Mr. Norris in his van to Codrington High School together with Marlene and Marsha Altman. The boys were driven to Lodge School. Harold Saunders (nicknamed Prof. Stringbeans) offering me my one and only cigarette puff, the best deterrent to Not Smoking Forever.

- Adults and children endlessly playing Canasta and the men, Poker.

- Jax, pickup sticks, hula-hoop, roller-skating and riding my bike in our neighbourhood, making and flying my own kite.

- The Drive-in

- Picking ticks off our dogs.

- Cheesecloths filled with milk hanging in the kitchen to make cottage cheese (milk came from local cows; only cheddar cheese and butter from New Zealand – no other dairy products available).

- Auntie Fela and Uncle Kuk (my father's brother) and their three sons arriving from Poland – found alive after the War!

- High Holiday services at the Altmans'.

- Sitting for our portraits to be painted by Mrs. Barrow, the Prime Minister's wife.

I currently live in Toronto, Canada with my partner, Demir. There are no children from my first marriage but I have a stepson from the current relationship. I have been a physiotherapist for more than 45 years and my special interest is the treatment of temporomandibular joint (jaw) problems. Unfortunately, my parents passed away two years ago. My sister, brother, and his children still try to attend Shabbat dinner every Friday night in my parents' house where my sister, Paulette, lives today.

My name is **Paulette** and I am the middle child of Fanny and Leib. In the past I have taught fitness, yoga and dance. The loves of my life are Jonathan, my life partner, and my cats, dogs, and birds. Currently, I am a dentist in private practice in Toronto, but I have previously taught at the Faculty of Dentistry, University of Toronto, and at dental conventions. My academic success is largely due to my parents' influence. My mother was always encouraging us to have professions in the medical field because when she was a prisoner in the concentration camps, people with medical knowledge were always treated better by the Nazis. My mom was far ahead of her time when it came to preventive medicine as she was always "shtipping" (stuffing) us with vitamins and cod liver oil, even in those days.

I, **Solomon (Sam, Sammy)** Pillersdorf was born in Barbados in the old Bailey Clinic on October 30, 1955. My parents had left the horrors of the Holocaust and war in Europe and arrived in paradise – Barbados, in the late 1940s. I attended Mrs. Jones' School and later went to Canada for further studies, graduating high school as an Ontario Scholar and obtaining a Bachelor of Science degree with Grade A standing from the University of Toronto. After graduating from The University of the West Indies Medical School with an Honours in Internal Medicine, I obtained my Internal Medicine and Rheumatology specialty degrees at McMaster University where I also did a clinical scholar year in epidemiology. I was an Assistant Clinical Professor of Medicine there; Head of Rheumatology Outpatient clinics and Head of Rheumatology training at the McMaster Medical Centre. I had a private practice in Guelph, Toronto, and Hamilton before retiring from medicine in 2010 when my wife, Rebecca, passed away. Our three children, Daniel, Sarah, and Benjamin consider Barbados their home away from home.

Since 2010, I have been active in the business arena with interests in the technology, real estate, mining, agriculture and securities sectors. I am a director and serve on the advisory boards of several publicly-traded and private companies.

My father had vivid memories of his childhood. Unfortunately, my memories of Barbados are somewhat limited. I remember feeling safe and supported by my family and by the whole Jewish community that met every Friday night for Shabbat services, and again most Sundays at Paradise Beach Club or at the Aquatic Club. I remember the privileged life of maids, nannies, and a chauffeur. On occasion, the chauffeur would cordon off a section of the yard, and cut the head off a live chicken to kill it before it was cooked for dinner. Although it seems quite morbid now, I use to look forward to this with glee as the headless chicken would run in circles for what seemed like several minutes!

At one point my parents bought a beach house in Bathsheba on the Atlantic coast where we would spend part of the summer. I remember Daddy trying to grow watermelon there; watching the bats at sunset swooping through the sky and checking for them behind hanging pictures when we returned to the house after a prolonged absence. We sometimes found a bat or two 'sleeping" behind one of the pictures. It was a toss up as to who would squeak louder, the bat or my mother.

Childhood memories are a tricky business. I remember the entrance to our house had a grand stairway that would take minutes to ascend and in the back yard there was a huge cliff with a panoramic view. When I returned as an adult, the stairway leading up to the house was a mere four steps and the back yard had a rise of about two feet compared to the neighbour's plot!

One of the nice legacies that Barbados has left those of us who grew up there is our lifelong friendships and relationships with all our cousins and friends with whom we continue to associate. This was doubly so for me because I returned to Barbados as a young adult for part of my medical training and in the process, was reintroduced to Barbados life.

# NAIMAN AND HANA/ANUTSA PULVER

**Naiman and Hanna Pulver, Barbados, ca. 1950s**
(Clara Paster Halpern photo)

Naiman and Hannah Pulver were among the Founding Members of the Barbados Jewish Community (1931-51) and came to the island from Romania after WWII.

## KIVA AND ESTEREA PULVER

Naiman Pulver's brother, Kiva, and his wife, Esterea, are listed among the Founding Members of the Barbados Jewish Community (1931-51). They came to the island from Romania after WWII. Their son, Bernard, was born in 1941.

# *MARTY AND ANITA REINGOLD'S STORY*
## Harold Saunders

Marty/Motel and Anita Reingold are listed among the Founding Members of the Barbados Jewish Community (1931-51).

The Reingolds came to the island from the United States and lived on Rockley New Road next door to the Saunders family. They had a son, Paul, and a daughter. Marty worked for Ernest Saunders at the Barbados Knitting and Spinning Mills where he helped maintain the machinery.

Betty and Max Konigsberg both remember Marty often coming to their home to chat with their father, Bernard Konigsberg. They also remember him helping their father when he purchased and renovated the Coronation Store on Swan Street.

The Reingolds did not stay in Barbados very long and returned to the US some time in the 1950s.

## *LEO AND CATHERINE RUBIN'S STORY*
Simon Kreindler
(Based on the recollections of James Altman, Aaron Truss,
Richard and Joseph Pilarski, and Paul Bernstein)

Leo Rubin is listed as one of the Founding Members of the Barbados Jewish Community (1931-51). Legend has it that during World War II he was among those responsible for burning the bodies of Jews gassed in Auschwitz. Leo's wife's name was probably Catherine.[113] I am not sure if she is the same person as Dr. K. Kathrina Rubin who is buried in the Barbados Jewish cemetery.

The Rubins probably came to Barbados in the late 1940s. Leo's business, the "Paradise Store," was located on the south side of Swan Street very close to Iancu Lazar's business. Apparently, Leo regularly attended synagogue and had a beautiful singing voice.

According to Aaron Truss, the Rubins were shunned by the Jewish community although the reasons for this are unclear. Aaron thought it might have had to do with what Leo supposedly did in Auschwitz but Richard Pilarski believes it was more likely because of the couple's unhappy relationship. Whatever the reason or reasons, it seems Motel Truss did maintain contact with Leo and the Pilarski family periodically entertained his wife and him in their home.

---

[113] The online Jersey Heritage collection has a 1977 Grant of Probate record for Catherine Semenow, wife of Leo Rubin, of Kimberley, St. Matthias, Christ Church (the contents of which are not publicly available) http://catalogue.jerseyheritage.org/collection/Details/archive/110280250/.

# ERNEST AND JEAN SAUNDERS' STORY
## Based on an interview with Harold Saunders
## by Simon Kreindler

**Jean and Ernest Saunders, Barbados, ca. 1950s**
(Rachel Pillersdorf Weisman photo)

Ernest Saunders (Szunyogh) was born into an extremely wealthy family in Munkacs, Hungary[114], in 1910. He attended yeshiva and wanted to go to Berlin to study medicine but his father told him that if he did, he would become a goy.[115] Instead, he brought him into the family business that sold linen and silk in stores all over Europe.

Eventually, Ernest left home, travelled to Holland and ended up in the same rooming house as Bernard and Ethel Konigsberg, Mina Zierler, and Srul Jacob Bernstein.

Ernest booked passage on a ship headed to Honduras but when it stopped in Jamaica someone asked him why he wanted to go there because there were frequent revolutions there. So he got off in Jamaica but because the island was British and he didn't have a visa, he had to leave temporarily, go to Haiti, and apply for re-entry from there.

---

[114]Munkacs became part of Czechoslovakia between 1920 and 1938; Hungary again between 1938-44; USSR from 1945-1991 and since 1991 is part of Ukraine. Wikipedia.org
[115] A Gentile.

In Jamaica, Ernest worked as peddler. He was still observant and kept kosher even though it wasn't easy. He saved his money and bought tickets for his family to join him, but sadly his father refused and everyone in the family, except for his younger brother, perished in Auschwitz. When his brother arrived in Jamaica, the British refused to let him off the boat and wanted to send him back to Germany. His brother went on to what was then British Honduras but soon after, Ernest received a cable saying he was very ill. When Ernest got to Belize, his brother couldn't recognize him and died not long after. Ernest arranged his burial in the Jewish cemetery there. For the rest of his life, Ernest struggled with guilt over the loss of his family and his father's decision to remain in Europe rather than come to Jamaica. He would never talk about it but his anger and disillusionment was evident in his giving up Jewish observance. After the War, Ernest went into business in Jamaica and with several partners started the Jamaica Knitting Mills, the first such business on the island.

In the early 1940s Ernest was planning a business trip to New York when a Hungarian refugee friend suggested he contact his cousin, a physician in Wilmington, Delaware. Ernest did and met the Aerenson family and their daughter, Jean. Ernest and Jean were married in Wilmington in 1944 and for a time lived in Jamaica. However, the Aerensons wanted Jean back in the US so Ernest and Jean eventually moved to Charlotte, NC, where Ernest went into business making T-shirts. A polio epidemic in Charlotte subsequently prompted them to leave and they moved to California where Ernest was one of the early importers of clothing from the Far East. In California Ernest met a Bajan who knew the families he had stayed with at the boarding house in Holland before the War as well as some Bajan Jews he had encountered in Jamaica. In 1949 Ernest and Jean immigrated to Barbados with Harold, then four years old, and Robbie, six months. Simon Altman met them at the airport.

Ernest started the Barbados Knitting and Spinning Mills with several partners, including Simon Altman and Aaron Karp, but the partnership didn't work out. He later partnered with a wealthy Lebanese Catholic man from Antigua that proved very successful.

**Harold Saunders' Bar Mitzvah.
L to R: Max and Minnie Aerenson,
Harold, Robbie, Jean and Ernest Saunders, Barbados, 1961**
(Robbie Saunders photo)

Harold left Barbados in 1963 to continue his education at the University of Miami. He had known Rabbi Bogomilsky[116] in Barbados and the Rabbi encouraged him to come to New York. For a while, Harold attended Yeshiva University but culture shock led him to transfer to George Washington University in Washington, D.C. Later he completed accounting training at the University of Toronto, met and married his wife, Ruth, and moved with her to Vancouver.

Harold and Ruth have two children, a daughter, Sherry, and a son, Danny. Sherry and her family live in Vancouver, and Danny and his family are in Israel.

Ernest and Jean left Barbados about 1974 and settled in Toronto. Jean died there in 1995 and Ernest in 1999.

---

[116] For more on Rabbi Bogomilsky, see the story of the Rebbe and his Emissaries in Chapter 6

## ROBBIE SAUNDERS' STORY
### Roberta (Robbie) Saunders

**Robbie and Jean Saunders, Barbados, 1949**
(Robbie Saunders photo)

I was born in Wilmington, Delaware, in 1949 and was six months old when our family arrived in Barbados. My father, originally from Czechoslovakia, thought Barbados would be a good place for his business.

I always tell friends that the Jewish community in Barbados operated as one large family. My parents played card six nights a week, rotating through each other's homes. Friday nights most everyone went to synagogue services. On Sundays, the community gathered at a chosen beach, usually the Aquatic Club or the Paradise Beach Club. After spending time at the beach my parents went home to take a nap.

My parents worked 5-1/2 days a week. My father owned the Barbados Knitting and Spinning Company on Roebuck Street, and my mother, the Style Shoppe on Broad Street. My immediate "family" lived in Worthing, Maxwell Coast, Garden Gap and Highgate Gardens.

My mother made wonderful desserts but my grandmother was the "chef" of the family. She also helped my mother in the dress shop when she and my grandfather would come to the island from Florida for their usual long visits.

**Robbie's Saunders' birthday party, ca. 1954.**
Back row: Fanny Pillersdorf and Evelyn Truss.
Next row: Jerry Steinbok, Maurice Kreindler, Molly Pulver, Felicia Lazar, and two unknown girls
Next row: unknown girl, Florence Pillersdorf, Linda Rosner, Hanna Wajchendler, Manea Truss, and unknown boy
Front row: Harold Saunders, unknown girl, Leon Truss, Robbie Saunders, unknown girl, Joe Truss, Paul Steinbok, Abraham Truss and Aaron Truss
(Robbie Saunders photo)

Family time usually centred around the dinner table. My mother taught the cook how to make my father's favourite European dishes. My father forbade dishes containing pork including the Bajan food my nanny brought from her home. As a child, I snuck out to the back porch to share Nanny's food. To this day, I consider these wonderful dishes my "soul food." My mother hired Nanny (the only name I ever called her) to take care of me when we arrived on the island and she had a profound impact on my life. She loved me unconditionally and I miss her to this day.

Growing up in Barbados greatly influenced who I am today. Most people grew up with an extended family that can include aunts and uncles. My aunts and uncles were members of the Jewish community who became an integral part of my life. I had non-Jewish friends in the neighbourhood but the unspoken message from my parents was not to get too close to them (to the point that my father directed my nanny to hold my hand whenever we went anywhere) and she did this until I was 12 years old!

**Robbie, Jean, Ernest, and Harold Saunders, Barbados, ca. 1959**
(Robbie Saunders photo)

I attended Mrs. Jones' elementary school and St. Winifred's School where my only Jewish friend was Eva Steinbok. My brother Harold attended Lodge School, a boarding school. Even though he was far away, I always felt close to him and he was fiercely protective of me. I always felt very loved by him and we remain close as adults.

I left Barbados at 15, spent my adolescence in Delaware, and attended Roosevelt Jewish Boarding School in Stamford, Connecticut. My parents wanted to be sure that I maintained my identity as a Jew and thought the US would be better for that.

I married Steven Jay Greenberg in 1967 at 18 years of age. We lived in Barbados for one-and-a-half years and then moved to Los Angeles, California. We divorced in 1981. My son, Michael, is 44 and my daughter, Kara, is 40. I have two beautiful granddaughters, Megan, four years old, and Ellie, two-and-a-half.

It is no surprise to me that I became a psychotherapist. I have studied the effects of survivor mentality and understand how the Jewish community may not have been sure enough of their own survival to support each other completely. They had to leave their homes that were not safe and came to an island that was very different from their homeland in every way. To this day I love hearing Yiddish being spoken as it takes me back to childhood. I loved my father's sense of humour and how the men all sat together on Sunday and laughed and talked in a language they could all share.

My mother brought us the American way of life and modern ideas that were sometimes received with ambivalence. She modelled how to be an independent, strong woman. My favourite aunts were Evelyn Truss and Fanny Pillersdorf. These two women loved me in powerful ways as they were themselves strong and powerful.

I'm not very religious but consider myself spiritual. That said, I do love the Jewish holidays and became a Bat Mitzvah at age 40.

As an adult, I understand how the community's Jewishness was primary to their identity. As a female child, it was difficult for me to understand. I have worked hard at healing this split within myself.

I have a Ph.D. in psychology and a Marriage and Family Therapy license. I have a private practice in Rohnert Park, California, and reside in Santa Rosa with my partner, Dr. Paula Solomon.

I consider myself very fortunate to be able to go home to Barbados every November to spend time with my childhood friends, Eva Steinbok, Florence Pillersdorf, and Aaron Truss.

# SALOMON AND FEIGA SCHOR'S STORY
## Simon Kreindler

I believe Salomon/Shlomo Schor was born in Poland. He was a friend of Judah Brzozek and both men had lived in Guatemala before coming to Barbados about 1933/34.

When I interviewed Ellen Brzozek Steinbok in Barbados in May 2016, she recalled that Salomon Schor had had a store on Swan Street in Bridgetown and that his wife, Feiga, was older than him. Max Konigsberg believes the Schors lived in Bridgetown, perhaps on Roebuck Street. Feiga Schor died in Barbados on August 12, 1942, and is buried in the Jewish cemetery in Bridgetown. Max Konigsberg recalled hearing that she had drowned and Clara Paster Halpern believes she drowned at the Aquatic Club.

Ellen Steinbok recalled that the couple's son, David, had oriental features and thought he might have been adopted. After Mrs. Schor died, Mr. Schor and David immigrated to Israel. Max believes they probably left Barbados in the early 1950s.

**Joseph Gerstenhaber, Joseph Kreindler, Edy Gerstenhaber
and Salomon Schor, Paradise Beach, Barbados, 1936**
(Kreindler photo archive)

Ironically, the Schors knew my maternal grandparents, Bertha and Joseph Gerstenhaber, from the time they and the Brzozeks had lived in Guatemala in the early 1930s. In fact, it was because the Schors and Brzozeks had immigrated to Barbados that my grandparents came there when they had to leave Guatemala in 1936. Salomon Schor introduced my parents and Yehudah Brzozek married them!

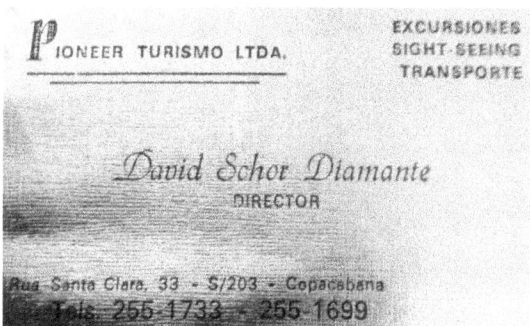

I tried to trace David Schor online but had no success. In 2016 Jimmy Altman showed me the business card (above) that he had been given some years earlier. He believed the person named on the card might have been the same David Schor who lived in Barbados in the 1930s.

The David Schor Diamante on the business card apparently operated a sightseeing business on Copacabana Beach in Rio de Janeiro, Brazil. I searched for his name but again came up empty-handed. When I asked Max Konigsberg what he remembered of David Schor, the one thing he recalled was that he had a taxi business although Max did not know where.

# HENRY AND CHANA (ZYLBERCWAIG) SILVER'S STORY
## Carole Joseph Silver

**Chana Silver**

Henry Silver was a favoured nephew of Hinda and Moshe Altman. He and his wife, Chana, accompanied the Altmans and their five children as they escaped the turmoil in Europe. Lublin had been their home in Poland and it saw the last of them as they embarked on their journey to Barbados.[117]

Henry and Chana married in Barbados and had two children, Sonia and Leon. Unfortunately, Henry passed away when Leon was eleven months old and Sonia almost three years old. Chana had no income and two young children to care for. She tried to continue Henry's work but it was too difficult so the Altmans supported her. Henry and Chana had always been very close to Mary and Louis Speisman and to Rose and Simon Altman. Leon grew up with the Altman children, Marlene, James (Jimmy), Marsha, and Steven.

Chana did baking for parties and in the Barbados Jewish community was known for her famous torte, made of layers of chocolate, biscuit-like dough, and custard. Leon and I tried to duplicate, it but although it was delicious, it was a poor copy.

---

[117] Although Henry and Chana may have left Lublin with Moshe Altman, they did not travel with him to Barbados. Moshe Altman arrived in Barbados in 1932, and Henry and Chana probably arrived in 1938.

**Sonia Silver, Betty Konigsberg, Dorothy Burak, and Rosie Zierler at a 1955 party at the Pasters' home in Barbados.**
(Betty Konigsberg Feinberg photo)

Leon and Sonia received a British-style education in Barbados. After graduating, Sonia immigrated to Canada. Meanwhile, Chana's doctor suggested that living in a cooler climate would probably help her high blood pressure. In February 16, 1960, she and Leon arrived in Montreal in the middle of winter. It was very cold!

On Leon's first day of work, he walked up and down the street, sure the address he was looking for was correct but confused by the strange name on the street sign: CHEMIN ST. JACQUES. A passerby eventually explained to him it was French for St. James Street, the very one he was searching for!

Chana and Leon lived in an apartment building on Lavoie Street in the Cote-des-Neiges area of Montreal. Leon had a daytime office job and attended McGill University at night. They reconnected with old friends from Barbados who had also left the island and come to Montreal. Chana began helping parents who needed help with their children when they went on holiday. When my sister was going to give birth and needed someone to take care of her older daughter, she hired Chana.

I met Chana several times when I went to my sister's home to take my older niece, Beverly, for a walk in her stroller. On January 1$^{st}$, 1962, my sister invited Leon and Chana to her house to celebrate Chana's birthday. My mom asked me to bring a parcel to my sister and that was when I first met Leon. I remember he was curious about my interest in newspaper ads for art galleries. I couldn't say that our meeting led to our becoming fast friends but not long after he asked me to accompany him to his boss' wedding. I accepted and we had a great time. When I needed a date for my friend's wedding, I asked him to come and he was happy to accompany me.

After that we didn't talk for about a year and then one day found ourselves on the same street corner. It looked like fate had extended us a hand. We saw each other for several weeks and then our relationship fizzled again. Later that year I was apartment hunting with my brother and his fiancée, and as we walked down Dupuis Avenue, I met Leon again. This time we started seeing each other on a regular basis and it never stopped.

**Carol and Leon's wedding, Montreal, December 1964**

Leon and I married on December 27, 1964. In 1965, Chana developed serious back pain and in June of that year was found to have lymphoma. Near the end of her life she would tell me that the baby I was carrying was to have her name but she didn't want to see me anymore. Leon visited her every day, never missing once, and I would go to support him.

Chana passed away in hospital on November 30,1965. Leon arranged the funeral and we sat shiva at our apartment. Sonia sat with Leon while I looked after them and welcomed family and friends. Sonia and Leon were not very close. They traveled in different circles and went their own ways after the mourning period ended.

On a cold February morning the following year, Leon counted my labour contractions and couldn't wait for our baby to be born. Because neither the baby nor my body was doing much after more than 6 hours, labour was induced and our daughter was born. And yes, her Hebrew name is Chana and her English name, Sharon. Two months later we moved into our new home in Chomedey, Laval, a Montreal suburb.

When Leon had to leave his job at the Bagel Bakery, I went back to my teaching job. One year later Leon was opening a new franchise store in the Montreal suburb of Baie d'Urfe when I discovered I was again pregnant. Our son, Howard Phillip, was born on May 18th, 1968. After the store became a success, I stayed home with the children but helped Leon when I could, taking shifts in the store so he could get some rest and quality time with our children.

We made our first trip back to Barbados when Howard was six weeks old. My parents accompanied us and we had a great time. As the children grew, we kept returning to Barbados every two years. We made a trip when I was pregnant with our second son, Mark, and when the air traffic controllers went on strike we had to fly to Burlington, rent a car, and drive home. The man sitting next me on the flight asked me if I was going to Montreal. I told him we were and no sooner had we landed than he took our luggage, piled it in his car and drove us to our door. Talk about guardian angels!

When the Quebec government brought in their new language laws in the early 1970s, all Leon's employees were forced to speak French to customers. We knew we had to leave Montreal, and in 1977 Leon was offered an opportunity to develop the franchise bakery in Ottawa. We moved there that August. We rented two houses before buying our home in the Riverside Park area of Ottawa. The children transferred schools and Leon worked long hours trying to set up a bakery in a huge building. I went back to university to finish my degree. One year later Leon quit his job and bought a small supermarket. He kept that business for nine years as it proved to be very lucrative. However, when the lease for the store was not renewed, he had to shut it down and get rid of all the merchandise, something he accomplished in record time.

Leon then started to dabble in real estate, buying properties that needed renovating and getting them ready for sale. Some of the houses he renovated were sold for twice what he paid for them. After listening to my nagging, he finally registered for the real estate course and became an extremely successful agent. He also created Silver Management Group Ltd. and hired people to renovate foreclosed properties before putting them up for sale.

After our children married and moved away, Leon and I would spend time taking trips abroad and just enjoying each other's company. Howard married

Rae-Ann and they had two girls, Brittany and Kaylee. Brittany graduated from Carleton University and is about to embark on her career. Kaylee is at college and will go to university later. After 20 years, Rae-Ann and Howard got divorced. Two years later, Howard met Lisa Johnson and they got married on September 24, 2016. Lisa has two boys, Charlie, 12, and Niko, 6.

In 1995 Sharon met Tim, and after a long dating relationship they married. They have four children, Jordan, Brianna, Mikah, and Jayden. When Jayden was nine, Sharon and Tim adopted two Inuit children who needed a home. Jordan and Brianna are now in college; Mikah is on a hockey scholarship at Kimball Academy in Meridien, New Hampshire; and Jayden attends a private high school that offers hockey training.

Mark married his high school girlfriend and they have two children, Zachary and Jackson, who attend the same high school.

In November 1999 Leon was diagnosed with terminal cancer. During the last three months of his life the children and I cared for him 24 hours a day. As much as he tried to be positive about his disease, it was taking its toll. He passed away on August 29, 2001. We had a hard time coping with the sadness. Sharon's youngest son, Jayden Leon, who is named after him and who also carries his Hebrew name, Shlomo Leib, was born nine months after Leon passed away. After Leon's death, our family never heard from Sonia or her family again.

# LAZAR AND TONI SPIRA'S STORY
### Sidney Spira

**Lazar and Toni Spira, Barbados, ca. 1950s**
(Sidney Spira photo)

**Samuel Spira**
(Sidney Spira photo)

My grandfather, Samuel Spira, was born in Ulanov, Poland, and died there on October 28, 1937. We have only one yellowed photo of him that hangs on our living room wall.

After his first wife died, Samuel married Yenty Steiner and they had two sons. The elder, Shimon (1875-1937), was born in Ulanov, married Hannah/Hennele and they had five children, Pepi, Bernhardt, Simon, Rosa, and Hella. My father, Lazar, was Samuel and Yenty's younger son. He was born April 10, 1890, in Ulanov and came to Vienna in 1906 or 1907 because he had relatives there. One of them who later moved to Berlin invited him to come there and help him sell eggs in the market. He gradually became a well-known egg wholesaler.

At age 36, my father met my mother, Toni Schmelzer, and they married in December 1926 in a civil ceremony in Berlin and again in 1927 in a local synagogue. I was born October 2, 1927, in Berlin where my parents had a happy and prosperous life in a nice apartment, surrounded by family and friends. I went to a Jewish school for a year before Hitler came to power. Prior to that, my mother had taken me to a spa in Marienbad, Czechoslovakia, every summer and my father would join us there. In 1935 he crossed the border illegally and went to Prague. His phone call to my mother made her cry and when I asked why, she told me we would never go back to Germany!

**Toni and Lazar Spira, Berlin 1927**

**Sidney's 1927 Birth Certificate**

**Sidney, Berlin, ca. 1933**

My father communicated with other Jews in Berlin, and he and my mother decided it would be better for them to leave Germany to live in a safer place. My father had business connections in London and we moved into a nice neighborhood there. I attended elementary school, and at my teacher's suggestion, changed my name from Siegbert to Sidney. I quickly became fluent in English.

In 1939 World War II started and Hitler began his conquest of Europe. England became the target of bombings that continued day and night, the so-called Blitzkrieg. I had my Bar Mitzvah in October 1940 during the horror of a heavy bomb attack.

My father was afraid that the Nazis would eventually try to invade England and decided to leave. He had heard about an island in the Caribbean called Antigua and in March 1941 we left on an old passenger boat, the "Akaroa." We travelled through U-boat-infested seas and after 14 days, arrived in Trinidad. We met some Jewish people who suggested we go to Barbados where there was a small Jewish community and excellent schools. We arrived there in April 1941.

Barbados was safe, and its beautiful sunshine and palm trees made it a paradise after what we had gone through. In Hastings my father found a small house with the name, "Elim Hastings." We soon felt at home and contacted other Jewish families in the neighborhood who were delighted to welcome us into their community.

**The Spira family feeding their chickens at "Elim Hastings," ca. 1942**
(Sidney Spira photo)

The first Ashkenazi Jew who had come to Barbados in 1931[118] from Lublin, Poland, via Amsterdam was Moshe Altman. He liked it so much that he had his family follow him and they made it their home. After other Jewish families started arriving, he opened his house on Harts Gap, Hastings, for services and High Holiday celebrations for which he had even acquired a Torah. The men prayed in a large room and the women in a smaller one. I had a very good voice and often participated in singing the prayers in front of everyone. Moshe was delighted to have an educated, joyful "landsman" like my father join the community and particularly appreciated the advice my father would periodically give him regarding his business.

My father started a small clothing business, the Hollywood Store, at 9 Swan Street in Bridgetown, the island's capital. The combination of his cheerful manner and my mother's help in selecting clothing for the female customers soon made it successful.

---

[118]Chapter 3 addresses the topic of the first Ashkenazi Jew(s) to come to Barbados and their arrival date.

**Hollywood Store, 9 Swan Street, Bridgetown**
(Sidney Spira photo)

**Hollywood Store, 9 Swan Street, Bridgetown**
(Sidney Spira photo)

I was enrolled in Harrison College and was the eldest of the Jewish boys there. The education was excellent and the headmaster, Dr. Haskell, and the other teachers were treasured by all of us boys.

Unfortunately, I did encounter some anti-Semitism in Barbados. One day some friends invited me to play tennis at the Barbados Yacht Club. Shortly after we started playing, the manager of the club took my friends aside and told them the Club objected to a Jewish boy playing there. He asked them to have me leave immediately! My friends were very embarrassed, but I did not want to make trouble and left!

My mother kept a nice home, serving all the meals she had learned to cook with her own mother, but kosher cooking was impossible, of course. In 1946 my father bought a beautiful, large villa, "Green Acres," at Worthing View, Christ Church, where we lived for 17 years.

After graduating from Harrison College, I decided to go to New York City. In May 1946, I applied to Columbia University, and in September was accepted by its School of Optometry. A cousin and I found a very large room in a nice apartment house near the university. My parents often came to visit, but separately because somebody had to stay and supervise the store in Swan Street.

In the fall of 1949 I graduated as a Doctor of Optometry. My degree was signed by no other than Dwight D. Eisenhower. General Eisenhower was President of Colombia University for one year before becoming President of United States.

After graduating I worked for a large optical company, and at the beginning of 1951, visited my parents in Barbados. My friends urged me to stay and I did. I opened an office on McGregor Street in Bridgetown and imported the necessary optical instruments and the latest eyeglass frames from New York. I became an immediate success, especially in the black community. The white community, however, always seemed to have a problem with me. Perhaps it was because I was a professional or perhaps it was that I was so outspoken. I recall a white dentist and contemporary who had a similar experience. Over time I realized that some of the white girls I tried to date had been forbidden by their parents to see me. Luckily, the tourist industry had started to thrive at the time and I became very popular with tourists. I also had many friends in the Barbados government and was often invited to their social events. Once a year I travelled to New York City on business and to enjoy that city's cultural events.

Meanwhile the island's Jewish population increased from the birth of children and the arrival of eight Jewish families who had survived the Holocaust. To accommodate the newcomers at High Holiday and other services, a large villa was rented in Rockley. At the time, there was a building in Bridgetown that had formerly been a synagogue, built in the 17$^{th}$ century by Sephardic Jews who had lived on the island. The Government had taken over the building and later offered to sell it back to the Jewish community. My father was one of the members who wrote to a Jewish agency in England asking for a financial contribution. As a result of their contribution, the old Jewish cemetery was kept in good condition.

The Jewish community gradually decreased as children graduated from high school, left for Canada to further their education, and did not return. Slowly, parents sold their properties and left to join them.

In 1963 I decided to leave Barbados and return to New York City because I saw no possibility of ever getting married on the island. An old friend suggested we open a business together and we did so on 14<sup>th</sup> St., Manhattan. My parents sold their business and their villa to Barclays Bank and joined me in New York. I met my wife, Annelene, in New York and we were married there in 1971.

**Sidney and Annie, 1971**
(Sidney Spira photo)

I took Annie to Barbados in 1995 to show her the places of my youth. I contacted Paul Altman, Moishe's grandson, whom I had known when he was a baby, and he and his wife, Rachelle, invited us for dinner at the beautiful villa they had bought from the Cunards. Paul also took us on a tour of Barbados to see all the changes that had taken place in the intervening years. Our former home, "Greenacres," had been torn down to make room for an office building. The five-acre parcel of land I had purchased and developed had been a big success and there were ten beautiful villas there to prove it. Had I stayed, I would have made a lot of money!

Paul Altman has been instrumental in restoring and refurbishing the old synagogue, now a landmark along with the old cemetery. He has also developed many large projects and in 2016 was knighted by the Queen of England! Sir Paul Altman! It was a pleasure meeting him again.

## *THE STAMMLER FAMILY*
### Hanna Templer Abramowitz, Max Konigsberg, and Betty Konigsberg Feinberg

Mr. Stammler was from Tarnof, Poland, and he and his wife came to Barbados via Trinidad after WWII. The Stammlers lived on Dayrells Road and had two children, a daughter, Ruth, and a son whose name no one in the current community can recall.

Mr. Stammler was apparently very religious. He studied the Bible and would often come to the Konigsbergs' home to talk with Mr. Konigsberg.

Max Konigsberg recalled his father, Bernard, being very impressed with how beautifully Mr. Stammler davened and would often have him take his place leading the services in shul. Max also remembers the Stammlers eating at their home during the High Holidays.

Neither Betty nor Max remembered what Mr. Stammler did for a living but thought he might have peddled. Max believed that the family went to Toronto after leaving Barbados.

The Stammlers are listed as Founding Members of the Barbados Jewish Community (1941-51).

## *MORRIS TAUB*

Morris Taub is listed among the founding member of the Barbados Jewish Community (1941-51) but unfortunately, none of the current members of the BJC remember him and I can find no information about him. The same is also true of:

## *LODDI AND ARANKA FRIEDMAN AND SON*

# ABRAHAM AND ELFREIDA TEMPLER'S STORY
## Hanna Templer Abramowitz

**Abraham (1952) and Elfrieda (1958) Templer**
(Stan Abramowitz photos)

My father was a travelling salesman in his hometown of Gorlice, Poland, where his parents owned a winery. He moved to the Free City of Danzig and met my mother who was working there as a bookkeeper. They married in the Great Synagogue in Danzig on December 15, 1936. Fortunately, my mother was able to bring their Ketuba (marriage certificate) to Trinidad in 1937 when she left Europe with me, an infant. My father had arrived months earlier and my maternal grandparents followed, leaving Danzig on August 3, 1939, less than a month before the outbreak of WWII.

**Abraham and Elfreida Templer's Ketubah, brought to Trinidad in 1937 and later to Barbados in 1950**
(Stan Abramowitz photo)

**Elfreida Templer's Shabbat challah cover, ca. 1800s**
**A wedding gift from her grandmother**
(Stan Abramowitz photo)

I spent the first 12 years of my life in Trinidad. My mother, Elfreida, and I left Port-of-Spain on a bright sunny morning in mid-February 1950, took a taxi to Piarco Airport, and boarded a BWIA (British West Indies Airways)[119] plane for the one-hour flight to Barbados. We landed at Seawell Airport where the weather was just as beautiful as it was in Trinidad. Departing the airport and driving along the rugged coastline with the sea on one side of the road, I was impressed by the various shades of blue and green of the calm Caribbean Sea. We passed well-known places: Oistins, Maxwell's, St. Lawrence Gap, Worthing, and Rockley on the way to our destination, Brown's Gap, in Upper Hastings.

Six months later my mother's parents, Zvi and Miriam Rehfeld, who were originally also from Danzig and who had been living near us in Trinidad, joined us in Barbados. On June 17, 1952, my father, a Mason (a member of the Solomon Temple Lodge), died and was buried the next day in the Jewish cemetery in Bridgetown.

I have fond memories of the time I spent in Barbados. We lived on Brown's Gap in Rockley and I was enrolled at St. Winifred's School where I studied hard and made many friends. One of them, Ingrid Friedman, lived in Navy Gardens not far from our home and we regularly took the bus to school together. On Thursday afternoons after school I would ride my bike up to Rockley New Road to take piano lessons from a very kind, patient lady who belonged to the Seventh Day Adventist Church.

---

[119] BWIA started daily airline service between Trinidad and Barbados in 1940 using twin engine Lockheed Lodestar planes. In 1947 the company was taken over by British South American Airways (BSAA), but a few months later the BWIA name was restored and service extended to other Caribbean islands using Vickers Viking twin (piston) engine planes. (Google)

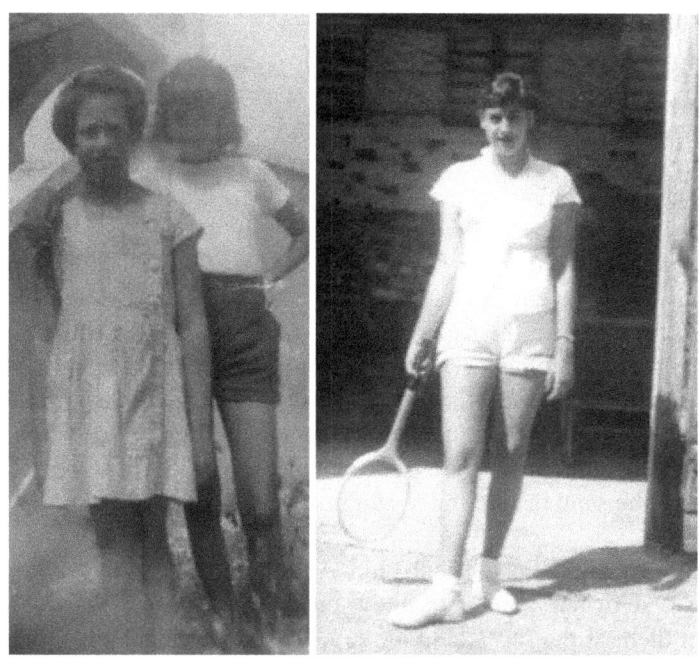

**Left: Ingrid Friedman and Hanna, Barbados, 1950
Right: Hanna on the tennis court at St. Winifred's, 1954**
(Abramowitz family photos)

In 1953 I had the opportunity to witness the elaborate, colourful decorations throughout Barbados celebrating the Coronation of Elizabeth II.

In the still of the morning of September 21, 1955, the quiet was shattered by the sound of a loudspeaker on a passing truck, advising people to turn on their radios to hear the storm warnings about an impending hurricane that was about to strike the island. On September 22, 1955, heavy rains began and Hurricane Janet struck Barbados causing millions of dollars of damage. Electric power was disrupted, the sugar cane crop was severely damaged, and poorly-built buildings were blown apart by winds of well over 200 km/hour. Highways were blocked, the airport was forced to close, and more than 50 people were killed. Although we were lucky not to be injured, we were greatly affected by this as we lived across the road from Rockley Beach.

Every year we would go to the home of the Altman family on Harts Gap to attend Rosh Hashana and Yom Kippur services. At the end of the Yom Kippur Service, we would break the fast together with a delicious slice of home-baked challah and pop or coffee for the adults.

After high school, I studied shorthand and bookkeeping at Miss Kinch's

Commercial School.

One of my treats on a Saturday morning was to take the bus to downtown Bridgetown to the Barbados Public Library to borrow a few books, as I was and still am an avid reader. A hobby of mine was stamp-collecting that I accomplished by exchanging stamps with pen pals around the globe.

Sunday mornings were often spent swimming and relaxing on the beautiful white sandy beach at The Barbados Aquatic Club. There I would see many of my Jewish friends with their parents. We would watch either a friendly game of water polo or a match between two teams. Then in the afternoon I would go to a movie at one of the local theatres with my friends or with my mother. Many weekends, holidays, and summers were spent swimming in the warm waters at Rockley Beach, sometimes trying to ride a large wave. Then my friends and I would lie on the sand drying in the sun in order to get a tan.

I was most fortunate to have friends like Angela and Betty Anne whose parents were racehorse owners, breeders, and trainers. Twice a year they would invite me to join them at the races held at the Garrison Savannah. As their parents knew the horses that were racing, they would give us tips on the chances of specific horses winning. The price of a bet for each race was $3.00. My friends and I would pool our money and place bets on a race or two – and hope our horse would come in. Sometimes we were lucky and won a few dollars.

My grandparents left Barbados on January 15, 1956, to join their many relatives in Israel. Two days later, on a beautiful, warm, sunny morning, I left on an Air Canada flight, bound for Montreal where I planned to live, and arrived on a very cold, snowy evening with the temperature at six degrees below zero Fahrenheit. I had never seen snow. Ten months later my mother joined me in Montreal.

On April 3, 1958, I got engaged to Stanley Abramowitz, the son of Mendel and Sonia Abramowitz of Montreal. On December 21, 1958, we were married by Rabbi Solomon Frank at the Spanish and Portuguese Synagogue in Montreal. He was assisted by Rabbi David Weiss, who had married my parents in 1936 in Danzig, and had escaped to Montreal before the start of World War II.

**Stan and Hanna's Wedding, Montreal, April 1958**
(Abramowitz family photo)

Our daughter, Arlene, came into this world in 1962 with severe anomalies and only survived three months. We then had three healthy sons, Mervyn, Alan, and Joel, all born at the Jewish General Hospital in Montreal.

When the political situation in Quebec started getting more complicated in 1970, we decided to move to Dundas, Ontario, with our three children. My mother joined us in 1982 but passed away in 1994, having suffered with Alzheimer's for about ten years. We are now retired and living in Burlington, Ontario, after having been in various businesses for many years. Our sons are all married and have given us six grandchildren, four girls and two boys.

A number of years ago we returned to Barbados and found tremendous change. It was not the same carefree place where I spent so many years, although the Bajan people were still very friendly, kind, obliging, and most caring. My children have visited the island on numerous occasions, enjoying Bajan hospitality and feeling very much at home there.

# MOTEL TRUSS' STORY

**Motel Truss, ca. 1980s**
(Dina Truss photo)

My name is Motel Truss. I was born in Ukraine, Russia, on May 17, 1910, in a small village not far from Kiev. My parents were ordinary middle-class people. My father was a teacher and "soifer" (a person who writes the Torah) and my mother was a housewife. Our family consisted of four children, three girls and one boy, of which I was the youngest. Soon after my birth, our family moved to Falesti, a small town in Bessarabia. The Jewish population of Falesti was a few thousand. Under the Tsar's regime, life for the Jews was unbearable. Most lived in "shtetls" (hamlets), were forced to live in certain areas, and were usually forbidden to own land. They lived by their wits.

In 1914 when the First World War broke out, the Tsar sent thousands and thousands of soldiers to dig trenches three kilometers from Falesti to prevent the Romanian invasion. The war on the Russian side was not going well. In 1917 the Russian Revolution broke out. The Jews in general felt relaxed, thinking that the situation for them would change for the better since they supported the Revolution. While the Revolution was in full swing, the soldiers were preparing a pogrom against the Jews with the help from the Gentiles. At the centre of the shtetl was a synagogue, a block from our home. Soldiers converted it to a barracks and were stationed there. Many soldiers were also distributed among the Jewish homes. The Jews started to organize a self-defense organization with the help of a Romanian spy (a Jew) who helped them buy ammunition from the soldiers. We were told that the pogrom would start on a Friday night and the Jewish self-defense group was ready. It was a winter night when the pogrom started. Two Jews were killed, one wounded, and 17 hooligans were killed. Our defense guard was very good - no deaths on our side. One day the Romanian army came and occupied our town and we had to get accustomed to the regime. For one thing, the pogrom stopped right away.

Years passed and the time came when I had to go into the army. Because I was the sole supporter of my family, I was allowed under Romanian law to serve five months each year for a period of five years rather than the usual two-and-a-half years. I was a travelling sales representative for a garment manufacturer, had a laundry business, and owned a cinema with a partner. I was doing very well.

In 1938 while still in the army, I received a mobilization notice to be ready to go to the front to fight. I knew that the Romanians were joining with the Germans. I discussed this with my wife[120], and we decided that I had to desert and leave. That was the only way we could save ourselves, but it was not going to be easy. I had to go to Bucharest to see a general medical doctor to whom I gave a bribe of 5000 lei to certify that I was sick. He gave me a paper saying that I had tuberculosis and that it was necessary for me to go to Paris for one year to improve my health. I could not tell them that I wanted to go away for good but really wanted to go to Trinidad.

I had very little time to put together a few thousand lei, and then went to Czernowitz to buy a ticket on the German boat, the "Kardileria," leaving for Trinidad via Paris. At the agency, a Jewish fellow by the name of Lerner was selling tickets. I did not know how he found out that I was a deserter. He asked everyone before leaving to make a statement of how much money each had. I had over $1,000 American that I could not declare officially. I had over 15,000 lei that I declared and all the jewellery I had. Everybody left for Hamburg to take the ship to go to France. Lerner kept me back and I got suspicious, so I asked him, "Mr. Lerner, two days have passed and I am going to miss the ship going to France. What is it?" He told me that he had a family, a wife and four daughters, and after this boat there will be another German boat leaving and he wanted to save his family. I did not have a choice and gave him the money. I asked him for a ticket to Trinidad that cost $150 American. He gave me the ticket and I asked him for a receipt as I did not have confidence in him.

I missed the boat from Hamburg and had to go by train to Poland, Germany, and then Paris. I went to an agency to confirm my ticket and was not surprised that the ticket was not valid. It was a good thing that I had the receipt to prove that I had really paid. They told me they would let me know when the boat would be ready to leave for Trinidad. I contacted the agency daily to find out

---

[120] Motel married his first wife, Feiga Kira, in Falesti, Bessarabia, in July 1934 and their son, Moisey/Misha, was born in 1936 (see Misha's story that follows).

when the boat was leaving. On December 19, 1938, I went in the morning as usual to find out the departure date and they told me it was leaving the next day at eight o'clock in the morning. I paid my hotel bill, packed my valises and was ready to leave the next day.

That night I went for a walk. It was late - close to eight o'clock. It was a lovely winter night. I was walking and looking at the show windows when I met the fellow who had helped me to translate in French. He was a very nice guy by the name of Israel. He said, "Motel, what are you doing here?" He told me my boat was leaving at 8 o'clock. I said "Yes, eight o'clock tomorrow." He said, "No, the agency fooled you." He phoned the shipping company right away and they told him that the boat had left already and that it was three kilometres from the harbour. They could not stop that ship but cabled it to slow down and to prepare a little boat. I took a taxi and he came with me. We got there quickly. I took the little boat and I was the last passenger to go to Trinidad.

I arrived in Trinidad on January 1, 1939. In the morning when I disembarked, there were three other passengers from Romania. We were told to come back later. We got suspicious and we found out that they had closed the immigration for tourism. We stole away from the ship and went to a Jewish boarding house owned by Mr. Rosner. It did not take long for the police to notify the Jewish community that four passengers had disappeared from the ship. The president of the Jewish community was Dr. Pulver and he knew where to find us. He came to Rosner and told him not to worry because we were going to leave before the ship returned from the United States of America in three weeks' time. We then discussed where each of us would go. One fellow went to Chile and the three of us decided to go to British Guiana, now Guyana.

We booked passage on an American ship leaving for British Guiana on January 15th. I got sick and could not go, but my two friends left. After three weeks, the German ship returned from the United States to go back to Germany. A doctor and two Nazis came with a policeman to pick me up and take me back to Romania. They did not know that I understood German. The doctor was a very good man. He took out a paper and started to write something, then asked them to please sign it. The two Nazis asked what it was he wanted them to sign. The doctor told them I had the Black Plague and was very contagious. If anything happened on the boat, they would be held responsible. The men ran away when they heard that. In the meantime, I got better.

I had to wait until February 15th to get a ship going to British Guiana. When I arrived, I discovered that immigration was closed. I hired a lawyer who spoke a little German like I did. We understand each other very well. I told him the whole story and I showed him when I had bought the ticket. He argued with the Immigration people that I had bought the ticket on January 15th. The new immigration law was passed on February 1st. He said that I was sick and could not make it on time. On this ground and for these reasons they let me stay.

The law in British Guiana was that I had to deposit $250 American in case I could not make a living and had to be sent back. I paid it and was left with $5 in my pocket. I could not contact my two friends as I did not know where they were. I went walking with my valises and was looking around when I saw a dry goods store marked "S. S. Khoury." The fellow inside looked Jewish, so I went in and asked if he was. He was. I was very happy and told him the whole story of what had happened to me. He introduced himself and said his name was Feferman. He said he was married and had two children. He had come from Brazil three months before and had peddled. He told me not to worry as I could stay at his home. I had to pay him $20 for board and lodging but because he did not have a bed, we had to buy one. On the way to his home, we stopped at a store and bought a small bed for $9.25. I only had $5 so he paid the difference. We then went to his home where I met his wife and children and we started to talk. He told me how he peddled and so on. The following day he asked me to go with him to the store where he worked and bring the receipt with me. When I showed Mr. Khoury that I had deposited $250 on that account, he took the receipt as a guarantee and gave me $100 in goods. That was enough to start peddling and I did very well.

In the meantime, I received a letter from my wife in Falesti saying that she could not sell the business nor the cinema as the Jews did not want to buy it. The Gentiles told her they would wait until the Germans came and then they would get it for nothing. I immediately booked tickets for my son and her, sent her money, and told her to leave everything as this would be the last boat. My son, a baby at the time, got sick so they could not travel. I booked another ticket for them via Italy. My wife left Falesti with the baby and went to Italy. By the time she got there, Mussolini had allied himself with Hitler that meant that no Italian boats could travel to an English port. They would be sent back to Falesti. This was the last I heard from my wife. In the meantime, I had prepared a house and had it furnished and ready so I do not have to tell you how I felt.

After two years of peddling, I opened a dry goods store and called it "The Russian Store." A few months later I opened a hotel by the ocean and called it "The Balalaika." I did very well. Suddenly in 1942 the police called to say they had a letter for me. The letter was from an English commissioner stationed in Kubuchev. My father-in-law explained that my wife and all the others were dead; that he and my son were the only survivors; and he asked for help. I requested permission to send 25 pounds sterling each month and did so for 11 months. After the 11th month, I received a letter from the English commissioner with the eleven drafts enclosed. He had not been able to contact my father-in-law; the Germans were preparing to invade; and they were packing to evacuate.

**Motel Truss' "Russian Store" that he operated in Georgetown, British Guiana, from 1942-1948**
(Aaron Truss photo)

That was the last I heard of my family and lost all contact with my son for years. When the war ended in 1945, I tried for many years to find him. In 1953 I learned he was alive when I went to Trinidad and met a Mr. Fishman. He told me his parents were alive and living in Siberia. I got their address and wrote and asked them if they knew my son. After a couple of months they replied that my son was alive and living with my brother-in-law and his wife in L'vov (Lemberg) but they did not know his address. Later I contacted a friend in Kishinev, Bessarabia, who gave me his address. I was then able to correspond with him, but it was not until 1967 that I was given permission to return to Russia to meet him. He was 34 years old, already married, and had a seven-year-old daughter.

In the meantime, I had remarried in 1943 and my business in British Guiana was doing well. In 1948 the country's government changed to Communism. I sold my building and business and went to Venezuela. I was there for a few weeks, but the climate did not agree with me because I had low blood pressure. I went back to British Guiana, then decided to go to Trinidad with my wife and three children.

In 1948 I started peddling in Trinidad and was there five years. In 1953 my good friend, Aron Karp, came to visit. He asked me if I would come to Barbados and stay a few months to run his store. He was not feeling well and needed to have an operation. After discussing it with my wife, I told him I would. I went to Barbados and started working in Aron's store, "The London Shop." After six months I sent for my family that by then consisted of five children. In the meantime Aron sold his building, and I decided to go to

Venezuela again. After six weeks there I started to be an agent. I was doing well but I got sick again. I had low blood pressure and the doctor warned me that if I wanted to live, I had to leave. I returned to Barbados and started to work with Mr. Kreindler. After the building where Mr. Kreindler had his store was sold, I went to work with the Pillersdorfs. After a time, Mr. Pillersdorf was expecting his brother, Kuk, to come from Poland, so I had to leave again and decided to open a handbag factory of my own, and later, a hat factory.

When I came to Barbados in 1953, the Jewish population numbered about 30 families of European origin - Polish, German, Russian, Hungarian, Romanian, English, and American. The first Jewish families came from Poland in 1932 and the others continued coming right up to the beginning of and after the Second World War. The Jews established themselves in business and factories, adapted themselves to the Barbadian way of life very well, and ensured a good future for their children and themselves.

There was an old Sephardic synagogue built by Portuguese Jews that had been sold and converted into offices. Not having a synagogue, the Ashkenazi Jews worshipped at the private residence of the Altman family. In 1969 I called a meeting at my home and everyone came and gave pledges totalling $23,500 to buy a house. We bought one for $28,000 and took out a mortgage to cover the balance. We converted the house into a synagogue that I designed and I also designed a new gate for the cemetery.

I do not think it is necessary to mention what I did in Barbados. I think everyone knows what part I took in the Jewish community. I want to thank everyone for giving me the honour of being your president and for being "gabai" and "cantor" for the High Holidays. May God bless you all.

**The M. Truss and Co. Ltd. Factory,
Hastings, Christ Church, Barbados, 1960**
(Aaron Truss photo)

**Motel Truss at the Barbados Exhibition, December 1966**
(Aaron Truss photo)

**The Truss and Karp families and friends in Barbados, 1955**
Back row, L to R: A friend of the Truss family standing behind her two children; Motel Truss with Aaron Karp leaning on him;
2nd row: Abraham Truss, Marilyn Karp holding Ronald and Stanley;
3rd row: Aaron Truss, Manea Truss and another Truss friend from Trinidad, holding her son's hands (her daughter is standing in front of Manea).
Front row: Evelyn Truss looking up at sons, Joe and Leon.
(Dina Truss photo)

## MISHA (MOISEY) TRUSS' STORY

**Misha (2016) and Musya Truss (ca. 2000)**

My name is Misha (Moisey) Truss. My father, Motel, was born in 1910 in Ukraine. When he was eight years old, his parents moved to Faleshti, Bessarabia, then a province of Romania. My grandfather was a teacher in the Jewish school there and my grandmother had a little store.

When my father finished high school, he became a businessman and opened a cinema in Falesti. He used to bring movies from Bucharest, the capital of Romania, to show in his cinema. He and his partner also owned a fabric store.

My father married my mother, Feiga Kira, in Faleshti, Bessarabia, in July 1934. She was a college graduate and worked in a government office. I was born in 1936.

**Misha, Feiga, and Motel Truss, Faleshti, Bessarabia, ca. 1937/38**
(Misha Truss photo)

In 1936/37, my father was drafted to serve in the Romanian Army. While in the army, he became sick and was put in a military hospital. He managed to escape from the hospital by bribing some doctors. He didn't return to his hometown but went to Paris, France. There he was able to get on a ship going to the West Indies. He had an old friend from his hometown of Faleshti who lived in British Guyana and that is where he was heading. When he arrived there, they were no longer accepting immigrants and he was in danger of being returned to Romania. However, a Jewish doctor proclaimed he had a dangerous illness and could not return to the ship. That is how he managed to stay in British Guyana.

He opened the "Russian Store" and once he got established, sent an invitation and tickets for my mother and me to join him there. It was 1939.... My mother and I left for Italy where we were supposed to board a ship going to the West Indies. Unfortunately, World War II had already started in Europe and we were returned to Romania.

In 1940 the Soviet Union took over Bessarabia that used to be a part of Romania. Bessarabia became part of the Soviet Republic of Moldova. In 1941 the War came to the Soviet Union, a nightmare for the Jewish population. Romania became an ally of Nazi Germany and they began an offensive on Moldova where we were lived. I remember the bombing and hiding in the basement. All the relatives on my father's side were killed, and my mother's sister and her family were killed as well. The Soviet authorities evacuated my mother, her parents, and me to Dagestan. On the way, we were bombed many times and many people died. We were lucky to survive the journey.

When we arrived at our destination, Makhachkala, Dagestan, my mother and I became very ill and ended up in the hospital. My mother died from high fever and starvation. I survived and was taken by my grandparents from the hospital. When the German offensive in the Caucasus started, we were moved to a small village. My grandparents and I got sick with typhus and were put in the hospital. There was a rumour that the doctors were poisoning Jews. As a small child, I was put in a bed with my grandmother. When she died, I was put in my grandfather's bed. Soon my grandfather died, as did my uncle, my mother's brother, who was severely wounded in the war.

I was left alone in the hospital. I saw my family die, but I was lucky to survive, thanks to a neighbour from our hometown who had been evacuated with us. She came to visit us in the hospital and the doctor told her that everybody had died, and if she didn't take me I would die too. She took me from the hospital and put me in the orphanage in the city of Derbent. It was 1942....

Motel Truss, my father, tried to find us during the War. He wrote and sent money to the British Embassy in Kuybyshev. (All embassies and Russian government offices were evacuated from Moscow to Kuybyshev since Moscow was under German attack). He was told that they couldn't find us, and most likely everybody was dead. He didn't know that I was still alive.

I was in the orphanage from 1942 to 1945. The woman, our neighbour, who put me in the orphanage, took me out when the War ended in 1945. She took me back to our hometown, Faleshti, Moldova, and I lived with her family for a few years. The first few years after the War were desperate, a lot of distraction, starvation. In school, we were fed potato skins. To get a loaf of bread, you had to stay in line all night until the morning. You could not get anything without special coupons.

When my uncle, my mother's brother, returned to Faleshti, I went to live with his family. I finished high school in 1954. My uncle's family moved to Lvov, Ukraine, and I went to the Polytechnic University there. Around that time my father somehow found out that I was alive and started searching for me through the Red Cross.

I married my wife, Musya, in 1959 and we moved to Leningrad. Our daughter, Lyuba, was born there in 1960. My father learned that our family was living in Leningrad and visited us there in 1967. It was the happiest time of my life, seeing my father for the first time.

**Motel and Misha, ca.1967**
(Misha Truss photo)

Thinking that his wife and son had died during the war, my father had remarried. He and his wife, Evelyn, had five children: Abe, Manea, Aaron, Joe and Leon. In 1954 they moved from British Guiana to Barbados.

My father and Evelyn visited us in Leningrad in 1975 and 1976. He wanted very much to bring my family and me to Barbados, but it was impossible to do so at that time. During his visit in 1976 we went to the Russian authorities and he left an invitation for me to visit him in Barbados. In 1977 I finally got permission to visit him in Barbados. I was so very happy to meet his family, my brothers and sister.

In 1979 my family and I decided to leave the Soviet Union. We got an invitation from my aunt who lived in Israel, and in 1980 after a year of rejections and many sleepless nights, were given permission to leave the Soviet Union. At the airport in Leningrad, they checked our two suitcases. They found that one was overweight and started to throw everything out. My wife was very upset and started arguing with the official who was going to call the police to arrest us. I begged him to forgive my wife, and tried to explain she was very stressed and had not slept the previous night. He told us we were lucky because had he called the police, we could have been stuck at the airport and missed our flight. At that time, we could not have gone anywhere else because we had been stripped of our citizenship and could have been put in prison without any rights. Finally, we were able to board the plane.

We flew to Vienna, stayed there a few days, then went to Italy. We lived in the suburbs, two hours outside Rome. I went to JIAS (Jewish Immigrant Aid Service), was interviewed by them and given a job. I helped with translation, processing documents, and delivering them to the U.S. and Israeli embassies, as well as the office of the United Nations. I worked for JIAS for six months for a small salary and during that time had to carry a gun. I would go to the train station at 5 AM and come back at 8 PM. While we were in Italy, my father helped by sending us some money. Finally, we received permission from the Canadian Embassy to come to Canada.

My father and my brother, Abe, met us when we arrived in Toronto in February 1981. I was happy to finally be with my father, Evelyn, my brothers, Abe and Joe, and my sister, Manea. The four years I got to spend with my father before his death in 1985 were the happiest years of my life.

My father died in Canada but is buried in Barbados, his home and the place where he lived and worked for many years. He was a prominent member of the Jewish community and a respected citizen of Barbados. Many attended his funeral, including members of the government of Barbados.

Even with all the help and financial support we got from my family after arriving, starting our new life in Canada was not easy. My father paid the rent for our apartment for the first year and Abe drove us to school and to grocery stores. I attended George Brown and Seneca Colleges and studied business, accounting, computers, and enhanced English. Pretty soon I got a job as a quality control inspector in an electronics company and worked for them for ten years. My wife, Musya, who had been a history teacher in Russia, washed floors and worked in grocery stores until she learned to speak English. She eventually got a job in a day care and worked there for 25 years. In 1996 I suffered a heart attack and quit my job.

In 1977 before we left the Soviet Union, I was able to visit my father in Barbados. While there, I met the Prime Minister, Tom Adams, who was a good friend of my brother, Aaron, then a member of the Barbados Parliament. I met with the representative of UNESCO who was interested in hearing about education in the Soviet Union and I attended a party at the home of the President of Barclay's Bank who gave me a gold pen and pencil set that I still have. The local newspaper printed a story about me, the first Soviet citizen to visit Barbados. The Ambassador of Israel wanted to meet with me, but I refused because I had been instructed by the Soviet authorities before I left not to meet with anyone from countries that didn't have diplomatic relations with them and I still had family in Russia.

We have now been living in Canada for 35 years. We are enjoying our retirement. We have taken cruises, travelled to Europe and to the Caribbean. Most important of all is to be healthy.

# *I REMEMBER WHEN - A TRIBUTE TO EVELYN TRUSS*
**Aaron Truss**

**Evelyn Truss**

I remember when I was six I suffered from asthma. Many, many nights when I had a bad asthma attack and could hardly breathe, gasping for breath and being so afraid, Mom would be by my side all night, rubbing me down with Vicks or some other concoction that she made up, and although I finally fell asleep from exhaustion, Mom would sit in a chair next to my bed.

I remember that feeling of just having Mom there was enough to make me feel better. Mom would say to me, "It's all right son, it's all right, son. Mom is here, Mom is here."

I remember when the five of us were all sick at the same time. Mom would run around from bedroom to bedroom, taking care of Abe, Manea, Joe, Leon and me. She worked tirelessly, efficiently, and calmly to nurse us all back to health and was always full of love for us. She stayed up night and day, day and night. There were times when she went without proper sleep for two or three days at a time but I never heard her complain.

I remember when I was eight and Mom was angry with one of her siblings over something to do with Granny. Mom came from a family of 13. Mom said on the phone, "A mother can take care of 13 children but 13 children cannot take care of one mother." I remember going up to her and holding her hand

and saying, "Don't worry, Mom, I'll always take care of you!" Tears came to her eyes and she hugged me. I always tried to take care of Mom and we always joked about what I told her so many years ago.

I remember when I was nine. One day when we came home from school, Dad was doing some renovations at home and there was a truckload of sand in the backyard. We could hardly wait to change our school clothes and play in it. Nothing less than king of the mountain is what we wanted to play. How does one separate children from sand? Shortly after we began playing in it with our neighbourhood friends we heard Mom's voice, "Don't play in the dead sand! You will all get chiggers." Mom repeated this a second time, but usually she would warn us three times before the licks started so we continued playing. I finally reached the top of the mountain of sand and there I was beating my chest like King Kong and shouting at the top of my lungs, "I am King of the Mountain; I am King of the Mountain." Suddenly, all the children scampered in every direction and before I knew what was happening, I felt this burning across my behind and there was Mom with a coucou stick in her hand. She gave me two more lashes, pulled me down the sand mountain and dragged me into the house where she declared, "I told you not to play in the dead sand because you will get chiggers. Go and bathe NOW!" Though I was crying, I was partly relieved because I knew I had received my lashes, but my brothers' turns were next. While bathing and crying, I could hear Mom calling Joe and Leon because no one escaped her hand. They both got the three lashes that I received plus three more for running away. We learned all about Mom's sense of justice and discipline at an early age.

I remember when I was 11 playing cricket in the yard after school with my two brothers and some friends. Mom was in the kitchen cooking soup. One of us hit the ball and it broke the kitchen window and dropped into the soup. Mom was stirring the pot and shouted in surprise. When she got outside, all she saw was a red Coca-Cola case that was the wicket and a wooden home-made bat lying on the ground and not a child in sight. Everyone had scampered for home except the three of us. Mom stood by the kitchen door, hands on her hips and called out to us. "Come into the house NOW." The three of us were hiding in the front patio and after her second announcement of "Come into the house, NOW!" we went in to face her. To our surprise she simply said, "I know it was an accident. Clean up all the glass, go inside, bathe and do your homework. Dinner will be late." She took the ball out of the soup, threw the soup away and started all over again. Mom taught us that when she said NOW she meant NOW. We learned that when she said jump, you asked how high or you ended up in more trouble than you were already in. Yes, she could be very fair. We got no licks that day, much to our delight,

just a stern look, but one of understanding as she muttered, "Boys will be boys!"

I remember when I was 12, I was really impressed with how Mom saved money. On a shelf in the kitchen she had small tins and on each was a label.... "Rent," "Electricity," "Telephone," "Redifusion," and "Aaron's Bar Mitzvah" (that she was saving for a year in advance). Every month she would take money out and pay her bills always on time. In those days she didn't have a chequebook. She paid her bills with cash and taught me to always pay bills on time.

I remember when I was sixteen I went out with friends and came home as the sun was coming up. I quietly opened the front door and sneaked into the house. Tiptoeing with shoes in hand, I walked to my bedroom. I started to close the door behind me and with a sigh of relief thought, "Thank God, Mom is asleep." As I closed the door and turned, I was startled to see her sitting on my bed. She asked, "Do you know what time it is?" And before I could answer, she added, "Have you any idea how worried I was?" Before I could answer, she continued, "Do you know I haven't slept a wink all night?" And before I could answer, "Where were you all night?" "I thought you were in an accident. Where did you go? Who were you with?" I had no chance to answer any of her questions because for one hour she chastised me and all I was able to say was, "I am sorry Mom, I am sorry, Mom, I am really tired and want to go to bed".... to which she replied, "Go to bed? I haven't slept for a whole night worrying sick over you and now you want to go to bed? I have things I want to tell you and you are going to listen!" Mom went on and on and on. There just wasn't any sleep for me that morning, and by the time she was finished lecturing me, the sun was shining. This was my punishment. NO SLEEP.

I remember when I was 17. I left Barbados to go to college in Montreal. I missed my parents very much, especially Mom. I wrote to her every single day and sometimes twice a day and on occasion, three times a day. I would forgo buying a snack or a piece of pizza or a hot cup of chocolate so I could buy stamps to write to her. We couldn't afford telephone calls in those days. Mom wrote me every week and sometimes twice a week. Once in a while, more often than not, she would send me $2 or $5 or sometimes $10. I knew she couldn't afford it and always wondered how she did it, but she was always generous, caring and loving.

I remember when I was 20 we had an Alsatian dog named Prince. Every day Mom would cook food for the dog. She always cooked rice mixed with gravy and large bones. In those days dog chow was not available, and if it was, it was too expensive. My brother, Joe, came home with a group of his friends at 1 AM. They were all hungry and seeing a big pot of food on the stove, freshly cooked with juicy bones, they sat down in the kitchen with pepper sauce and demolished this huge pot of food. When Mom woke up that morning, her first thought was that one of us had fed Prince. After both Leon and I said we didn't feed the dog, she checked with Joe and that was when she discovered that he and his friends had eaten Prince's food. Joe's friends said, "That was delicious food you cooked, Mom Truss. It was one of the best meals we've ever had." When Mom explained to them that it was the dog's food they ate, they replied "Too bad for the dog! The food was absolutely delicious!" To this day, Joe and his friends refer to Prince's food as one of the best meals of their lives. So it was with Mom and her cooking. She loved to cook and she cooked well.

Mom was the disciplinarian in the family. My father beat us once, with a tie... yes, with a tie. Although Mom was fair, she was strict, and she tried very hard to ensure that "the punishment never outweighed the crime," as she would put it. She had the "fastest hands in the West" as we would put it. Even though she said, "Boys will be boys!" she showed zero tolerance when we fought and she never took sides. She would beat all of us at the same time. Mom never asked who was right or wrong. We all received the same licks and punishment because brothers should never fight each other. She taught us that if we fought, "Peter would pay Paul and Paul would pay for all." That was another lesson we all learned from Mom.

I remember how wise Mom was. If any of us pretended that we were not well in order to miss a day of school, Mom would allow us to stay home but we could not leave the house during the day or go out to play in the afternoon. Mom would say if you were too sick to go to school, then you were too sick to go out and play. If you pretended to be sick on a Friday, God help you, because you spent the entire Saturday in the house and sometime Sunday as well. No wonder we seldom missed school. Mom's wisdom would stand to this day.

I remember Mom insisted we all sit down for dinner together at 6 PM Mondays to Fridays. She used to say, "A family that eats together stays together" and there were no exceptions. On Sundays, there was always the traditional Sunday lunch. Rice and stew, pork, baked chicken, macaroni pie, fried plantains, salad, and coleslaw, to name but a few dishes. "Food for days!" as our friends said of Mom's Sunday lunch.

When we went out with Mom and Dad, Mom made us go to each and every person, kiss them, and say hello. Before we left, we went through the same routine. We learnt good manners from Mom who would say, "Manners maketh man."
When our friends dropped in to visit, Mom always fed them. There was always food in our house and Mom always made everyone feel welcome. Our home was always "open house." I remember coming home one day and finding five or six sailors that she picked up on the street or at the bus stop. She brought these strangers home for a good home-cooked meal. Mom always said,

"Someday when my children grow up and leave Barbados, someone, somewhere will give them a meal." She taught us charity and that charity began at home.

When Errol Barrow (Uncle Errol, as we lovingly called him,) would drop in for a visit, he would sit in the kitchen and chat with Mom while she prepared a meal for him - chow mein or cook-up rice with pig tail or curry and roti, salt fish and bakes or black pudding and souse - a meal fit for a Prime Minister. Both Mom and Uncle Errol enjoyed these visits and he spent many hours in our home talking politics, women's affairs and business. Uncle Errol never missed a party or function at our home. Mom loved him and he loved her.

I remember going to school every day in Mom's small Volkswagen. Leon, Joe and I had to sit in the small compartment behind the backseat so that she could pick up everyone at each bus stop on the way into Bridgetown. Even when the little VW was full, Mom would still stop and ask everyone in the car to scotch around and make room for one more. I remember arriving at school one day and the entire school watched as 13 people climbed out of the little VW so that the three of us could get out from the little space behind the backseat. It was quite a sight, just like you would see in a circus. Mom taught us to never leave anyone at the bus stop. Always stop and give people a lift.

I remember so much more about Mom and the lessons she taught us in life. Be generous, be kind, be considerate, be compassionate, but most of all be human. I still remember and practice these lessons, Mom.

For those of you who knew Mom, think of the good times you shared with her, think of the happy days - it is what she would've wanted. She never dwelled on the sad things. During the most difficult period of her life when she was dying of cancer, she still had her sense of humour, and through it all she never complained. Not once. Mom showed true grit to the very end. She showed strength and courage that set an example for all of us to follow.

Mom..Mom.... there will never be an answer because I no longer have Mom. I have to get used to that but it hasn't quite sunk in yet. Mom is no longer here.

Mom, we miss you very much.
Mom, we love you very much.
May God bless you and keep you safe.
You were a good Mom.
We will always remember you.
You will always be in our hearts.

I love you, Mom.

# AROUND MY MOTHER'S TABLE
## Joe Truss' Story

It was the best of times, it was the best of times.

What I remember most about life as a member of a minority- Russian-Jewish-Chinese in a predominately black population, and as a member of a tiny Jewish community in a predominantly Christian society on the tiny British Caribbean island of Barbados, is how open our home was to all of our friends who were Jewish, non-Jewish, white and black, and in particular the relationships that were built and nourished around my Mom's table of food.

Our father, Motel Truss, was part of the Eastern European Jewish Diaspora that travelled to North and South America and the Caribbean in the early '40s. His journey took him first to British Guiana (now Guyana) where, after the war, he was informed that his first wife and son had been killed in Russia. He met and married our Guianese-born, Chinese mother, Evelyn (nee Hing). Abraham, Manea and Aaron were born in British Guiana, then the family moved to Trinidad where I was born and then Leon followed. In 1952 the family settled in Barbados permanently. In the meantime, Dad had received word that his son, Misha, was alive, and in 1980 we managed to get his wife, Musea, daughter, Lubya, and him into Canada. Misha and Musea still live in Toronto.

## *School Days*
At a certain school age, Dad began giving us a weekly allowance that ranged from 50¢ to $1. This was the first discretionary income any of us had and we spent a lot of it on bubble gum cards and shopping at the Woolworth's "Five and Ten."

In Barbados hurricanes were not common events, but we usually experienced the high winds and rain of other hurricanes that tended to pass north of us. As a result, we rarely got hurricane days off from school but in September 1955, Janet, a Category 5 hurricane hit Barbados. I was six years old and only remember leaving our house by the ocean and going to a friend's concrete bungalow on high ground where other families had also gathered. There were lots of kids and lots of excitement. Barbados eventually declared a state of emergency as Janet left massive devastation in its wake.

Aaron, Leon, and I attended the Barbados Academy, a.k.a Rudder's School. I found school interesting and engaging, and I did well enough to have a special place created for me at Harrison College where I could study the science subjects that the Barbados Academy did not offer. At the time, I thought I would go to medical school but due to a personality conflict with the school's first

Barbadian headmaster, I ended up leaving Harrison College. Although I achieved the required number of O level and A level GCE credits for admission to university, I decided to find a job rather than continue my education. My mom was devastated but later came to accept my decision.

After three months working at the Royal Bank of Canada in Bridgetown, I received a call from Norman Barrow who told me he was forming a new band and was looking for a drummer. I joined the band as drummer and this led to my becoming a career musician in a pop dance band.

## Saturday morning cartoons in the theatre
When I was about ten years old, both downtown theatres, The Plaza and The Empire, used to show cartoons and Horror B Movies (called serials) from 9 AM 'til noon. After the movies, we would go into Bridgetown, meet upstairs at Goddards, get something to drink, and wait for Mom to bring us home.

## Sundays
Sundays were the days when we had family picnics, often in Bathsheba on the east coast of the island. I remember a particularly hairy time when there were ten of us in a Volkswagen Beetle. The car couldn't make it up Horse Hill so we all had to get out and push it up the hill. At the top we all piled back in and headed off.

We often also went to the Aquatic Club on Sundays. There was a pier that extended out into the ocean, supported by huge concrete columns. Aaron, Leon and I would fish off the pier with our friends. We used flexible branches as rods and caught little fish called Jacks that were the perfect size to eat. We would cut the bait with a razor blade, bait our hooks, and when we had a bite, would jerk the rod up, yanking the fish out of the water. We would grab the squiggly fish in one hand, take the barbed hook out of its mouth and with our thumb and forefinger snap its spine at the base of its head. It was exciting to sit on the pier and watch a school of jacks come into sight and then feeling them nibble on our lines. Each of us could catch about a dozen fish on a good day. Afterwards we would take our catch home, gut them and fry them – head, tail, and all, then we ate them. As we would say, "dat was sweet fuh so". (We all learned to speak proper Bajan.)

In the evenings when the water was calmer, the floodlights would be turned on and large crowds would gather on the pier to watch water polo games. The water was so clear you could see the sandy bottom and the big sea turtles that would casually make their way under the swimmers' feet. Sometimes a manta ray or a sleek barracuda, like stealthy fighter planes, would swim into the area. All the swimmers would scramble out of the water, then jump back in again once the invaders retreated.

The Aquatic Club also had a second story deck with a huge dance floor. This was where I saw my first live Bajan band, *The Pete Jones Combo*. It was also the first time I'd seen drums and bass guitar in a live band.

The Paradise Beach Club was a very upscale place where we sometimes also went on Sundays. It had a beautiful beach, an entertainment area, and a huge bar. The Club often put on big floor shows that were standard at most hotels and clubs at the time. Sometimes the entertainment included dancing, something we all loved to do. Paradise Beach Club was also a place where Bar Mitzvah parties were sometimes hosted, although most took place at the large hotels. All our family's Bar Mitzvahs took place at home. Preparation was a frenzy of activity - folding blue and white crepe streamers and hanging Stars of David, with lights lying on the tables, etc. There was always live music and dancing, but the main event was always "Evelyn's food." No caterer or chef even at the best hotel, could compare to our Mom's table.

## *Christmas and Chanukah*
Christmas was the biggest holiday of the year. It was particularly hard for us kids who felt we were missing out on something because we were Jewish. Although Chanukah was observed at home, Mom and Dad made one concession – allowing us to have Christmas gifts like all the other kids. Chanukah was observed but without the exchange of gifts, and instead we exchanged gifts, opening them on Christmas Day. Dad would not allow us to have a Christmas tree so every Christmas we piled into the car and drove around the neighbourhood admiring the Christmas trees we could see through open windows.

## *Summer Vacations*
Summer vacations were the most special - practically three months of leaving home at 9 AM and coming home just in time for dinner. Life was carefree and although there was always something new to do, we often went back to our favourite games – cricket or kneel-down marble cricket - played with a carved, handmade, half-size bat and a red Coca Cola box as the wicket. The batsman played kneeling and the bowler bowled underarm with a softball or large marble or taw[121]. Sometimes we pitched marbles. Leon was king of the pitchers. I wasn't too bad myself, and he and I would often go home with pockets full of our friends' marbles. In one of the games players could be heard to shout, "Down taw no brush!" That meant wherever your marble landed – be it behind a rock or under a leaf – you had to pitch from that position without clearing anything away.

---

[121] A fancy marble.

Often during the summer, our friend, Leon Silver, who was like a big brother would visit from Canada. Leon loved cricket and I remember him once bringing us a baseball bat from Canada. We had never seen one, and although he tried to teach us to play baseball, it didn't take.

During the summer, there was always the sea and sun. We lived on or near the beach all our early lives and there were strict rules about swimming in the ocean. We could never swim alone or when it was rough, and never at Bathsheba which was famous for its undercurrents, rough water, and big waves. Of course, we were all good swimmers and I swam in school competitions. We had no coaching or training but just swam as fast as we could. Later when I owned a speedboat, Aaron and I got into waterskiing and we would ski from Carlisle Bay to Paradise Beach Club.

Another of our activities was to 'lime' – to hang out – although calling this an activity might be overstating it. It was far more about attitude, a way to hang out at the mall before there was a mall. At some point, we all entered the age of swagger and became Saga Boys. I remember as a young teenager trying to leave the house in my short sleeve shirt with my collar turned up which was a sign of cool in those days. Mom would stop me, turn my collar down and roll up my short sleeves. "The other way around" she said, "you look like a bad boy."

## *Coming of age*
Before my Bar Mitzvah, Mom and Dad travelled to Venezuela for Mom's conversion to Judaism. Unknown to us four boys, even though we were circumcised at birth, we had to be ritually re-circumcised[122] to be proclaimed officially Jewish. Two rabbis were brought in from New York, and one by one, in order of decreasing age, we entered the cutting room not knowing what was going to happen. We were asked to drop our pants and with what seemed like an X-Acto knife, the top part of the foreskin was cut until blood was drawn. Afterwards we each had our own ritual immersion in the ocean at a public beach. Being pre-Bar Mitzvah, I took it in stride as a religious initiation, but I think my older brothers might have felt humiliated by the whole experience.

The legal age to get a driver's license was sixteen. I was driving at fifteen using Aaron's license and I think Aaron did the same thing using Abraham's license. We loved driving and loved cars. At one time Aaron had a big Pontiac convertible complete with an eight-track player. It was so cool. Together with all my friends, I would stop at Accra Beach and retract the convertible top. The Barbadians had never seen anything like it!

---

122 For more details, the reader is referred to the story of the Rebbe and his Emissaries in Chapter 6.

Abraham and I also had a motor scooter and a small sports car that I tried to take apart a few times. After reassembling it and finding there were still some parts left over, I knew that mechanical engineering was not to be my profession.

## The girls and the good times we had

Undoubtedly, when it came to girls and growing up, Aaron epitomized the Casanova of the day. The only opportunity we had to hold hands with a girl was in a movie theatre. My earliest attempts to "get the girl" were made sitting in a dark theatre usually with friends or a chaperone. It would take me half the movie to put my arm around the chair behind the girl's shoulder. Sometimes the movie would end and I still hadn't succeeded. By then my arm would be asleep and so numb it wouldn't have mattered.

When we were teenagers, the theatre was also where we could hang out and smoke cigarettes in the back rows. I smoked my first cigar in the theatre and it was the first time I literally turned green. It was also the last time I ever did that. The same thing happened to me with rum. I got drunk and could not touch the stuff for years.

In my late teens, I would occasionally receive hand-me-downs, something we were used to in our family - except shoes because Mom said everyone had a different way of walking and so we always got new shoes. We received our first suit for our Bar Mitzvah. Dad would take us to The London Shop for the obligatory three measurings and fittings. The store was owned by Aron Karp and Dad had worked for him before he got into his own business.

By age 17 I was ready to leave home. Although Aaron and Leon were still at home, Abraham had left and Manea was in Canada. My parents found an ingenious way to keep me with them. They allowed me privacy without having to leave by building a room for me on a concrete platform on the beach in back of the house. It was made of concrete blocks and had one window, a sink, electricity, and running water. With a pull-out couch/bed and my stereo, it became a meeting place for my friends and the occasional adopted visitors – "freaks" who ended up in Barbados with no money and no place to go. It was also a place where I could listen to my music and where I started my extensive record collection.

## Nightclubs and nightlife

Because Aaron was in the hotel and nightclub business and I was a professional musician, we both spent a lot of time enjoying the nightlife separately and together. In the process, we made long-lasting friendships with an element of the Barbadian population of whom many in the Jewish community were not even aware.

The Island Inn was a well-known club and the location of one of my first paid gigs as a musician. Each nightclub had its own special night. Saturday nights the Merry Men played at the Caribbean Pepperpot. On Tuesdays, The Sandpebbles were at the rooftop of the Caribee Hotel. Monday night was Island Inn night and there would be a live band, MC, a full floorshow with limbo and belly dancing with Madame Yvette. Other clubs I played at and that we frequented included the Hilton and Sandy Lane Hotels, the Beau Brummel, Mary's Moustache, the Bearded Fig Tree, Coconut Court, Pandora's Night Club, and later, the outstanding club of the day – Alexandria's Night Club.

Aaron and I would sneak out our bedroom window after everyone else had fallen asleep and put a pillow under the sheet in case Mom were to look in. We would go out to clubs or ride and race motorcycles with our friends. Most of the time we went to parties. Occasionally, we would find Mom sitting on the front veranda waiting for us when we got home. No matter how late it was when this happened, we knew we were not going to sleep any time soon.

Old Year's Night was a very big deal – Mom and Dad always went out with a large group of friends. After my Bar Mitzvah, I was once allowed to join them but generally we kids would go to a big public party at The Crane or Marine Hotel, celebrate midnight there, then go to a house party for the rest of the night. New Year's Day was one of the few times Mom allowed us to stay in bed as long as we wanted.

## *Musical influences*

My earliest musical influences came from my Jewish heritage and going to synagogue on Friday nights where I learned many Jewish melodies. Although I also heard West Indian music from Trinidad, I related more to Jewish music in those formative years.

For my Bar Mitzvah in 1962, I composed the music for my own Haftorah. Although we attended shul on Friday nights and learned the Hebrew alphabet in 'Sunday School', we never learned to read Hebrew fluently or understand it. Instead we learned our Haftorahs by listening to a recording of a cantor singing it and a transcription of the words in phonetic English.

**Joe Truss' 1962 Bar Mitzvah invitation**

(Joe Truss photo)

In my case we couldn't get a recording of my Haftorah although I had the phonetic English translation. I composed my own music from what I'd been hearing all my life and sang a totally original Haftorah. Louis Speisman was my 'religious mentor' during the years leading up to my Bar Mitzvah and he began teaching me how to put on tefillin. He led the prayers the day of my Bar Mitzvah and could not believe that this little Chinese boy was singing a Jewish melody. He kind of adopted me afterwards and I almost had my own bedroom at the Speisman home, spending many nights there.

Uncle Louie, as we all called him, had a favourite breakfast – half-cooked scrambled eggs, soft and runny. (I now eat my own version of soft, runny spicy morning eggs.) He also had a habit of putting his teeth in his top pocket when he smoked or played poker and sometimes had to be reminded to put them back in his mouth afterwards!

The Barbados Police Band often played concerts in the open band shell on the Rockley boardwalk, and hundreds of people would bring chairs and come to listen. This was my early connection to big-band classical music.

The first radio on the island was a service called Rediffusion, a closed-circuit one-channel radio. A wire ran into the house and into a large box with only one knob. We would hear British and American hits over Rediffusion. It was a mix of Jewish music and music from Rediffusion that most influenced me when I was growing up. Dad played an accordion that he had brought with him from Russia and there was always an organ in the house. We, therefore, all grew up learning how to pick out tunes.

Although Abraham and Aaron had music lessons, I never did. Even so, my interest in music was keen from an early age. An older friend of Abraham's who played the guitar and sang would come and play for us. I hounded him to teach me one particular song on the guitar so he taught me the first four chords – C, A min, F, G7 – and then how to play the song. I discovered that you could play almost any song with these four chords. When I was about eight, I heard Elvis Presley's *Ain't Nothing but a Hound Dog* and hounded an older girl I knew until she wrote out the lyrics so I could pretend to be Elvis.

In the early days, I played in a band with Aaron and later in a number of others including the Young Ones, the Heart Beats, the Staccattos, the Sandpepples, Musicians Union, and the Bachelors.

Aaron had the voice and personality to be a good singer but never pursued it. He convinced himself that I had musical ability and he did not. Abraham drove us crazy for a short time learning to play the tenor saxophone. Although he probably had the most developed taste in 'good' music and listened to classical, we were all relieved when he gave it up. Leon played keyboard by ear and even though he never played in a band, still plays when he can. I don't think Manea ever took up an instrument but she was a terrific dancer and nothing made my friends and me happier than to dance with her when she visited from Canada.

At about age 13, I won my first music competition, a Rediffusion talent contest at which Emil Straker, leader of The *MerryMen*, was a judge. It was the first time I'd ever had piano accompaniment. I went with my little guitar and played two songs, one of which was *Devil Woman* by Cliff Richards – another C, A min, F, G7 chord song. So now I was a little guitar player/singer with a sweet, high voice and it prompted all my school friends to say I sounded like a girl. I won in my age category and this started my actual 'performance' career. From then on, I just wanted to play in a band.

The first instrument I played was lead guitar and later I moved on to bass guitar. I had the second bass guitar on the island for a pop band. I didn't know how to tune it properly so I tuned it my own way. My tuning gave me notes lower than E on the E string and I learned a song by knowing what the positions were on the bass guitar. Later when I learned how to properly tune the bass, I had to relearn how to play from scratch.

In 1967 I got a call from Norman Barrow. He was starting a band and needed a drummer. Norman and I formed the *Sandpebbles* together with John Gibbs and Brian 'Bam' Marshall. Along with other bands of the time, the *Sandpebbles* heralded in a new era of live music on the island. Lots of bands were playing everywhere in hotels and clubs and at private parties. It was wild in those days.

In my later teenage years, Harry Wajchendler was one of my best friends. We were at Harrison College together for a couple of years and shared similar musical interests. To put a place marker on this, he and I listened to the Beatles' *Sgt. Pepper's Lonely Heart's Club Band* together for the first time and played music together. Outside of my family, Harry and his brother Irving were the only two members of the Jewish community who knew firsthand about this period of my life.

Of all the bands I played with, the *Sandpebbles* were the best known and most successful. Not only were we 'famous' in Barbados (big fish in a small pond), but we travelled and performed around the Caribbean and as far away as London, England, where we spent about three months in 1969. On our return Aaron organized a huge welcome home gathering in the VIP Lounge of the Barbados Airport and I remember signing the guest book close to where the Beatles had signed not long before. We were met by reporters and photographers, and interviewed for *The Advocate* newspaper and for the radio.

The conquering heroes had returned. We were a big deal! My dad and the other parents came out and I think they were impressed with the whole thing. After this it seemed my dad relaxed about my living this lifestyle. During my time with the *Sandpebbles* we recorded two LPs and several singles, garnering early hits for the group. After I left, the *Sandpebbles* became even more successful and made many more LPs and hit singles.

One of my great joys has been to become reacquainted in Ontario with musicians I played with as a young musician in Barbados – including Franc Mosbaugh, Roger Gibbs, Andy Earle, and recently, Louis Weatherhead. Though I stopped playing professionally in 1972, today I drum with two local musical groups, *Abbey North Drummers* and *5th Business*, a modern, rock-influenced band.

## *Open house and home*

Before Mom and Dad settled at Atlantic Shores, the last place where they lived in Barbados, we had moved almost a dozen times in less than 20 years. Other than two of those times, we were always on the beach and it occurs to me now how keen my father's instincts were about the benefits of living by the ocean. He loved his early morning swim and was an ardent gardener.

I have especially fond memories of Sunday morning lunches, picnic-style, at our home. We always greeted everyone who came to visit with a kiss and anyone older than us was called either auntie or uncle. After lunch, the adults would play cards (the men, poker and the women, Canasta) and money was always put aside to be donated to Israel. We were told that Barbadian Jews per capita were the second largest contributors to the State of Israel. Meanwhile we kids (including Hannah, Harry and Irving Wajchendler, sometimes Paul and Jerry Steinbok, Harold and Robbie Saunders, Richard, Joseph, and Alex Pilarski, Joel, Stanley, Ronald and Annie Karp) would go off together to play on the beach, walk on the reef at low tide, or play games in the backyard which was usually also on the beach. Harry Wajchendler and my brother, Leon, were both very accident-prone, so many Sundays there would also be an emergency run to the hospital for stitches or other ministrations.

## *Food*

So now about the food. Our family always ate dinner together. There was no valid excuse for not being there. We all loved the food and wanted to be there.

Through her journey from country to country, our mom developed a diverse and highly hybridized cuisine that made eating at home a joy for us, our many friends, and guests. Not that we ever had to try curried gefilte fish, as the European Jewish menu was always properly honoured, but having said that, Passover may have been the only meal where curry was not served! Dad was quite addicted to his curry, and as I remember, whatever else was being served, there was always curry and rice on the table. There would be a meat curry and a potato curry. One of his favourite breakfasts was hard-boiled eggs with cook-up salt fish. I remember that our house was one that was most favoured for a drop-in visit by our friends. Often we would have double sittings for dinner. Although our friends convinced us that they came to play with us because they liked us, I do wonder now how much the food had to do with it!

Spend enough time at Mom's table and you would have had fungtsi soup, barley soup, cook-up soup (with "kosher" pigtail), fried fish steaks, chow mein, cook-up rice, peas 'n rice (with more "kosher" pigtail), and there were the stews including oxtail, pepper pot, and the ever-present curry dishes including curry channa, fried fish, fried chicken, Chinese chicken, ginger chicken, pork ribs and pork chops, breadfruit cou-cou and flying fish, rotis, fish cakes, black pudding 'n souse, metemgee, fried plantain, pumpkin fritters, big green salads with cucumbers and tomatoes, avocados the size of pumpkins and texture like cheese, fresh fruit and salads with papaya, mangoes, bananas, watermelon, ackees, guavas, golden apples, sugar apples, soursop, oranges, and apples (only around Christmastime).

During the month of December there would be vendors with carts and trays piled high with apples all along Broad Street and Swan Street. In fact, all of Bridgetown smelled like one big apple. It was lovely and the smell of apples still reminds me of Christmas in Barbados.

There were the special meals connected with the Jewish high holidays like gefilte fish, borscht, matzo ball soup, and those matzo biscuits that we ate with cheese or jam and peanut butter during Passover.

There were some really delicious cakes. One worthy of mention was a multi-layer cake made with about 20 thin circular cookies, with a layer of chocolate, then cookie, then vanilla pudding, then cookie, then chocolate, etc. The whole thing was covered in chocolate. When cutting through it, it looked amazing and tasted even more so!

### An Idyllic Life
Looking back, I realize we led an idyllic life. We had all the necessary things – a safe and secure environment, life outdoors with sea and sun, family values,

love and caring, discipline and sharing, a good education system, and the cultural traditions of my Jewishness.

For me, part of this idyllic life was having many role models, and most importantly, those in my own home. In terms of my siblings, my eldest brother, Abraham, my Big Brother, was my earliest mentor in things spiritual and he introduced me to meditation. Part of the allure was that he had built himself a small windowless shack in the back yard that was kept under lock and key. We were not even allowed to ask him what was inside that room. It was his meditation room.

Each of us boys wanted to be the favourite of our only sister, Manea, and that was also true for my friends who thought she was the most gorgeous creature in the world. In a house of five children, she was also the only one with a separate bedroom while we boys all had to share. We never minded though as she was our only sister and Mom and Dad never showed favouritism among the children. After Manea moved to Montreal, she would visit Barbados annually and that was always a huge treat for all her brothers.

Aaron was closest to me in age, and we shared many of the same friends. He was always my protector and was an awesome Karateke. Leon was younger, didn't quite make it into our age group, and suffered from the "youngest child syndrome." I always admired his calm demeanour - he was very laid back. As a youth, he was the best marble pitcher and later became a world-class athlete. My family was always very close and we have maintained strong links with each other over the years.

### The Last Sip...

As youngsters, we knew that there were some things that adults were allowed and we children were not. Smoking, drinking alcohol, and coffee. I don't remember who started it - it might even have been me, but one day one of us asked Dad if we could have the last sip of coffee that was left in the bottom of his cup. Once this started, it was natural that we each had to have our turn.

That last sweetest sip of coffee from my father's cup portended not the end of the last generation of Jewish immigrants who founded thriving and successful communities like the one in Barbados in which I grew up, but the beginnings of new generations of communities connected by the richness of our Jewish heritage. Here's to the next cup!

### Postscript

More than a decade after my 1962 Bar Mitzvah I too joined the Barbadian Jewish exodus. Many of us in our late teens and early 20s moved to Canada, the United States, and other countries. In 1978 I moved to Ontario, Canada. Years later my parents relocated to Toronto where Mom's table continued to be a gathering place for the Truss extended family and friends.

I married Canadian-born Judith Macdonald, and together we raised a beautiful daughter, Ziska Marnie Truss, born in 1980, who is now married to Steve Schwab and is the mother of our grandson, Zaiden.

In 2001 Judy and I separated, and I have since been partner and spouse to Christine Cullen who has two grown children – Rob and Meg Cullen. Between us we have six grandkids who bring so much joy to our lives – Keira, Larry, Alyssa, Isabel, Sebastien and Zaiden.

I have been largely self-employed since I traded the music business for retail and then consulting. I went back to school and completed an MBA. My most significant professional achievement was to help build a business called Team Syntegrity Int. AG. Together with the inventor of Team Syntegrity, Prof. Dr. Stafford Beer, his partner Allenna Leonard, friends Alan Pearson and David Beattie, my partner Christine Cullen, Dr. Fredmund Malik and his staff, and many other dear colleagues and friends, we were able to take this brilliant protocol called *Syntegration* successfully to market and help organizations of every conceivable type. I continue my involvement with this work in the field of management cybernetics.

# *LEON TRUSS' STORY*
## Interviewed by Simon Kreindler, Barbados, May 2016

**Leon Truss, Barbados, 2016**
(Simon Kreindler photo)

When I was little, my family lived at Coconut Court, Hastings. One of our neighbours had a dog and I remember each day after school we would annoy him by dragging our rulers along the pailing[123] that separated their property from ours. One day my friends and I were pitching marbles when the dog got out from behind the pailing. They saw him coming and ran. I didn't realize what was happening until he jumped on me. Dr. Storey needed 56 stitches to patch me up and told my parents I was very lucky as the bites had been close to my jugular vein. Next day I was again pitching marbles with my friends but the experience has left me with gaps in my recall of other early life events.

I attended Mrs. Kinch's Primary School and then went on to the Barbados Academy, formerly the Rudder School. After completing my O Levels[124] in 1968, I spent two years studying accounting at Shaw's Business College in Toronto. Initially, I lived with the Wajchendlers, later with the Pilarskis, and each day took two buses and two subways to school, a long, unpleasant trek that I suffered through, especially in winter.

I had planned to stay on another six years and get my Chartered Accountancy designation but I was going out with my first love, Desiree, to whom I am now married, and was only able to see her about once a year when I came back to

---

[123] A corrugated steel fence.
[124] The Oxford and Cambridge Ordinary level exams that all secondary schools required for graduation and universities required for admission.

Barbados on vacation. I could not see myself being separated from her for such a long time.

I came back to Barbados and took a job with Scotia Bank where I was making $200/month, a lot of money at the time. I spent a year at the Bank, then joined my brothers, Abraham and Joe, who wanted to start a business selling goods wholesale by the carton. It was a revolutionary idea at the time, but the economy was such that people just could not afford to buy things in such large quantities so the business never really got off the ground.

For a couple of years, I ran a small restaurant near my parents' fabric and haberdashery store, "Charming Lady," on James Street, but gave it up to get involved in a plastic bag manufacturing business. The man who started the business was from Guyana and had manufacturing plants in Guyana and Suriname. To take advantage of the government's five-year, tax-free incentive, his company needed to have Bajans as majority owners. He offered my brother, Aaron, and me a partnership in which we would own 51% of the business and he would have 49%. He would provide the equipment and technical expertise and we would be responsible for marketing the bags. As it turned out, he sent us very old equipment and three technicians who lived in terrible conditions in the company's office and whom he paid next to nothing.

Within a year there were all sorts of problems with the bags and customers started returning them. Our partner came to us and told us the business was losing money and either he would buy us out or we could buy him out. We didn't have the capital to buy him out so he took complete advantage of the situation and bought us out for a dollar! Almost immediately he brought in new equipment and carried on with the business. Not long afterwards we discovered there was a legal loophole in our earlier agreement. We sued him and got a settlement of $340,000. He never spoke to us again. Aaron and I used the funds to get bank financing for a plastic bag business of our own which we launched about 1974/75. Later, after two fires seriously damaged our facility, we got out of manufacturing and I now sell bags manufactured by others.

S.K. note: Leon was too modest to mention it but for years he has been an avid squash player and was the Barbados over-60 squash champion.

# ABRAHAM AND HELEN WAJCHENDLER'S STORY
Hannah Wajchendler Oliver,
Harry Wajchendler, and Irving Wajchendler

Helen and Abraham Wajchendler, Barbados, 1970

## Grandparents
Paternal: Isaac Wajchendler and Cirla Wajchendler, Skarżysko-Kamienna, Poland
Maternal: Nusyn Jankiel (Jacob) Rajfer and Chana Gitla (Hannah) Rajfer (nee Pinczowska), Staszow, Poland

## Parents
Abraham Adek Wajchendler, June 20, 1922, Skarżysko-Kamienna, Poland
Helen Chajuta Chaja Wajchendler (nee Rajfer), November 11, 1920, Staszow, Poland. Married: Turkheim, Germany, 1945. Both are Holocaust survivors whose journey took them from Poland to Germany to France to Trinidad in 1949 and to Barbados in 1949.

Helen Wajchendler had four brothers in Trinidad who left Poland before the War and who arranged for Abraham and her to continue to Barbados after they were unable to obtain residency upon arriving in Trinidad.

After arriving in Barbados in 1949, Abraham peddled dry goods. After a few years, he and Helen opened The General Store, 1 Swan Street; later, the Coronation Store, 15 Swan Street; then Textile Town, 20 Tudor Street.

At the Coronation Store, Abraham began manufacturing uniforms, caps, and clothing for Barbados Light and Power and others. Then he founded Barbados Draperies on the Textile Town premises, supplying many hotels, businesses, and individuals. This operation was expanded to a factory at Wildey, St. Michael, in partnership with his son, Irving. Customers included Princess Margaret, UK Prime Minister Sir Anthony Eden, and Sir Errol Barrow.

***Anni (Hannah) Oliver (nee Wajchendler)***, born in Turkheim, Germany, 1947
Spouse: Clifford Oliver, born in South Africa 1952

***Harry Wajchendler***, born in Barbados in 1950
Spouse #1: Dr. Francoise Derman, born in Nancy, France, 1957. Our son, Ber Dov Wajchendler, born in Nancy, France, 1986
Spouse #2: Susan Wajchendler (nee Goldenberg), born in Toronto, Canada, 1954
Our daughter, Amy Samantha Wajchendler, born in Toronto, 1995
Susan's son (my stepson), Jordan Matthew Gluckstein, born in Toronto, 1988.
Grandchildren: Ber Wajchendler and Lucie (nee Bertinet) Wajchendler's children: Liam and Yael, both born in Nancy, France, in 2011 and 2014 respectively

***Irving Wajchendler***, born in Barbados in 1955 (one week after Hurricane Janet)
Ex-Spouse: Jeannette Wajchendler (nee Altman), born in Australia, 1956
Their children:
    Lauren Rachael Guyon (nee Wajchendler), born in Barbados, 1984 her daughter, Gabrielle, born in Toronto, 2016
    Sarah Gayle Bernholtz (nee Wajchendler), born in Barbados, 1987 her daughter, Charlotte, born in Toronto, 2015
    Shaina Lisa Wajchendler, born in Barbados, 1988
    Elliott Zvi Wajchendler, born in Barbados, 1990

***Hannah***: Saint Winifred's; Jewish College in Chicago; conveyancer, housewife, and business partner in Toronto

***Harry***: Harrison College; University of Toronto (BSc); York University Schulich Business School, Toronto (MBA); Insurance industry financial reporting; information technology: corporate consulting, small-medium business application development

***Irving***: Harrison College; York University (BA Economics), Toronto; construction and furniture manufacturing in Barbados

## NARRATIVE DETAIL

Our parents loved Barbados, the people, the climate, the Jewish community. They often said that after they experienced the horrors of the slave labour and concentration camps in Germany and Poland, Barbados was a perfect paradise. Once they could afford it, they travelled extensively, including to Israel several times.

### Family Memories:

- Evening country drives with ice cream stops (Defreitas on Bay Street or White's Snackette)
- Aquatic Club (Bentley drinks) or Paradise Beach every Sunday and Hilton Hotel later on
- White House Inn for chicken-in-the-basket after Paradise Beach
- Rented summer vacation houses in Bathsheba or Cattlewash
- Edgewater Hotel buffet lunch and pool
- Stayed in guest house at Kingsley Hotel over Christmas
- Crane Hotel vacation and visits to Sam Lord's Castle
- Members of Sandy Lane Hotel Beach Club
- Roodal's and Sundown drive-ins, movie matinees at Empire, Plaza, and Globe cinemas
- Parents frequently played canasta and poker with other members of Jewish community.
- Our father went to shul every Friday night with whichever children were available.
- Our family celebrated and went to shul for all the Jewish holidays.
- Evening drive to Oistins to deliver merchandise to customers and then visit the fish market to buy flying fish, dolphin (mahi mahi), king fish, red fish, smelts, and occasionally 'sea eggs' (urchin roe)
- Sunday evening visit to Humphreys bakery to buy coconut turnovers, rock cakes, and bread
- The Jewish ladies did needlepoint around the pool at the Hilton and Helen contributed a beautiful piece to Shaare Tzedek shul in Rockley.
- We toured and dined on the Israeli cruise ships, 'Israel' and 'Jerusalem' with others in the Jewish community as guests of the captain. Before the deep-water harbor was built, boarding the ships involved going there by an open-sea launch. Thrilling! Bought Elite Israeli chocolate onboard – a real treat!

### Cuisine

- Traditional Jewish food – Friday night chicken and matzoh ball/kreplach soup; gefilte fish; onion cookies; apple or peach cake
- Barbados – flying fish and coucou with okras, rice and peas, curry chicken, pumpkin fritters, pumpkin soup, breadfruit, bread pudding, mauby, and Ribena beverage

## Jewish Holidays
- Went to Aaron and Marilyn Karp's or Simon and Rose Altman's homes for Passover celebrations.
- Also went to the Buraks' and Konigsbergs' for High Holidays.

## Family Connections
- Trinidad and then Chicago – Helen's three brothers (her fourth brother, Harry, died in Trinidad before she arrived from Europe)
- Toronto – Abraham's two sisters who emigrated from Israel.
- Israel – Abraham's father (Isaac) until his death in 1955. He is buried in Haifa.
- Israel – Helen's first cousins in Tiberias and Kibbutz Ma'ale Hahamisha near Jerusalem

## Shoah victims
Helen's parents - Nusyn Jankiel (Jacob) Rajfer and Chana Gitla (Hannah) Rajfer (nee Pinczowska) in Auschwitz, in 194?.
Abraham's mother (Cirla) – died of typhus in Szydlowiec ghetto in Poland in 194?.
Abraham's grandmother and younger sister (who had polio) perished in Treblinka concentration camp in 194?.
Abraham played violin for fellow prisoners and brought the violin to Barbados.

## Barbados residence
1949-1954: Oistins (above a store), Worthing
1955-1957: Sunrise Drive, Pine Hill, St. Michael
1958-1967: Highgate Gardens, St. Michael (built by Abraham)
1969-1989: Rendezvous Ridge, Christ Church (built by Abraham)
1990-1995: Four Square Townhouses, Rockley Resort, Christ Church

## Hurricane Janet
In September 1955, this devastating tropical storm hit the island at Category 3 force. It would later reach Category 5! We evacuated the main floor to our concrete basement just in time. Helen was very pregnant with Irving, born one week later. The roof was entirely blown off, all the windows were blown out, and we lost all of our furniture and possessions. The owner of the house

generously accommodated us in a beach house on Maxwell's Coast for a few months while the house was rebuilt.

## Outside the Jewish community
Abraham and Helen visited friends for afternoon tea and attended charity functions at Government House. Helen was an amazing cook and baker and her culinary creations were loved by all. She and Abraham held frequent dinner parties for the Jewish and non-Jewish communities.

At the Hilton Hotel Abraham met Abraham Waksman, a Rutgers scientist who discovered the powerful antibiotic, streptomycin (anti-tuberculosis drug), for which he was awarded the Nobel Prize in Medicine. Abraham and Helen invited his wife and him for dinner and they spent a day with us at our vacation house in Cattlewash. Harry took a long walk on the beach with Professor Waksman who lectured him on his research. At the tender age of 16, Harry was overwhelmed by the subject matter!

## At the Movies
'Island in the Sun': Helen and Abraham were invited to the end-of-filming cocktail party where they mingled with Harry Belafonte, Dorothy Dandridge, James Mason, Joan Fontaine, and Joan Collins. Professional photos were taken of Helen and James Mason and of Abraham and Joan Collins. When 'The Tamarind Seed' was filmed, Abraham, Helen, and Irving socialized with Julie Andrews and Omar Sharif. Abraham supplied drapes for the movie set which, as a part of the script, went up in a blaze.

## Growing up in Barbados
Hannah, Harry, and Irving played with and socialized with many non-Jews and Jews which was always positive and fun. We did not experience any anti-Semitism to speak of. A notable exception, however, is that we were excluded from the Yacht Club.

There were many activities we enjoyed growing up, including cricket, football, table tennis, tennis, road tennis, tree-climbing, building treehouses and tents in the woods, water-skiing, surfing, belly-boarding, body surfing, motorcycle trail riding, woods and forest hiking, cave exploring, Aquatic Club pier games and diving, snorkeling, spear-fishing, pier and sailboat fishing, scuba diving, ocean sailing, bicycle racing and touring. A notable adventure was a coastal day hike that Harry, Joel Karp, and Roger Hill did from Burke's Beach (by the Aquatic Club) around South Point to East Point Lighthouse in St. Philip. We also explored the hills and Joe's River in Cattlewash, including Fat Pork Hill, and climbed Round Rock to demonstrate our athletic prowess.

We went to dances at hotels and private homes (fetes), parties with Jewish community friends, and we performed in rock bands (Harry founded the Staccatoes).

Hannah and Harry took piano and art lessons from Ms. Violet Spencer who was a crisp 70 at the time. Hannah also took ballet and performed in recitals at St. Winifred's.

All of us children have many happy memories of our life on the island. Barbados will forever be in our hearts as a very special place and our first home.

**The Wajchendlers, Toronto, 2014**
Standing L to R: Irving's son, Elliot Wajchendler, Irving's girlfriend, Michelle Shanker, Irving Wajchendler, Cliff Oliver, Sarah (girlfriend of Irving's stepson, Jordan Gluckstein), Jordan Gluckstein, Harry's wife, Susan Wajchendler, Anni Wajchendler Oliver
In front of them, Harry Wajchendler
Front row, squatting: Irving's son-in-law, Remy Guyon, Harry's daughter, Amy Wajchendler, Lauren Wajchendler Guyon,
Irving's daughter, Shaina Wajchendler
(Harry Wajchendler photo)

# *ROSALINDE ZIERLER-WEINBERGER'S STORY*
### Daniel and Joe Weinberger

**Rose and Joe Weinberger**
(Betty Konigsberg Feinberg photo)

Rosalinde ("Roz" or "Rosie") was born in Barbados on January 4, 1940. Her mother, Mindla ("Mina") Adler, and father, Jacob Zierler, originally from Poland, were living in Holland before the Second World War. Mina's first cousin was Ethel Schiffman, married to Bernard Konigsberg. In the face of rising anti-Semitism, the families decided to leave Poland and Holland before the start of the War, ending up in Barbados. When Roz was born, Mina nearly died in childbirth and was advised not to have another child. The homes of the Zierlers and Konigsbergs were just a few doors down the road from each other so Roz was never really an only child. The Konigsbergs had four children who were like siblings to Roz and together their families immersed themselves in the Jewish community of Barbados.

**Mina and Jacob Zierler, Barbados, ca. 1950s**
(Dorothy Burak Rosenthal photo)

Their community was steeped in tradition, having been founded centuries earlier by Jews from Spain. In the Jewish cemetery near the synagogue there can be found many headstones with Spanish/Sephardic family names dating back to the 1600s. The Jewish community living in Barbados in the 1940s was made up of about 30-35 families, mainly Ashkenazi Jews, who practiced the traditions taught to them back in Europe. Roz's childhood was a blend of traditions – Jewish culture/Yiddishkeit and Caribbean soul. They grew their own vegetables, raised chickens and pigeons, and prepared them in the traditional kosher way, with her father acting as a "Shochet" – kosher slaughterer. Roz's father also performed for the Jewish community the ritual of the "Shomer", one who watches over the body of a deceased until its burial. Her playground was the ocean, just a short walk from her home, and nature was her backyard.

**Rose in her backyard, Barbados, ca. 1953**
(Betty Konigsberg Feinberg photo)

**Betty Konigsberg and Rose Zierler, Barbados 1950s**
(Daniel Weinberger photo)

Roz had a natural talent for music, languages, and art, which flourished in the environment provided by Barbados. She sang at school, she sang at synagogue. She was an enthusiastic dancer, blessed with natural rhythm, always the first on the dance floor when the music started. She had great admiration and respect for the locals in Barbados. She learned all about the plentiful flora and fauna of the island and beyond. Roz was a voracious reader. The first 16 years of her life spent in Barbados provided a blissful upbringing that implanted a nearly-permanent smile on her face and sunny disposition in her heart. The sun and the sand, the sounds and the tastes, the voices, people and culture of Barbados were programmed into her genes and never left her, even after moving to Canada.

In 1956 at the age of 16, Roz and her parents moved to Montreal, Canada. Roz, an extremely bright student, was accepted into Sir George William University (now Concordia University) at that early age. During her studies, she focused on areas related to art and architecture to nurture her artistic talents and passion. She eventually worked in a supporting role for prominent Montreal architects. In 1961 she met Joseph ("Joe") Weinberger, a young Holocaust survivor from Hungary who had recently immigrated to Canada from London, England. They married on June 22, 1964, and when the time came to have children, Roz's strong dedication to Joe and family led her to leave her job and raise the children full-time. Her intellect and knowledge base was the stuff of legend. She was an accomplished bridge player, Scrabble enthusiast, and crossword puzzle-solver, filling in the words just as fast as she could write.

**Rose and Betty Konigsberg Feinberg**
(Daniel Weinberger photo)

Roz's passion for music and art was ever-present. Throughout her life she sang in choirs, sang to her children, and led the singing at all the family events and religious occasions. For two decades Passover Seders were prepared in Roz's Passover kitchen, with the aunties cooking and singing, regaling family with tunes from the islands. This was the highlight of Roz's year. She would prepare the annual round-up of every family member, whose numbers eventually swelled to over 50, saying a few words about their significant events from the past year.

Her love for nature and the ocean never abated. Although living in Canada, she and Joe would travel to Barbados from time to time, taking their three children (one daughter, Debbie, and two sons, David and Danny) on several occasions to show them where she grew up. Early on in their marriage they spent summers with family friends north of Montreal in "cottage country", renting a tiny cottage on a small lake. Eventually they built a home there, designed by Roz, so they could spend weekends "up north" year-round. This country home became a focal point for the family-at-large for many years and was a site of peace, calm, fun and frolic for all their friends. She was always drawn to the water. Roz painted many scenes of the lake and the flowers and trees, as well as many barns, many of which hang on the walls of family and friends. Later they spent time regularly in Florida at an apartment on the ocean. Roz could not stay away from the ocean for too long: the salty, blue waters were her connection to her childhood, to her Barbados.

She practiced fine arts, becoming an accomplished painter and sculptor. She painted at home and at the country house. Roz took lessons in art classes and was even under the tutelage of the famous Polish painter, Rita Briansky. Roz was instrumental in commissioning a glass carving of Briansky's most famous painting of a walking Talith - prayer shawl (the "Guf", meaning "body") for permanent display at House of Israel, the synagogue near their country home in Ste. Agathe, Quebec. She eventually spent more and more time painting and sculpting in a studio, with some of her pieces being exhibited and sold at art galleries. There were many works commissioned by friends and even by corporations. One of her sculptures was acquired by the famous tennis player, Chris Evert Lloyd, on one of her visits to a Montreal art gallery and another sculpture is still on display at the Montreal headquarters of Pratt and Whitney.

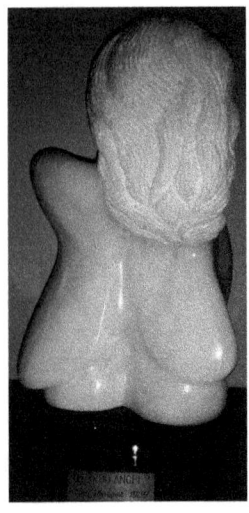 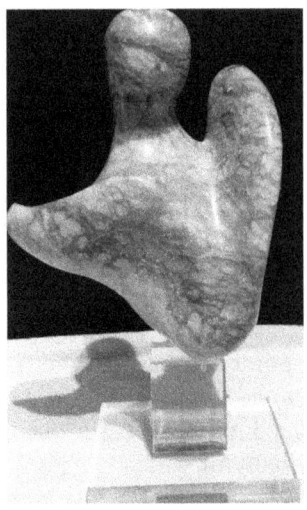

**Rose Zierler Weinberger's sculptures**
(Daniel Weinberger photos)

Roz was also well known for knitting kipas. Over the decades she made hundreds of kipas for family and friends, rarely relying on a set pattern. The designs came from her imagination and were flawlessly translated to the head cover. To this day, you see dozens of men at Roz's family synagogue in Montreal wearing her kipas. On one famous occasion during the 2000 US presidential election, Roz was attending synagogue near their Florida apartment. She saw the vice-presidential candidate, Joseph Lieberman, but wasn't impressed with the kipa he wore. She knit one especially for him and sent it to him. It was warmly received and recognized by a letter from him (on official US Senate stationery, no less,) thanking her for her gift.

The influence of Barbados was evident in Roz's passions and mannerisms. She had an encyclopedic brain and was a treasure-trove of information about all subjects. She had an affinity for flowers and birds, which she learned about and was exposed to extensively in Barbados. She knew the names of all the species and painted countless images of them.

She expressed herself in unique ways, always providing a glimpse into her Bajan childhood. Her ear for music allowed her to excel at learning languages. In addition to being taught English and Yiddish, over the years she learned French and Spanish along with some Hebrew, German and Hungarian. The most remarkable aspect of this talent was her ability to adopt various accents and dialects of these languages. But she was probably best known by her family and friends for her Bajan accent, the accent of her home. Although at most times she would speak English in a dialect worthy of the Queen, all it took for her to slip into a heavy Bajan accent was the presence of her cousins/siblings or a random encounter with someone, anyone, from any one of the Caribbean islands. The familial, free and laid-back attitude associated with Barbados was a cornerstone of Roz's personality. She was never too shy to strike up a conversation with strangers because everyone was her neighbour, her friend, her extended family. But if you happened to be from the Caribbean, then you were truly her best friend, whether you realized it or not. And if you were originally from Barbados, well, then you were her sister or brother, without question.

At too young an age, when she was around 63 years old, Roz became afflicted with ALS (Lou Gehrig's disease). She never lost her joie de vivre, and barely acknowledged her illness. The disease can quickly become devastating but Roz didn't suffer in the way most with ALS do. Her physical strength deteriorated but she was still able to function and travel. With the loving care provided by Joe, she continued to enjoy life. In the fall of 2006 they travelled to Florida, still a regular occurrence for them. In her weakened state, Roz developed complications from her illness and passed away on November 3, 2006, in Florida, not far from the ocean, her first and favourite playground. She was blessed with an idyllic childhood, a loving and doting husband for over 43 years, three adoring children, and 11 grandchildren, all of whom could tell you stories! They all remember her unique personality, her zest for life, and will forever associate her with the "islands." There is always a sense of pride when they tell their friends that their Jewish grandmother of Polish descent was born and raised in Barbados.

## *DAVID AND ANNE ZLOTOWITZ'S STORY*
### Clara Paster Halpern and Jack Pasternack

**David and Anne Zlotowitz, Toronto 1979**
(Clara Paster Halpern photo)

David Zlotowitz was one of the Founding Members of the Barbados Jewish Community.[125] Paltiel Paster (David's brother-in-law's brother) brought David to Barbados not long after the Pasters themselves arrived on the island.

Jack Pasternak was a child at the time David came to live with them and recalls him being short and of slight build. David and Ephraim Burak were the only single men in the Jewish community at the time and were friends.

David left Barbados for New York about 1947 and ran a successful "schmatta"[126] business in Harlem. He married Anne and they had two children. In the 1970s when Jack was working for Imperial Oil in New Jersey, he and his wife, Ricky, reconnected with David.

Sadly, Anne was killed in a freak highway accident (probably in the early 1980s) when a car driving in the opposite direction crossed the median and landed on theirs.

Jack believes David died in New York sometime in the 1980s.

---

[125] Memorial Board of Founding Members of the BJC in Shaare Tzedec Synagogue, Barbados.
[126] A self-deprecating Yiddish term for the clothing industry. Literally, a rag.

# CHAPTER 5
## From Peddling to Retailing and Manufacturing
### Simon Kreindler

Most of the Ashkenazi Jewish men who came to Barbados in the 1930s and 40s started out as peddlers, including Moses Altman, Srul Jacob Bernstein, Harry Burak, Aron Karp, Bernard Konigsberg, Bunia Korn, Joseph Kreindler, Paltyel Pasternak, Shlomo Schor, Moses Steinbok, and Abraham Wajchendler.

Joseph Kreindler had peddled in Curacao, and Motel Truss in British Guiana and Trinidad before coming to Barbados. A handful of the early immigrants such as Yehudah Brzozek, Moses Mass, Oscar Pillersdorf, Ernest Saunders, Lazer Spira, Moses Steinbok and Motel Truss never peddled but went directly into retail businesses in Bridgetown or started small factories.

For generations, peddling was an established Jewish occupation in rural communities in Europe and it came to America with the tide of immigrants who arrived there in the 19th century. As they made their rounds, many of these men (and peddlers were almost exclusively men) developed skills they would later turn to good use in retail businesses.

Peddling was "a start-up occupation that provided an excellent first step towards stable and prosperous careers…it required going into the homes of customers and (convincing them) to buy something…needles, threads, lace, ribbons, mirrors, pictures, picture frames, watches, jewelry, eyeglasses, linens, bedding, and other sundry goods…."[127]

Between the two World Wars, deteriorating economic conditions and increasing anti-Semitism in Europe resulted in a wave of Jewish emigration. Some Jews were able to emigrate to the US before the Johnson-Reed Immigration Act was passed in 1924 [128] but many were forced to look elsewhere. Some went to South and Central America while others found refuge in the Caribbean, especially in Jamaica, Curacao, Trinidad and Barbados.

Both Yehaudah Brzozek and Shlomo Schor had lived in Guatemala, Central America, before coming to Barbados in the early 1930s. I suspect they left Guatemala after its anti-Semitic president, Jorge Ubico, introduced legislation

---

[127] Hasia Diner http://www.immigrantentrepreneurship.org/entry.php?rec=191
[128] There was a lot of anti-immigrant feeling in the US at the time and the Johnson-Reed bill limited the number of immigrants from Europe to 150,000 per year. "As rumours made their way through the shtetls and cities in Eastern Europe that the US wasn't going to let any more immigrants in, many made a mad dash to the northern European ports to sail…before it was too late."
http://www.museumoffamilyhistory.com/mfh-imm-jbs.htm

in 1932 ordering the expulsion of all peddlers, most of whom were Jewish. Although the actual expulsion was later averted, Ubico prohibited peddling in Guatemala and many of the country's Jews emigrated.

The Jewish peddlers in Barbados were a determined and ambitious bunch. They would not allow their lack of fluency in English to be an impediment and knew that if they were going to bring their families from Europe they had to succeed. They bought whatever goods they could afford from merchants in Bridgetown and got started. Initially they visited homes in and around the capital but as they got to know the lay of the land, gradually extended their range. Bajans appear to have responded remarkably positively to them and none of the stories in this book even hint at them encountering hostility or customers who didn't pay for their purchases. In fact, I recall my father having only praise for the Bajans with whom he dealt when he was peddling. He spoke about how warmly he was received and even recalled one homeowner who regularly offered him a cold drink when he passed by her home.

Whether travelling on foot, bicycle, or employing a pushcart, the peddlers were likely regarded as something of a novelty. In September 2007, a contributor to the online Barbados Free Press Blog recalling his early life on the island, remembered "Mr. Kreindler (peddling) haberdashery items – combs, buttons, ribbons, needles, thread, etc."[129] as he rode his bicycle with a suitcase strapped to the carrier from Bridgetown to Speightstown.

Peddling was physically demanding work. It involved walking or riding many miles, sometimes in scorching heat. At the end of the day, the peddler would return "home" (wherever that happened to be), take something to eat, and hope to get a few hours sleep before it was time to start all over again the next day. Recalling his time peddling in Barbados in the 1930s, Bernard Konigsberg would later later tell his daughter, Betty, "There's not one stone on this island that's not covered with my tears."

After accumulating enough money to pay for his family's passage from Europe, the peddler continued working and saving to achieve his next objective - renting a store and stocking it with sufficient merchandise to start a retail business. Shirts, pants, socks, underwear, hats, belts, blouses, yard goods, lace, ribbons, and notions were some of the more common items retailed by these early shopkeepers.

When their children were old enough to be left with a nanny or had started school, wives typically joined their husbands in the business. Because theft was always a problem in retail establishments, having a second family member to

---

[129] http://barbadosfreepress.wordpress.com/2007/03/28/barbados-free-press-under-attack-again/

help keep an eye on the merchandise was a necessity.

The majority of the Jewish men who started out peddling in Barbados eventually ended up running retail businesses on Swan Street[130] and nearby High, Palmetto, and Roebuck Streets. Some later opened businesses on Broad Street, the island's main shopping thoroughfare.

A few of the more entrepreneurial men opened manufacturing facilities that made men's and women's clothing as well as hats, handbags, and underwear. From time to time, proprietors would give up their retail establishments either to do something else, try a new location, or as began to happen with increasing frequency in the 1950s follow their children when they left the island to work or continue their education elsewhere. When this happened, it was not uncommon for one of the other Jewish families to take over the location and start doing business under a new name.

What follows is a list of the early Ashkenazi retailers in Bridgetown based on information culled from contributors' stories. Some owners gave their businesses names while others were known only by street number or the owner's surname. I have tried to include as many store names and street numbers as possible and as many of the original and subsequent owners as I could uncover. Exactly when various businesses first opened and when they ceased to operate was a challenge as many of the stories did not include this information. In some cases, I took the liberty of making an educated guess.

## *EARLY RETAIL BUSINESSES*

About 1932 Moses Mass opened "The Russian Store" at 9 Swan Street. When the Mass family left Barbados for British Guiana in 1943, the location was taken over by Lazar Spira who renamed it "The Hollywood Store."

---

[130] According to Warren Alleyne in his book, "Historic Bridgetown," Swan Street acquired its name in 1657 and was probably named after the surveyor, John Swan. The Barbados Pocket Guide notes it later came to be known as Jews' Street because of the many successful (Sephardic) Jewish merchants who had shops and businesses there. At the time, imported goods form Europe were in high demand and the Jews literally had exclusive control over their importation. Most of the Sephardic merchants lived on the upper level and their businesses were on the ground floor. When the Ashkenazi Jews began opening businesses on Swan Street in the 1930s, they also used the ground floor for business but the upper levels were used as warehouses for their goods.

After peddling for a while, Moses Altman opened the Royal Store on High Street in the early 1930s. The store was later taken over by Oscar and Edna Pillersdorf ca. the early 1940s and still later by Oscar's brother, Kuk Pilarski, after he came to Barbados from Poland in 1957.

Oscar Pillersdorf later opened the Colony Store on lower Broad Street and after starting his Reliance Shirt Factory on Palmetto Street, his wife, Edna, took over running the store.

In the 1930s Bunia Korn had a store on Swan Street (or possibly High Street near Swan Street). Later his son-in-law, Chaim Rosner, joined him.

In the early 1930s Yehudah Brzozek opened a leather goods store on Palmetto Street.

About 1935 Joseph Kreindler opened the "Jubilee Store" on High Street near Swan Street.

In the late 1930s Jacob and Mina Zierler opened a business at 8 Swan Street next door to Moses Mass' "Russian Store."

Also in the late 1930s, Louis Speisman had a store on Swan Street. Unfortunately, its name and location are unknown.

In the late 1930s Leon Bernstein opened "The Sandal Shop" on High Street at Swan Street.

About 1939 Bernard Konigsberg opened "The Coronation Store" at 15 Swan Street. The location was later taken over by Abraham Wajchendler; subsequently by Helen and Mauricio Raizman; and then by Paul Bernstein who named it "Stitches." Paul still owns the building as of 2016.

23 Swan Street was owned by Louis Speisman and rented it to Simon and Rose Altman who named it "Altman's."

30 Swan Street was also owned by Louis Speisman and rented to Simon and Rose Altman. It was known as "Altman's Bargain House." When Simon and Rose gave it up, Iancu Lazar rented it and renamed it "Lazar's Society Store."

In the 1930s Srul Jacob Bernstein ran "The Shopping Centre" on the south side of Swan Street across from where the Barbados Hardware was located (now the DaCosta Mall). The store number would probably have been in the high 30s on Swan Street.

In the late 1930s Paltyel Pasternak operated a dry goods store at 42 Swan Street and when his cousin, Yehudah Brzozek, left Barbados for Australia in 1948, Paltyel took over his Palmetto Street store and continued to run it as a leather business.

About the early 1940s Harry and Sonia Burak opened their "Lucky Store" at 14 Swan Street. They later had two other stores on Swan Street, one where the R. S. Nicholls and Co. Ltd. Haberdashery store had been and the other across the street from the Lucky Store.

Gustav Feldman's "Swan Store" was located at 50 Swan Street.

Aaron and Marilyn Karp's "London Shop" operated at three different locations on Broad Street. It is unclear where the first location was but the second was at 29 Broad Street and the third on lower Broad Street.

About 1946 Joseph Kreindler closed the Jubilee Store on High Street and opened the "Modern Dress Shoppe" at 6 Broad Street.

Around 1949 Henry and Deborah Altman opened the "Broadway Dress Shop" on upper Broad Street. They sold it around 1966.

From the early 1950s Jean Saunders ran her "Style Shoppe" on upper Broad Street, upstairs at the Women's Self Help and across from the Broadway Dress Shop.

About 1951 Abraham and Helen Wajchendler opened "The General Store" at 1 Swan Street. Later they took over "The Coronation Store" from Bernard Konigsberg and subsequently opened "Textile Town" at 20 Tudor Street.

In 1956 Rose Altman purchased 8 Broad Street and "Altman's Dept. Store" was born and remained in business at this location until 1998.

Around the 1960s Joe Simon, Iancu Lazar's son-in-law, who had previously rented on Tudor Street, opened a store on Swan Street.

In the early 1960s the CIBC purchased the building where the Modern Dress Shoppe was located at 6 Broad Street to build a new head office. Joseph Kreindler moved the business across the street to 29 Broad Street, the former location of G.W. Hutchinson and Co. Ltd.

## *FACTORIES*

In the late 1940s Oscar Pillersdorf started the Reliance Shirt Factory on Palmetto Street.

In the 1950s Helen Bernstein Raizman started Drapery Secialists. She was later joined by her sons. Originally located in Pelican Village near the deep-water harbor, the factory was later moved to the Grazettes Industrial Park.

Moses Steinbok started The Eileen Shirt Factory about 1950. It was originally located next door to his home on Palm Beach and later moved to Roebuck Street in back of Harrison College.

In the early 1960s Motel Truss opened a hat and handbag factory, M. Truss and Co., that was located in the Grazettes Industrial Park next to Oran Ltd.

Ernest Saunders and partners, Ferdie Shoul of Antigua, Ram Kirpalani of Trinidad, and Leon and Paul Bernstein started the Barbados Knitting and Spinning Mills, located at the corner of Spry and Roebuck Streets (where the Central Bank is now located) and his Carifta Industries was across the street from it.

Abraham Wajchendler founded Barbados Draperies at 20 Tudor Street in Bridgetown, supplying hotels, businesses and individuals. The operation was later expanded to a factory at Wildey, St. Michael, in partnership with his son, Irving.

## *OTHER*

After a successful career with Crown Life Insurance Company of Canada in Trinidad and Barbados, Leon Bernstein retired and built Goodwood Apartments near Accra Beach. He was later appointed the first chairman of the Barbados Development Bank.

## *SOME LATER BUSINESSES*

In the early 1960s Marshall Oran founded Oran Ltd., originally in Grazettes and now in the Harbour Industrial Park.

Paul Koves started Koves and Company in the late 1960s or early 1970s, a garment manufacturing business that was located in the Harbour Industrial Park.

In the 1960s Jay and Leila Newman started Zylcraft Optical, a factory making eyeglass frames in a building on Bay Street owned by Paul Altman.

In the late 1970s or early 1980s Stan Hoffman was manager of Barbados Children's Wear, a factory that made children's garments that were shipped offshore.

In 1983 Goldie Spieler started "Earthworks Pottery" in the parish of St. Thomas. She is now semi-retired and the business is run by her son, David.

"Swiss Art" watches, located next to Correia's on Broad Street at Prince William Henry Street, was owned by Joseph Burgida, a Holocaust survivor who came to the island with his wife, Judith, in the 1960s. After Joseph died in 1991, the business was sold to Jennifer Truss. Judith Burgida now lives in Israel.

# EARLY JEWISH RETAILERS ON SWAN STREET
## (1930s -1950s)
**(Adapted from a hand-drawn map by Paul Bernstein with help from James Altman)**

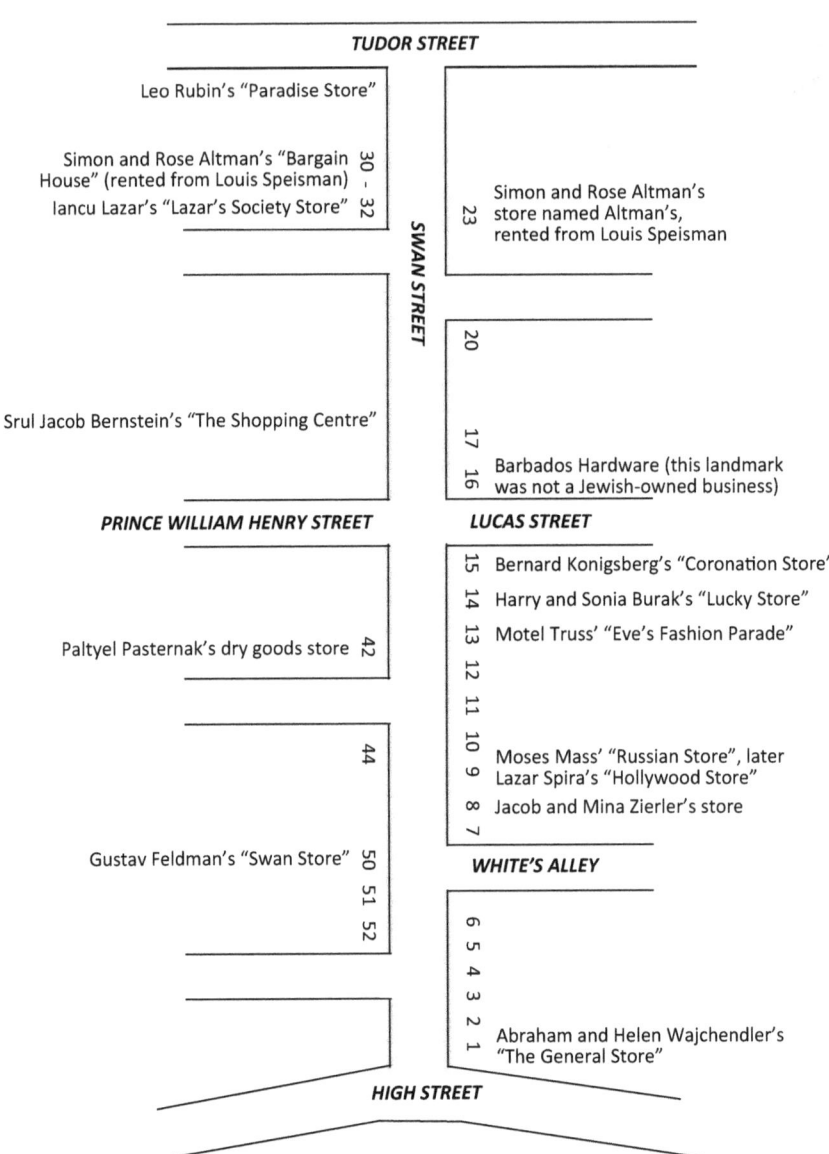

# CHAPTER 6
## Some families who came to Barbados in the 1950s and later
### Simon Kreindler

As North American economies rebounded following World War II, the Caribbean saw a huge increase in tourism and Barbados became a choice destination for airlines and cruise ship companies. Some Jewish visitors liked what they saw and decided to open businesses. Others, drawn by the weather and beautiful beaches, saw the island as a great place to retire.

In the 1970s government tax incentives encouraged the establishment of new businesses that brought Jewish investors and created new employment opportunities for Bajans.

In the past 25 years, Barbados has welcomed offshore business and entered into favourable tax treaties with a number of countries further boosting foreign investment.

What follows are the stories of some families who came to Barbados in the 1950s and later. At least two of them were closely related to founding families - Marshall Oran, who married into the Miller/Altman family and Kuk Pilarski, Oscar and Leib Pillersdorf's brother.

Others came to Barbados for a variety of reasons. Each of their stories is unique but one feature they all shared was their connection to the Jewish community. For some, that connection was more superficial and for others it went deeper. Again, I have chosen to arrange the families in this group alphabetically.

# HY BLOOM'S STORY
## Hy Bloom and Internet sources

Hy Bloom was born in Ottawa in 1921, the eldest of his parents' three sons. His father was a custom tailor who was barely able to support his family.

Hy first encountered the fascinating world of sound as an eight-year-old under the guidance of his father. In elementary school he built basic microphones. Frequent visits to the library and regular attendance at various radio shops augmented his Lisgar Collegiate education. After working at the National Research Council and spending time in the army, he opened "Soundmaster" that became a very successful amplifier business. Simultaneously, he ran a recording studio that attracted many musicians and singers.

Hy's father died in 1956. Hy and his mother had cared for him during the last six years of his life and his own health had deteriorated. When he heard about Barbados' wonderful climate he decided to visit the island. He stayed at the Crane Hotel and paid eight dollars per day for a room and meals!

Hy wanted to say kaddish[131] for his father and asked hotel staff if there were Jews or a synagogue on the island. No one knew. He tried the telephone book hoping to find a Jewish name but was unsuccessful. He had been to Bridgetown searching for a shop with a Jewish name but doubted that Altman qualified. Then his luck changed. He and a fellow traveller he had met at the hotel took the bus to Bridgetown where his friend went searching for an oversized sport shirt. They went into Altman's Department Store and luckily were served by Simon Altman. Hy studied Simon's face as he tried fitting his friend with a shirt and thought he could be Jewish. Since Hy was fluent in Yiddish, he said to Simon in Yiddish, "What a big slob!" Simon grabbed and hugged him saying, "You speak Yiddish!" As Hy recalled, "My Barbados world changed at that memorable moment."

Simon invited him for Friday night services the next evening and asked Hy to meet him when the store closed. They drove to the Aquatic Club where Simon had a quick swim before getting into his Sabbath clothes which he kept in a locker there. Simon told Hy about the small shul he had built in back of his house on Harts Gap and invited him to join his family for dinner before services. Hy noted that the Altman dining room could accommodate approximately 20 guests and that Rose, Simon's wife, had prepared gefilte fish and delicious

---

[131] An ancient Jewish prayer sequence regularly recited in the synagogue service, including thanksgiving and praise and concluding with a prayer for universal peace. (Google)

chicken soup. There was also a beautifully sculpted challah that had been made by Humphreys Bakery.

The local community and Jewish tourists filled the small shul and members took turns conducting the service. Afterwards, everyone sat on the front lawn and sang songs. It was Hy's first Erev Shabbat in Barbados and it gave him the opportunity to experience the warmth and sincerity of the community.

In 1966 Hy built a beautiful home in St. James and recounted the cute story of how his friends, Dr. Jack Berman and his wife, Birdie, had accompanied him to the island for the planned housewarming. They brought many Jewish delicacies with them and Evelyn Truss helped them through customs, brought them to the new house, and loaned them her car. Next day the entire community celebrated with them. That evening Evelyn told Hy that her daughter, Manea, who had been married a few days earlier, wanted to use the house for her honeymoon. Hy agreed and "happily" moved into the Trusses' home with the Bermans.

In 2014 Hy recalled having visited Barbados at least 50 times, spending time with his many Jewish friends there, and attending many of the community's weddings, bar mitzvahs, and funerals.

Hy concluded his story by listing the names of the families in the community that he remembered: Simon and Rose Altman and their children; Aaron and Marilyn Karp; Iancu and Tony Lazar; Mr. and Mrs. Rubin; Abraham and Helen Wajchendler; Louis and Mary Speisman; Oscar and Edna Pillersdorf; Marshall and Anita Oran; Yankel Bernstein; Leon and Kitty Bernstein; Motel and Evelyn Truss and their children; Benny and Leah Gilbert; Moses and Helen Steinbok; Mr. and Mrs. Green; Goldie Spieler; Henry and Deborah Altman and son, Paul; Joseph and Sara Kreindler; Bunia and Sophie Korn; Joe and Felicia Simon; Paul and Visia Paster; Lazar and Toni Spira and son, Sidney; Luzer and Brancia Gross; Ernest and Jean Saunders, and the Lubavitcher rabbis who came to the island in 1961.

Postscript: Hy Bloom died in an Ottaw nursing home on July 19, 2017, four days after his ninety-sixth birthday.

# HAL AND MICHELLE BLUMENFELD'S STORY
First published in the Connecticut Jewish Ledger in September 2013 and reprinted here with permission

**Hal and Michelle Blumenthal and children, Barbados, 2005**
(Hal Blumenthal photo)

Dr. Hal Blumenfeld is Yale professor of neurology, neurobiology and neurosurgery, and director of the Yale Clinical Neuroscience Imaging Center. But every High Holiday season since 1995, Blumenfeld has exchanged his white lab coat for the tallit and kippah of a lay rabbi – in Barbados.

Blumenfeld leads Rosh Hashanah and Yom Kippur services at Shaare Tzedek, a small, rabbi-less Conservative synagogue in the Christ Church parish outside Bridgetown. He is a shaliach tzibur – Hebrew for "a person sent by the community," and someone familiar enough with Jewish religious services to stand in for a rabbi.

A native of California, Blumenfeld grew up in Glen Cove, Long Island, where he cut his teeth as a shaliach tzibur at the Conservative synagogue led by his father, Rabbi David Blumenfeld. The Harvard- and Columbia-educated physician and neuroscientist joined the Yale University School of Medicine faculty in 1996.

After living in Westville for more than a decade, Blumenfeld and his wife relocated to White Plains, N.Y. so that their three children could attend SAR Academy in Riverdale. This year marks the 18th High Holiday season that the doctor and his family have spent on the island.

"Our children have grown up knowing Barbados as the only place they've experienced the High Holidays," Blumenfeld says. "When they draw pictures for Rosh HaShanah in day school, the other kids draw the usual symbols of the holiday — shofar, apples and honey — and our kids draw beach, sail, sun."

Barbados was already a familiar place when Blumenfeld met his wife, Michelle Brody, whose family traveled regularly to the island when she was growing up. Blumenfeld's father was working for United Synagogue of Conservative Judaism in the '90s and mentioned the Barbadian congregation to his son, a practiced shaliach tzibur since his teenage years. With no permanent rabbi, Shaare Tzedek was looking for a lay leader.

"I'm not formally trained as a rabbi or cantor, but I had a strong Jewish education and with my father being a rabbi, I knew enough about the prayers and the siddur to play the role," says Blumenfeld, who has led services in New Jersey and Boston synagogues as well. "It's my other professional beat, different from anything I do in New Haven. My wife and I were very happy to go."

Blumenfeld sees a mix of congregants at "True Blue," the original name of the house purchased to serve the Shaare Tzedek congregation: native-born Barbadian Jews, Jews by choice, non-Jews who are curious about the services and the religion. He sees attrition as well, but there are always newcomers to the Jewish community. "In the time we've been there, the composition has changed but the size has stayed the same," he says. "Children are born and new people move in from Israel and other places."

Blumenfeld describes his family's Jewish community-away-from-home as "very warm, welcoming, and close."

"It's a very unique community, a mix of people who came in the '30s and built on the foundations created by their 17th-century predecessors. It still has the feeling of being a special, remote enclave of Jews practicing Judaism in a unique locale, and maintaining a very strong connection to Jewish tradition – and at the same time, being integrated into Bajan society."

There's a good reason that the Blumenfelds are invited back year after year, says Jewish communal leader Paul Altman, a Shaare Tzedek congregant and close friend. "As usual, Hal was brilliant!" he says. "He and his wife Michelle and their three children are a part of our extended community. Hal is a very learned scholar and always includes wonderful and deep messages in his sermons."

## *Our Welcome by the Jewish community of Barbados*
### Hal Blumenfeld

The voice on the other end of the telephone was warm, vibrant and strong. There was a harmonious mix I'd never heard before - a deep Caribbean accent flavoured with Yiddish expressions and most of all, a warm, engaging and welcoming spirit. This was my interview in 1997 when I was invited to join the Jewish community of Barbados and lead the High Holidays services—a wonderful privilege that I've enjoyed along with the rest of my family ever since.

We arrived, my wife, Michelle Brody, and I, with our then-infant daughter, Eva, and were immediately embraced by the members of the community. Our sons, Jesse and Lev, each joined us a few years later and became part of our traditional annual pilgrimage.

We have learned that the Jewish community of Barbados, like my initial encounter on the phone, is a unique blend of Caribbean and ancient Jewish tradition; of cultures ranging from Barbados to Israel; of the Eastern European shtetl, and of other countries around the world. Since our arrival, the community members have greeted us warmly each year in the synagogue, in their homes, and on visits throughout the island. The community clearly has a strong sense of "hachnasat orchim" or welcoming hospitality, rooted in our tradition going back to the times of Abraham and Sarah. Over time, we have formed close bonds with everyone in the community. We can honestly say that the Jewish community of Barbados is now like family for us, a loving connection that transcends distance and time.

The strong spirit of the community is also felt in the synagogue during services where everyone participates and there is a certain energy in the room. In my first year in Barbados standing on the bimah, I was pleased when I reached certain prayers to hear a surge of strong voices joining in with a Galitzyanishe lilt mixed with Bajan and modern Hebrew. I can still hear the echoes of these voices resonating through the years even though some of our older members have left us. Still, the singing in the synagogue continues, blending the present and the past. And young children play freely in the synagogue, hiding under the podium on the bimah, coming in and going out to play with lizards or frogs in the yard, or to enjoy a lollipop or card game in the back room before rejoining us for shofar blowing or other key moments in the service.

We have enjoyed many wonderful and special community activities over the years, including communal holiday meals on Rosh Hashannah, Shabbat, or after Yom Kippur (organized with great spirit and delicious contributions from community members); preparations to build the sukkah behind the synagogue; repair of prayer books by the children; celebrations of community historical milestones; completion of historical restoration; exciting projects at the original synagogue site in Bridgetown; and dedication of a new sefer torah for the community.

Having been a part of the community these past 20 years we have seen how passionately it wants to preserve its Jewish past while moving forward. Some things change over time but I believe and hope that the welcoming charitable spirit embodied by our Jewish tradition, blended with Bajan, Israeli, and other international culture, will continue to thrive in the Jewish community of Barbados for many years to come.

# ERIC AND PENNY BOWMAN'S STORY

**Eric and Penny Bowman, 2016**
(Penny Bowman photo)

Eric was born in England in 1937 and immigrated to Canada with his family in 1948. Penny was born in Toronto in 1941 and she and Eric married in 1961. Before retiring in 2005, Eric practiced law in Toronto for 47 years while Penny was the coordinator of the Interior Design Department at Seneca College for over 20 years.

Eric and Penny first got to know Barbados while vacationing there in 1966 and soon fell in love with the island's sun, sand, sea, and friendly people. Initially, Penny spent three months there each winter and Eric would commute from Toronto, often bringing the children during their winter school break.

In 1986 Penny was invited by the Barbados Community College to be an educational consultant for their Division of Fine Arts to help raise its standards through curriculum development and training of tutors. She also worked with various interior designers and architects on the island, designing, refurbishing, and redecorating homes. A former nurse and weight management counsellor, Penny led support groups and classes for men and women in Barbados who needed help with weight and health issues, and for more than 20 years volunteered with the Open House program of the Barbados National Trust, talking about the history and furnishings of the island's heritage homes.

For Penny, Barbados was home for many years before Eric felt at home there. She made friends in the island's arts and educational community and in the Barbados Jewish community. They bought a house in Rockley Country Club in

1986 and when Eric retired, began spending six months there each year and are now Barbados residents.

Besides law, Eric's passion is the history of Barbados and particularly its Jewish community. He often leads Friday night services at the Share Tzedek Synagogue in Rockley and at the Nidhe Israel Synagogue in Bridgetown during the tourist season. He speaks and lectures about Jewish practice to church groups, schools, service clubs, etc., and has represented the Jewish community at multi-faith services at the University of the West Indies and at Independence Day services. He is very involved with the Barbados National Trust, and like Penny, also volunteers at their Open House program.

Penny and Eric observe kashrut; hold Shabbat afternoon Torah and discussion classes at their home; and often host observant visitors to the island on Shabbat. Both enjoy leading tours at the Nidhe Israel Synagogue, the Jewish Museum and the mikvah in Bridgetown. Penny participates in synagogue services and bakes fat-free, sugar-free cakes for Jewish holidays.

When the mikvah was discovered, Penny found it to be her "spiritual place." She lectures about its history and has occasionally assisted other women in experiencing the spiritual feeling of its water.

As Penny says, "Barbados is not just an island in the Caribbean. It is my home and place of healing and helping. The members of the Barbados Jewish community are my extended family."

## *ROBERT AND DEL FLAM'S STORY*
### Karen Flam

**The Flams, ca. 1980: Harold, Donald, Karen, Charles, and David
Sitting: Dell and Robert**
(Karen Flam photo)

In 1940 newlyweds Robert and Dell Flam moved from New Brunswick to Chandler, Quebec, a small town on the Gaspé Peninsula. That year Abitibi Price, the world's largest newsprint company, was building a pulp and paper mill there and a deep water harbour to accommodate the ships transporting giant rolls of paper to customers such as the New York Times and the Miami Herald. Robert knew that little Chandler would need a store to supply Abitibi's workers and their families with clothing, home supplies, and dry goods. Flam's Store was born and both the business and the family thrived in Chandler for 30 years.

Robert and Dell had five children: David in 1941, Charles in 1942, Donald in 1943, Harold in 1944 and Karen in 1954. There were virtually no Jews within hundreds of miles of Chandler. The Jewish shopkeeper in small-town Canada and the United States is a well-known phenomenon. The Flams travelled to New Brunswick or Nova Scotia to celebrate the Jewish holidays and all five children attended various boarding schools and Young Judea summer camps. All of them visited Israel after graduating high school and before starting university, something neither Robert nor Dell did until 1980.

Eventually Robert began searching for a warmer winter destination. Gaspé winters were long, dark, and unusually cold. He visited south Florida, Cuba, the Bahamas, the Caymans and Mexico in his quest to find a place. Dell joined him at each location but they couldn't find what they were looking for.

In 1968 they decided to try a new destination recommended by Alex Konigsberg, a close law school friend of their son, Charles, and some other Montreal business acquaintances. On arrival in Barbados they headed to the Rockley Hotel. Their taxi driver suggested returning the next day and giving them a tour of the island. Their friendship with him (Mr. Yardey) lasted until he passed away many years later. Robert and Dell fell in love with Barbados, particularly Robert.

In December 1968 David and Barbara Flam were married and decided to honeymoon in Barbados. They stayed at the Rockley Hotel and fell in love with the island. As avid golfers, they truly enjoyed the course at Sandy Lane.

In 1969 and 1970 Robert and Dell returned to Barbados and Rockley Beach several times. They spent hours with Mr. Yardey driving around the island searching for the perfect property to buy. Robert began attending Friday evening services at "True Blue" (Shaare Tzedek) and he and Del found the Jewish community very welcoming. By then they were convinced that Barbados was the place for them. By the time Karen was about to finish high school in Montreal and leave for college, they were ready to retire to Barbados. In 1971 Robert heard through friends that a Montreal businessman was interested in selling his home in St. Peter. He went to Barbados to see it, returning to Chandler with Polaroid photos of the house and property. He and Dell purchased "Green Valley" at the top of Gibbs Hill and moved there permanently in the fall of 1971. It was a wonderful spot, close to beautiful Mullins Beach, Sandy Lane's golf course, and Speightstown.

Robert and Dell became hosts extraordinaire to their children, grandchildren, relatives and friends, and constantly had a house full of guests. They enjoyed 38 years of happiness in their new home and fully participated in the rich and vibrant life the island offered.

Dell lived in Barbados until she was 83 years old. She died in November 1994, after spending the final three months of her life in hospital in Montreal. Robert remained in Barbados until his health began to fail in 2009 at which point it was impossible for his kids to care for him from afar. He left Barbados kicking and screaming and spent the last two years of his life in a long-term care home in Montreal, missing his daily swims in the Caribbean and sunrise visits to his backyard orchid house. He passed away in December of 2011 at age 90.

# *JACOB HASSID'S STORY*
## Interviewed by Simon Kreindler, Barbados, May 8, 2016

**Jacob Hassid**

Jacob came to Barbados in 1996 to open a branch of Diamonds International (DI), an Israeli company whose clientele were cruise ship passengers and whose business followed the ships' ports of call.

Initially DI focused on St. Thomas and St. Maarten, and later Cozumel, then virgin territory but today one of the largest tourist destinations in the world. The fourth island DI focused on was Antigua where Jacob helped set up their business.

Jacob and his wife, Michal, were married in 1995 and initially lived on St. Maarten. They subsequently moved to Barbados (DI's fifth island destination), because they wanted to start a family in a country that was safe, had good medical care and a stable government.

From the outset, Jacob felt warmly received by Bajans, not only in the way they greeted him on the street but also by the way they responded when he would ask for directions. Michal had a more difficult time adjusting to being away from her family in Israel and was initially quite homesick.

When Jacob and Michal were setting up the company's first location in Bridgetown, the landlord knew they were Jewish and introduced them to Jimmy

Altman. Jimmy told them about the shul and introduced them to the Jewish community.

At the time, Jacob and Michal were in their 20s, and Jacob remembers meeting many of the community's Founding Members and being impressed. Each had an interesting story to tell and he felt a great deal of respect for them. In particular, he recalled Henry Altman, Robert Flam, Helen Reisman, Oscar Pillersdorf, and others who are no longer with us. Their closest friends in the community were Anita and Jimmy Altman and Leah and Benny Gilbert, all considerably older than Michal and him.

When DI began doing business in Bridgetown, established merchants such as Cave Shepherd and Harrison's were not at all happy. Cave Shepherd's subsidiary, Colombian Emeralds, was a direct competitor. Harrison's had its own jewellry and watch division, and Louis Bayley had Little Switzerland. DI became the target of their animosity, and while Jacob could appreciate that they did not like having him as a competitor, he felt very isolated. Things slowly changed, however, and today DI enjoys excellent relationships with all these companies. Interestingly, the children were the catalyst that brought about the change. Clement, Noi and Shelley all attended Montessori School and later, St. Gabriel's. When Clement first began socializing with other Bajan children at school, including the children of some of DI's competitors, the animosity Michal and Jacob had been experiencing began to dissipate. Clement was invited to birthday parties and his friends' parents gradually got to know Michal and Jacob. They recognized they were decent, good people and before long they became friends. Over time they developed warm relationships. Although the children recently moved to Israel with Michal (and Clement joined the Israel Defense Force), they still keep in close touch with their friends in Barbados.

Jacob and Michal always observed kashrut and the children embraced the practice. Sometimes Jacob would pick up kosher meat (for which he had a special import license) on one his frequent overseas trips, but the family was also quite happy eating fish, etc. When the children slept over at friends' homes, their parents would call to ask Michal and Jacob what their kids could eat. When there was a bonfire and hotdogs were being served, Michal and Jacob would send kosher hotdogs for them to eat. The children's friends respected their observance as did their parents.

With regard to the children's Jewish education, Michal and Jacob did the best they could under the circumstances. The Hassids' home was Jewish and everyone knew it. There was a mezuzah on the front door; they kept kosher

and they celebrated Shabbat and all the holidays. On Fridays Michal would bake challah and in the evening, would light Shabbat candles. Jacob said kiddush before dinner and later they would sing Shabbat songs, then go to shul and celebrate with the rest of the community. When Jacob drove the children to various places, he tried to use the time to teach them about some aspect of Judaism. His only regret is that he was not able to do more.

Jacob, who recently stepped down after 6 years as President of the Barbados Jewish community, described the experience as a great privilege and honour. He was touched that the community had accepted him so warmly and offered him the opportunity to be their leader. As president, he tried to be governed by what he perceived as the community's needs and challenges, the biggest of which was the diversity of the membership and the fact that it had important and long-established family relationships and traditions. When all was said and done, however, he felt the community was too small to be self-perpetuating without accepting change. Keeping the various factions together while trying to implement this had been his biggest challenge.

Other challenges included finding adequate burial space for members; Jews whose family wanted them buried in the cemetery even though they were not members of the community; dealing with the burial of a non-Jewish spouse of a Jewish member; and the problem of conversion. The community's constitution required conversion according to the guidelines of the Conservative Movement but there had been cases where a majority of the members refused to accept such a conversion because they did not approve of the rabbi/rabbis who oversaw it.

In spite of the above challenges, Jacob worked hard to keep the community's flame alive, create excitement, and ensure member participation. He is optimistic the community will survive but believes that change is inevitable. As one example of how this might come about, he noted the recent interest Chabad had shown in getting involved in Barbados, an interest he had tried to encourage.

## STANLEY AND JOAN HOFFMAN'S STORY
**Simon Kreindler and Internet sources**

Stanley and Joan Hoffman came to Barbados about 1978/79, accompanied by their daughter, Samantha. The couple also had two sons who never lived in Barbados. Stan was the manager of Barbados Children's Wear, a factory that made children's garments that were shipped offshore.

In the late 1970s and early 1980s, the Hoffmans ran a Hebrew school in their home. When they later divorced, Stanley married an Indian woman from Guyana.

Joan died of cancer in Barbados. Samantha married an Englishman, Paul Fogelman, later divorced him, and moved to England.

## PAUL AND PRISCILLA KOVES' STORY
**Leah Pillersdorf Gilbert and Internet sources**

Paul Koves was born on January 21, 1920, and married Priscilla Champagne, a native of Somerset, Manitoba, in 1951. After travelling to Venezuela and various other countries in the Caribbean, they settled in Barbados and jointly founded Koves Company Ltd., a highly successful garment factory where Pricilla was the head designer.

According to Leah Gilbert, Koves and Company produced smocked dresses for girls. The company employed a large number of cottage industry workers and shipped the finished garments to high-end stores in Europe. An article in the March 14, 1977, edition of the Caribbean News reported that Koves and Co. "had just shipped 6000 dresses to England and Ireland and had orders for another 18,000. Each order was estimated to cost around $90,000 (BDS). The company was selling nightgowns, negligees, panties and toddlers' dresses." By 1984 a faltering world economy forced Koves and Co. into receivership.

Paul Koves apparently died a pauper in a Barbados nursing home on June 12, 2003. He is buried in the Jewish cemetery in Bridgetown. Priscilla returned to Canada and died in Winnipeg, Manitoba, on November 16, 2015, at age 95.

The couple had two daughters, Anita and Yvonne, the latter now a successful singer-songwriter in Canada.

# JAY AND LILA NEWMAN'S STORY
## Leah and Benny Gilbert, Simon Kreindler, and Internet sources

**Jay and Lila Newman**

The Newman family came to Barbados from the US in 1965 and lived on Atlantic Shores. Jay and Lila had three children, Jory, Sindy, and Amy. Jay started Zylcraft Optical, a factory that made eyeglass frames in a building on Bay Street which he rented from Henry Altman.

The Newmans returned to the U.S. about 1980 and Jay opened a silver polishing business, Pikesville Silver and Antiques, in Baltimore, Maryland. According to an article in the March 12, 2015, Baltimore Jewish Times, "while in the Caribbean…(Jay) became well-versed in the art of silver polishing when the family's silver was constantly getting tarnished by the harsh tropical climate. Having regularly used the machinery in his manufacturing plant to polish glasses, he decided to apply the same practice to his silver. When he returned to Baltimore, he decided to make a business out of his hobby." At Pikesville Silver and Antiques, Jay did the polishing and Lila looked after the books.

When Jay retired in 2003, son, Jory, and his wife, Barbara, took over the business and ran it until they later retired and moved to Florida in 2015.

Lila Newman died on July 12, 2001, and Jay Newman on September 2, 2014. Both are buried in Baltimore, MD.

# MARSHALL AND ANITA ORAN'S STORY
Gilda Oran

**Marshall Oran, Barbados, 2016**
(Gilda Oran photo)

Marshall Oran's ancestors settled in Boston, Massachusetts, after arriving in the US from Europe. In 1980 shortly before his son, Scott's wedding, Marshall learned from a cousin that he was a Kohen.[132] In 2003 his daughter, Gilda, verified this when she went "ancestor hunting" and found the headstone of her great-grandfather, David Oransky, which identified him as "David haKohen" (i.e., David the Kohen).

In 1953 Marshall was a 21-year-old Air Force captain, just home from Korea when he met Anita Miller at a YMHA dance in Miami. It was love at first sight and they got married in Miami on June 19, 1954. Their children, Gilda and Scott, were born in Miami. Marshall worked for Alterman Transport Lines as a practical engineer, servicing the refrigeration units (ThermoKing) on their long-haul trucks.

---

[132] Descendant of Aaron, the first Jewish priest

**Marshall and Anita Oran's wedding, Miami, June 19, 1954**
(Rose Altman photo archive)

Marshall described his family as non-observant Jews – the type sometimes referred to as "Three-Day Jews, observing Rosh Hashana, Yom Kippur, and Passover."

Years ago, when Gilda asked him why they had not belonged to a synagogue, he reminded her that she had attended a synagogue preschool and that they would have joined one when Scott was closer to his Bar Mitzvah (a choice typical of many American Jews), but coming to Barbados had placed them in a warm and caring Bajan Shtetl where Friday night services were and still are the norm.

In 1963 Anita's sister, Rose, and her husband, Simon Altman, were thinking of immigrating to the US and asked Marshall if he was interested in coming to Barbados and managing their two stores, Altman's Department Store on Broad Street and the Bargain House on Swan Street. After talking it over with Anita, they decided it was a good idea, given that Marshall had gone about as far as he could at ThermoKing. In May 1963 Marshall moved to Barbados and the rest of the family followed in June.

The family's arrival coincided with the Barbados Jewish community's decision to rent "Tru-Blue," the bungalow in Rockley that subsequently became Shaare Tzedek Synagogue.

Even though Simon and Rose subsequently changed their minds about emigrating, the Orans stayed on in Barbados. Meanwhile, Marshall's mother, Sarah, moved into their home in Miami, and Simon and Rose's three eldest children, Marlene, James, and Marsha lived with her while they attended high school there.

In 1967 Sarah Oran moved to Barbados and lived with Marshall, Anita, and the children. Gilda recalled that her grandmother was "known for her brownies, her Shake n'Bake chicken, her watch dogs, Bulova and Timex, and for her ability to listen with a caring heart." Although she was older than many of the other Jewish women in the community, she made friends with them and often played Canasta with Mary Speisman, Edna Pillersdorf, Evelyn Truss, and Tony Lazar.

Marshall recalled that when Simon and Rose decided not to emigrate he had only been in Barbados a few months but he loved the island and still does. According to him, "The US was my mother; Barbados, my bride." It was around that time that "fate and destiny stepped in." Marshall recalled he had gone next door to visit Louis Speisman and was sitting on an aluminum chair when Uncle Louis said, "Nu! What ya goin' to do? You have a wife, you have two children, and you have to make a living." Marshall replied, "You know, it doesn't look too difficult to make this chair." Within three months he had produced his first chair and sold it to Simon Altman for the "massive price of $6." In fact, Rose Altman still had it until 2015 when Marshall bought it back from her. "That was the beginning of Oran Ltd. I was very fortunate the timing was correct."

Years later, after Oscar Pillersdorf and Benny Gilbert had served their terms as President of the Barbados Jewish Community, Marshall was elected to this office and served several terms. During his tenure he recalled facilitating the process by which the BJC became part of the Conservative Movement (United Synagogue for Conservative Judaism) that in turn led to the connection with Prof. Hal Blumenfeld who has been leading High Holiday services at Shaare Tzedek for the past 20 years. During Marshall's tenure, the community also brought in scholars from Israel and rabbis to convert children and women from mixed marriages.

Although acknowledging that the community has had its share of challenges and others it still faces, Marshall is optimistic. According to him, "G-d is looking after this community." He commends the current President, Jacob Hassid, for the leadership he has provided and for the work he is doing in preparing Steven Altman and his own son, Scott, to do the davening at Friday evening services.

# GROWING UP IN OUR BAJAN SHTETL
## Gilda Oran

(Gilda Oran photo)

In 1963 my parents, Marshall and Anita Oran, moved to Barbados from Miami, Florida, with my brother, Scott, and me. I was eight years old and Scott was five. My mother's sister, Auntie Rose (Altman), had been there since 1946 when our Auntie Chuma (Averbuch), who lived in Trinidad, brought her from the US and introduced her to Uncle Simon (Altman).

There are pictures of us visiting in 1959 and my father admits he fell in love with the island even then. In my memory, multiple stories circulate about how long we were supposed to remain in Barbados - long enough for Dad to ship his pick-up truck from the US; short enough for my grandmother, Sarah Oran, to move into our house in Miami. In 1967,she moved to Barbados to live with us and remained there until her passing in 1996.

But move we did! And what an adventure! I say I grew up in a shtetl, a small European village. Except for my parents and a few others, the adults in the Barbados Jewish community had emigrated from Europe, some in the 1930s, others in the 1940s. For the most part, they spoke to one another in Yiddish or Yinglish (Yiddish and English), probably with the intention of ensuring that we children would not understand. However, I did learn to understand and speak Yiddish quite proficiently (though reading it is somewhat difficult).

In the beginning we lived with Auntie Rose and Uncle Simon, along with cousins Marlene, Jimmy, Marsha, and Steven at Macabbee, the original

Altman house in Harts Gap, Christ Church. There were 10 of us, not counting the multitude of guests whom Simon and Rose often invited over.

My Altman cousins had friends of all ages who would come over and 'hang out'. The 'big kids' would congregate in the playroom on the side of the main house (later made into an apartment for Mom, Dad, Scott, and me) where there was a ping-pong table and record player.

By the early 1960s, most of the children who had either been born on the island or arrived from Europe when they were very young were then in their teens or early 20s. They graduated high school and moved either to Canada or the US to attend university and in some cases their parents had moved with them, especially to Toronto and Montreal. Within a few years of our arrival, there were only a few of us remaining: Scott and me; Annie and Ronald Karp; Jerry Kreindler; Jorge, Dan, and Martin Raizman; Abraham, Joe, Martin, and Esther Steinbok; and Irving Wajchandler. (Forgive me if I have left anyone out from that era.)

## Community Life
The World Zionist Organization played an integral part in Jewish life in Barbados, particularly in the adults' social life. About once a month (I think), they got together at someone's home to play cards and socialize. For example, the men would play poker on the patio at Auntie Mary and Uncle Louis Speisman's home while the women played Canasta over on the Altman side of the gate. We children learned to play both games in case they were short a player or someone needed to leave the table. Otherwise, we would wander around.

## Community Outings and Get-Togethers
Sundays were family day. The main place to gather was at the Aquatic Club (the current Radisson Hotel) where, after changing, everyone young and old would hang out on the beach. It was during these outings that Felicia (Lazar) Simon taught me how to swim (no idea why an eight-year-old from Florida had not learned this beforehand).

The youngsters would walk over to 'The Pot,' a cage in the ocean where hot water exited the Barbados Power and Light Company's cooling system. After swimming, we would walk along the pier where ice cream was sold. Sometimes we went to the end of the pier where there was an upstairs bar and the bartender would serve us Bentleys (lemonade and bitters) with extra cherries. Sometimes we climbed out the windows and dove into the ocean. (It is very shallow now but was much deeper in those days).

Other community outings included swimming and the buffet lunch at Sandy Lane Hotel, Paradise Beach Club, The Crane, Sam Lord's Castle, or Edgewater Hotel. I remember going to Cattlewash for lunch at the Kreindlers' and we 'young ones' driving in Aaron Truss' convertible, with the top down at full speed down the East Coast Road! And then there was lunch at the Trusses' when they lived at the bottom of Rendezvous Hill...and we would swim and then come in for lunch.

There were a few unique community outings and experiences I remember, in particular, one arranged by Uncle Aaron Karp. We all met at the Careenage and went on a daylong boat trip up the West Coast - it may have been a glass bottom boat, but it was a novel experience!

Sometimes around Passover (during the Easter school break) or in the summer, families created the bungalow experience and rented houses – either in Cattlewash or near Paradise Beach Club. One year I think there was a flu epidemic and I remember a bunch of us kids having to sleep at the Karps' house near Paradise Beach Club—I think we had cots set up in the screened-in porch and Aunt Marilyn (Karp) took care of us all.

## Shabbat and Jewish Holidays

### Friday Night Supper
Shabbat supper was always a mega-affair, with the 10 of us family members to start, along with multiple guests from all around the world. Preparations began first thing in the morning. Mrs. Keiser (Kiki), the Altmans' nanny, would make thin, square noodles, which she prepared from dough she made and rolled out on the yellow table that had been a fixture in Auntie Rose's kitchen. The dough was so thin it was almost transparent and she then cut it into small squares. There was chopped liver, eggs, and onions as an appetizer, along with chicken soup and matzah balls. We would eat all this quickly so we could be in shul by 7:30pm.

It is my understanding that before we arrived, Friday night and holiday services were held at Macabee, but my memories include only those at True Blue/Shaarei Tzedek on Rockley New Road. (It was not until 1988 that Nidhe Israel was restored. I remember the building being a dilapidated warehouse, all boarded up except when you peeked in and could see the marble floors.)

### Friday Night Services
As I remember, services were held on Friday night with men sitting on one side, women on the other, and children all over. Highlights for me were Uncle Louis Speisman's rendition of Yigdal and Mr. Lazar's Shalom Aleichem (the sounds still resonate!). Everyone attended, even if you went first to services and then out with your friends afterwards.

### Jewish Holidays

The Jewish holidays were central to our Jewish lifestyle. Services were led by whoever could daven - my memories include Uncle Simon (Altman), Uncle Louis (Speisman), Uncle Oscar (Pillersdorf), Mr. Pilarski (not sure when he left...but I remember during the Aleinu he was the first person I ever saw drop to his knees and have others help pick him up).

Of course, we children would not remain inside the shul for the entire service. Behind the main house there was an orchard with plum trees where we would run around and have plum fights. One of the most vibrant memories was of Eva Steinbok who always had a basket of food and toys for her siblings which she would share with all of us. I remember her taking us for walk up the hill (north of the house) and supervising us while we ran around up there.

## Yom Kippur

There was a rite of passage during Yom Kippur - the goal was to be willing to fast enough to be allowed to use the Limacol that was placed throughout the synagogue to 'revive' you when you felt faint. But the highlight of Yom Kippur was the Break-the-Fast afterwards - with Mrs. Truss' coffee, which she would brew in a HUGE pot and serve with brown sugar and evaporated milk. To this day, my own children ask me to make it for our after-fast get-togethers, served with thick slices of bread and butter!

## Passover

Passover was unique but now that I have been a Judaic Studies teacher all my adult life, I am amazed at how we learned none of the symbolism. In fact, I do not remember reciting the Four Questions (Mah Nishtana) or hiding the Afikomen. What stands out were the preparations. At least six weeks before the holiday, Auntie Rose would set up her raisin wine. This involved placing several cups of raisins in sugar and water and leaving it until Passover. The raisins at the bottom of the container gradually absorbed the sugar water and floated to the top. Then when they were saturated, they would sink back to the bottom. This process would repeat itself for the six-week period. The wine was sweet without being too alcoholic for us children.

Another pre-Passover preparation was ordering the matzah and other food items for the community. People would place their orders with the Altmans and when the shipment arrived, would come over to their house to pick them up.

A vivid memory is how Auntie Rose kashered her dishes for Passover. She would place a huge washtub on the kitchen floor, place a stone in it, and then pour in pots and pots of boiling water. She would then wash every dish, pot and pan. I don't remember anyone keeping kosher except the Newman family from Baltimore who imported their meat from the US. For our community, what was considered kosher meat was taking the regular meat from the butcher (remember the one in Cheapside?) and sprinkling salt on it to draw out the blood.

But the absolute most amazing part of Auntie Rose's holiday food array was her homemade gefilte fish. She would clamp her food grinder to the table and grind a variety of white fish. (Until recently, my sister-in-law, Sharon, Scott's wife, borrowed the grinder to make her version.) Auntie Rose's gefilte fish was amazing (even if it did have the thick jelly on it). And a favorite snack - schmaltz (rendered chicken fat) on matzah, sprinkled with salt (the very thought of which could clog your arteries!).

## Hebrew School (or lack thereof)
While I often have heard stories from the generation "above" me about their Hebrew school experiences, in my day there was no one around who had time or was able to teach us Hebrew. I do remember one summer Harold Saunders was home from college and taught some of us the beginning of the alef bet and to read some prayers. For the most part, we used transliterations. When it was time for Scott to study for his Bar Mitzvah, cousin Jimmy (Altman) transliterated his Haftorah and we purchased a recording for Scott to follow along and to memorize it.

## Bar Mitzvahs
To my recollection, Bar Mitzvahs had to start on Saturday morning at 6 a.m. so the service would be over in time for the adults to open their stores in Bridgetown.

## Jewish Bridgetown
The stores of the Jewish community members in Bridgetown were places where I could always find a 'family' member who would have a hug for me, a story to tell or something encouraging to say, especially when I would come back from university in Toronto or Miami, and 'do the rounds.' Included here were:
The Altman family: Altman's Department Stores on Broad Street and Swan Street
The Karp family: The London Shop
The Kreindler family: Modern Dress Shoppe
The Lazar family: on Swan Street, and
The Saunders family: Style Shoppe on upper Broad Street and Barbados Knitting and Spinning Mills

Growing up in our Bajan shtetl was an experience like no other. Often you hear stories of families who went to South America or other islands. But Barbados was unique - was it because we were allowed to practice our religion freely? I attended Queen's College, and along with some other girls who were either

Brethren or Seventh Day Adventists, were permitted to skip the morning assembly where the Lord's Prayer was always recited. Was it because the language of the land was English rather than Spanish or Dutch like the other islands? Was it because the Jewish community was an extended family, even if you weren't directly related? Whatever the reason, I believe the culture in which I was raised had a significant effect on who I am, on my Jewish practice, and on my outlook on life. As Margaret Mead said, it DOES take a village to raise a child…and the village that helped raise me was our Bajan shtetl.

## KUK AND FELA PILARSKI'S STORY
### Joseph Pilarski

**Fela and Kuk Pilarski, Toronto 1968**
(Joseph Pilarski photo)

My father was born on November 29, 1914, in Rutki, a small village near Lwów, Poland, now part of Ukraine. There were four brothers, Oscar, Bum (who was shot by the Nazis), Naftali Andrew (Kuk), and Leib. There were also six sisters. His family was poor.

My father only managed a grade four education and started working when he was 10 to help support his family. Later he worked in a hardware store in Lwów. He had a wife and two daughters who were lost during the War. As a young man, he joined the Polish army and when Poland fell he joined the Russian army. He was twice decorated for bravery in the face of enemy fire but laughed it off when he told us the stories of how he got the medals.

After the War, he returned to Lwów as an administrator, allocating apartments to survivors. He met my mom when she asked for an apartment for her family (which he provided). They were married three days later. My mom always joked that when she met my dad she couldn't even afford underwear. He used to jokingly say that was the reason he proposed.

My mom was born on December 5, 1918, in Lwów and lost her first husband to the Nazis. She had become an accountant and had a good life before the War, but when it came to Poland, she spent three years hiding in a hole they dug in the basement of their home (that was now occupied by a Polish family). They lived in daily fear of discovery - her parents, a younger sister and brother.

When my mom came to Barbados in 1958, she cried for a whole year. She was used to city life, theater, and opera in Poland, and on many occasions, told me the story lines of all the famous operas. Barbados had no theater, no opera, and no nightlife. She felt trapped. Many years later in Canada she would look back on her years in Barbados, fondly referring to them as her Camelot.

Every Wednesday night was Canasta night for the ladies, hosted on a rotating basis by all the Jewish families in Barbados (of which there were about 50 at that time). My father was a bridge lover and organized games with his playing partners, among them Mr. Hammond, the then-headmaster of Harrison College.

At parties, mixed alcoholic drinks were not served. An overused common joke was; "You want a gin and tonic?" If the answer was yes, you would be told, "Go to the Aquatic Club!"

Besides bridge, my father was keen on political debate and was an avid student of history. He read a lot and was knowledgeable about many topics despite only having a grade four education. He was also very wise. I still quote him today: "Everyone has his own truth." And "Let stupid people die stupid." On the outside he appeared austere but he was very gentle and softhearted.

Bathsheba was to us what Florida is to Canadians. It was a long trip and we would go there on special occasions. Sometimes Oscar and Edna would rent a cottage and sometimes we would visit the Kreindlers who also had a cottage there. On one occasion, we were a procession of three cars going to Bathsheba and we stopped to take a break. My father looked back at the cars of Leib, Oscar, and ours and said, "I wonder what our father would say if he saw us like this, each with his own car?" Three years after Richard and I went to Canada to study, our father sold everything in Barbados, just when he was starting to make a lot of money. He said what good was the money if our family was not together.

Looking back at our time in Barbados, it was indeed our Camelot. There is a popular song called "Beautiful Barbados" and in it a line that says: "You'll find rest, you'll find peace in Barbados..." And we did.

# *JOSEPH PILARSKI'S STORY*

(Joseph Pilarski photo)

My family lived in Wroclaw, Poland. My father, Andrew, was the president of a conglomerate that he created for the Polish government and my mother, Felicia, was the Vice President of the state-run chimney-sweeping services.

I was born in Wroclaw in 1947, preceded by my elder brother, Richard, who is 14 months older. Our younger brother, Alex, was born in 1953. My father liked to name his children after great men. Richard was named after the Lion Heart, I after Stalin, and Alex after Alexander the Great.

We had a beautiful apartment in Poland and my father had a chauffeured limo at his disposal. One of his company's enterprises were amusement parks so there was a lot of weekend fun for us children and we were treated like royalty by the staff.

In my early childhood, I became an avid stamp collector. The first memories I have of Barbados are the beautiful stamps that I got from the letters we received from my father's eldest brother, Oscar Pillersdorf. Because Pillersdorf was hard to pronounce in Polish, my father changed our name to Pilarski.

My father had turned down many requests by Oscar to join him in Barbados, as we were very comfortable in Poland. However, when the Russians invaded Hungary in 1956, he saw the writing on the wall and shortly after, accepted Oscar's invitation to visit. My father and I arrived in Barbados in April 1957

on the Boeing "Whispering Giant." The trip from Warsaw via London, Greenland, and Bermuda took 44 hours.

As I recall, the Barbados airport was just a row of green wooden barracks. Our ride from the airport in Oscar's car, a navy Vauxhall, took us through sugar cane fields as my uncle briefly explained the sugar cane industry. At that time sugar was still the island's principal industry and Great Britain bought all its output.

We arrived at my uncle's house, a white three-bedroom bungalow on Rockley New Road and there waiting for us was my father's younger brother, Leib, and his wife, Fanny. For the first time, I heard my father being called "Kuk" the name by which he was known in his family. We were also greeted by my uncle and aunt's two black maids. I had never seen a black person before our brief stop in Bermuda. I remember one of the maids, Beckles, preparing my bed for me. At one point when she used her chin to fold a white sheet I fully expected to see a black smudge on the sheet.

My mother and brothers joined us a year later in April 1958. My father and I were already living on our own in a rented three-bedroom aquamarine bungalow called "Lochdale" and Oscar had set up my father in his own store, The Royal Store, on High Street in Bridgetown.

**Richard, Joseph, and Alex Pilarski,
Barbados, ca. 1958**
(Joseph Pilarski photo)

When my family arrived on the Polish ship, "Batory," the deep-water harbour did not exist so small boats brought them to the arrival terminal.

School was a priority and so I spent my summer at Mrs. Jones' private prep school before being admitted to Harrison College, an all-boys' school of some 700 students. Richard caught up on his English at the Barbados Academy before joining me at Harrison College in 1959.

**Joseph, Fela, Kuk, Richard, and Alex,
Barbados, 1960**
(Joseph Pilarski photo)

We both represented our school in track and field (shot putt) and I also represented the school in swimming and water polo.

Our daily routine as a family was this: Around 8 AM my father drove us to school, then went on to open the store. We would stay in school until 3:30 PM and then walk to the store and hang out until closing time. At 5 PM we all went home together for dinner. Traffic was horrible even then. Apparently, Barbados was already famous for having more cars per mile of road than any other country in the world. When we got home, dinner would be ready and the table set. Our meals consisted of salad, vegetables and rice with a shrimp or chicken curry, the simple local one with curry powder, not the sophisticated East Indian type.

Most middle-class households could afford a staff of four helpers: a cook, cleaner, gardener and chauffeur. Usually the cook or cleaner was provided with living quarters. At that time labor rates for most household jobs were $6 Barbados per week. While that sounds like very little, most Bajans lived rent free, in a one-room wooden house with no electricity or running water. Food was cheap - cou cou (cornmeal) and stew with black eye peas and breadfruit or squash. Alternatively, there was salt fish and rice. With rice at 10c per pound, $6 went a long way. Fruit was free (from the trees) and included banana, paw paw (papaya), mango, golden apple, local cherries, aki (Guinep), local plums, coconut, etc.

The only other expense was clothes. The most expensive clothes served the dual role of wedding and funeral attire. Bajans were big on funerals and saved all their lives for a huge taxi procession when the time came.

Saturday was the busiest day at the store so we all went together to help. Stores closed by 1pm – loosely enforced by the police. We did a lot of business with last-minute shoppers with the doors officially closed. On Saturdays we did three to five times the volume of the preceding week. All the country folk would come to town to shop. Their wallets consisted of a length of cloth that was tied in knots. In between the knots were coins of different denominations. When paying for goods they would patiently untie one knot at a time until the required amount sat on the counter.

I was usually in charge of the shoe department. I remember one Saturday a countrywoman wanted a pair of shoes in size 8. I couldn't find it so as a joke I brought her two size fours - a joke that gave me my first life customer. Every Saturday she would bring a new friend and ask her to order size 8 shoes!

Sunday was "beach day" for the whole Jewish community. We would all meet at the Paradise Beach Club or in later years at the Aquatic Club. I remember one year some high waves hit the shore and threw the bathers violently onto the beach. A scary moment followed by a surreal comic scene of the ladies of our community wandering dazed on the beach with their one-piece bathing suits at their ankles!

# SHELDON AND LAURELL SALCMAN'S STORY
### Interviewed by Simon Kreindler, Barbados, May 2016

**Laurell and Sheldon Salcman, 2016**
(Laurell Salcman photo)

The Salcmans came to Barbados from Toronto, Canada. Shelly, an Orthodox Jew, is a lawyer and property developer with business interests in many countries. In 2013 he set up an international business corporation in Barbados because he liked the island's extensive network of tax treaties. Having business interests and children living in several countries, he and his wife, Laurell, spend a lot of time travelling. It was therefore important for them to be in a place with a good communications network and from where it would be easy to travel to Canada, Europe, and elsewhere.

On their first visit to the island, they went to Big B (now Massy Stores Supermarket in Worthing) and the first item they saw when they walked through the door was Sabra-brand hummus. Shelly turned to Laurell and said, "It's a sign that we'll be ok, don't worry!" Originally, one of their biggest concerns was whether they would be able to find kosher food in Barbados, but they soon found this would not be a problem. Although they sometimes bring some kosher cheese and bread with them from North America, they have found an enormous number of kosher products on the island. Shelly contrasts the situation with Martinique where they have good friends whom they frequently visit. There everything is brought in from Europe and none have hechshers (Kosher Certification). At Massy many of the products come from the United States, and it's easy to pick up kosher bagels, cream cheese, yogurt, etc.

Shelly notes that PriceMart, which is partly owned by Costco and has stores throughout the Caribbean and South America, carries many of Costco's Kirkland products, including pizza crusts complete with pizza sauce, pasta, eggs, etc. One of the few concerns he had early on was finding kosher milk because milk is often not 100% pure cow's milk. As it turned out, Pine Hill Dairy's milk is, and Shelly appreciates the strict regulations and controls the island imposes on this industry.

Shelly says his routine in Barbados is always the same. He gets up in the morning, says his prayers, then goes to the office for the day. When he comes home, he and Laurel have dinner and then they relax. In this respect, evenings in Barbados are different from other places like Jerusalem, Toronto, or New York where there is always something going on in the evening. In Barbados, there is nothing to do in the evening.

Laurel has enjoyed the adjustment to living in Barbados. Waking up to the sound of the sea and surf is part of her rejuvenation from an otherwise busy lifestyle involving frequent travel. She fills her free time with exercise classes and seeing friends. In a relatively short time Shelly says he and Laurell have come to feel welcomed and integrated. Because there is little else to do in the evening, they often socialize with friends for coffee or dinner.

The fact that there have been Jews on the island since the 1650s gives the Salcmans a feeling of continuity, and as Shelly says, "It feels good to be part of a community that has this history." He expresses great respect for the Jewish community because he recognizes it is not easy to be Jewish in Barbados, certainly compared to many other places in North America.

## GOLDIE SPIELER'S STORY
Adapted by Simon Kreindler from Goldie's book, "Becoming No Ordinary Pottery - The Story of Earthworks Pottery"
(with additional information from Internet sources)

**Dave and Goldie Spieler at Earthworks Pottery, Barbados, 2016**
(Goldie Spieler photo)

Goldie Leiken was born in 1932 and grew up on a small dairy farm outside Ottawa. Her father, Harry Leiken, was a Russian immigrant who in 1936 became the founding president of the Agudath Israel Synagogue in Ottawa.

After completing high school, Goldie studied art at the Ontario College of Art in Toronto, and after returning home, met Ted Spieler. He was originally from New Jersey and operated a family-run, wholesale grocery business, Universal Confectionery, in Ottawa. Goldie and Ted married in February 1955 and their son, Dave, was born in 1959.

In 1966 Ted suffered a massive heart attack and died suddenly. His family had never cared for Goldie and showed her little sympathy or support. Her own friends, however, were very caring and one couple even invited Dave and her to spend Christmas and New Year's with them at their rented housekeeping cottage in Barbados.

That brief visit was life-changing for Goldie. She fell in love with the island and she and Dave returned the following year for six months. Dave started school in Barbados and Goldie started painting again. After a brief return visit to Ottawa, Goldie decided to make Barbados her home and the simultaneous offer of a job teaching art at Queens College in Bridgetown sealed her decision.[133]

In 1968 Goldie purchased an acre of land high up on Shop Hill, St. Thomas, overlooking the Caribbean. It was an area of the island that had always appealed to her artistic instincts and she was happy to be able to design her own home that she named "Shalom."

Goldie was first and foremost a water colourist and tapestry-maker. Her interest in pottery came only later and stemmed from her curiosity about the items Bajan artisans were making that she could use at home. After several visits to Chalky Mount in St. Andrew, she realized that the small group of potters working there were carrying on traditions that had come down to them from ancestors who were brought to the island from Africa as slaves more than 300 years earlier. Unfortunately, none of the younger generation of Chalky Mount men had any interest in learning the craft.

Recognizing that the demise of the Chalky Mount pottery would be a major cultural loss for Barbados, Goldie built and equipped a studio adjacent to her house with the assistance of several knowledgeable friends and arranged with one of the senior Chalky Mount potters, Clement Devonish, to start using it. Unfortunately, the kiln was not able to achieve the required temperatures to fire the clay, and while Goldie and Dave were on vacation in Israel, Clement left and returned to Chalky Mount.

Goldie set about trying get funding to establish a facility to train local potters. Because Chalky Mount was so remote, she wanted to set it up on her property in St Thomas. CADEC[134] liked her idea but ultimately chose to locate the new facility at Chalky Mount and brought in a trained US potter to run it.

While construction slowly dragged on, Goldie invited the new director, Bob Lanman, to stay at "Shalom" and he asked permission to use her studio to start training the students. This proved to be a fortuitous development as Bob and his students built a proper kiln capable of high-temperature firing.

It was in the process of watching this first group of students and with encouragement from Bob that Goldie made her first pinch pot – a tentative effort that launched her on an entirely new career and gave birth to Earthworks Pottery in 1983.

---

[133] Goldie later taught art at St. Winifred's School, Codrington High School, and Harrison College.
[134] Christian Action for Development in the Eastern Caribbean

In late 1981 Goldie was staying with her father in Ottawa while recuperating from bunion surgery. He had apparently been feeling increasingly disillusioned with Goldie's failure to become financially independent and resented her repeatedly turning to him to bail her out when she could not pay her bills. In the course of a seemingly trivial exchange about the death of a movie star she had long admired, her father exploded and called her a parasite! Goldie was devastated and returned to Barbados feeling deeply depressed.

Searching for answers, she began attending Sunday morning services at St. James Methodist Church with her old friends, the Blanchettes. Reflecting on her life she realized that even though her father was a highly-respected member of their synagogue in Ottawa and a pillar of the Jewish community, she had never felt moved by Judaism the way she now felt moved or cared for by the church. By February 1982, she felt she had been "fully adopted into the Family of God" and knew Jesus cared for her. In fact, his caring had given her the strength and confidence she needed to support herself and not have to ask her father for anything ever again. Jesus had brought her back to Judaism with pride in the bloodline she had wanted to walk away from in 1982 and her faith had increased her desire to connect with Israel. Becoming a "Messianic/ Completed Jew" now connected her even more closely to G-d.

The growth of Earthworks Pottery progressed slowly but steadily over the next several years. In 1989 Dave gave up his full-time teaching position at Harrison College and joined Earthworks. At the time, Goldie was feeling overwhelmed with all the administrative chores, in addition to being the pottery's creative force. Combining their respective skills proved a good move, and not long after, they decided to expand the physical plant to make more room for storage, work space, glazing, displays, and retail sales. Dave introduced new product lines and equipment, and made Earthworks more efficient. He improved their marketing and created colourful brochures that were placed on the activity desks of the island's many hotels. Sales increased and more staff was hired.

In 1996 Goldie was awarded the Ernst and Young Entrepreneur of the Year Award, an honour that validated her ability to be self-sustaining and simultaneously contribute to the preservation of the island's pottery tradition.

Goldie and Dave have been members in good standing of the Barbados Jewish community since 2000. In 2006 Goldie decided to act on a long-held desire to make aliyah[135] and purchased an apartment in Jerusalem. She now spends several months there each year. Dave, his wife, Shawna, and their two children

---

[135] To make Aliyah is to become a new immigrant to Israel. Goldie began visiting Israel in the 1960s and after many visits finally made aliyah in 2006.

now live at "Shalom." Goldie built a smaller house for herself on the property and is now Earthwork's emeritus potter!

# ORIAL AND ANTHONY SPRINGER'S STORY
Orial Springer

**Orial and Anthony Springer, Barbados, May 2016**
(Simon Kreindler photo)

Anthony and I were both raised in Christian families - he was Catholic and I was Evangelical. I converted to Catholicism after marrying him in 1985. We both served on the Barbados Christian Counsel's Marriage Encounter and were trained counsellors.

Both of us were troubled by questions for which Christianity had no answers or offered answers that made no sense (such as the issue of life after death). Anthony lost interest in Catholicism and felt he was lacking something spiritually. He embarked on a search of other religions and came to feel that Judaism was the only one that followed all of God's commandments. It was also a way of life. He became acquainted with Stephen Miller, a convert and member of the Barbados Jewish community, who recommended that he consult Rabbi Bernhard Pressler in Miami about his interest in converting.

I noticed a positive change in Anthony after he started visiting the synagogue and began his Skype sessions with the rabbi. My curiosity led me to start sitting in and participate in his intense weekly Skype sessions. Every week Rabbi Pressler tested us on all aspects of Jewish history and our reading of the prayers in Hebrew. We also had to explain why we wanted to convert to Judaism.

At the end of months of rigorous preparation, we flew to Miami with Shirley Ramjit, Vimla Haynes, and Stephen Miller, Jr., where we were questioned on our knowledge of Judaism and subsequently converted in the presence of three rabbis. Anthony and I were remarried and took new names, Anthony (Joshua) and I (Ruth).

Christianity teaches that if you are not Christian, you are doomed to eternal torture, a belief I always found troubling. My grandfather and my best friend were not Christians, but they were kind and good individuals. It really bothered me that God would sentence them to eternal suffering because they chose not to be Christians. Judaism, on the other hand, stresses the importance of our relationship with God and with each other.

Nothing could have prepared us for the difference between how Jews react to non-Jewish visitors to their synagogue and how Christians respond to non-Christians coming to their church. Christians are eager to welcome you into their fold but Jews are the extreme opposite. There were times when we felt invisible and often unwelcome. We even thought we were victims of racism. However, as we consistently attended synagogue, our opinion changed. Just like Naomi tried to dissuade Ruth from converting, Jews follow this practice because of the inherent challenge of being a Jew. As we continued going to the synagogue, our opinion and outlook changed. Not only were we welcomed with warmth but I was eventually elected the first Black secretary of the Barbados Jewish Community.

Everyone is now supportive of me, as evidenced by our strong attendance at and participation in the monthly potluck dinners which I organized to boost attendance and by the weekly emails I receive from members giving feedback on articles that I share.

Anthony, Shirley, Vimla, Stephen Jr., and I can truly say that we have an awesome community.

# CHAPTER 7
## Some Notable People and Interesting Events that Impacted the Barbados Jewish community

**Errol Walton Barrow (1920-1987)**
Barbados' first Prime Minister and his possible Jewish roots
**Simon Kreindler and Internet sources**

Errol Barrow served in the Royal Air Force during World War II and after the War studied law in England. He returned to Barbados in 1950 and was elected to the Barbados Parliament in 1951 as a member of the Barbados Labour Party (BLP).

In 1955 Barrow founded the Democratic Labour Party as a progressive alternative to the BLP. He became its leader in 1958 and the party won the parliamentary election in 1961. Barrow served as Premier of Barbados from 1961 until 1966 when, after leading the country to independence from Great Britain, he became Prime Minister. He served continuously in that capacity as well as stints as Minister of Finance and Minister of Foreign Affairs for the next ten years.

During his tenure, the DLP government accelerated industrial development, expanded the tourist industry to reduce the island's economic dependence on sugar, introduced National Health Insurance and Social Security, and expanded free education to all levels.

After another landslide victory in 1971, the DLP returned to the electorate in 1976 for a mandate after two years of bitter controversy over constitutional amendments put forth by the government. A general economic downturn that affected most countries in the hemisphere contributed to a shift in public sentiment and the party was defeated.

In May 1986 after 10 years in opposition, Barrow was re-elected as Prime Minister in a landslide victory in which the DLP won 24 of 27 seats in the House of Assembly. A year after his re-election, Barrow collapsed and died at his home on June 1, 1987.

Barrow was a friend of many of the island's Jews and a staunch supporter of the State of Israel. For years he claimed to have Jewish roots and, as noted earlier in this book, often quipped about the connection between his success and his Jewish ancestry.

Barrow claimed he was a descendant of the Baruch Lousadas, a Jewish family whose roots go back to pre-Inquisition Portugal. He also claimed that his great-grandfather, Simon Barrow, who was buried in the Nidhe Israel Cemetery had changed his name from Baruch to Barrow. These claims remain to be verified.

In 2016 two Barrow gravestones were uncovered during excavation work for the Synagogue Block Redevelopment Project that may have some relevance to Barrow's claim. One stone is inscribed "Sarah Barrow, widow of Joseph Barrow who departed this life on the 19th March 1814" and the other "Sacred to the memory of Sarah, wife of Haim Barrow, who departed this life the 12th of September 1823."

# THE BENDAS OF ISLINGTON, ENGLAND
## The Jewish Ancestry of Genevieve Adams, Widow of Former Prime Minister Tom Adams
### Genevieve Adams

**Tom and Genevieve Adams 1977**
(James Altman photo)

My great-great-grandfather, Anton Benda, son of Saligman Benda of Bavaria, arrived in London in 1846. He was a merchant in the City of London, importing Oriental goods, mainly from Japan.

In 1853 he married Frances Mandelbaum, the daughter of David Mandelbaum of Bavaria. Their marriage in London was officiated by the Chief Rabbi.

In 1855 Anton became a naturalized British citizen and declared himself to have been "a loyal subject of the King of Bavaria" prior to taking British citizenship. Anton and his wife, Frances, had eight children; the eldest, Sigmund, was my great-grandfather.

Sigmund "married out" in 1885 to Annie McNicoll and they had two sons, Douglas (my grandfather) and George.

Douglas married my maternal grandmother, Edith Ada Winder, in 1901 and they had one child, a daughter, Hazel Edith, who was my mother. Douglas Benda may have been an early example of British Jews who fought in the First World War in a regular, i.e., not specifically Jewish, army division. He suffered from being gassed in that war and died a few years later in 1924, leaving my grandmother a single working mother for the rest of her life.

My mother, Hazel Edith Benda, married Philip Turner in 1937 and they had two daughters, Genevieve and Antonia. I, Genevieve, met and married Tom Adams when we were both working at the BBC in London. In 1963 we came to live in Barbados and 13 years later he became Prime Minister.

The first generation of Bendas born in England had settled in Islington, North London, and later ran their import business from a large extended family home in the same area of North London. The numerous family members remained scattered over a relatively small area of North London for many years.

Recently I finally managed to connect with a surviving third cousin, descended from Dudley, the youngest son of Anton and Frances Benda, and even now he is living in Watford just on the northern edge of London. However, he is not importing Oriental goods!

I believe that Benda is originally a Czech name and therefore it is reasonable to assume that they had emigrated to Bavaria (then a separate nation) from Czechoslovakia before making their way to England. As far as I can tell, they appear to have been economic migrants rather than fleeing from any specific persecution.

# ISRAEL BRODIE, CHIEF RABBI OF THE UK (1948-1965) AND MRS. BRODIE, VISIT BARBADOS
Simon Kreindler and Internet sources

**Rabbi and Mrs. Brodie on arrival in Barbados.
L to R: Aron Karp, Mrs. Brodie, Sidney Spira, Bunia Korn,
Rabbi Brodie, Geoffrey Lebens, Oscar Pillersdorf, and Lazar Spira**
(Anne Karp Zeplowitz photo)

Israel Brodie, Chief Rabbi of the United Kingdom from 1948-1965, and Mrs. Brodie visited Barbados in the late 1950s. Leah Pillersdorf Gilbert remembers her parents entertaining them at their home on Rendevouz Ridge when she was a teen. Rabbi Brodie later officiated at her marriage to Benny Gilbert in London in 1965.

Israel Brodie was educated at Balliol College, Oxford. He served as Rabbi of the Melbourne Hebrew Congregation in Australia from 1923-1937 and was influential in establishing the Zionist Federation of Australia in 1927. During WWII, he was evacuated from Dunkirk and finished the War as Senior Jewish Chaplain, aka, Forces Rabbi. Brodie became Chief Rabbi of the United Kingdom soon after WWII ended and faced a difficult time when the British Mandate in Palestine came to an end. A dignified man of great presence, he was regarded as a mellifluous preacher. He had impeccable English connections and was a freemason, rising to the senior appointment of 'Grand Chaplain' in the United Grand Lodge of England.

Through the Conference of European Rabbis, which he founded and led, Brodie took a significant part in rebuilding the religious life of European Jewry after the Holocaust. He undertook a number of tours throughout the Commonwealth, and strengthened the community in a quiet but significant manner, although the closing years of his tenure were overshadowed by religious dispute. Brodie banned Rabbi Dr. Louis Jacobs from becoming principal of Jews' College after he questioned the Orthodox notion that the Bible had been written by the hand of God. On his retirement, Brodie was knighted "for services to British Jewry," the first Chief Rabbi to be so honoured, even though his predecessor was appointed to the restricted membership of the Order of the Companions of Honour.

# MEMORIES OF HURRICANE JANET, SEPTEMBER 22, 1955
### Simon Kreindler and Internet sources

Any Bajan who was more that a very young child in 1955 probably remembers the arrival of Hurricane Janet that smashed into the south coast of the island the morning of Thursday, September 22nd. Packing winds of 125 mph, it flattened homes, uprooted trees, knocked out electricity, and crippled communications. Thirty-eight people lost their lives, more than 2,000 were left homeless, and the island suffered $5 million in damages.

The Royal Theatre in Worthing was destroyed and one observer describing the hotels in the Hastings area noted, "Verandahs were piled high with sand....and fish were floating in the flooded ground floor lounges. The restaurant at the Royal-on-Sea Hotel in Hastings that had been built on piers in the (ocean) vanished and the hotel was left roofless. The manager's beautiful bungalow had shifted on its foundations and the roof lay shattered in the middle of the street. Further up the road I saw the home of a distinguished merchant completely cut in two as if from bomb damage."[136]

**Hanna Templer Abramowitz** remembers that morning when "the quiet was shattered by the sound of a loudspeaker on a passing truck advising people to turn on their radios to hear the warnings of a hurricane that was about to strike the island. Next day heavy rains began and Hurricane Janet struck Barbados, causing millions of dollars of damage. Electric power was disrupted, the sugar cane crop was severely damaged, and poorly built buildings were blown away by winds of well over 200 km/hour. Highways were blocked, the airport was forced to close, and more than 50 people were killed. Although we were lucky not to be injured, we were greatly affected as we lived across the road from Rockley Beach.

---

[136] Winifred K. O'Mahony, http://www.britishempire.co.uk/article/hurricanejanet.htm

"Roseview," the Templers' home and "Grandview,"
their neighbours' home, after Hurricane Janet
(Hanna Templer Abramowitz photos)

**The Royal Theatre, Worthing, Christ Church, after Hurricane Janet**
(Hanna Templer Abramowitz photo)




**The Royal Hotel, Hastings, after Hurricane Janet**
(Hanna Templer Abramowitz photo)

**The Royal Hotel, Hastings, Christ Church, after Hurricane Janet**
(Hanna Templer Abramowitz photo)

**Leah Pillersdorf Gilbert** remembers her uncle, Henry Altman, and his son, Paul, coming to their home for the duration of the hurricane. "My mother put mattresses in the hall and the children were supposed to stay there. My father tied a rope to the handle of the glass-panelled front door, then to the leg of the piano, and then to the handle of the kitchen door. We children thought it was great fun!

At one point the chattel house in back of us folded like a pack of cards and the entire roof sailed into our verandah and down the steps. It really was a miracle it didn't break the glass in the same door to which the rope was tied.

After the storm passed, we went next door to Paul's house to see if there was any damage. The roof had leaked and the chandelier was full of water and dead beetles. We promptly named it beetle soup!"

**Louis Burak** remembers, "We left our house and went to stay with the Spiras. Their house had shutters so we thought that we would be safe there. The Konigsbergs were also there. We peeked out through the shutters and saw the Royal Theatre collapse. When the storm was over, we returned home to find that our house had not sustained any damage."

**Robbie Saunders** was six years old when the Hurricane hit Barbados. "I remember Fanny and Leib Pillersdorf and family came to stay at our house in Garden Gap. Florence and I were very excited but scared. I also remember looking out the window just in time to see our next-door neighbour's roof go flying off, carried by the strong wind. We were told later that they were all huddled under their dining room table."

**Rachel Pillersdorf Weisman** was nine when Janet struck. She remembers when "Paul, Henry, and Deborah (Altman) moved into our house, next door to theirs. We also had our maids and gardener with us.

All the rooms of our house opened off a central hallway. Mattresses were placed on the floor of the hall and all the bedroom doors were closed. The end of the hall opened onto our living and dining room. Before the hurricane hit, large wooden planks were nailed across each bank of windows in every room.

We had a baby grand piano in the living room. There was rope tied to the patio door that was wrapped around the piano's legs. When the hurricane hit, it took everyone in the house to hold onto the rope in order to prevent the patio door from pulling open.

Across the field behind our house was a row of three chattel houses. I remember seeing the roof of the first one being lifted off and dropping onto the field in front of it. Then the walls fell out and finally a family ran out and into the second house. A similar thing happened to the second house, and when its walls fell, I remember seeing someone still sitting on the toilet! The two families then ran into the third house. This one held or perhaps the worst of the wind was by then over.

The rest of the time we children spent playing or sleeping on the mattresses.

The next day we went to investigate the damage to Uncle Henry's house. I don't remember much except that the crystal chandelier over the dining table that consisted of a bowl with crystals hanging from it was full of water and beetles. We declared it 'beetle soup" and thought that was very funny."

**Betty Konigsberg Feinberg** remembers being awakened by a siren at 3 or 4 AM and then Redifusion coming on air much earlier than normal. "At first there was just rain. My father and I went downtown to board up his store the best we could. On the way home, we tried to pick up some milk and bread but the stores were already pretty empty.

Because our home had many windows and no shutters, my parents were reluctant to stay there so our family, the Pasters, Buraks, and Zierlers all went to the Spiras' home that did have shuttered windows. When we got there, it was about 10:30 or 11 AM and the wind was already so strong we could hardly close the car door or get up the Spiras' front stairs. Before long, the wind started howling and it was quite disturbing especially for Ellen who was only eight years old at the time and could not understand what was going on.

The strong winds continued for several hours, then died down in the afternoon. When we finally could get outside, the Royal Theatre on the Worthing Main Road, directly behind the Spiras' home, had been blown to bits. We had earlier seen parts of the red velvet curtains that covered the stage flying around and now we could see uprooted seats from the theatre scattered everywhere.

When we left the Spiras to return home, their yard and the street were covered with sand that the wind had blown inland from Worthing Beach. Getting home was problematic because there was lots of debris from fallen trees and branches everywhere. When we finally got there, we found someone's chattel house in our backyard - pots, pans, and even a man's shaving stuff!"

**Dorothy Burak Rosenthal's** memories of Janet were somewhat different. "Not at all scary but rather exciting. My parents closed up our home as best they could and we all got into the car and drove to the Spiras' home. The Spiras had shutters on their windows whereas we did not so there was more protection at their house.

Mr and Mrs. Spira were away on a trip and Sydney was at home alone. The Konigsberg family also went to the Spiras' as did others. To me, it was an exciting adventure. It was so much fun being with the other kids. We played and entertained ourselves while the adults spent their time together, probably worrying.

I remember looking out the window as the tall coconut trees flipped back and forth from side to side touching the ground, left then right like a blade of grass, not a tall mighty tree.

And then there was the amazing sight of the roof of the Royal Theatre, a block away, lifting off, piece by piece, and blowing away. Then the walls started falling. It was unbelievable. Scary and astonishing to see the building where we had seen so many movies just fall apart.

After the hurricane passed, we went outside to see the damage. There was no damage to the house. The cars that had been parked outside were also fine but all around there was destruction, damaged homes, fallen trees, broken roofs and fences, and most amazing of all, thick sand all over the streets blocks away from the ocean.

When we arrived home, happily the only damage was a broken fence. We were lucky for many other people had suffered greatly."

**Ellen Konigsberg Schapiro:** "I was eight years old when Hurricane Janet hit the island. Although I was very young, I have very vivid and distinct memories of that frightening experience. For me, the story of Hurricane Janet began the night before the hurricane actually hit the island.

I was outside watching my father water the flowers in the front garden, which was something that he did almost every night. One specific thing stood out for me that night. It was a very hot, humid, and dense evening. The clouds were darker than usual and hung low in the sky. The island was completely still. The usual breeze was absent and not a leaf moved on the trees. My father told me that when the weather changed like this, it was often because something was brewing in the atmosphere that could mean bad weather was on the way.

A short while later I remember standing at the kitchen door facing our backyard that was enclosed by a wall. It seemed to me that there were hundreds of birds perched on the wall. I had never seen this before. It was explained to me that when there was turbulence in the ocean, birds tend to fly inland.

In the middle of the night our family was awakened by very loud knocking at the front door. When my father opened the door, he found Mrs. Burak standing there soaking wet. Heavy rains had already started falling and she was in a complete panic. She told my father that we were expecting a hurricane and urged him to start preparing accordingly.

My father immediately drove to his store on Swan Street to board it up. When he returned home, I remember him climbing up on a ladder, and with my sister, Betty's help, sealing the windows of our house with cardboard and newspapers. The windows needed to be protected to prevent the glass from splintering, and the wind from entering and destroying the house. My mother was in the house preparing for evacuation. I remember feeling very frightened by the scene unfolding in front of me.

We then drove to the Spiras' house that was supposedly sturdier and had windows with shutters (unlike our house which only had glass windows). I remember that the Burak and Zierler families were also at the Spira house.

The second most frightening experience that night occurred at the Spiras' home. My mother and sister got out of the car and went into the house. By the time my father came around to get me, the winds had already increased and the car started to shake from side to side. My father was trying to pull the car door open towards him but the wind kept pushing the car door back in. I will never forget the look of sheer panic and terror on my father's face as he struggled with the door and the wind. He finally got the door open, picked me up, and ran into the house. Inside, he walked around with a plastic tablecloth folded under his arm that I later learned he had planned to use to cover me in case we had to run out of the house.

Another memory that stands out in my mind was peeking through the shutters with Betty and seeing the curtains and chairs from Royal Theater (located behind the Spira house) sailing through the air. That night I slept between my mother and father. I remember hearing the house creaking and feeling the plaster falling on our heads from the ceiling. The next day we returned home. The drive took a long time because the streets were covered with sand from the high ocean waves that brought it inland, and also, large trees had fallen and lay in the middle of the road.

When we finally got home, we were shocked to see our house. It had been white when we left it but now was an ugly shade of green because the wind had blasted it with grass and leaves. Thank goodness, the house was in pretty good condition, except for my parents' flooded room. Apparently, a cement block had landed on the roof and fallen into their bedroom. We realized later that the cement block had come from our neighbour's house. In our backyard, we also found this same neighbour's toothbrush, shaving utensils, some clothing and a toilet seat!

I don't remember much after the storm except that it took the island a considerable time to rebuild. Although Hurricane Janet touched down on the island 61 years ago, and I was only a very young child, it made an indelible impact on my life. It is a memory and experience I will never forget."

# THE REBBE AND HIS EMISSARIES
Simon Kreindler, James Altman, Larry Rosenthal, and Aaron Truss

The Rebbe, Menachem Mendel Schneerson[137]
and his emissary, Rabbi Pesach Bogomilsky

"In 1959 the Rebbe sent Rabbi Shmuel Pesach Bogomilsky to the Caribbean in order to help strengthen the islands' Jewish communities. Upon landing at the airport in Barbados, Rabbi Bogomilsky met an *estranged Jew* who sought to develop a relationship with the Rebbe. Little did he know that this one small connection would lead to some very big achievements".

The above quote is from a Chabad Lubavitch video[138] in which Rabbi Bogomilsky recalled his initial visit to Barbados in 1959. Louis Speisman was the "estranged Jew" who met him at the airport and I presume Rabbi Bogomilsky referred to him as "estranged" because Louis had told him he "didn't wear tfillin; didn't keep Shabbos; and didn't keep kosher."

---

[137] Menachem Mendel Schneerson (April 5, 1902 – June 12, 1994), known to many as the Rebbe, was a Russian Empire-born American Orthodox Jewish rabbi, and the last Lubavitcher Rebbe. He is considered one of the most influential Jewish leaders of the 20th century. As leader of the Chabad Lubavitch movement, he took an insular Hasidic group that almost came to an end with the Holocaust and transformed it into one of the most influential movements in world Jewry, with an international network of over 3,000 educational and social centers. The institutions he established include kindergartens, schools, drug-rehabilitation centers, care-homes for the disabled, and synagogues. Schneerson's published teachings fill more than 300 volumes and he is noted for his contributions to Jewish continuity and religious thought, as well as his wide-ranging contributions to traditional Torah scholarship. He is recognized as the pioneer of Jewish outreach. Google search

[138] The video was brought to the author's attention by Larry Rosenthal who saw it at the Montreal Torah Centre (Chabad) in Hampstead, Quebec, in the summer of 2016. The video was part of a presentation about the Rebbe's early efforts to spread Yiddishkeit in the Caribbean through the emissaries he sent there.

Apparently, towards the end of his visit, Louis asked Rabbi Bogomilsky if he would mention him to the Rebbe because the Rebbe could "pull (him) out of this (estranged state)." Louis would later travel to Brooklyn, stay with Rabbi Bogomilsky's parents, and have an audience with the Rebbe, a meeting that led to a long correspondence between them.

In subsequent years Rabbi Bogomilsky visited Barbados many times usually with an associate/assistant rabbi. They always stayed with the Speismans and took the opportunity to raise funds for Chabad Lubavitch. In order for them to have kosher milk, Simon and Rose Altman borrowed a cow from a Mr. Reid, a Bajan gentleman who lived near the Altmans on Harts Gap, and tethered it in the Speismans' backyard. The rabbis would milk the cow themselves. Ironically, Mr. Reid had befriended Moses Altman (Simon's father) when he first came to Barbados and would take him on the bar of his bicycle when he first began working as a peddler.

Jimmy Altman recounted how, after he learned to drive his parents' car, he would take the rabbis to the beach at the Hilton Hotel for an early morning swim so they could wash away some of the grime they accumulated wearing their traditional black suits all day long.

**Clipping from the Barbados Advocate, July 25, 1961, describing Rabbis Bogomilsky and Swved's hope to "reawaken interest in Judaism in the island's Jewish population."**
(Newspaper clipping courtesy of James Altman)

In 1961 Rabbi Bogomilsky and Rabbi Chaim Swved attended Jimmy's Bar Mitzvah in Barbados.

**Rabbis Swved and Bogomilsky with other guests at Jimmy Altman's Bar Mitzvah, Barbados 1961**
(Anne Karp Zeplowitz photo)

In the Chabad Lubavitch video referred to above, Rabbi Bogomilsky noted that (in 1961) there were 18 Jewish males in Barbados who had not had a "kosher" circumcision. In due course, a mohel was brought in to address this matter and the ritual was carried out in Louis Speisman's home.

With one possible exception, the boys had previously been circumcised by their family physicians. Joe Truss was 12 years old at the time and recalled, "One by one, in order of decreasing age, we entered the cutting room, not knowing what was going to happen. We were asked to drop our pants and with what seemed like an exacto knife, the top part of the foreskin was cut until blood was drawn. Afterwards we each had our own mikvah in the ocean at a public beach." Joe's brother, Aaron, was 13 at the time and recalled that "the mohel only drew a small amount of blood from our penis.... cut our hair like a baby's and dipped us in the ocean while the Rabbi said some prayers."

Jack Mass was 22 and happened to be visiting his uncle and aunt, Aaron and Marilyn Karp, at the time. He had a very different experience. "I was cut with a plain cuticle scissors, maybe dipped in disinfecting alcohol, before the procedure. I was told it would not hurt (but) how did anyone even know? For something that supposedly would not hurt, one could hear my scream for days after. There was no numbing (and) no precautions (taken) to prevent infection, save the healing powers of the Caribbean seawater into which I was told to wade. I remember taking myself to a doctor on my return to Miami. He asked why I had submitted to the procedure. When I told him, he just looked at me in disbelief. It is one thing for an infant to undergo circumcision but quite another for an adult to experience something so painful and traumatizing. Who received God's glory for it? The rabbi? Louis Speisman? My uncle? All I know is that I could have lived very nicely without it."

In the Chabad video, Rabbi Bogomilsky quotes Louis Speisman's cable to the Rebbe in New York following the procedure: "Today you have removed the reproach of Barbados." According to Rabbi Bogomilsky, this was a play on the words Joshua used when he circumcised the Jewish men after they crossed the river Jordan. The Rebbe wrote back to Louis saying, "Greetings to all the chasidim, may they live and be well."

When Louis Speisman died in 1976, the Barbados Jewish community asked Rabbi Bogomilsky to officiate at his funeral, and with the Rebbe's endorsement, the funeral was delayed until he was able to arrive.

# CHAPTER 8
## Where do we go from here?
## The Future of the Barbados Jewish Community
### Simon Kreindler

Opinion regarding the future of the Barbados Jewish community is divided. Some are discouraged by what they see as escalating assimilation and loss of interest in Jewish practice. Others are more optimistic and believe that growth and renewal are possible. Although descendants of the original Ashkenazi families are being lost to assimilation, some believe the community can still attract new members and want to see it move it forward.

Jimmy Altman, the former treasurer of the BJC and grandson of Moses Altman, is pessimistic: "As the senior members our community pass on, it appears the Yiddishkeit our parents and grandparents brought with them from Europe in the 1930s will soon be lost. Many in the younger generation have intermarried, and there has been a decline in their practice of Jewish traditions and dedication to the synagogue. Unfortunately, I do not foresee the continuation of a meaningful Jewish community in the future."

Jacob Hassid, who recently stepped down as President of the Barbados Jewish Community, has witnessed the community's evolution over the past two decades. He has seen the challenges it faces but is optimistic about the future. As he [139] notes, "The membership (is diverse) and…the community has important and long-established family relationships and traditions. When all is said and done, however, the community is too small to be self-perpetuating without introducing some changes." Jacob worked hard to "keep the community's flame alive, create excitement, and ensure member participation." He is optimistic it can survive and hopes the recent interest shown by Chabad in getting involved in Barbados will soon be realized.

I believe Jacob highlights the crux of the problem - one that Jewish communities in other jurisdictions are also facing, viz., how to engage the younger generation and make Judaism more relevant. If communities cannot accomplish this, then the likelihood is they will continue to suffer attrition and eventually die.

Change and renewal will mean embracing converts who care about Judaism and are prepared to complete the necessary course of study in preparation for conversion. Jewish communities elsewhere have embraced converts and the point has repeatedly been made that they often prove to be more committed Jews than those born into the faith. Judaism needs committed followers. If

---

[139] See Jacob Hassid's story in Chapter 5.

Bajans want to embrace Judaism with all its lofty expectations, I believe the Jewish way is to welcome them.

I share Jacob's view that Chabad could also be very helpful to the BJC. It can offer educational programs for the children and teach the adults about day-to-day Jewish practice and observance. In other jurisdictions Chabad has been able to bring assimilated families back to to the fold and they might be able to do the same in Barbados. In combination with a group of dedicated converts, Chabad could well breathe new life into the Barbados Jewish community.

## APPENDIX 1

## LEADERS OF THE BARBADOS JEWISH COMMUNITY

Moses Altman (1932 - 1948)
Oscar Pillersdorf (1948 - 1975)
Motel Truss (1975 - 1982)
Benny Gilbert (1982 - 1992)
Marshall Oran (1992 - 1995)
Joseph Steinbok (1995 - 1997)
Rachelle Altman (?1997 - ?)
Jacob Hassid (2011 - 2017)
Scott Oran (2017 - )

# APPENDIX 2

## Group Photos of the Barbados Jewish Community from the 1940s to the 1960s

**Mina Zierler's Sunday School ca. 1944/45**
Front row L to R: Alex Konigsberg, Louis Burak, Clara Paster,
Betty Konigsberg, and Rosie Zierler
Middle row: Unknown boy with camera, Max Konigsberg,
unknown girl and boy
Back row: David Miller and Samuel Brzozek

**Some Members of the Barbados Jewish community
Seawell Airport, 1948**
Back row, left to right: Mary Brzozek, Miriam Brzozek, Miriam Bernstein, Clara Paster, Wisia Paster, Fanny Pillersdorf, Paltyel Paster, Mary Speisman, Oscar Pillersdorf, Major Kopel (Israeli visitor), Szol Bernstein, Moses Altman, ?, Leib Pillersdorf, Bernard Konigsberg, Yehudah Brzozek, Esther Bernstein, Ethel Konigsberg holding Ellen
Front row: Alex Konigsberg, Jack Paster, Max Konigsberg, Bunia Bernstein, Sonia Burak, Dorothy Burak, Rose Zierler, and behind her, Louis Burak, Helen Bernstein, Mina Zierler, Samuel Brzozek, Sam Mass
(Betty Konigsberg Feinberg photo)

**The Altman Family, Barbados, ca. 1948**
Front row: Edna Pillersdorf holding Rachel and Hinda Altman holding Leah
Middle row, standing: Rose Altman (holding Jimmy), Mary Speisman,
Simon Altman (holding Marlene), and Doris Kaplan (holding Marty Kaplan).
Back row: Jack Kaplan, Fanny Pillersdorf (standing behind Rose),
Leib Pillersdorf
(Marsha Altman Glassman photo)

**Davening at "Macabee," ca. 1951/52**
Back row L to R: Dr. Pulver (Tony Lazar's father), Zvi Rehfeld (Hanna Templer Abramowitz's grandfather), Mauricio Raizman, unknown, Moses Steinbok, Paul Steinbok, Paltyel Pasternak, Srul Jacob Bernstein
Middle row: Bunia Korn holding Linda Rosner, Henry Altman, Kiva Pulver, and behind him, Mr. Stammler, Leon Silver
Front row: Harold Saunders, Bernard Pulver, Jacob Zierler
(Ellen Konigsberg Schapiro photo)

**Leah Pillersdorf's Birthday party, Rockley New Road, Barbados ca. 1952**
Back row: Edna Pillersdorf, (unknown lady behind her two children,)
Marilyn Karp, Tony Lazar, Helen Wajchendler (holding Harry),
Chana Silver (hidden), Sonia Silver (holding Steven Altman),
Betty Konigsberg (holding Stanley Karp), Rosie Zierler, & Anutsa Pulver.
Front row: Jocelyn & Jimmy Parris (Pillersdorf neighbours),
Ellen Konigsberg, Paul Altman, Joel Karp, Leah Pillersdorf, and behind her,
Rachel Pillersdorf, Hanna Wajchendler, Molly Pulver, Harold Saunders,
Vicky Pulver held by unknown girl, Felicia Lazar, and Leon Silver.
Standing in front of Leon: Robbie Saunders,
Marlene Altman, and Jimmy Altman.
Sitting in front of Marlene is her sister, Marsha
(Rachel Pillersdorf Weisman photo)

**An Evening at the Zierlers' Home in 1953**
Left to Right: Mina Zierler, Toni Spira, Sara Kreindler, (unknown,)
Lazar Spira, Harry Burak, Jean Saunders, Motel Reingold,
Ethel & Bernard Konigsberg, Sonia Burak, Anita Reingold, Joe Kreindler
(Betty Konigsberg Feinberg photo)

**Children of the Barbados Jewish community, ca. 1952**
Back row, left to right: Sonia Silver, Rochelle Tepper, Bernard Pulver, Felicia Lazar, Leon Silver, Paulette Tepper, Kathlyn, Dina (in front) and Joan Bernstein
Front row: Rachel and Leah Pillersdorf, Ellen Konigsberg, Harold Saunders, Paul Steinbok, Molly Pulver (behind Paul Steinbok), Linda Rosner, Marlene Altman, Marsha Altman, Jimmy Altman (behind Marsha), Paul Altman, Ruth Stammler

**Young Women of the Barbados Jewish community, ca. 1954**
L to R: Rochelle Tepper, Dorothy Burak, Clara Paster, Rosie Zierler, Betty Konigsberg, Sonia Silver, Peggy Kreindler

**Rosh Hashannah 1954, Ladies of the BJC at "Macabee"**
Back row, L to R: Ellen Steinbok, Marilyn Karp,
Elfreida Templer, Mary Rosner, Hannah Templer,
Edna Pillersdorf, ?, ?. Mina Zierler,
Chana Silver, Miriam Bernstein, ?, Anutsa Pulver, ?
Front row, seated: Sonia Burak, Sara Kreindler, Wisia Paster,
Mary Speisman, Rose Altman (holding Steven), Ethel Konigsberg

**Sunday School, Barbados Jewish community, ca. 1955**
Back row: Rose Altman holding Steven, ?, Mary Speisman, ?,
Rosie Zierler, Dorothy Burak, Sonia Silver, Betty Konigsberg, Leon Silver
Second row: AbrahamTruss, Ellen Konigsberg, Maurice Kreindler, ?,
Harold Saunders, ?, ?, ? Felicia Lazar
Third row: Paul Reingold, Paul and Jerry Steinbok, ?, ?, ?,
Linda and Molly Rosner
Front row: Eva Steinbok, Stanley Karp, Joel Karp, ?

**Paltyel and Wisia Pasternak's 1956 Anniversary Party**
Back row, L to R: Mina Zierler, Mary Speisman, Aron Karp,
Wisia and Paltyel Pasternak, Jacob Zierler, Srul Jacob Bernstein,
Bernard and Betty Konigsberg
Middle row: Ellen and Moses Steinbok, Leib and Fanny Pillersdorf,
Sophie and Bunia Korn, Leon Silver, Mary Rosner
Front row: Harry Burak and Helen Wajchendler
(Harry Wajchendler photo)

**Simon and Rose Altman's Seder, "Macabee," Harts Gap, 1957**
Going around table from bottom: unidentified serviceman from the US base in St. Lucy, Mr. & Mrs. Lustgarten's daughter, Sonia Silver, hidden man and woman, Warren Sondon, Fanny and Leib Pillersdorf, Mr. & Mrs. Lustgarten from Venezuela, Rose and Simon Altman, Mary & Louis Speisman, Aron & Marilyn Karp, Morris Berman (Marilyn Karp's father), unknown couple, Jimmy Altman
(Anne Karp Zeplowitz photo)

**Clubbing in the 1950s**
Upper photo: Abraham Wajchendler, Rose Altman, Mary Speisman,
Lazar & Toni Spira, Helen Wajchendler, Jean & Ernest Saunders
Lower photo: Standing, Aron Karp & Benny Gilbert
Seated: Simon Altman, Ernest Saunders, Moses Steinbok, Motel Truss,
Iancu Lazar and Kuk Pilarski

**The Next Generation, 1961**
Clockwise from L to R: Stephen Lebens, Jerry Steinbok, Steven Altman, Paul Steinbok, Jimmy Altman, Joel Karp, Stanley Karp, Harry Wajchendler, and Ralph Lebens

## APPENDIX 3

## Bar Mitzvah Photos, 1930s – 1960s

**Jack Pasternak's 1948 Bar Mitzvah,
Ocean View Hotel, Rockley, Barbados**

Left side of long table, clockwise: Simon and Rose Altman, unknown, Mary and Louis Speisman?, unknown

Head Table, left to right: Clara Paster, Wisia Paster, Jack Pasternak, Paul Paster, Mr. and Mrs. Brzozek

Right side of long table, clockwise: unknown, unknown, unknown, unknown, Mrs. and Mr. Alexandor (from Montreal), unknown, Kitty Feldman

**Abraham Truss' 1957 Bar Mitzvah, Flint Hall, St. Michael**
Front row, L to R: Leon Truss, Paul Steinbok, Abraham Truss,
Marlene Altman, Aaron Truss, Manea Truss, Joe Truss
Middle row: Unknown boy, Hanna Wajchendler, Harold Saunders,
Sophie Korn, Ellen Steinbok, Mary Rosner, Leon Silver, unknown,
Motel Truss, Moses Steinbok? Evelyn Truss

**Aaron Truss' 1960 Bar Mitzvah**
Clockwise: Marilyn Karp, Aaron Truss, Oscar Pillersdorf,
Sophie and Bunia Korn, unknown, Edna Pillersdorf and unknown

**James Altman's 1961 Bar Mitzvah**
L to R: Rose Altman, James, Geoff Lebens, and Simon Altman

**Joel Karp's 1963 Bar Mitzvah, "Las Palmas", Rockley, Christ Church**
L to R: Joel's grandparents, Morris and Gussie Berman, Marilyn Karp, Joel, Rachel Pillersdorf, and Aron Karp

**Leon Truss' 1963 Bar Mitzvah**
Back row, L to R: Joe Truss? Jerry Steinbok, Mary Speisman, Edna Pillersdorf, Rose Altman, Leah Pillersdorf, Jack Mass, Miriam Bernstein, and Evelyn Truss
Front row: Issy Tepper, Ron Karp, Harry Wajchendler, Stanley Karp, and Leon Truss
(Rachel Pillersdorf Weisman photo)

**Stanley Karp's 1965 Bar Mitzvah**
L to R: Iancu Lazar, Stanley, Marsha Altman, Geoff Lebens,
Aron Karp, and Mary Speisman
(Anne Karp Zeplowitz photo)

# APPENDIX 4

## Ashkenazi Burials in the Barbados Jewish cemetery

Adda, Maximillian Joseph, 1985 - 1997
Altman, Deborah, Dec. 8, 1914 - Jan. 7, 1998
Altman, Henry, Apr. 23, 1913 - July 20, 2008
Altman, Moshe, 1888 - 1949
Altman, Simon, May 19, 1920 - July 5, 1976
Altman, Rose, Apr. 1, 1923 - May 9, 2016
Benjamin, Edward Adrain, Dec. 23, 1908 - Nov. 13, 1997
Benjamin, Joan Rebecca, Feb. 24, 1915 - Jan. 31, 1994
Bernstein, Miriam Laja, Nov. 18, 1899 - Aug. 22, 1967
Bernstein, Srul Jacob, Nov. 1, 1899 - May 16, 1974
Bernstein, Szol, May 7, 1907 - Sept. 6, 1974
Bomsztajn, Jakub Josef, Jan. 22, 1899 - Aug. 8, 1968
Burak, Ephraim, 1905 - Feb. 19, 1951
Feldman, Gustav Getzel, 1897 - 1978
Fletcher, Pamelia Elizabeth, Apr. 8, 1931 - Oct. 3, 2012
Fletcher (Fleischer), Peter, Sept. 16, 1921 - May 30, 2002
Friedman, Joseph, Oct. 20, 1903 - Jan. 5, 1950
Gross, Lazar, Mar. 16, 1897 - July 9, 1968
Karp, Aron Louie, Mar. 21, 1915 - Apr. 7, 1967
Karp, Marilyn, Nov. 12, 1926 - Feb. 19, 2013
Koves, Paul, Jan. 21, 1920 - June 12, 2003
Lazar, Iancu, Sept. 24, 1907 - June 17, 1992
Lazar, Toni, Jan. 1, 1911 - Mar. 22, 1997
Oran, Anita, Apr. 26, 1935 - Aug. 8, 1997
Oran, Marshall, Jan. 9, 1932 - Feb. 27, 2017
Rubin, Dr. K. Cathrina
Schlesinger, Carlotta
Schor, Feiga? - Aug. 12, 1942
Silver, Hersh, Mar. 15, 1909 - Feb. 2, 1943
Simon, Adrian Aaron, Dec. 12, 1972 - July 7, 1974
Speisman, Louis, Nov. 25, 1906 - Aug. 18, 1976
Speisman, Mary, Apr. 5, 1915 - May 5, 1985
Steinbok, Moses Aron, Jun. 15, 1915 - Apr. 18, 1991
Truss, Motel, May 17, 1910 - Nov. 13, 1985
Wajchendler, Abraham, June 20, 1922 - Oct. 4, 1990

## *Memorial Plaques in honour of Former Members*

Pillersdorf, Elka, July 30, 1917 - May 15, 1990 (Toronto, Ontario)
Pillersdorf, Oscar, Nov. 8, 1908 – Sept. 4, 1999 (Toronto, Ontario)
Bernstein, Helen, Nov. 7, 1930 - Oct. 8, 2011 (Barbados)
Bernstein, Leon, Mar. 24, 1924 - Dec. 4, 2000 (Toronto, Ontario)

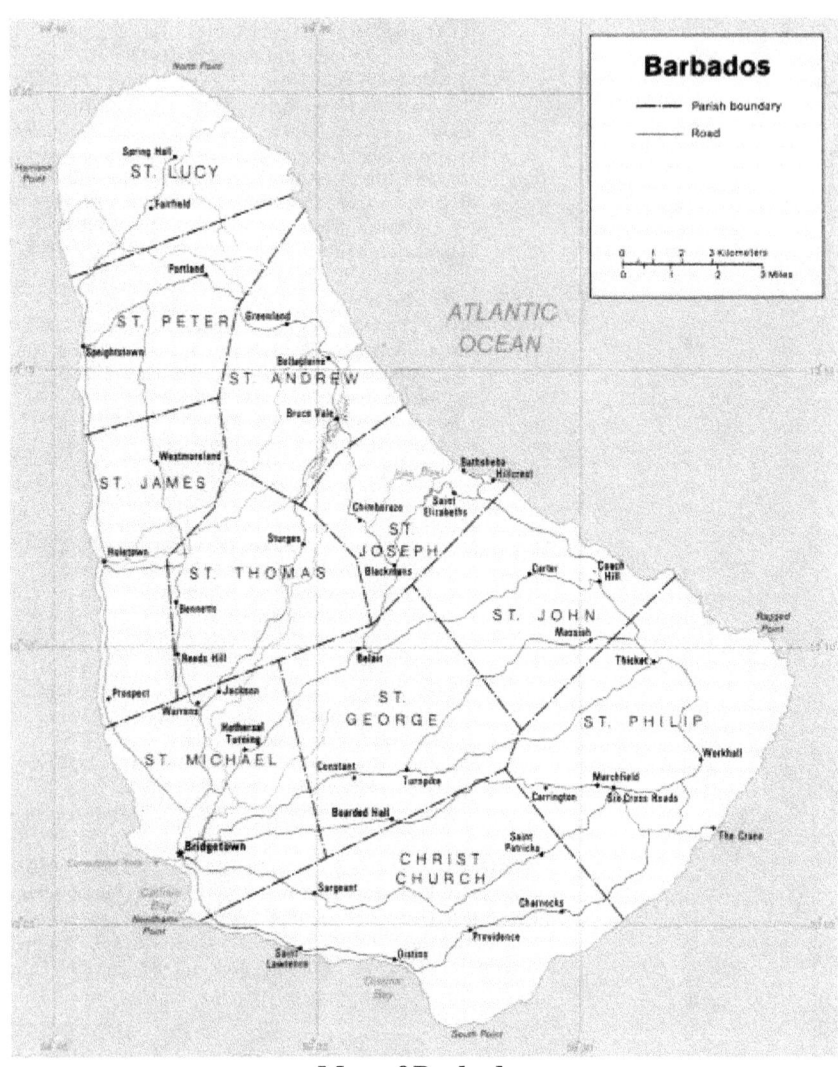

**Map of Barbados**
(Geography and Map Division, US Library of Congress)

# INDEX

"f" refers to photograph.

## A

Aarons, Leon, 96
Abbedi (sic) (new settler), 29
Aboriginal workers in lumber camp, 210, 211f
Abramowitz, Stanley, 274–75, 275f
Adams, Genevieve (née Turner), 15f, 377f, 378
Adams, J. M. G. M. "Tom" (Prime Minister), 14–17, 21, 21f, 22–23, 25, 37, 288, 377f, 378
Adda, Maximillian Joseph, 423
Adler, Mindla ("Mina"), 317
Aerenson, Jean, 246
Aerenson, Max, 245f
Aerenson, Minnie, 245f
Aerenson family, 246
Alexandor, Mr. and Mrs. A. J., 220, 416f
Alleyne, Margaret, 55
Alleyne, Warren, 24
Altman, Abby (Abigail), 37, 72–73
Altman, Adam Colin, 70, 72
Altman, Anita (née Vatch), xiv, 60, 68, 74f, 346
Altman, Deborah (née Tintpulver), 27, 33–34, 35f, 36, 44, 329, 335, 385, 423
Altman, Donna (née Pooler), 70
Altman, Ellen (née Ganzman), 70
Altman, Henry Judka Hersz, 27–28, 28n19, 29, 32, 32f, 33, 35f, 36–38, 42, 42f, 44, 52f–53f, 60, 62, 71–73, 255, 329, 335, 346, 350, 385, 403f, 423
Altman, Hinda, 29, 38, 42, 42f, 52f, 54f, 60, 61f, 62, 71, 81, 255, 402f

Altman, J. Henry, 10–11, 12f
Altman, James Chaim, 15, 15f, 38, 62, 74–80, 255
Altman, Jimmy, xiv, 27, 44, 64, 68, 74f, 92, 125, 203f, 253, 346, 354–55, 358, 391, 391f, 394, 402f, 404f, 406f, 411f, 413f
Altman, Leah, 402f
Altman, Marlene Estelle, 38, 44, 62, 64, 68, 71, 125, 195f, 203f, 238, 255, 354–55, 402f, 404f, 406f, 417f
Altman, Marsha, 38, 40, 44, 62, 64, 69, 72, 125, 203f, 238, 255, 354–55, 404f, 406f, 422f
Altman, Mary (née Lea/Leah)), 68
Altman, Moses (Moshe), xii, 10, 27–29, 32–33, 37–38, 42–43, 50, 52f, 53, 59–60, 61f, 62–63, 71, 81–82, 82n47, 83, 113, 128, 131f, 147, 169, 208, 208f, 255, 264, 264n107, 325, 328, 391, 394, 397, 401f, 423
Altman, Paul Bernard (Sir), 15, 18f, 21–22, 22f, 22n15, 25, 27, 33, 35f, 36–37, 44, 46–47, 55, 55f, 72, 195f, 196, 203f, 267, 335, 337, 385, 404f, 406f
Altman, Rachelle, 37, 397
Altman, Rina, 37, 72–73
Altman, Rochelle, 50
Altman, Rose, xiii, xiv, 28, 33, 38–39, 44, 56, 59f, 60, 61f, 62, 70, 74, 76, 110f, 114, 130, 147, 194, 206, 255, 314, 328–29, 332f, 334–35, 352–54, 356–58, 391, 402f, 408f–409f, 411f–412f, 416f, 419f, 421f, 423
Altman, Ryan Jacob, 68, 72
Altman, Sean Noah, 68, 72

Altman, Simon (Szymon), 27, 29, 32–33, 36, 38–39, 42, 42f, 44–45, 51, 53, 53f, 56, 59f, 61, 61f, 62–65, 71–74, 76, 110f, 118, 125, 130, 147, 194, 246, 255, 314, 328, 332f, 334–35, 352–55, 357, 391, 402f, 411f–412f, 416f, 419f, 423
Altman, Stacy, 70
Altman, Steven Lawrence, 38, 44, 62, 64, 70, 72, 125, 203f, 255, 353–55, 404f, 408f–409f, 413f
Altman family, 42f, 44, 273, 281, 333, 358, 400f, 402f
Altman Glassman, Marsha, 27, 59, 64f
Altman Kaplan, Doris (Dyna Ita) (née Altman), 29, 38, 42, 42f, 52f, 62, 71, 81, 81f, 255
Altman Mansour, Stacy, 70–71
Altman Pillersdorf, Elka (Eda, Edna) (née Altman), 29, 38, 42, 42f, 52, 52f, 62, 73, 255
Altman Speisman, Mary (née Altman), iii, 27, 29, 38, 38f, 39, 41, 52f, 54, 54f, 61f, 62, 64, 67, 71–72, 203f, 255, 335, 353, 355, 401f–402f, 408f–412f, 416f, 421f–423f
"Altman's Bargain House" (Swan Street), 328, 332f
Altman's Department Store (Swan Street), 32, 34f, 62, 64–66, 66f, 77, 78f, 328, 332f, 334, 352, 358
American Jewish Historical Society, 3
American Women's Club, 49
Andrew, Julie, 315
Angela, 154
Apfeld, Tina, 107

Aquatic Club, 41, 46–47, 56, 67, 78, 102, 106–7, 138, 156, 164, 171, 181, 194, 216, 220, 238–40, 248, 252, 274, 296–97, 313, 315, 334, 355, 361, 366
Aruba (Dutch West Indies), 44, 168
Ashkenazi businesses and factories
  Barbados Draperies, 312, 330
  Barbados Knitting and Spinning Mills, 87, 243, 246, 248, 330, 359
  Drapery Specialists, 89–90, 330
  Earthworks Pottery, 331, 369f, 371–72
  Eileen Shirt Factory, 98, 98n57, 99f, 330
  Goodwood Apts., 330
  Koves and Company, 330, 349
  M. Truss and Co., 282f, 330
  Oran Ltd., 330, 353
  Reliance Shirt Factory, 45, 328, 330
  Swiss Art, 330–31
  Zylcraft Optical, 331, 350
Ashkenazi families, founding, xiii, 31, 394
Ashkenazi immigrant men, xiii. See also peddlers
Ashkenazi Jews
  "Names of the New Settlers in Barbados," 27–30
Ashkenazi Jews, burials of, 424
Ashkenazi retail businesses
  "Altman's Bargain House," 328, 332f
  "Altman's Department Store," 32, 34f, 62, 64–65, 66f, 77, 78f, 328–29, 332f, 334, 352, 358
  "Broadway Dress Shop," 33–34, 34f, 36, 62, 329
  "Colony Store," 45, 50, 55, 328

"Coronation Store," 89, 129, 153, 155f, 243, 311–12, 328–29, 332f
Dry goods store, 219, 329, 332f
"Eve's Fashion Store," 332f
"The General Store", 311, 329, 332f
"The Hollywood Store," 264, 265f, 327, 332f
"Jubilee Store," 171, 172f, 328–29
"Lazar's Society Store," 328, 332f
"London Shop," 114, 114n60, 116, 116n, 117, 117f, 122, 171n, 281, 299–300, 329, 359
"Lucky Store," 102, 329, 332f
"Modern Dress Shoppe," 173, 173f, 174, 174f, 175, 180, 186, 196–97, 329, 359
"Paradise Store," 244, 332
"Reliance Shirt Factory," 45, 328, 330
"Royal Store," 43, 45, 328
"The Russian Store," 206, 280, 280f, 285, 327–28, 332f
"S. S. Khoury" (dry goods store), 279
"The Sandal Shop," 328
"The Shopping Centre," 83, 328, 332f
"Stitches," 328
"Style Shoppe," 248, 329, 359
"Swan Store," 329, 332f
"Textile Town," 311–12, 329
Ashkenazi retailers and business people
Altman, Henry and Deborah, 329
Altman, Moses (Moshe), 328
Altman, Rose, 329
Altman, Simon and Rose, 328, 332f
Bernstein, Leon, 328, 330
Bernstein, Paul, 328, 330
Bernstein, Srul Jacob, 328, 332f
Brzozek, Yehudah, 328–29
Burak, Harry and Sonia, 329, 332f
Burgida, Joseph, 331
Feldman, Gustav, 329, 332f
Hoffman, Stan, 331
Karp, Aaron and Marilyn, 329
Konigsberg, Bernard, 328–29, 332f
Korn, Bunia, 328
Koves, Paul, 330
Kreindler, Joseph, 328–29
Lazar, Iancu, 328
Mass, Moses, 327, 332f
Newman, Jay and Leila, 331
Oran, Marshall, 330
Pasternak (Paster), Paltyel (Paul), 11, 12f, 30, 214, 214f, 215, 215f, 216, 217f, 218–19, 219f, 221, 325, 329, 332f, 403f
Pilarski, Kuk, 328
Pillersdorf, Oscar and Edna, 328, 330
Raizman, Helen and Mauricio, 328
Raizman family, 330
Rosner, Chaim, 328
Rubin, Leo, 244, 332f
Saunders, Ernest, 330
Saunders, Jean, 329
Shoul, Ferdie, 330
Simon, Joe, 329
Speisman, Louis, 328, 332f
Spieler, Goldie and Dave, 331
Spira, Lazar, 327, 332f
Steinbok, Moses (Moishe) Aron, 330
Truss, Jennifer, 331
Truss, Motel, 330, 332f

Wajchendler, Abraham, 328, 330, 332f
Wajchendler, Helen, 329, 332f
Wajchendler, Irving, 330
Zierler, Jacob and Mina, 328, 332f
Ashkenazic Jewish community, 45
Austro-Hungarian Empire, 167
Averboukh, Chuma, 44, 60–61, 208, 354
Averboukh, Louver, 60–61, 208

B
Baeza, Mr., 9–10
"The Balalaika," 280
Bannister, Delbert, 110
Bar Mitzvah photos (1930-1960s)
　Aaron Truss' 1960 Bar Mitzvah, 418f
　Abraham Truss' 1957 Bar Mitzvah, Flint Hall, 417f
　Jack Pasternak's 1938 Bar Mitzvah, Ocean View Hotel, 416f
　James Altman's 1961 Bar Mitzvah, 419f
　Joel Karp's 1963 Bar Mitzvah, "Las Palmas," Rockley, 420f
　Leon Truss' 1963 Bar Mitzvah, 421f
　Stanley Karp's 1965 Bar Mitzvah, 422f
Barbadian Jewish Diaspora, xiv, 307
"Barbados, Home to a Fascinating Jewish History" (Canadian Jewish News), 23
Barbados Advocate newspaper, 16, 392f
Barbados Ashkenazi Jewish community, v, 33, 83
Barbados Board of Tourism, 17–18, 18n14, 24, 77
Barbados Children's Wear, 77
Barbados Deep Water Harbour, 197
Barbados Development Bank, 86, 330
Barbados Draperies, 312, 330
Barbados Globe newspaper, 5
Barbados Hardware, 83, 87, 329
Barbados Jewish cemetery (Bridgetown), 3n4, 11, 11n12, 12–15, 16f, 23, 25, 41, 63, 73, 76, 83, 87, 92, 93f, 108, 108f, 112, 200–201, 244, 246, 252, 267, 272, 318, 349. See also Nidhe Israel Cemetery; Petition of the Barbados Jewish community
　Ashkenazi burials in the cemetery, 423
　memorial plaques in honour of former members, 423
　synagogue and cemetery, sale of, 9–10
Barbados Jewish community, iii, v, xiii, xiv, 12, 14f, 15, 17–18, 17f, 25–27, 50, 75, 79, 105, 157, 201, 203f, 219, 241–44, 255, 269, 324, 347, 352–53, 372–75, 393–95, 397, 399–413
　Altman family (1944/45), 400f
　children of the community, (ca. 1952), 406f
　clubbing in the 1950s, 412f
　davening at "Macabee" (ca. 1951/52), 403f
　founding members, iii, 27–30, 30n23, 31, 83, 157, 201, 241–44, 324, 324n114, 346, iiin1
　future of, 394–95
　group photos (1940s to 1960s), 399–413
　leaders of, 397

Leah Pillersdorf's birthday party (1952), 404f
members at Seawell Airport (1948), 401f
Mina Zierler's Sunday (ca. 1944/45), 400f
next generation (1961), 413f
Paltyel and Wisia Pasternak's 1956 Anniversary Party, 410f
Rosh Hashannah 1954, ladies of the BJC at "Macabee," 408f
Simon & Rose Altman's Seder, "Macabee," Harts Gap (1957), 409f
Sunday school (ca. 1955), 409f
Zierlers' home (1953), gathering at, 405f
Barbados Knitting and Spinning Mills, 87, 243, 246, 248, 330, 359
Barbados Labour Party, 78, 375
Barbados Museum and Historical Society, 3, 4n, 7, 11, 37, 41n29
The Barbados National Trust, 15, 26, 37
Barbados Police Band, 303
Barbados Public Library, 104, 174, 196, 274
Barbados Water Polo League, 137–38
Barbados Yacht Club, 47, 194, 265, 315
Bargain House, 62
Barrow, Carolyn, 119–20, 120f, 238
Barrow, Errol Walton (Honourable), 15–16, 21, 21f, 23, 86, 119–20, 120f, 293, 296 375f, 375–76
Barrow, Haim, 376
Barrow, Joseph, 376
Barrow, Norman, 304

Barrow, Sarah, 376
Barrow, Simon, 23, 376
Bata Shoe Store (Broad Street), 112
Bauer, Chava, 97
Bayley, Corin, 24
Bayley, Louis, 346
Beattie, David, 308
Beaudoin, Alex, 156
Beaudoin, Caroline, 156
Beaudoin, Mathieu, 156
Beckles (maid), 363
Beer, Stafford, 308
Belafonte, Harry, 315
Benda, Anton, 377–78
Benda, Douglas, 377
Benda, Dudley, 378
Benda, Frances, 377–78
Benda, George, 377
Benda, Hazel Edith, 377–78
Benda, Saligman, 377
Benda, Sigmund, 377
Benjamin, Edward Adrian, 423
Benjamin, Joan Rebecca, 423
Berman, Birdie, 335
Berman, Gussie (née Rosenkavich), 114, 420f
Berman, Jack, 114, 335
Berman, Morris, 114, 411f, 420f
Bernholtz, Charlotte, 312
Bernholtz, Sarah Gayle (née Wajchendler), 312
Bernstein, Ann, 85
Bernstein, Bunia, 401f
Bernstein, David, 87
Bernstein, Dina, 83f–84f, 85, 406f
Bernstein, Esther, 401f
Bernstein, Helen, 29, 83, 85, 88, 90, 401f, 423
Bernstein, Joan, 84f, 85, 406f
Bernstein, Kathlyn (Ginger), 84f, 85, 85f, 406f
Bernstein, Kitty (née Gonsalves), 83f, 85–86, 335

Bernstein, Leon, 29, 83, 83f, 85, 85f, 86, 89, 328, 330, 335, 423
Bernstein, Louis, 87
Bernstein, Matthew, 87
Bernstein, Miriam Laja, 29, 82, 82f, 83, 83f–84f, 85, 89–90, 401f, 408f, 421f, 423
Bernstein, Paul, 28, 82, 83f, 85, 87, 89, 328, 330
Bernstein, Samuel Paul, 83, 85
Bernstein, Shaul (Szol), 87, 401f, 423
Bernstein, Sidney Lewis (Lord), 15
Bernstein, Sonia, 87
Bernstein, Srul Jacob, 11, 12f, 28, 28n21, 29, 82, 82f, 83, 83f, 83n48, 84f, 87, 89, 131f, 158–59, 169, 245, 325, 329, 332f, 403f, 410f, 423
Bernstein, Tola, 83, 84f, 85
Bernstein, Yankel, 59, 75, 128, 335
Bernstein Raizman, Helen, 83f, 89
Bernstein Tepper, Tola, 83f
Best, Lorenzo, 138–39
Bethell, Freddie, 188
Bevis Marks Synagogue (London, England), 9
Billie, Stephan, 230
Blackman, Shanika, 87
Blanchettes, 371
Bloom, Hy, 334–35
Blumenfeld, David (Rabbi), 336
Blumenfeld, Eva, 336f, 338–39
Blumenfeld, Hal, 79, 336, 336f, 337–40, 353
Blumenfeld, Jesse, 336f, 338–39
Blumenfeld, Lev, 336f, 338–39
Blumenfeld, Michelle (née Brody), 336f
Bobby (dachshund), 39

"Bognor" (Paster family's home), 225, 226f–227f
Bogomilsky, Shmuel Pesach (Rabbi), 76, 247, 247n106, 390, 390f, 391, 391f–392f, 393
Bomsztajn, Evelyn, 92
Bomsztajn, Jakub Josef, 30, 92, 92f–93f, 423
Borenstein family, 33
Borer, Eliana Aviva, 73
Borer, Nathan Joshua, 73
Borer, Rebecca Sophie, 73
Bornstein, Celia, 48
Bornstein, David, 48
Bowman, Eric, 341, 341f, 342
Bowman, Penny, 341, 341f, 342
"Breezely," 172, 173f, 176, 180–81, 183–84, 183f, 186, 193
Briansky, Rita, 321
Bridgetown Synagogue, 2–3
A Brief History of The Jewish Settlement in Barbados (Singh), 17–18, 24
Broadway Dress Shop (Bridgetown), 33–34, 34f, 36, 62, 329
Brodie, Israel (Chief Rabbi), 379, 379f, 380
Brodie, Mrs., 379, 379f
Brody, Michelle, 39, 337
Brzozek, Judah, 252
Brzozek, Judko (Yehudah), 29–30, 94, 94f, 94n53–55, 95, 95f, 96, 96f, 97, 131f, 169–70, 215, 253, 325–26, 328–29, 401f
Brzozek, Mary, 94, 94n52, 95f, 96, 401f
Brzozek, Miriam, 94, 94f, 94n52, 95, 95f, 96, 96f, 401f
Brzozek, Mr. and Mrs., 416f
Brzozek, Samuel, 94, 95f, 400f–401f

Brzozek, Sarah, 94, 95f, 96
Brzozek Steinbok, Ellen, 94, 95f, 97, 252
Burak, Brian, 107
Burak, David, 156, 156f
Burak, Dora, 100
Burak, Elana, 107
Burak, Emma, 156
Burak, Ephraim, 29–30, 103–4, 108, 108f, 131f, 423
Burak, Erin, 156
Burak, Fred, 105f, 107
Burak, Harry, 11, 12f, 29–30, 100–101, 100f, 102f, 104–5, 106f, 107–8, 325, 329, 332f, 405f, 410f
Burak, Louis, 100–103, 103f, 104–5, 107, 110f, 178f, 203f, 385, 400f
Burak, Michelle, 107
Burak, Sonia, 30, 103–4, 106f, 107, 329, 332f, 405f, 408f
Burak family, 314
Burak Rosenthal, Dorothy, 100–101, 100f, 102–4, 106–7, 106f, 108, 149f, 155f, 178f, 203f, 256f, 386–87, 407f, 409f
Burak Stein, Hellen, 108
Burgida, Judith, 331

C
Canada, 18, 39–40, 48, 57, 67, 73, 122, 128, 132, 140, 143, 145, 148–49, 151, 164–65, 174, 190, 216, 222–24, 231, 235, 239, 256, 267, 274, 288, 295–96, 298, 300, 304, 307
Canadian Jewish News
  "Barbados, Home to a Fascinating Jewish History," 23
Carew, Hugh, 45, 76
Carib Flying Fish, 219, 219f

Caribbean Conservation Association, 15
Carr, Charmian, 196
Carter, Harcourt, 171
Cave Shepherd (department store), 346
Cernauti, Romania, 30, 167, 167n74, 169–70, 199, 199f
Chabad Lubavitch movement, 75
Chalky Mount (St. Andrew), 370
Champagne, Priscilla, 349
"Charming Lady" (James Street), 310
Chemtob, Tali, 68
Chevra Kadish, 49, 49n34, 200
Christian families, 373
Christian merchants, 5
Christian society, 295
Christianity, 374
Christians, 7, 140, 168, 186, 373–74
Clarke, Belle, 107
Clarke, Howard, 107
Clarke, Jeremy, 107
Clarke, Lewis, 107
Codd's House, 26
Codrington High School, 64, 176, 238, 370n121
Colbert, Claudette, 196
Coleman, Edward D., 3
Collins, Joan, 315
Colony Store (lower Broad Street), 45, 50, 56, 328
Coral Ridge Memorial Gardens (Christ Church), 25
Coronation Store (Swan Street), 89, 129, 153, 155f, 243, 311–12, 328–29, 332f
Crane Hotel, 46, 56, 98, 107, 152f, 164, 194, 216, 313, 334
Cromwell, Oliver, 2
Cullen, Christine, 308
Cullen, Meg, 308
Cullen, Rob, 308

Cumberbatch, Mr., 87
Cumberbatch, Shanika (née Blackman), 87
Curaçao (Dutch West Indies), 30, 167–68, 325, 325n117
Czernowit (Bukovina), 167, 167n74, 172, 199, 277

D
Dandridge, Dorothy, 315
Deed of Conveyance (1664), 3
Derman, Francoise, 312
Devonish, Clement, 346, 370
Diamonds International, 50, 62, 345
Dias, Lewis, 2–3
Diner, Hasia, 325
Displaced Persons' Camp (Europe), 199
Drapery Specialists, 89–90, 331
Drummond, Mrs., 196
dry goods store (Swan Street), 62, 66, 129, 135, 206, 216, 279–80, 329, 332f
Dubarsky, Haley, 107
Dubarsky, Howard, 107
Dubarsky, Miranda, 107
Dutch West India Company, 2

E
Earle, Andy, 305
Earthworks Pottery, 331, 369f, 371–72
Eastern European Jewish Diaspora, 295
"Easy Boy," 77
Eileen Shirt Factory, 98, 98n57, 99f, 330
"Elim Hastings," 263
Elizabeth II, Coronation of, 273
Emancipation Bill, 26
Empire Cinema, 182
Emtage, Mr., 83
Erla (household help), 219, 225

Ernst and Young Entrepreneur of the Year Award, 371
"Eve's Fashion Store" (Swan Street), 332f

F
Feferman, Mr., 279
Feinberg, Bernard, 39
Feinberg, Betty, 39
Feinberg, Diidi (Dyan) Ellen, 150
Feinberg, Howard, 150
Feinberg, Jack, 146f, 149–50
Feinberg, Nolan, 150
Feinberg, Ronald, 150
Feinberg, Shayne, 150
Feldman, Carolyn, 110
Feldman, Gustav Getzel, 29–30, 109, 109f, 110, 329, 332f, 423
Feldman, Julien, 110
Feldman, Kate, 30, 109, 109f, 110
Feldman, Kirsten, 110
Feldman, Kitty, 416f
Feldman, Leslie, 110
Feldman, Nicola, 110
Feldman, Rolf, 30, 109, 110f, 111, 111f
Feldman, Ruth, 30, 109–10
Feldman, Verna (née Schwartz), 110, 111f
Fenichel, Debbie, 192f
50th World Jewish Congress (Jerusalem, 1986), 17–18
Fishman, Mr., 280
Flam, Barbara, 344
Flam, Charles, 343, 343f, 344
Flam, David, 343, 343f, 344
Flam, Dell, 343, 343f, 344
Flam, Donald, 343, 343f
Flam, Harold, 343, 343f
Flam, Karen, 343, 343f
Flam, Robert, 343, 343f, 344, 346
Flam's Store, 343
Fletcher, Pamelia Elizabeth, 423
Fletcher (Fleischer), Peter, 423

The Flying Fish Club, 33
Fogelman, Paul, 348
Fontaine, Joan, 315
Foss, Merlyn, 178–79, 213
Foundation School (Church Hill), 119
Frank, Solomon (Rabbi), 274
Fraser, Henry (Sir), 23
Free Masons in Barbados, 121
Freidman, Morris, 105
Freidman, Solomon, 104, 106f
Fridman, Leib, 100
Friedman, Edith, 30, 112, 112f
Friedman, Ingrid, 112, 112f, 272, 273f
Friedman, Joseph, 29–30, 112, 112f, 423
Friedman, Perel, 233
Friedman, Shaindel, 233
Friedman, Sidney, 233
Friedman, Tzeitel, 233
Friedman, Yetty, 233, 237
Friedman, Yosef, 233

G
Ganzman, Ellen, 70
"Gearbox," 77
The General Store (Swan Street), 311, 329, 332f
George (gardener), 225
Gerstenhaber, Bertha, 169–70, 253
Gerstenhaber, Edy, 170f, 253f
Gerstenhaber, Joseph, 169–70, 170f, 253, 253f
Gerstenhaber, Sara, 30, 94n53, 95, 95f, 95n56, 169–70
Gibbs, John, 304
Gibbs, Roger, 305
Gilbert, Benny (Bernard), 15, 17, 17f, 48, 48f, 49–51, 79, 335, 346, 353, 379, 397, 412f
Gilbert, Eli Simon, 73
Gilbert, Ian Michael, 73
Gilbert, Leah, 335, 346, 349

Gilbert, Mya, 73
Gilbet, Riley, 73
Gittel Winogora, Miriam, 94
Glassman, Daniel, 69, 69f
Glassman, David Isaac, 69–70, 72
Glassman, Eliana Nicole (Eliana Nurit), 70–72
Glassman, Jesse Alexander (Yishai Alexander), 70–72
Glassman, Liat Dania, 69–70, 72
Glassman, Marsha (née Altman), 69, 69f
Glassman, Samara (née Lazarus), 70
Gluckstein, Jordan Matthew, 312, 316f
"Golf View" (Rockley New Road), 35, 35f, 36
Gonsalves, Kathlyn/Kitty, 85
Gonzalves, Mrs., 184
Goodwood Apts., 330
Graham, Dr., 121
Great Depression, 171
Green, Adam, 192f
Green, Kevin, 192f
Green, Matthew, 192f
Green, Mr. and Mrs., 335
Green, Samara, 192f
"Green Acres" (Christ Church), 266–67
Greenbaum, 29
Greenberg, Ellie, 250
Greenberg, Kara, 250
Greenberg, Megan, 250
Greenberg, Michael, 250
Greenberg, Steven Jay, 250
Gross, Bertha, 29
Gross, Brancia (née Kreindler), 30, 199, 199f, 200, 335
Gross, Lazar, 29–30, 199, 199f, 200, 335, 423
Guyon, Gabrielle, 312
Guyon, Lauren Rachael (née Wajchendler), 312

Guyon, Remy, 316f
G.W. Hutchinson Ltd, 174

H
"Hall of Justice" (Supreme Court), 14–15, 26, 37
Hallam, Henry, 5, 5n7
Halpern, Danielle, 227
Halpern, Karen, 227
Halpern, Noa, 227
Halpern, Norman, 221, 225f, 227
Halpern, Ryan, 227
Halpern, Talia, 227
Halpern, Wendy, 227
Hammond, Mr. (Harrison College headmaster), 361
Hammond School of Dancing, 47
Harrison College, 36, 45, 58, 87, 95, 105, 110, 119, 125, 132, 137–39, 143, 186, 195, 203, 220, 265, 295–96, 304, 312–13, 364, 371
Harrison's (department store), 346
Haskell, Dr. (Harrison College headmaster), 265
Hassid, Chabad, 347
Hassid, Clement, 346
Hassid, Jacob, 50, 345, 345f, 346–47, 353, 394–95, 397
Hassid, Michal, 345–47
Hassid, Noi, 346
Hassid, Shelley, 346
Haynes, Vimla, 373–74
Hebrew School, 107, 125, 131, 147, 156, 193, 348, 358
Herzl's grave (Israel), 120, 120f
Herzog, Yaacov, 39, 39n27
Hill, Roger, 315
Hirsch, Roza/Zozo, 217
Hirscheimer, Andrea, 223
History of Barbados (Schomburgh), 1
History of the Middle Ages (Hallam), 5, 5n7

Hoffman, Joan, 77, 348
Hoffman, Samantha, 348
Hoffman, Stanley, 77, 331, 348
Hollywood Store (Swan Street), 264, 265f, 328, 332f
Holocaust, 31–32, 32n26, 113–14, 131, 160, 206, 230–31, 233, 239, 266, 320, 380
Hudson, Gerald, 47
Humphrey's Bakery, 67
Hurricane Janet, 74, 273, 312, 314–15, 381, 382f–384f, 385–89
Hutchinson, W. St. C., 10, 14, 36–37
Hutchinson family, 11, 11n12

J
Jacob, Abraham, 1
Jacobs, Louis (Dr. Rabbi), 380
Jamaica Knitting Mills, 246
James, Earl of Carlisle, Lord Proprietor of Barbados, 1
Jewish diaspora, xiv, 295, 307
Jewish ghetto (Australia), 96
Jewish Immigrant Aid Service (JIAS), 287–88
Jewish Monumental Inscriptions in Barbados (Shilstone), 2–3, 24
Jewish Museum, 20f, 25
Jews of London, 2
Jivotovsky, Annat, 107
Joel, Rabbi, 73
Johnson, Lisa, 259
Johnson-Reed Immigration Act (U.S., 1924), 167, 325, 325n117
Journal of the Barbados Museum and Historical Society (1942), 7
Journal of the Barbados Museum and Historical Society (1948), 3

Jubilee Store, High Street (Barbados), 171, 172f, 328–29

## K

"Kahal Kadosh Nidhe Israel" (Jewish congregation), 4
Kaplan, Abbadi, 29
Kaplan, Doris, 402f
Kaplan, Jack, 29–30, 62, 81, 81f, 402f
Kaplan, Leah Rebecca, 81
Kaplan, Martin (Marty) Spencer, 81, 402f
Kaplan, Matthew Ari, 81
Kaplan, Michael Slater, 81
Karp, Aaron (Ari), 123, 169, 174n81, 209, 212–13, 246, 281, 283f, 300, 314, 329, 335, 356, 379f, 411f
Karp, Alan, 213
Karp, Alexander Louie, 123, 125–26
Karp, Annie, 305, 355
Karp, Aron Louie, 29–30, 45, 71, 114, 115f, 116, 116f, 117–18, 118f, 121, 121f, 122, 410f, 412f, 420f, 422f, 423
Karp, Caroline, 123
Karp, Chaya Raizel, 123
Karp, David, 213
Karp, Dina, 114, 206
Karp, Jessica Michelle, 123, 126
Karp, Joel (Yosef) (Rabbi), 71, 114, 119f, 121f, 123, 124f, 305, 315, 404f, 409f, 413f
Karp, Jonathan David, 123, 126
Karp, Joseph, 114, 206
Karp, Marilyn (née Berman), 71, 73, 113, 113f, 114, 115f–116f, 117–18, 119f, 121, 121f, 122, 213, 256, 283f, 314, 329, 335, 404f, 408f, 411f, 418f, 420f, 422f, 423
Karp, Matthew Jason, 123, 126
Karp, Moshe, 123
Karp, Raizel (née Altman), 114
Karp, Ronald, 71, 114, 119, 119f, 121f, 123, 124f, 125, 125f, 283f, 305, 355, 421f
Karp, Samuel James, 123, 126
Karp, Sarah, 123
Karp, Shmuel, 123
Karp, Stanley, 71, 114, 119, 119f, 121f, 123, 283f, 305, 404f, 409f, 413f, 421f–422f
Karp, Theresa (Terry), 123, 125, 125f
Karp family, 62, 283f, 359
Karp Zeplowitz, Anne (Hannah), 71, 113, 119f, 121f, 124f
Kassner, Doris, 121f, 206, 212–13
Kassner, Richie, 212–13
Kassner, Sheryl, 121f
Katz, Maxine, 224
Katz, Mr., 98
Keiser, Mrs, (Kiki), 64, 356
Kellman, Ruby, 118–19
Kent, Erica, 68
Kent, Jackson, 68, 71
Khoury, Mr., 279
Kindertransport, 202, 202n96
"King Dyal," 77
Kira, Feiga, 277n109, 279–80, 284–85, 285f, 286–87, 295
Kirpalani, Ram, 330
Kollek, Teddy, 76
Konigsberg, Alex, 129, 130f, 132, 135, 140–41, 143, 143f, 144, 144f, 145–46, 148, 150–51, 152f, 178f, 344, 400f–401f
Konigsberg, Bernard, 29–30, 45, 62, 75, 89, 127, 127f, 128–29, 131f, 134–37, 139–41, 142f, 147–48, 150–51, 154f, 164, 243, 245, 268, 317, 325, 328–29, 332f, 401f, 405f, 410f
Konigsberg, Charlie, 144

Konigsberg, Ethel (née
  Schiffman), 30, 127, 127f,
  128–29, 130f, 135, 147, 151,
  154f, 245, 401f, 405f, 408f
Konigsberg, Hannah, 144
Konigsberg, Jonathan (Jon), 144
Konigsberg, Lori, 144
Konigsberg, Max, xiv, 30, 127–32,
  130f, 134, 134f, 136, 136f,
  137–41, 142f, 146, 148–51,
  243, 252, 254, 400f–401f
Konigsberg, Mr., 45
Konigsberg, Natalie, 144
Konigsberg, Shirley, 134, 134f
Konigsberg family, 152f
Konigsberg Feinberg, Betty (née
  Feinberg), 56, 103f, 106,
  106f, 130–31, 130f, 131–32,
  134, 140–41, 143, 146–47,
  146f, 148, 148f, 149, 149f,
  151, 152f, 178f, 190, 203f,
  243, 256f, 268, 319f–320f,
  386, 400f, 404f, 407f, 409f–
  410f
Konigsberg Schapiro, Ellen, 129,
  132, 134, 141, 146–47, 150–
  52, 152f, 154f–156f, 387–88,
  401f, 404f, 406f, 409f
Konigsbergs, 314
Kopel, Major, 401f
Korman, Shlomo, 228–29
Korn, Baruch/Bunia, 29, 157,
  157f, 158, 160f, 169, 325,
  328, 335, 379f, 403f, 410f
Korn, Bertha, 29, 157, 157f, 158,
  160f
Korn, Buny, 29
Korn, Gertie, 159
Korn, Mr. and Mrs., 418f
Korn, Myrla/Mary, 29, 158, 158f–
  159f, 161f
Korn, Sophie, 335, 410f, 417f
Koves, Paul, 30, 331, 349, 423

Koves, Priscilla (née Champagne),
  30, 349
Koves, Yvonne, 30, 349
Koves and Company, 331, 349
Kreindler, Aden, 192f
Kreindler, Brancia/Bertha, 199
Kreindler, Corry, 192f
Kreindler, David Michael, 191–92,
  192f
Kreindler, Dina, 170
Kreindler, Edy, 170
Kreindler, Eliana Fenichel, 192f
Kreindler, Jacob Fenichel, 192f
Kreindler, Jerry, 174, 186, 190,
  355
Kreindler, Jonathan Andrew, 191–
  92, 192f
Kreindler, Joseph (Joe) Chaim, 28,
  30, 94n53, 95, 95n56, 141,
  167, 167f, 168–70, 170f, 171,
  171f, 172, 172f, 173, 173f,
  174–75, 180, 181f, 182, 190,
  193, 196, 199, 253f, 325,
  328–29, 335, 405f
Kreindler, Kayla, 192f
Kreindler, Lisa Sharon, 191, 192f
Kreindler, Maurice, 174, 186, 190,
  193, 193f, 194, 194f, 195,
  195f, 196–97, 203f, 249f,
  409f
Kreindler, Noah, 192f
Kreindler, Peggy, 45, 112f, 171,
  173f, 174, 176, 176f, 177,
  177f, 178, 178f, 179–81, 181f,
  182–83, 190, 194, 213, 407f
Kreindler, Ruby, xiv, 180f, 191,
  191f, 192, 192f
Kreindler, Sara (née
  Gerstenhaber), 112f, 167f,
  170, 171f, 173f, 174–75, 180,
  181f, 182, 184, 190, 193, 196,
  335, 405f, 408f
Kreindler, Simon, xiii– xiv, 112f,
  173f, 176, 180, 180f, 181,

181f, 182–84, 183f, 185f, 186–87, 188f, 190, 191f, 192, 192f, 195, 203f, 394–95
Kreindler, Willie, 200
Kreindler family, 359, 361
Kreindler (Green), Lisa, 192f
Kriegel, Alter (Rabbi), 69
Kuk, Naftali Andrew, 360

L
Lago Oil refinery (Aruba), 168
Lancut, Peggy (née Kreindler), 179
Lancut, Shalom/Shlomi, 179
Lancut, Sharon, 179
Lancut, Shelley, 179
Langer, Ella (née Schondorf), 68
Langer, Liam Samuel, 68, 71–72
Langer, Marlene (née Altman), 68
Langer, Simon Louis, 68, 72
Langer, Stan, 68
Lanman, Bob, 370–71
"Las Palmas," 118, 420f
Layne, Winston E., 4, 4n6, 5, 10, 24
Lazar, Felicia, 30, 249f, 355, 404f, 406f, 409f
Lazar, Iancu, 30, 201, 201f, 328, 335, 422f, 423
Lazar, Tony, 30, 201, 201f, 335, 353, 404f, 423
Lazar family, 359
"Lazar's Society Store" (Swan Street), 328, 332f
Lazarus, Samara, 70
Lea (Leah), Mary, 68
Lebens, Ann, 45, 195f, 202, 203f, 204
Lebens, Edith, 202, 202f, 204
Lebens, Geoffrey, 45, 62–63, 76, 194, 202, 202f, 203, 203f, 204, 379f, 419f, 422f
Lebens, James, 419f
Lebens, Mr., 156

Lebens, Ralph, 45, 202, 203f, 204, 413f
Lebens, Stephen, 202, 204, 413f
Leiken, Goldie, 369
Leiken, Harry, 369, 371
Lennon, John, 197
Lennon, Sean, 197
Leonard, Allenna, 308
leper colony, 92
Lerner, Mr., 277
Lesser, Basya, 123
Lieberman, Joseph, 322
Ligon, Richard, 2, 24
Lloyd, Chris Evert, 321
Lodge School, 64–65, 88, 186–88, 188f, 189, 195, 238, 250
London Shop (Bridgetown), 114, 114n60, 116, 116n, 117, 117f, 122, 171n, 281, 299–300, 329, 359
Lousadas, Baruch, 376
Lubavitch, Chabad, 390, 390n125
Lubavitch community, 119
Lubavitcher Rabbis, 335
The Lucky Store (Swan Street), 102, 329, 332f
Lustgarten, Mr. & Mrs., 411f

M
M. Truss and Co. Ltd. Factory, 282f, 330
"Macabee" (Harts Gap, Christ Church), xiii, 10, 33, 36, 39, 44, 62–63, 74, 131f
Macdonald, Judith (Judy), 308
MacKenzie, Doug, 185–86
Mahon (housekeeper), 130, 132, 154, 154f
Malik, Fredmund, 308
Malka Monka, Esther, 60
Malke, Faige, 101
Malke Lachover, Faige, 100
"Mallows" cottage (Sandy Lane), 37

Mandelbaum, David, 344
Mandelbaum, Frances, 344
Manis, Howard, 144
Manis, Jordyn, 144
Manis, Lindsay, 144
Manis, Lori (née Konigsberg), 144
Manis, Sydney, 144
Mann, David, 166
Mann, Harry, 166
Mann, Jonah, 166
Mann, Laura, 166
Mann, Lyla, 166
Mann, Melissa, 166
Mansour, Danny, 70
Mapps College (St. John), 88, 90
Marshall, Brian 'Bam,' 304
Mary's Moustache, 300
Mason, James, 315
Mass, Aaron, 206
Mass, Alan, 178–79, 213
Mass, David, 178–79, 213
Mass, Dina (Dyna), 27–28, 28n20, 29, 59, 83, 205f, 206, 207f, 208, 208f, 209, 211–12, 212f, 213
Mass, Dora, 205f
Mass, Helen, 114, 116f, 206, 207f, 212f, 213
Mass, Hyman, 205, 205f, 212
Mass, Jack, 114, 206–9, 211–12, 212f, 213, 393, 421f
Mass, Joseph, 114, 206, 212–13
Mass, Merlyn (née Foss), 178–79, 205, 213
Mass, Moses, 27–28, 28n20, 29, 83, 205, 205f, 206, 208f, 209, 212, 212f, 213, 327, 332f
Mass, Moshe, 59, 114
Mass, Peggy (née Kreindler), 178, 190, 194
Mass, Rochelle (née Tepper), 178, 178n83, 213
Mass, Samuel (Sam), 28, 45, 114, 178–79, 190, 194, 205, 205f, 206–7, 207f, 208–9, 212, 212f, 213, 401f
Mass family home (Georgetown, British Guiana), 209, 209f
Mass Kassner, Doris (née Mass), 28, 114, 116f, 121f, 206, 207f, 212, 212f, 213
"Massiah" (Speismans' home), 40f, 64
Mauer, Harry, 149
Mauer, Lucy, 149
Mauer, Michael, 149
Mauer, Shirley, 142
Maxwell, Jas, 1, 1n3
McCormack, Mrs., 220
McKenzie, Mrs., 185–86
McNicollm Annie, 377
Mead, Margaret, 359
Medveier, Rivka, 87
Menachem Schneerson, Mendel (The Rebbe), 390f, 393
Mercado, Abraham de, 2
Mercado, David Raphael de, 2, 4
Miller, Anita, 60, 61d, 351
Miller, David, 60, 61f, 400f
Miller, Harry, 61f
Miller, Stephen, 373
Miller, Stephen (Jr.), 373–74
Miller Altman, Rose Diane (Dyna Raizel), 59–61, 61f, 62–65
Miller (Monka), Pauline, 60
Miller (Monka), Sara Lily, 60
Miller (Monka), Simcha Bunem, 60
Ministry of Tourism and Environment, 17
Minutes of Council of Barbados (1654), 2
Minutes of Council of Barbados (1655), 2
Miss Hart's Primary School (Worthing, Christ Church), 64, 184, 184n88, 185, 185f

Miss Kinch's Commercial School, 95, 207, 274, 309
Modern Dress Shoppe (Broad Street, Bridgetown), 173, 173f, 174, 174f, 175, 180, 186, 196–97, 329, 359
Moishe Steinbok's factory, 105
Montefiore, John Castello, 7, 7n9
Montefiore Fountain (Coleridge Street), 7, 7f, 7n9
Moore, Danny, 122–23
Mosbaugh, Franc, 305
"Mr. Mac," 185
Mrs. Jones' School, 57, 238–39, 250, 364
Mrs. Kinch's Primary School, 309
Mrs. Smith's Primary School, 119, 125
Mrs. Webster's school, 220
Mutchnik, Erica (née Kent), 68
Mutchnik, Jackson Kent, 71–72
Mutchnik, Mark Aron, 68, 72
Mutchnik, Marlene (née Altman), 68
Mutchnik, Yerachmiel (Rachmi), 68

N
"Names of the New Settlers in Barbados," 27–30
Nation Newspaper (1984), 16
"New Settlers in Barbados," 29–30, 53n50, 82
Newman, Amy, 350
Newman, Barbara, 350
Newman, Cindy, 350
Newman, Jay, 331, 350, 350f
Newman, Jory, 350
Newman, Leila, 331, 350, 350f
Nidhe Israel Cemetery (Bridgetown), 3, 3n4, 6f, 12, 13f–14f, 19f, 71. See also Barbados Jewish cemetery

Nidhe Israel Museum, Bridgetown, 102f
Nidhe Israel Synagogue (Bridgetown), 6–8f, 18, 19f–20f, 21, 23, 25, 32, 37, 63, 71, 78–79, 342, 376. See also Barbados Jewish cemetery
  Adams, J. M. G. M. "Tom," 14–17, 21, 21f, 22–23, 25
  Altman, Paul Bernard, 15, 18f, 21–22, 22f, 22n15, 25
  Artisans' Workshop building, 26
  The Barbados Jewish community, 26
  The Barbados National Trust, 26
  Barrow, Errol Walton, 15–16, 21, 21f, 23
  "Building of Special Architectural or Historic Interest," 15, 16f
  donations for restoration, 18
  50th World Jewish Congress (Jerusalem, 1986), 17–18
  marble laver that stood at the entrance, 6f
  Mikvah, restored, 20f, 25
  Montefiore Fountain with Synagogue in background, 7f
  Petition of the Barbados Jewish Community, 14–15f
  picture 1925, 8f
  seven men who facilitated the return of the cemetery to the Jewish community, 12, 13f–14f
  Social Hall building, 26
  synagogue, restored interior of, 19f
  synagogue and cemetery, restored, 19f
  synagogue and cemetery, sale of, 9–10

synagogue and cemetery, saving, 16–17
"Synagogue Burial Grounds Committee," 11
synagogue interior after construction (1833), 6f
Synagogue Restoration Project, 16–17, 25–26
The Tabor Foundation (Barbados), 25–26
UNESCO World Heritage status, 23, 23n17, 26
Norris, Mr., 238
Norwood, Andrew, 3

O

Ocean View Hotel (Christ Church), 168, 195f, 220, 416f
Okna, Bukowina, 167, 199
Oliver, Anni (Hannah) (née Wajchendler), 312
Oliver, Clifford, 312, 316f
O'Mahony, Winifred K., 381n124
O'Neale, Mrs., 184
Oran, Anita (née Miller), 62, 72, 335, 351, 352f, 353–55, 423
Oran, Gilda, 351–52, 354–55
Oran, James, 352–53
Oran, Marlene, 352–53
Oran, Marsha, 352–54
Oran, Marshall, 15, 50, 62, 64, 330, 333, 335, 351, 351f, 351n120, 352, 352f, 353–54, 397
Oran, Sarah, 352–54
Oran, Scott, 351–55, 358
Oran Ltd., 330, 353
Our Calypso Shtetl (Pillersdorf), 43, 43n30, 44

P

Padriski, Dora, 205
Paradise Beach, Barbados, 170f
Paradise Beach Club, 41, 46, 67, 78, 119, 156, 158, 168, 170, 181, 194, 238–39, 248, 253f, 297–98, 313, 356, 366
"Paradise Store" (Swan Street), 244, 332
Parris, Jimmy, 404f
Parris, Jocelyn, 404f
Parris, Mrs., 55
Pasternak (Paster), Alana, 223
Pasternak (Paster), Andrew, 222–24
Pasternak (Paster), Chaim, 214
Pasternak (Paster), Clara, 30, 214, 215f, 216, 218, 221, 400f–401f, 407f, 416f
Pasternak (Paster), David, 224
Pasternak (Paster), Emily, 223
Pasternak (Paster), Esther, 214
Pasternak (Paster), Jack, 30, 103f, 214, 215f, 218, 218f, 219–23, 227, 324, 401f, 416f
Pasternak (Paster), Melissa, 223
Pasternak (Paster), Mr., 324
Pasternak (Paster), Paltiel (Paltyel) (Paul), 11, 12f, 29–30, 62, 75, 106f, 214, 214f, 215, 215f, 216, 217f, 218–19, 219f, 221, 325, 329, 332f, 335, 401f, 403f, 416f
Pasternak (Paster), Rowena (Ricky) (née Wiseman), 218f, 221–24, 324
Pasternak (Paster), Steven, 222–23
Pasternak (Paster), Wisia (Visia) (Vishka) (Vera) (née Ribakovsky), 30, 106f, 214, 215f, 216–19, 221, 335, 401f, 408f, 416f
Pasternak (Paster), Zozo, 221
Pasternak (Paster) family, 226
Pasternak (Paster) Halpern, Clara (née Pasternak), 94n53, 95n88, 103f, 112, 178f, 190,

214, 216–17, 219, 221, 225, 225f–226f, 227, 252
Pasternak (Paster) passport photos, 215f
Pasternak (Paster) store, 219
Pearson, Alan, 308
peddlers
   Altman, Moses (Moshe), 325, 328
   Bernstein, Srul Jacob, 325
   Brzozek, Yehaudah, 326
   Burak, Harry, 325
   Konigsberg, Bernard, 325
   Korn, Bunia, 325
   Kreindler, Joseph, 325
   Pasternak (Paster), Paltyel (Paul), 325
   Schor, Shlomo, 325–26
   Steinbok, Moses (Moishe) Aron, 325
   Wajchendler, Abraham, 325
peddling, 325–27
Peters, Ryan, 216f
Petition of the Barbados Jewish Community presented to Governor W. L. Savage, 14–15f. See also Barbados Jewish cemetery
"Pikesville Silver and Antiques", 350
Pilarski, Alex, 45, 57, 305, 362, 364f–365f
Pilarski, Andrew, 362–63
Pilarski, Bum, 360
Pilarski, Cook, 122
Pilarski, Fela, 45, 57, 122, 360, 360f, 361, 365f
Pilarski, Felicia, 362–63
Pilarski, Iancu, 412f
Pilarski, Joseph, 45, 57, 305, 360–62, 362f, 363–64, 364f, 365, 365f, 366
Pilarski, Kuk, 45, 328, 333, 360, 360f, 365f, 412f

Pilarski, Lazar, 412f
Pilarski, Lieb, 360, 363
Pilarski, Oscar, 360, 362–63
Pilarski, Richard, 45, 57, 195f, 305, 357, 361–62, 364, 364f, 365, 365f, 366
Pilgrim, Mr., 182–83, 183f
Pillersdorf, Avraham (Abraham) (Buom), 53, 228–29
Pillersdorf, Benjamin, 232, 237, 239
Pillersdorf, Daniel, 232, 237, 239
Pillersdorf, Edna (Eda, Elka) (née Altman), 35, 42, 42f, 44, 44f, 46f, 50–51, 54f, 56, 61f, 62, 71–73, 328, 330, 335, 353, 402f, 404f, 408f, 418f, 421f, 423
Pillersdorf, Faigy, 228–29
Pillersdorf, Fanny (née Friedman), 231–37, 239, 249f, 251, 363, 401f–402f, 410f–411f
Pillersdorf, Fanta, 232
Pillersdorf, Fela, 238
Pillersdorf, Florence, 195f, 231, 233, 237–39, 249f, 251
Pillersdorf, Joel, 420f
Pillersdorf, Leib, 228, 228f, 229–35, 239, 333, 401f–402f, 410f–411f
Pillersdorf, Mya, 51
Pillersdorf, Naftalie ("Kuk"), 57, 228–29, 238, 281
Pillersdorf, Oscar (Schie Wolf), 11, 12f, 29–30, 35, 42–44, 44f, 45, 46f, 50, 50f, 53, 53f, 54, 54f, 56, 61f, 62, 73, 75, 92, 228, 234, 281, 328, 330, 333, 335, 346, 353, 357, 359, 362–63, 379f, 397, 401f, 418f, 423
Pillersdorf, Paulette (Polly), 231, 233, 236, 238–39
Pillersdorf, Rebecca, 239

Pillersdorf, Riley, 51
Pillersdorf, Ruhel, 237
Pillersdorf, Sarah, 232, 239
Pillersdorf, Solomon (Sam, Sammy), 231, 238–40
Pillersdorf, Zeidy, 232
Pillersdorf Gilbert, Eli, 48–49, 51
Pillersdorf Gilbert, Ian, 48, 51
Pillersdorf Gilbert, Leah Rose (née Pillersdorf), 35, 43–46, 46f, 47, 47f, 48, 48f, 49, 54, 55f, 57, 61f, 73, 92, 155, 203f, 379, 385, 404f, 406f, 421f
Pillersdorf Weisman, Rachel (née Pillersdorf), 35, 44, 46, 46f, 47, 47f, 51, 54, 55f, 56–57, 73, 155, 203f, 228, 385–86, 402f, 404f, 406f, 420f
Pinsky, Courtney Summer, 69
Pinsky, Drew, 69
Pinsky, Noah Jason, 68
Plantations Ltd., 175
Polly (dachshund), 39
Pooler, Donna, 70
Prescod (domestic helper), 118
Pressler, Bernhard (Rabbi), 373
Pulver, Anutsa, 47, 404f, 408f
Pulver, Bernard, 403f, 406f
Pulver, Dr., 278, 403f
Pulver, Esterea, 242
Pulver, Hana/Anutsa, 30, 241, 241f
Pulver, Kiva, 242, 403f
Pulver, Molly, 30, 47, 249f, 404f, 406f
Pulver, Naiman, 30, 47, 241, 241f
Pulver, Vicky, 30, 47, 404f
Purity Bakeries, 87, 164

Q
Queen's College, 47, 58, 95, 119, 202, 204, 225, 227, 359

R
Radio Distribution (Barbados) Ltd., 41n29
Raizman, Calena, 90
Raizman, Dan, 82, 88, 88f, 89–90, 355
Raizman, David, 90
Raizman, Helen, 86, 89, 328
Raizman, Jorge, 88–91, 355
Raizman, Martin, 88–89, 355
Raizman, Mauricio, 88–90, 328, 403f
Raizman, Raquel, 90
Raizman family, 331
Rajfer, Chana Gitla (Hannah) (née Pinczowska), 311, 314
Rajfer, Nusyn Jankiel (Jacob), 311, 314
Ramjit, Shirley, 373
Ramsey, Penny, 47
Recife Jewish community elder, 2
Recife's Jews, 2
Rehfeld, Miriam, 272
Rehfield, Zvi, 272, 403f
Reid, Mr., 391
Reingold, Anita, 243, 243f, 405f
Reingold, Marty/Motel, 243, 243f, 405f
Reingold, Paul, 243, 409f
Reisman, Helen, 346
Reliance Shirt Factory (Palmetto Street), 45, 328, 330
Ribakovsky, Wisia (Vera), 214
"Righteous Among the Nations," 32, 32n26
Rollock, Sam, 36
Rosenthal, Amanda, 107
Rosenthal, Arieh, 107
Rosenthal, Catherine, 107
Rosenthal, Florence, 107
Rosenthal, Larry, 107
Rosenthal, Liam, 107
Rosenthal, Martin, 107
Rosenthal, Samantha, 107

Rosenthal, Shawn, 107
Rosmarin, Barbara, 107
Rosner, Chaim, 158f, 159–60, 160f–161f, 164–66, 328
Rosner, Herman, 159–60
Rosner, Jacob, 159
Rosner, Linda, 158f, 159, 161, 162f, 165, 249f, 403f, 406f, 409f
Rosner, Mr., 278
Rosner, Myrla (Mary), 160f, 164–66, 408f, 410f, 417f
Rosner Mann, Molly (née Rosner), 158, 158f, 161, 162f–163f, 165, 409f
Royal Hotel (Hastings), 384f
Royal-on-Sea Hotel (Hastings), 381
"Royal Store" (High Street), 43, 45, 328, 363
Royal Theatre (Worthing), 381, 383f, 386–88
Royal Yacht Club, 47
Rubenstein, Anna, 96
Rubin, Catherine, 244, 244n104
Rubin, Devorah, 60
Rubin, Jacob, 60
Rubin, K. Kathrina, 244, 335, 423
Rubin, Leo, 244, 332f, 335
Rudder's School, 295
"Russian Store" (Swan Street), 206, 280, 280f, 285, 328, 332f

S
"S. S. Khoury" (dry goods store), 279
Salcman, Laurell, 367, 367f, 368
Salcman, Sheldon (Shelly), 367, 367f, 368
Samuel, Wilfred S., 2
"Sanctuaries in the Sand" (Caribbean Travel and Life), 27–28
"The Sandal Shop," 328

Sarjeant, Marlene (née Altman), 39, 68
Sarjeant, Peter, 68
Saunders, Danny, 247
Saunders, Harold, 29–30, 203f, 238, 246–47, 247f, 249f, 250, 250f, 305, 403f–404f, 406f, 409f, 417f
Saunders, Jean (née Aerenson), 30, 245, 245f, 246–47, 247f–248f, 249, 250f, 251, 329, 335, 405f, 412f
Saunders, Roberta (Robbie), 30, 203f, 246, 247f, 248, 248f, 249, 249f, 250, 250f, 251, 305, 385, 404f
Saunders, Ruth, 247
Saunders, Sherry, 247
Saunders family, 359
Saunders (Szunyogh), Ernest, 29–30, 87, 245, 245f, 246–47, 247f, 248, 250, 250f, 330, 335, 412f
Savage, Alfred William Lungley (C.M.G., Governor and Commander-in-Chief), 11, 13–14f
Schapiro, Bram, 156
Schapiro, Hallie, 156
Schapiro, Livia, 156
Schapiro, Michelle, 156, 156f
Schapiro, Peter (Pedro), 151, 151f, 156, 156f
Schapiro, Robert, 156, 156f
Schiffman, Ethel, 127, 317
Schlesinger, Carlotta, 423
Schmelzer, Toni, 261
Schneerson, Rabbi, 39, 39n28, 75
Schomburgh, Robert, 1, 24
Schondorf, Ella, 68
Schor, David, 29, 252–53
Schor, Feiga, 29, 252, 423
Schor, Salomon (Solomon) (Shlomo), 29, 94n54, 169,

170f, 252, 252f, 253, 253f, 325–26
Schor Diamante, David, 253–54, 253f
Schwab, Steve, 308
Schwab, Zaiden, 308
Schwartz, Verna, 110
"Sea Island Cotton" shirts, 219
"Seashell," 36
"Semach David" (Speightstown synagogue), 4, 4n5
Sephardic community, xiii n2
Sephardic synagogue, 281
Shaare Tzedek Synagogue (Christ Church), iii n1, 10, 11f, 27, 40, 70, 78–79, 90, 313, 324n114, 336–37, 344, 352–53, iiin1. See also "True Blue"
Shanker, Michelle, 316f
Shapiro, Dr. and Mrs. Saul, 69
Sharif, Omar, 315
Shilstone, Eustace M., 2–3, 9–11, 12f, 24, 37
Shilstone Library, 37
Shirmax fashion organization, 142
"The Shopping Centre" (Swan Street), 83, 329, 332f
Shor, Salomon, 29
Shoul, Ferdie, 330
Silver, Brittany, 259
Silver, Carole Joseph, 255–59, 257f
Silver, Chana (Sharon) (née Zylbercwaig), 30, 71, 255, 255f, 256–58, 404f, 408f
Silver, Charlie, 259
Silver, Henry, 255
Silver, Hirsch (Herschel), 29–30, 71, 423
Silver, Howard Phillip, 258–59
Silver, Jackson, 259
Silver, Jayden Leon, 259
Silver, Kaylee, 259

Silver, Leon, 71, 255–59, 298, 403f–404f, 406f, 409f–410f, 417f
Silver, Mark, 258–59
Silver, Niko, 259
Silver, Rae Ann, 259
Silver, Shlomo Leib, 259
Silver, Sonia, 56, 71, 149f, 178f, 255–56, 256f, 257, 259, 404f, 406f–407f, 409f, 411f
Silver, Zachary, 259
Silver family, 62
Silverman, Adam Howard, 68
Silverman, Anita (née Altman), 68
Silverman, David James, 68
Silverman, Gabriel, 68
Silverman, Joseph Dylan, 68
Silverman, Lauren Shari, 68
Simon, Felicia, 335
Simon, Joe, 329, 335
Singh, Don (author), 17–18, 24
Skeete, Dr., 104
Slater, Marjorie Ann, 81
Solomon, Paula, 251
Solomon Temple Lodge, 272
Sondon, Warren, 411f
Spanish Inquisition, 2
Speedbird House (Bridgetown), 36
Speisman, Fanny, 55, 57
Speisman, James, 62
Speisman, Leib, 29, 45, 55, 57
Speisman, Louis, 30, 38–41, 38f, 44–45, 61f, 62, 64, 67, 72, 75, 118, 255, 303, 328, 332f, 335, 355, 357, 391, 393, 411f, 416f, 423
Speisman, Mary (née Altman), 27, 38f, 39–41, 44, 61f, 62, 67, 72–73, 203f, 255, 335, 353, 355, 401f–402f, 408f–412f, 416f, 421f–422f, 423
Spencer, Violet, 316
Spergel, John, 132

Spieler, Dave, 331, 369, 369f, 370–72
Spieler, Goldie (née Leiken), 331, 335, 369, 369f, 370, 370n121, 371–72, 372n123
Spieler, Shawna, 372
Spieler, Ted, 369
Spira, Annelene (Annie), 267, 267f
Spira, Bernhardt, 261
Spira, Hannah/Hennele, 261
Spira, Hella, 261
Spira, Lazar, 11, 12f, 29–30, 75, 106f, 260, 260f, 261, 262f, 263–64, 264f, 266–67, 327, 332f, 335, 379f, 405f, 412f
Spira, Mr., 206, 387
Spira, Mrs., 387
Spira, Pepi, 261
Spira, Rosa, 261
Spira, Samuel, 260–61, 260f
Spira, Shimon, 261
Spira, Sidney (Sydney), 29–30, 178f, 261, 262f, 263, 263f–264f, 266–67, 267f, 335, 379f
Spira, Simon, 261
Spira, Toni (née Schmelzer), 30, 106f, 206, 260f, 261, 262f, 263–64, 264f, 335, 405f, 412f
Spira's home, 386–88
Spitz, Dan, 70
Spitz, Kai Joseph (Hai Yosef), 70–72
Spitz, Liat Dania (née Glassman), 70
Spitz, Riley Alexis Lydia (Rachel Leah), 70–72
Springer, Anthony (Joshua), 373, 373f, 374
Springer, Hugh (Sir, Governor General of Barbados), 50f
Springer, Orial (Ruth), 373, 373f, 374

St. John, Harold Bernard (Prime Minister), 24
St. Winifred's School, 102, 112, 148f, 155, 155f, 163f, 176, 250, 272, 370n121
Stamler (sic) (new settler), 29
Stammler, Mr., 268, 403f
Stammler, Ruth, 268, 406f
Stammler family, 30
Steinberg, Alan, 213
Steinbok, Abraham, 98, 99f, 355
Steinbok, Cecelia, 97
Steinbok, Ellen (née Brzozek), 97, 97f, 98, 252, 408f, 410f, 417f
Steinbok, Esther, 98, 99f, 355
Steinbok, Eva, 98, 99f, 250–51, 357, 409f
Steinbok, Helen, 335
Steinbok, Jacob/Yankel, 97
Steinbok, Jerry, 98, 99f, 195f, 203f, 249f, 305, 409f, 413f, 421f
Steinbok, Joseph, 50, 98, 99f, 355, 397
Steinbok, Martin, 98, 99f, 355
Steinbok, Moses (Moishe) Aron, 29–30, 95, 97, 97f, 98, 99f, 325, 330, 335, 403f, 410f, 412f, 417f, 423
Steinbok, Paul, 96–98, 99f, 203f, 249f, 305, 403f, 406f, 409f, 413f, 417f
Steinbok, Pinchas, 97
Steinbok, Sonia, 97
Steinbok, Toba, 97
Steinbok, Toby, 97
Steiner, Yenty, 261
"Stitches," 328
Stock, Beverley, 94n52, 96
Stock, Jack, 96
Storey, Dr., 309
Stoute, Edward, 24
Straker, Emil, 304
"Style Shoppe," 248, 329, 359

sugar mill, 4
"Swan Store" (Swan Street), 329, 332f
Swiss Art, 330–31
Swved, Chaim (Rabbi), 391, 391f–392f
Synagogue Block Redevelopment Project, 376
"Synagogue Burial Grounds Committee," 11

T

The Tabor Foundation (Barbados), 25–26
Taub, Morris, 269
Templar (sic) (new settler), 29
Templer, Abraham, 30, 270f–271f
Templer, Alan, 275
Templer, Arlene, 275
Templer, Elfreida, 408f
Templer, Elfrieda (née Rehfeld), 30, 270, 270f–271f, 272, 272f, 274–75
Templer, Joel, 275
Templer, Mervyn, 275
Templer Abramowitz, Hanna, 30, 112, 268, 270, 272–73, 273f, 274–75, 275f, 381, 408f
Tepper, Anne, 83f
Tepper, Issy, 83f, 195f, 421f
Tepper, Leopoldo, 30, 83f
Tepper, Paulette, 83f, 406f
Tepper, Rochelle, 83f, 178, 178n83, 213, 406f–407f
Textile Town, 311–12, 329
Tint-Pulver, Deborah, 33
Tint-Pulver Altman, Deborah, 72
Tissenbaum, Vivian, 144
Tissenbaum Konigsberg, Vivian, 143f, 145
Toynbee, Arnold, 39
A True and Exact History of Barbados (Ligon), 2

"True Blue" (Rockley New Road), 10, 40, 63, 76–77, 337, 344, 352. See also Shaare Tzedek Synagogue
Truss, Aaron, xiv, 1f, 15, 15f, 15n13, 18f, 57, 92, 195f, 244, 249f, 251, 283f, 287, 289–95, 299–300, 303–4, 307, 310, 356, 393, 417f
Truss, Abraham (Abe), 203f, 249f, 283f, 287–89, 295, 299–300, 303, 307, 310, 409f, 417f, 418f
Truss, Desiree, 310
Truss, Dina, 283
Truss, Evelyn (née Hing), 115, 116f, 249f, 251, 283f, 287–89, 289f, 290–301, 305, 307, 335, 353, 417f, 421f
Truss, Jennifer, 18f, 331
Truss, Joe, 249f, 283f, 287–89, 292, 295–302, 302f, 303–8, 310, 393, 417f, 421f
Truss, Leon, 249f, 283f, 287, 289, 292, 295, 298, 300, 304, 309, 309f, 310, 417f, 421f
Truss, Lyuba, 286, 295
Truss, Manea, 249f, 283f, 287–89, 295, 300, 304, 307, 335, 417f
Truss, Moisey/Misha, 277n109, 279–80, 284, 284f, 285, 285f, 286, 287f, 288, 295
Truss, Motel, 29–30, 30n23, 75, 115, 121, 244, 276, 276f, 277–81, 282f–283f, 284–85, 285f, 286, 287f, 288, 292, 295, 297–300, 305, 307, 330, 332f, 335, 397, 412f, 417f, 423
Truss, Musya, 284, 284f, 286, 288, 295
Truss, Ziska Marnie, 308
Truss family, 283f
Turner, Adam, 107

Turner, Antonia, 378
Turner, Charlene (née Rosenthal), 107
Turner, Fred, 107
Turner, Genevieve, 378
Turner, Joshua, 107
Turner, Philip, 378
Twain, Mark, 23–24

U
UNESCO World Heritage Site, 23, 23n17, 26
University of the West Indies (Jamaica), 89n51, 110, 125, 239, 342

V
Vatch, Anita, 68
Vienna, 167, 199, 202, 261, 287

W
Wajchendler, Abraham Adek, 30, 89, 121, 311, 311f, 312–13, 315, 325, 328, 330, 332f, 412f, 423
Wajchendler, Amy Samantha, 312, 316f
Wajchendler, Ber Dov, 312
Wajchendler, Cirla, 311, 314
Wajchendler, Elliott Zvi, 312, 316f
Wajchendler, Hanna, 247f, 305, 312, 316, 404f, 417f
Wajchendler, Harry, 304–5, 312, 314, 316, 316f, 404f, 413f, 421f
Wajchendler, Helen Chajuta Chaja (née Rajfer), 30, 311, 311f, 313–15, 329, 332f, 335, 404f, 410f, 412f
Wajchendler, Irving, 304–5, 311–16, 316f, 330, 355
Wajchendler, Isaac, 311, 314
Wajchendler, Jeannette (née Altman), 312
Wajchendler, Leon, 305
Wajchendler, Liam, 312
Wajchendler, Lucie (née Bertinet), 312
Wajchendler, Shaina Lisa, 312, 316f
Wajchendler, Susan (née Goldenberg), 312, 316f
Wajchendler, Yael, 312
Wajchendler family, 49
Wajchendler Guyon, Lauren, 316f
Wajchendler Oliver, Anni, 316f
Waksman, Abraham, 315
Ward family, 168, 168f78
Weatherhead, Louis, 305
Weinberger, Danny, 321
Weinberger, David, 321
Weinberger, Debbie, 321
Weinberger, Joseph ("Joe"), 317f, 320–21, 323
Weinstein, Saren, 156
Weisman, Gideon Solomon, 73
Weisman, Jonathon Jacob, 73
Weisman, Rachel (née Pillersdorf), 58
Weisman, Simon, 58
Weisman Borer, Sara Arielle, 73
Weiss, David (Rabbi), 274
Weissmuller, Johnny, 196
Wilkie (Bajan), 168
Williams, Ralph "Bizzy," 89, 89n51
Winder, Edith Ada, 377
Wiseman, Rowena (Ricky), 221
Wolofsky, Samara, 68
Women's International Zionist Organization, 41, 64n38
Women's Multi-National Group, 79
World Zionist Organization, 355

## Y

Yarden Borer, Kalanit, 73
Yardey, Mr., 344
Yearwood, Henry Graham, 9–10
Yiddish theatre group, 45
Yiddishkeit, 79, 189, 318, 390n125, 394
Yitzhak, Chaim, 100–101
Yitzhak, Ephraim, 100
Yitzhak, Helen, 100
Yitzhak, Leib, 100
Yitzhak, Mina, 100–101
Yitzhak, Morris, 100–101
Yitzhak, Nissel, 100
Yitzhak, Solomon, 100–101
Yitzhak, Sonia, 100–101
Yitzhak, Zvi ben Avraham (Harry), 100
Young Men's Progressive Club, 47
Yvette, Madame, 300

## Z

Zeplowitz, Abigail, 122
Zeplowitz, Irwin, 122–23
Zeplowitz, Nathan Avi, 122
Zierler, Jacob, 29–30, 129, 147, 317–18, 318f, 328, 332f, 403f, 410f
Zierler, Mina, 30, 129, 130f, 131, 147, 245, 318f, 328, 332f, 401f, 405f, 408f, 410f
Zierler, Paltyel, 410f
Zierler, Wisia, 410f
Zierler Weinberger, Rose (Rosie) (Rosalinde) (Roz) (née Zierler), 56, 106, 106f, 129, 130f, 146f, 147, 149f, 178f, 190, 203f, 256f, 317, 317f, 318–19, 319f, 320–21, 321f, 322, 322f, 323, 400f, 404f, 407f, 409f
Zlotowitz, Anne, 324, 324f
Zlotowitz, David, 29–30, 218, 324, 324f
Zylcraft Optical, 331, 350

## *ABOUT THE AUTHOR*

Simon Kreindler was born and grew up in Barbados. After graduating from The Lodge School in 1957, he studied marine biology at McGill University in Montreal before entering medical school there. In 1971, after completing postgraduate training in adult and child psychiatry in the United States, Simon, his wife, Ruby, and their children returned to Canada. They settled in Toronto where Simon has been in private practice for the past 46 years.

Simon has been researching his family's history for more than 25 years and in 2013 published a memoir for his children and grandchildren, incorporating much of what he had discovered. The story of how his parents got to Barbados in the 1930s inspired him to acquire and record the stories of their European Jewish contemporaries on the island which ultimately led to the publication of this book.

Simon and Ruby have three children and eight grandchildren, all of them living in Toronto.

www.ingramcontent.com/pod-product-compliance
Lightning Source LLC
Chambersburg PA
CBHW070714160426
43192CB00009B/1183